BREAKING RANK

A Top Cop's Exposé of the
Dark Side of American Policing

NORM STAMPER

NATION BOOKS
NEW YORK

For James Norman Stamper, Everett Eugene Stamper,
and Matthew Todd Stamper

BREAKING RANK
A Top Cop's Exposé of the
Dark Side of American Policing

Published by
Nation Books
An Imprint of Avalon Publishing Group
245 West 17th Street, 11th Floor
New York, NY 10011

AVALON

Nation Books is a co-publishing venture of the Nation Institute and
Avalon Publishing Group Incorporated.

This memoir is a product of the author's recollections and is thus rendered as a subjective
accounting of events that occurred in his/her life.

Library of Congress Cataloging-in-Publication Data is available.

ISBN-10: 1-56025-855-1
ISBN-13: 978-1-56025-855-1

9 8 7 6 5 4 3 2 1

Book design by Maria E. Torres

Printed in the United States of America
Distributed by Publishers Group West

CONTENTS

POLICING THE POLICE

THE POLITICS OF POLICING

CONCLUSION • 391

INTRODUCTION

WHAT DO YOU SEE when you picture a "safe" America? I envision infants born into a loving, nurturing world—to women whose reproductive rights are protected by law. Children and teens who exhibit consideration for themselves and others. Citizens who question, challenge, and disagree with one another—nonviolently. Men who refuse to abuse women. Gun violence gone from our homes and streets, our schools and workplaces. Law enforcers, from the beat cop to the U.S. Attorney General doing their jobs properly, applying their imagination, playing by the rules. I see Americans, black, white, straight, gay, expressing themselves freely, pursuing happiness as they define it. I picture an America safe from consumer, environmental, and political, as well as predatory crime—and free from the specter of an overzealous, overreaching, moralistic government.

Einstein defined insanity as doing the same thing over and over, and expecting different results. That pretty much sums up this nation's law enforcement approach to public safety. Take drugs, for example. How much more evidence do we need that America has *lost* its "war on drugs," even as we keep our cops slogging away on the perilous front lines? Or prostitution: How likely is it that hookers and their johns will decamp the sex industry any time soon? Or guns: I heard Barry Goldwater rail against controls some 35 years ago because "it would take 50 years to get rid of handguns." Or *men*: What are the chances that we American males will accept full responsibility for the breathtaking levels of violence in our society, and *do* something about it? Or racist cops: Do we honestly believe we've seen the last Rodney King, Abner Louima, Amadou Diallo incident?

Problems like these *can* be solved. It's possible for a police force to be tough on crime and still treat people with dignity and respect. But not with the same politics, the same paramilitary infrastructure, and the same inbred cop culture that *produce* police incompetence and misconduct. What's needed is an honest examination of the failures of our justice system, along with the will and the courage to employ radically different—but theoretically sound—approaches to their solution.

How? By *breaking rank*, by questioning long-accepted ways of doing business, and by taking direct action to change the system.

+ + +

I had impressions of the law and "lawmen" long before I became a cop. As a kid, I was in some kind of trouble just about every day of my life. Most of my behavioral problems were handled not by the police but by my parents (unevenly), or by teachers and coaches (more constructively, on the whole). Still, despite an anemic rap sheet I had enough early contact with "the Man" to cultivate some major hostility toward the police.

I grew up in National City, a small town of car lots, slaughter-houses, meat packing plants, and navy bars at the southern city limits of San Diego, 14 miles from the Tijuana border.

At nine, I had my first contact with two of NCPD's finest. My friend Gary and I, weary of shooting out streetlights with our slingshots, meandered over to Kimball Park to kick over the portable Little League fence, again. We'd finished off about a third of the job when a black-and-white Dodge shot out from behind the visitors' dugout and swooped down on us from the left field foul line. One of them seized the cigarettes I'd lifted from my mother. The driver cop, the talker, ordered us to put out our smokes and replace the fence. The two men sat in their car, supervising us, tiny orange dots lighting up their faces as they inhaled mom's Chesterfields. When we finished, the talker ordered us, with great profanity, never to set foot in the park again. I had to agree with my pal when he said, as the black-and-white drove off, leaving us in a cloud of dust, "I *hate* those fuckers!"

When I was sixteen a National City cop wrote me a citation for doing seventeen miles an hour through a fifteen-mile-an-hour intersection. (Later, I would learn the technical term for such a ticket: *chickenshit*.)

A year later I watched a San Diego police officer jab his finger into the chest of the lead singer of our R&B band and call him a "splib" and a "motherfucking nigger."

In my late teens I sat glued to the tube as Birmingham Bull Connor sicced his dogs on peacefully assembled civil rights demonstrators. I saw well-dressed Negroes—women in Sunday frocks, men in white shirts, skinny ties, and porkpie hats, even children—get clubbed to the ground, kicked, bitten by police dogs, and sprayed with fire hoses. It felt like *I'd* been kicked in the stomach.

At nineteen and twenty I was burglarized, three times. The police took forever to show up, and when they did the one in a suit mumbled something about the "Mezicans" who lived up the steep bank from my apartment. They took no prints, no shoe impressions, not even notes. They arrested no one, recovered none of the hundred or so jazz and R&B LPs that were my most prized possessions. (To this day I still feel the sting of that loss, along with a powerful case of resentment. Not so much toward the burglars— they did *their* job.)

And where were the cops when my old man was beating the snot out of his sons? Our house at 2324 K Avenue was the site of multiple and continuing felonious acts. But even if they'd been called (our neighbors certainly heard what was going on) the cops wouldn't have done a thing.

People talk about "bad apples" in police work. To me the whole barrel was moldy. Not once, growing up, did I have a positive contact with a police officer. I'm not claiming I was an angel, not saying my behavior didn't contribute to my "anti-police" attitude. It's just that I got neither protection nor service from my local police. All I got was no respect.

So why did I become one of them? I needed a job.

+ + +

I was twenty, freshly married, working as a kennelman at the National City Pet Hospital. My eighteen-year-old bride and I lived in an apartment on the grounds. Dottie wasn't overjoyed with the arrangement—the barking dogs, the yowling cats, the odors. And the pet owners rapping on our bedroom window in the middle of the night: a woman to inform me that Mitzi's nose was warm, that she "just doesn't seem herself lately," the owner of a kitten wondering if Tangerine needed her rabies shot before traveling to

Mexico, a party animal demanding to know why his new puppy, bloated and comatose, wouldn't wake up after being fed a bowl of Bud. It was time for a new home, a new job.

I passed each phase of San Diego's civil service testing, which took a couple of months. At the end of the process I was scheduled to meet with the chief of police himself.

I walked down the long, terracotta-tiled corridor of the old police headquarters on West Market to the "corner pocket." The police chief, a white-haired, wrinkled man, squinted at me through rheumy eyes and thick horn-rimmed glasses. "Tell me, son, why do you want to be a policeman?" I'd been practicing for this all morning, I was ready.

"To help people and prevent crime and—and *mayhem.*" The word, which a lieutenant had scolded me for misusing during my civil service interview (think not chaos and disorder but split lips and slit ears), was lodged there in my brain, like a song you can't shake. The chief shook his head.

"That's what they all say. 'I want to *help* people.' Tell me the real reason you want to be a policeman."

"Really, sir. I've thought about it a lot. I really *do* want to help people. Like when they get robbed and so forth."

"Do you know what a robbery is?"

"Sure. It's when somebody, like, breaks into your apartment and steals your things."

"That's a burglary son. A robbery is a little more—personal. But you'll have plenty of time for all that in the academy . . . *if* I decide to hire you. Tell me, why should I hire you?"

"Because I'm a hard worker? Because I care about people? Because . . ."

"Are you asking me these things, or telling me?"

"*Telling* you, sir." I tried to be emphatic but my voice cracked in the middle of "telling." The assistant chief, a large man with a crew cut who'd been sitting in silence off to the side, laughed, explosively. I blushed. And fumed. I didn't need this shit. I could become a fireman. Or, God forbid, go back to working with Dad on his construction sites, something I'd done every summer from age eight to sixteen.

"Well, you've made it this far," said the chief. "I guess I'll go ahead and take a chance on you. But you remember this." He crooked a finger at me.

"You're on probation for a year. That means I can fire you just as quick as I've hired you. You understand?"

"Yes, sir." My voice cracked again and the assistant chief laughed again, a little softer this time.

"Well, welcome aboard, son." The chief stood up, wincing. Maybe he had a trick knee too; mine was from football. I'd lied about it on the application. The chief hobbled out from behind a prison-industries desk the size of a jury box and smiled at me as we shook on it. He seemed like a really nice guy.

Although I was thrilled, I honestly didn't get it: Why in the world would Chief Wes Sharp hire *me*? Later I learned that SDPD was hard up for cops at the time. It's a cyclical thing, police hiring. Three months later, the budget closing in on him, the city manager demanding "economies" for the rest of the fiscal year, Sharp never would have welcomed me aboard. But he was hurting for cops in the field.

+ + +

I brought my new identity home from Albert's Uniforms in two brown paper shopping bags. As soon as Dottie left for work I tried it all on. I was jolted by the image in the full-length mirror on the back of our bedroom door. But I would be a *different* kind of cop, I told myself. Sensitive and compassionate, responsive and responsible. I would catch people who stole from or hurt other people. I would not write chickenshit tickets. I would never use the "N" word, or act unprofessionally.

I practiced a few quick-draws with my imaginary six-shooter and then pulled on my new raingear: rubber boots, a yellow coat, a yellow rain cap with a floppy visor. I looked like a 170-pound canary.

The police academy was a catalytic, values-jarring, life-changing experience. The staff and most of the instructors, cops all, were charismatic and sarcastic, comical and irreverent. I aspired to be just like them. And bowed enthusiastically to their authority.

What about all those accumulated grievances, all that fear and loathing of cops? They evaporated overnight. My top priority, my only priority, was to please or at least not piss off these cool new people in my life. To that end,

I spent hours studying the academy manual and spit-shining my new regulation plain-toed black shoes.

A few weeks into the academy I began to feel the rumblings of something I'd never felt before: self-confidence.

There was no greater confidence-builder than overcoming my fear of firearms. I'd performed dismally at the range, and had failed to qualify in our first "shoot." The rangemaster, Sergeant A. B. Davis, who sounded a bit like Sean Connery but looked nothing like him, ordered me to take my six-inch .38 Smith and Wesson revolver home and "dry-fire" it, over and over. "An schqueeze that trigger, Schtamper. Schtop jerking it. Itch not your goddamn dick." I got home that evening and unloaded the pistol (counting the six bullets in my hand at least half a dozen times). I picked a tiny smudge on the living room wall of our new apartment, took aim at it, and started dry-firing. *Click-click-click.*

My right hand was cramped, bruised, and cracked, but I went on to qualify. In fact, by graduation day I was the number-one shooter among SDPD recruits. (I would have been first overall but for an El Cajon cop who later got busted for pulling burglaries on his beat, on duty. I've always prided myself on being the number-one, non-felon marksman in the Forty-Ninth San Diego Police Academy Class.)

After twelve weeks at the academy I was out on the streets on my own, at last. I loved it. Chasing calls, writing tickets, wrestling drunks, pinching the occasional burglar or stickup man. And letting the bad guy know who was boss. Our instructors had drilled it into us: it was *us* against *them*, good guys versus bad guys. I knew which one I was, and set out to prove it.

I didn't give a moment's thought to how the job might be affecting me. Within months (was it weeks, *days?*) I was saying and doing things I'd never said or done before in my life. Not nice things, not proper things. But, oh my lord, was it fun! Screwing people around, laughing and joking about it after shift with my peers. My favorite stunt? Choking people out. I'd jab my right forearm against their throats, spin them around, hoist them up on my back, and squeeze with all my might. Then I'd whisper into their ears as they lost consciousness, "You're gonna *die*, asshole."

I'd been on the job a little over a year when I pinched a nineteen-year-old puke who'd had the nerve to question my authority.* I'd busted him for a violation of Section 647(f) of the California Penal Code—drunk in a public place and unable to care for himself or the safety of others. In those days people arrested on that charge pled guilty and paid their twenty-nine bucks. Not this kid (I was three years his senior). A month after the arrest I received a subpoena. No problem—I knew exactly what to do.

On the trial date I sauntered into the county courthouse, sidled up to the deputy prosecutor, and suggested with a wink and a poke that he dismiss the case. *Why?* he demanded to know. Because it was a skinny pinch, I told him. He asked if the kid had actually been drunk. What kind of a question was that? "No, not really. But he was a puke. He called me a pig."

The attorney peered at me through his tortoiseshell glasses and said, "Does the Constitution of the United States mean anything to you, Officer Stamper?"

I was furious, as angry as I'd ever been in my life. But my rage quickly turned to embarrassment. How could I have come so far from my pre-cop views and values? By the time I slithered down the stairs of the courthouse and out into the bright sunshine, I was saturated in shame.

+ + +

That slap-down in the courthouse, coupled with other developments in my personal life (such as junior-college classes that were leading me to question, at least tentatively, some of the things we did in police work) triggered an abiding commitment to reform. Of myself, initially. Then of everyone else, the whole rest of that tainted, unholy institution called American policing.

---

* We dealt in pukes and assholes in those days. A puke was a longhaired youth who flipped you off, called you a pig, or simply had that "anti-establishment" look about him. An asshole, on the other hand, was a doctor, a lawyer, or a clean-cut blue-collar worker who gave you lip as you wrote him a ticket—or who disagreed with your informed take on current events. The world was conveniently divided into "good people" vs. pukes and assholes. There were, of course, regional, as well as generational, differences in the vocabulary of the cop culture. In the eighties, for example, *Hill Street Blues* Detective Mick Belker's, "Sit, hairball!" or "Freeze, dogbreath!" was drawn directly from the streets of New York (and widely copied in PDs throughout the country).

+ + +

After a few years as a hydrophobic gasbag, haranguing my fellow cops and confessing our private sins publicly, I resolved to actually *study* my profession. My goal was to come up with more effective, more humane ways to get the job done.

The investigation was experiential: every shift on the streets was a learning experience. A couple of coworkers and I would regularly debrief the incidents we handled, including the almost nightly riots and mini-riots in the black community, plus all those civil rights and antiwar demonstrations. It wasn't always easy but we did learn things, and we applied the lessons to our practice.

I also studied my field academically, researching and analyzing our laws, police procedures and police administration, political science, leadership, social and organizational change, systems theory. Later, I attended and spoke at numerous national and international conferences on policing, and visited and consulted with several dozen police agencies, often conducting "organization development" and leadership workshops for them. I taught at the police academy, and at San Diego State University, the University of California at San Diego, and the University of Washington. I wrote a dissertation, later published, on the "professed values versus the observed behavior" of American big-city police chiefs.* I came to Seattle in 1994 as a police chief with a Ph.D. in leadership and human behavior.

With each new badge, each new phase of learning, I developed a deeper and keener understanding of this: the most intractable problems of my field—racism, sexism, misogyny, homophobia and other brands of bigotry, fear, brutality, corruption, organizational ineptitude, even individual incompetence—are rooted in the *system* of policing, a system that includes the laws police are called upon to enforce.

+ + +

---

* *Removing Managerial Barriers to Effective Police Leadership.* Police Executive Research Forum, 1992.

As my former colleagues will happily attest, I was never a cop's cop. But throughout my career I witnessed many officers who consistently performed the job with inspiring mastery. They're the kind of police officers who make a difference in the lives of the people they were hired to serve. My love for these cops is a major motivation behind this book. That they continue to get the job done lawfully and humanely, in spite of senseless laws, dim-witted policies, and childish workplace pressures, is something of a minor miracle.

It's a thing of beauty to watch these cops work with kids and parents, the homeless, the mentally ill. To observe their creativity and enthusiasm for community policing, and their talent and courage as they track down and capture the genuinely dangerous among us. Rarely did a day pass in my career that I didn't register the humor, humanity, and compassion of these officers. Or their willingness to sacrifice all for a risky and delicate mission: in my thirty-four years I helped bury more than two dozen police officers slain in the line of duty.

+ + +

Who are the instructors I remember most vividly from my academy days? The ones who told stories. You couldn't get those guys (not a woman among them) to cough up a theory or a principle if their lives depended on it. Not that I wished for them to turn academic on us: Their tales made the streets come alive. They educated, amused, frightened, and inspired us with images of what we'd face in the real world when we'd finally hit the streets. The instruction may have lacked a tidy theoretical foundation but it was compelling, entertaining, and unforgettable.

Today, the best academy instructors still tell tales, but they weave relevant theories into those stories, helping new cops understand *why* they're expected to do, and not do, certain things. These instructors also get their students out of the classroom and into "mock scenes," simulations that help recruits get a taste of what it's going to be like to collect evidence at a robbery, make a felony hot stop, or enter a stranger's living room to interrupt family violence. In this book I set out to do something of that for you: to help you *imagine* what it's like to be a beat cop, or a police chief.

+ + +

I've approached *Breaking Rank* not only as a memoir but thematically and polemically, introducing in each chapter a critical issue facing community-police relations and the justice system.

"My aim is to agitate and disturb people," wrote the philosopher and writer Miguel de Unamuno. "I'm not selling bread, I'm selling yeast." *Breaking Rank* provides "yeast" for those who seek to help this country move toward more effective, humane, and progressive policing.

CRIME AND PUNISHMENT

CHAPTER 1

AN OPEN LETTER
TO A BAD COP

On April 26, 2003, Tacoma Police Chief David Brame shot and killed his estranged wife, then turned the gun on himself. His eight-year-old daughter and five-year-old son witnessed the event.

Dear David:

What was it like just before you did it, inside that cocoon you'd spun around your brain? Had you convinced yourself it was a private matter, nobody else's business? Were you at peace? I want to understand, David, I really do, as one ex–police chief to another. One ex-spouse abuser to another.

You were angry, I get that. Crystal had filed for divorce. It made headlines. You saw your name attached not to the talented, visionary police chief you imagined yourself to be, but to the portrait of a monster. Unlike thousands of other abusive men in high places and/or respected positions, you got outed. Until that Saturday afternoon your public persona had been that of a sophisticated, well-mannered civic leader.

The murder-suicide was hardly private, as you would have known all too well. It shook your city to the core, David. Women's groups are demanding answers and sweeping reforms. The mayor and city council are scrambling to cover their tails. The guy who made you chief, the city manager? He's been fired. Crystal's family is suing the city for $75 million. Tacoma's insurance company is threatening not to pay (remember, Chief, those premiums don't buy coverage for the *criminal* actions of our employees). The FBI is investigating charges of impropriety in your hiring, as well as your ascension to the chief's office. Your beloved hometown is reeling, people are saying it'll take years to recover. Of course, you don't have to worry about the "collateral damage" you caused.

All your chiefly chatter about "valuing diversity," treating citizens and your employees with dignity and respect—that wasn't the real you, was it? I mean you *raped* a woman, for crying out loud. Someone you dated back in 1988. True, you got off on some bogus "he said/she said" internal affairs finding (and the inexplicable failure of your boss to submit the case to the prosecutor)—but you *confessed* to the crime. I heard that you broke down in a face-to-face meeting with your victim, sobbed to her that you were a "born-again Christian," that you were "very truly, terribly sorry" and would "never, ever do that again."

But there were other women. Your own employees. One had begun making noises about your having sexually harassed her; it seems you promised her a promotion if she'd share the sheets with you. You pestered another female employee to join you and your protesting wife in a three-some. That would have been more recent, well after you'd pinned on your chief's badge in January 2002.

Wife beating, rape, sexual harassment. You couldn't live with it, could you? Being disgraced publicly. Most likely losing the job you'd politicked so hard to win. Possibly going to prison. You weren't just angry, were you? You were scared—to death.

I'm curious, David. Where did you get your attitudes about women? About wives? Employees? Dates? Was it from your parents? Are you aware a therapist convinced a judge that your children shouldn't be left in the care of their paternal grandparents? They're afraid of your mother. They say she's been violent with them. What do you make of that? Did Mom beat you when you were a kid? Not to get *too* psychological, but did she help turn you into a misogynist?

How about your dad? Did he mistreat you? If so, I can relate. My old man beat me often. Usually it was with his belt but sometimes it was his fists or his foot or the back of his meaty construction worker's hand. I remember the worst beating as if it happened this morning. It left me bloodied and cowed. Not until my forties did I come to realize that my father was a criminal, his "discipline" a felony.

That's my story, David. Not all of it, of course. (I haven't told you how Mom would send my brothers and me out to the apricot tree to pick a switch when we'd been bad. It hurt like the devil, I can tell you that, against our bare backs and bare legs. And she'd have this absolutely *ferocious* look on her face when she lit into us. But I choose to believe she did it to protect us from Dad. It was like they'd cut this deal between them: If she did it during the day he wouldn't be required to do it that night.) Anyway, like I said, that's *my* story. I wish you could tell me yours.

I wish I knew whether, like so many of us, you were beaten as a boy. Was your dad, the Tacoma policeman, physically violent with your mom? With you? I know I'm dwelling on it here, but answers to these questions are of consequence, they really are.

Research over the past three decades supports the conventional wisdom: Witness your parents fighting? Statistically, you're likely to grow into a batterer yourself. Beaten as a child? Odds are you'll beat your own kids. If you're both a witness to and a victim of family abuse, your chances of becoming a partner beater and a child abuser, unless you have some remarkable coping skills or some other adult to turn to for support, are off the charts. And, God forbid you should grow up in a household where violence is the norm—spousal assault, child abuse, an everyday vocabulary of violence ("Eat those peas or I'll kick your ass," "Wipe that smirk off your face or I'll slap it off"), and, yes, megadoses of TV and video game violence. If you come from that kind of home, the chances are slight that you'll *not* settle differences with your fists or a hammer or a gun. (Either that, says the research, or you'll turn out pathologically passive.)

So, those questions about your upbringing are important, David. But the answers, no matter how heart-wrenching, don't let us off the hook. Not for how we behave as grown-ups. They'll never excuse what you did to Crystal, even before April 2003. Let's talk about your behavior first. Then we can compare notes.

The pushing, the threats to kill her, the choking (four episodes in the year before you murdered her), the angry display of your firearm—I hate to say it but that stuff's not all that uncommon among male cops, or men in general. But you did some certifiably weird things, too. You sent her flowers with no card . . . so you could study her reaction. You timed her every trip from the house. You checked the odometer on her car. You accompanied her to the bathroom, and into her gynecological exams. You weighed her daily. You handled all the money, giving her a miserly allowance then accounting for it like a cross between Scrooge and Attila the Hun. I wonder, David, if you also:

- Listened in on her phone conversations?
- Read her mail?
- Followed her?
- Interrogated her when she got home, demanding to know what she did, who she was with?
- Expected or demanded sex when she didn't want it?
- Selected her friends for her?
- Prevented her from having friends?
- Threw the family kitten or puppy against the wall?
- Scissored up her photos?
- Threatened to leave her?
- Screamed at her?
- Glared at her?
- Made a fist, shook it in her face?
- Gave her the silent treatment?
- Compared her body to photos in magazines?
- Threw things?
- Punched holes in the wall?
- Left a threatening note?
- Forced her to have sex when she was asleep?
- Called her a whore?
- Made yourself unavailable to watch the kids when she was counting on you?
- Took the car, leaving her unable to get where she needed to go?
- Refused to allow her to have male friends?
- Accused her of flirting, or of having an affair?
- Sabotaged family/social affairs?
- Blamed her for financial problems, or troubles with the kids?
- Told her she was a bad mother?
- Told her she was a lousy lay?
- Told her she was mentally ill?
- Made light of your abuse, minimizing its effects?

- Forced her to watch pornography?
- Told her you were in charge, that your home was your castle?
- Told her it was the alcohol or the drugs that made you do it?
- Told her that if you couldn't have her no one could?
- Idolized her?
- Obsessed about her all the time?
- Flew into rages?
- Went cold, and stayed cold?
- Drove recklessly with her (and/or the kids) in the car?
- Failed to give her messages from people who called?
- Defined and dictated her role as mother, homemaker?
- Got jealous when she bought new clothes, put on makeup, got a new hairstyle?
- Goaded her into talking about other men, then condemned her no matter what she said?
- Checked the phone bills for suspicious calls?
- Refused to stop the car when she requested it?
- Followed her to work?
- Questioned or threatened her coworkers?
- Used sex to "make up" for your violence, expecting her to forgive you?
- Pulled the phone out of the wall?
- Fought in front of the kids?
- Used violence against her?

The whole world knows the answer to the last two questions. But, how about the other stuff on that long, depressing list? You're familiar with these behaviors, right? If not from your own home then from the annual domestic violence conferences we sponsored in Seattle? I wouldn't be surprised if there are some conference handouts gathering dust in the filing system of your old office. It would credit people like Michael Paymar, and his book, *Violent No More: Helping Men End Domestic Violence*. Had you read Paymar's book, David? Did you see yourself in those pages? I certainly did—I saw *me* in them.

I've been married and divorced, three times. I recall what it was like to be provoked, the rage that welled up inside when I felt jealous or possessive or disrespected or—insecure. I did things I regret, and since I'm not shy about judging you I'll tell you what they are.

I *screamed* profanities at my wife—in front of the kids (two stepchildren from the second marriage, my own from the first); turned cold, gave her the silent treatment; slammed my fist into the wall; interrogated her when she returned home—surely she'd been sleeping, or at least flirting, with someone else; glared at her; drove at breakneck speeds with her in the car; lifted her and moved her when she refused to get out of a doorway so I could leave (a favorite tactic: get to the car, roll the windows down, and motor like a madman into the mountains or the desert). Which wife? Doesn't matter. I behaved the same way with each, habitually.

The worst thing I ever did, from where I sit, was to stand above the woman I loved and rain down madness upon her. I was carrying my seventh or eighth badge by then, each new professional milestone symbolizing, in my delusional mind, the parallel progress I'd been making in "personal growth," in "enlightenment." My partner was asleep at the time, on a futon on the floor. She hadn't returned my calls, wouldn't commit to some office holiday function I'd felt professionally obligated to attend. She had *ignored* me. So, I towered some six feet above her in a darkened room and *ROARED!* Berating her, accusing her, intimidating her. All I lacked was the belt.

It's tempting for me to minimize these behaviors, to slough them off as "nonviolent," because nobody got a cut or a bruise—much less a bullet to the brain. But, make no mistake, David: Shouting, threatening, intimidating are all forms of violence. You know this as well as I do. We both saw it throughout our careers as cops. Big men, loud men, scary men—looming over their women, making them quake in fear. I picture the difference in physical space you and Crystal take up in your respective coffins. You, a six-foot, 175-pound man. Your wife, five feet tall, all of a hundred pounds. Don't tell me the way we "talked" to our respective spouses wasn't violent.

Escalation of nonphysical abuse into physical attacks and physical injury is not automatic, but it happens often enough to be predictable and of deep concern to the women being raged against. And to the children who witness it, shrinking in the corner. And to a whole society overrun by violence.

I don't want to be presumptuous, David, but I think I know where you and I parted company: You seemed to believe what you did was okay because you were in charge. The king of your castle. The *patriarch* in a dismally dysfunctional patriarchal society that licenses men to command rather than communicate.

Mary Nõmme Russell writes in *Confronting Abusive Beliefs: Group Treatment for Abusive Men*: "An abusive man's belief in the centrality and separateness of the self precludes a definition of his behavior as abusive by disregarding effects of this behavior on his partner. His belief in the superiority of the self permits him to devalue his partner [as] well as to justify abusiveness as a necessary defense to his threatened superiority. An abusive man's belief in deservedness of the self provides justification for abuse when his needs are not met."

Wow. If you'll pardon my saying so, David, that describes you to a T. Your total self-centeredness, your sense of superiority and entitlement.

Me? I'll own the self-centeredness, the "centrality of self" that Nõmme Russell writes about—I was one self-absorbed, narcissistic sonofabitch (I see myself today as a recovering self-absorbed, narcissistic sonofabitch). But I never believed myself to be superior to my partner. Or that I was entitled to hit her. My actions may not have communicated it but I always felt, with each partner, that we were equals.

Alas, what you and I may have felt about our motives matters not a whit. It's how we acted that matters.

There's another major difference between us, my colleague: I got help, you didn't. While I never entertained the thought of physically attacking my partner I knew it was in there, percolating: the potential for physically wounding violence. Psychotherapy was a great gift. It helped me understand and deal with the sources of my childhood wounds, and my adult insecurities. It informed me that my parents' "discipline," especially my father's, was as unlawful as it was ineffective. It reinforced my fundamental belief in the moral (and liberating) value of true gender equality.

And it erased any excuse I may have had for my behavior: *I* was responsible, not Mommy, not Daddy, not God, not Twinkies, and *certainly* not my partner, for how I acted.

I wish for Crystal that she'd had a chance to know you as an equal, David. I wish that same thing for all partners in their relationships. Especially the wives of cops.

Your crimes triggered a feeding frenzy among the local media. Reporters started sniffing and snooping even before you and Crystal were in the ground (your wife lay in the hospital until they lowered you into your grave, and at that moment she died). The press was eager to learn how many other cops were abusing their partners. Yeah, I know, reporters are bottom feeders, but you can hardly blame them in this case. I mean, you were the top cop in town; if you were guilty of domestic violence, what did that say about other men in blue?

The Seattle Post-Intelligencer ran a week-long series "exposing" the fact that cops are at least as likely as other men to commit domestic violence. (Next, they'll be telling us there are racists in policing.) In fact, more recent research reveals that cops are far more likely than non-cops to be domestic abusers. Yet, police officers are far *less* likely to get busted for DV. Why? Because they're trained to fight, to take charge, to *manipulate*. They know how to inflict excruciating pain that leaves no marks. And they have guns. Their wives aren't stupid.

A police wife also understands that if her husband is convicted of domestic violence he'll lose his gun. In police work, if you lose your gun you lose your job. And since a "cop" is not merely *what* he is but *who* he is (tragic, but true), the implications are ominous. A DV conviction would take away his identity, his reason for living. Talk about your ultra-dangerous situation.

Look at how long it took Crystal to file for divorce. Her family and friends think it was because of your role as a cop, especially a high-profile cop. I think so, too.

But her reticence could also have been for any of the "conventional" reasons many abused women don't "just up and leave." If there are "fifty ways to leave a lover" there must be an equal number of reasons for staying with an abuser. Anna Quindlen cites several in her best-selling novel *Black and Blue*. And Michael Paymar weighs in with more:

- She's afraid she'll lose her kids
- She's accepted his apologies and promises, and figures he won't do it again
- She feels pressured by her religion or her family to stick it out
- He's made threats, and she believes he'll act on them

- She still loves him
- She hasn't the money to leave
- She feels she's to blame
- She believes he'll commit suicide
- She doesn't think she'll find another partner
- She believes the negative things he has said about her, and hasn't the self-confidence to take control of her life
- She has no support system, no place to go, no one to talk to
- She doesn't trust the police or the courts to help
- She thinks abuse goes with the territory
- She doesn't want to be a failure, in her eyes or in the eyes of others

These realities have prompted Paymar and others to redefine the question: *Why doesn't she just leave?* becomes, *In what ways is a woman* trapped *in an abusive relationship?*

You know, there's an irony here, David. More than any of your predecessors you seemed to take DV seriously. Most police chiefs don't. They talk a good game but it's a rare chief who puts the needed time, energy, money, and imagination into DV prevention and enforcement. Do you remember what I inherited in the department thirty-two miles north of yours?

When I got to Seattle in 1994, robbery detectives were handling DV follow-up investigations. *Robbery dicks!* As a *collateral* duty. No wonder DV ranked at the bottom of the food chain within the department. The very structure of the organization proclaimed domestic violence the lowest of the low-priority assignments. One detective, unburdened by sensitivity, told me, "You spend your days handing Kleenexes to some sobbing broad whose old man gave her what she deserved."

Them was fightin' words to my ears. I went back to my office that very afternoon and wrote out the skeleton of a plan to put an end to family violence in Seattle.

My colleagues said it was foolish to set a goal of *ending* domestic violence. Why? Because it couldn't be attained. Goals need to be reachable, they said, otherwise your cops and the community and the politicians get frustrated. I chose to think differently: I *wanted* people to get "frustrated" when we fell short. Every time a wife is battered, a date is raped, a child is scalded, an elder is abused, we *should* be "frustrated." Hell, we should be goddamn *outraged!*

In 1985 the U.S. surgeon general declared family violence a national epidemic. The American Medical Association and the U.S. Centers for Disease Control and Prevention took a similar stand. *Violence and the Family: Report of the APA* [American Psychological Association], *Presidential Task Force on Violence and the Family* (1996) supports the notion that DV is indeed a national epidemic (see sidebar below).

At least 25 percent of all American homes play host to domestic abuse; one of every four men has used or will use violence against a partner during

---

DOMESTIC VIOLENCE IN AMERICA

Nearly one in every three adult women experiences at least one domestic violence assault as an adult.

Four million American women are victims of a serious assault by an intimate partner during an average 12-month period.

Every year about 600,000 men are arrested for violence against women.

Women are six times less likely to report violence by an intimate partner than by a stranger.

At least 1,300 women are killed each year by an intimate partner (mostly by handguns); spotty reporting leads some experts to put the number at between 1,500-4,000.

Every year approximately 3 million cases of child abuse are reported to official agencies such as child protective services.

Approximately 1,300 children die of child abuse or neglect every year.

Fifty-seven percent of children under 12 who are murdered are killed by a parent.

In a given year, 3.3 million kids are exposed to violence by male family members against their mothers or female caretakers.

Sixteen to 34 percent of girls and 10 to 20 percent of boys are sexually abused, most by a family member or trusted family friend.

A family member is involved in nearly one-third of the murders of people aged 60 or older.

---

the life of their relationship; 30 percent of all female homicide victims are slain by their partner or former partner. And, children witness 80 percent of the DV assaults against their mothers.

What comes up for me, David, when I think about why I did not become a physical batterer of my children (including a son who's kind enough not to recall the one firm swat to his butt I gave him when he was four) or of my intimate partners was that my old man didn't start his "lickings" until I was four or five. I read somewhere that if a parent starts beating a kid at, say, one or two or three that child's likely to be one seriously mucked-up adult. The Boys Club of National City also helped, a lot: If I wasn't hunkered down in the front row of the Bay Theater (or out terrorizing the neighborhood with my slingshot), I was at the Boys Club playing basketball, building balsa wood CO_2 land-rockets, and absorbing important life lessons from Coach Frank Leinsteiner and Director Jay Sutcliffe—two men who, unknown to them (and to me, at the time), were my own personal models of male decency and nonviolent communication.

Plus, I never saw my father beat my mother. I don't believe he ever did.

I know this is "personal stuff," David, me jabbering on about our moms and dads, our upbringing. Most cops like opening up about their private lives as much as they enjoy a lecture from the Rev. Al Sharpton. But violence in the home *is not private*. Who you voted for, what you read, what you watch on the tube, what you do when you get naked (kept within, ahem, prudent boundaries)—that's private. Domestic violence is as much a *public* crime as auto theft or a drive-by shooting.

In the early 1970s, clueless that I myself fit the profile of a DV offender, I began to speak out against domestic violence, including child and elder abuse. I was motivated by memorable moments on the beat: a husband who stabbed his wife to death because his dinner was late; a man who allowed his elderly father and his father's twin brother to rot away in a converted garage full of human and dog feces; a buffed-out hod-carrier who whipped welts onto the faces and backs of his six children (all under the age of ten) before binding his diminutive wife at the wrists and ankles, then beating her face into an unrecognizable mush; a mother who shook her baby so hard she produced "boxer's" or "shaken baby" syndrome—which causes a slow degeneration of nerves and other neuropsychological defects in children as they grow.

I spoke out everywhere, David, sharing my personal story (the sanitized Norm-as-kid-victim version at that time), rallying others in support of additional resources for prevention, shelters, child and adult protection services, vigorous enforcement and prosecution.

A huge leap forward in my comprehension of the scope, nature, and consequences of domestic violence—and in my commitment to doing something about it—came in 1980 when in Duluth, Minnesota, a small group of daring and dedicated women formed the "Domestic Abuse Intervention Project." Remember that time, David? Every police chief in the country seemed to have heard about DAIP. Not that they were all that happy with the implications: the identification by the police of a "primary" aggressor, screening for serious threats and/or injuries, mandatory arrests of primary aggressors—it all meant more work for us. But it gave us a clearer, and far more comprehensive picture of the crime of domestic violence—and what to do about it.

Some DAIP theories have been challenged, in most instances by their own ongoing research and analysis, but also by such observers as the late Susan Sontag, the ACLU, and former San Diego police sergeant Anne O'Dell, now an internationally recognized DV expert. They've all raised questions about the most fundamental of DAIP's positions, namely that the primary aggressor in a DV incident be hooked up and taken to jail in *all* cases that result in serious threats and/or physical injury. It's smart theory, predicated on the safety of the victim/survivor and on holding the batterer accountable. All states now have either mandatory or "warrantless" arrest laws. These statutes have saved countless lives. But they can backfire. Busted in front of their partners, some men whose sense of "centrality, superiority, and deservedness" will sit fuming in their jail cells. Plotting deliberate, lethal revenge.

Another problem with mandatory arrests: Cops often make mistakes trying to figure out who the primary aggressor is (this is one of Sontag's concerns; see "Fierce Entanglements" in the November 17, 2002, issue of *The New York Times*). Scratches on a man's face may have been put there by an unprovoked partner. But they could also be the product of a woman defending herself—against being choked to death, for example. I know of a case where a con-wise DV suspect plunged a knife into his own gut just as the cops walked up to the house. Guess who went to jail that night? Clue: It wasn't the husband.

And the ACLU, of which I am a card-carrying, dues-paying member, argues that *requiring* the police to arrest someone too often leads to false arrests. It's the only law on the books that denies cops the discretion to sort out the facts and circumstances of a given case, and to make a case-by-case judgment about what to do. That's bad law, says the ACLU. I agree, in principle. The discretion to arrest, or not, allows professional cops to make prudent, case-by-case decisions that further the causes of victim safety, offender accountability, and justice.

Yet, as a society we're so far behind the curve in protecting women and children that physical-custody arrests *must* be imposed on police, at least for now. It's kind of like affirmative action. You work hard to remedy the problem, even if it requires crude measures; once you've achieved success you can (and should) drop the program. We're not there yet in the battle against racism, or domestic violence.

That being the case, I shook up my department in Seattle. I took DV away from the robbery dicks (and put them back to work on their first love), ripped off detectives from various units within the Investigations Bureau, set up a formal domestic violence unit, recruited a smart, aggressive lieutenant to run it, gave her a virtual blank check to develop the unit—and to staff it with the very best people. I made the DV unit part of a newly formed "Family and Youth Protection Bureau," headed by an assistant chief.

Within a year, twenty-five investigators were working DV cases exclusively, with almost as many additional detectives specializing in stranger-on-stranger sexual assaults—far more than any other centralized investigative function. Each investigator received intensive training, some in specialties that helped establish them as national experts in such areas as stalking, elder abuse prevention and enforcement, computer-based "lethality testing" (to help us predict which of the 10,000 or so annual DV calls in Seattle were most likely to result in death or serious injury), protection orders, even a "DV fugitive" strike team that went out in full uniform, ballistic helmets, and high-powered rifles to take down DV suspects who'd failed to show up in court or who had violated restraining or protection orders.

That last one was partly for show, I admit. It symbolized my priorities, and sent a clear signal to the cop culture that DV enforcement is not social work, it's genuine crime-fighting police work. But it also bowed to the reality that the most risky moment in the life of a DV case is when the guy finally faces facts: when it dawns on him that she really doesn't want him, that she's leaving him—for good. Isn't that right, David? That's also the moment when cops who attempt to intervene are most likely to get blown away. You and I both know a "family beef" is one of the most dangerous 911 calls that are broadcast over the police radio.

Speaking of which: we trained our radio dispatchers, too. Remember those tapes you listened to in your office, David? The type that get played on *60 Minutes* or the local newscast? A woman or a kid is on the line begging us to get there, now! Before Daddy strangles Mommy. Those tapes always give me the willies. They drive home the absolute need for our phone operators and dispatchers to know *exactly* what to say and do, and what not to say or do. (Lessons I'll not repeat here, or anywhere else outside of a training classroom, for fear that some batterer will pick up on our tricks.) Employees who take these calls are forced to make rapid, life-and-death decisions. They need intensive, ongoing training to help them make the right call.

One test of a police department's sophistication in handling DV calls? The number of "mutual combat" arrests, where both parties are showing injuries and the cops can't figure out which one is the *primary* aggressor (who may or may not be the person who "started" the fight—an irrelevancy, in law). When that happens, both parties get carted off. If the number is high (say, 20 or 15 or even 5 percent), you're looking at a very badly trained department. I don't know what Tacoma's average was; I heard you were working to reduce it, David. In Seattle, we averaged a fraction of 1 percent, the result of having effectively trained our entire patrol force.

We developed new investigative procedures and purchased new equipment (including cameras used in "time-lapse" fashion to get pictures of injuries both in the moment and in the days ahead—when bruises and other injuries often turn even more gruesome-looking).

We hired DV advocates, handpicked, specially-trained civilians who cleaned up blood, arranged for medical appointments, found shelters or other lodging and child care, secured transportation and cell phones, comforted and educated and guided women through the legal and other entanglements they faced. Our advocates worked with battered women's programs and survivors of DV incidents to fashion a specific *safety plan* for an endangered woman and/or her children (the ingredients of which I'll also keep secret).

The Seattle Police Department (SPD) reached out to the rest of the criminal justice system, as well, and to the broader "DV community." This is where I think chiefs need to set the example, David. We've been there, we've seen the effects of domestic violence. Our physical presence, our active participation in systemwide efforts is vital. There's no kind way to say this: You were a no-show on that DV council you'd agreed to join. The effects of your absenteeism? You contributed *squat* to the cause. You didn't help your own department improve its performance in combating DV. You lost personal credibility. Apart from all that, I can't shake the thought that you might have *learned* something. Something that, who knows, might have stopped you before it was too late.

To toot my own horn, I served as cochair of our local DV coordinating council and as a Clinton appointee to the National Advisory Council on the Violence Against Women Act—and *nothing* in my Palm Pilot was more important than making those meetings, even though it meant thrice-yearly trips to the other Washington. I'm glad I attended the sessions: I learned something new at every single one. That happens when you rub elbows with the experts.

We constantly swapped research data, anecdotes, and expertise. And we struggled together in common pursuit of answers to such thorny questions as: What do you do with clergymen who, invoking a fundamentalist interpretation of scripture, blame and shame victims of wife battering, who urge these women to do a better job of looking pretty for and obeying their husbands? And how do you penetrate the thick skulls of high school, collegiate, and professional male athletes in order to teach them that it is not their God-given right to fondle, rape, or batter the women in their lives?

One member of our national group, the National Football League's chief psychologist, a former tackle, started off like the sport's chief apologist. Several of us wanted to choke him, but, given the nature of the forum (and the man's size), we thought better of it. Soon enough, however, he came around, and in the end scored a big TD for us: NFL sponsorship of a powerful anti-DV ad.

Not that that solved the problem—read today's paper. If it's not there, it was in yesterday's or it'll be in tomorrow's: Some boneheaded jock slaps his wife and tears her dress off at a party, or rapes a groupie, or smashes up his girlfriend and her apartment. That tearjerker NFL TV spot notwithstanding, we still see countless owners, coaches, athletic directors, teammates, and alumni boosters make excuses for criminals who happen to be athletes. *That ain't the Bubba Bob I know; the Bubba Bob I know is a role model, a pillar of decency and decorum . . . Chainsaw didn't mean to do it, he was drinkin' that whiskey and snortin' that nose candy . . . It's Merle's first time away from home, the boy just got carried away . . . Boys* will *be boys.*

Something else, David. After killing your wife, and damaging your kids for the rest of their lives, you took the coward's way out. Maybe you think you held yourself "accountable" by taking your own life. But all you did was spare yourself the humiliation and degradation of public knowledge of your abuse of women, especially the wife you purported to love. It was a dishonorable thing to do, your suicide. At least O. J. stuck around—a living, respirating reminder of his dead wife. Every time we see that smug mug on the golf course we can use the image as inspiration to redouble our efforts to make women safe. And to hold men like us accountable.

I know you said you were religious, David. I'm not. I don't belong to any church but I'm a spiritual creature, and I believe in a higher power I'm happy to call "God." I believe all God's creatures have souls. I believe in redemption, the opportunity for those of us who've done wrong to try to make ourselves right with the universe—and with our partners, if they'll have us. But that seems possible only if we do the work. You didn't do the work, David.

Sincerely,
Norm

+ + +

I'm at a meeting on Capitol Hill, in Seattle. I get beeped. There's been a shooting. An address shows up on my pager. I know right where it is. It's across the street from "Common Ground," a social services agency that oversees the safe transfer of children in joint custody cases—you know, mom drops the kid off at 8:00 A.M., dad picks her up fifteen minutes later. Dad returns the child at 5:00 P.M., mom picks her up at 5:15. That way mom and dad never have to see each other.

I glide my vehicle under the outer perimeter tape held high by two of my officers and pull up to the inner perimeter. A car is parked facing south in the northbound lane, its driver's door open, the dome light on. Lt. Harry Bailey says, "I thought you'd want to roll on this one, boss." He's right, he's wrong. Behind the wheel of the car is the sprawled body of a woman, dressed in business attire. She's dead. In back, buckled snugly into her car seat, a little girl about two. White tights, patent leather shoes, plaid skirt, puffy nylon jacket. Dark curly hair, long eyelashes, the face of an angel. Her eyes are wide open, her two little fists clenched. She's also dead, shot through the chest.

It was a little after five, a dark, moonless evening when Melanie Edwards had picked up Carli from this "safe house." Her estranged husband, Carl Edwards, had dropped the child off fifteen minutes earlier. Then he stuck around, lying in wait. When the mother and daughter got to the car he shot them both, most likely Carli first so that mom would be forced to watch. Then he sped off.

A week or so later, as a California Highway Patrol officer approached him in Marin County, Edwards shot and killed himself.

Melanie Edwards did everything right. She got a protection order. She moved out of the house. She connected with and got help from a battered women's shelter. She kept her new location secret from Carl. She even seized his gun and turned it over to Seattle police. She arranged for the hassle-free transfer of Carli at the beginning and end of her workday—something she was forced into doing because a clueless judge ruled that Carli's daddy had a right to see his daughter, even in the face of an amply justified protection order. To learn more about why this happens, read Professor Sarah Buel, founder and codirector of the University of Texas's Domestic Violence Clinic (see especially

"Access to Meaningful Remedy: Overcoming Doctrinal Obstacles in Tort Litigation Against Domestic Violence Offenders," *Oregon Law Review,* No. 83, 2005.) Buel has spent twenty-six years in the courts as an advocate and prosecutor. Her examples of the "acculturated non-empathy" of lawyers and judges are as jolting as they are revolting. To repeat: Melanie Edwards did everything right.

What is it with these fathers? David Brame names his son, "David, Jr.," and five years later kills the boy's mother in front of the kid. Carl Edwards names his *daughter* after himself, then shoots her. What else can we conclude: To men such as David Brame and Carl Edwards and God knows how many others, families are disposable property.

+ + +

Let me guess, if you're a certain kind of man you've already blown a gasket. Yes, you say, it's horrible what *some* men do to their wives and children. But, not *all* men are like Brame or Edwards. Men are also beaten and battered, knifed or shot by their women partners. If you're a certain kind of male cop you're especially impatient for me to acknowledge this, to say *something* about these women, the female DV offenders you encounter on the job—the ones who scream and rant and spit and hit.

They're out there, believe me. Misogynist cops call them *nags, cunts, bitches, ball-busters.* Even before "primary aggressor" became part of our lexicon I encountered several such women. In fact, I choked one out one night. Her name was Kathryn Knox. She was beating the crap out of my partner after she'd beaten the crap out of *her* partner, a good-sized male.

My heart goes out to any man who's been falsely arrested, maliciously prosecuted, wrongly convicted. An injustice is an injustice.

But hear this, guys: domestic violence is overwhelmingly a *male* problem. Look at the numbers. In about 15 percent of DV cases the woman goes to jail. Many men say that that number underestimates the incidence of women who batter men. I say bullshit.

Often, women are arrested because they've committed the "crime" of self-defense. Or, they've simply had enough and decided to retaliate. Sorry, man, but if your partner comes at you as you sleep off a drunk, after having sliced her with a box-cutter, thrown hot coffee in her face, or blackened her eye—and she puts a 12-gauge shotgun under your chin and pulls the trigger . . . let's just say you don't want me on your jury.

And how many men are *actually* afraid of their female partners? Some, to be sure (I'd rather not have to face Kathryn Knox again). But, most? I doubt it. Men are simply bigger, meaner, scarier, better acculturated to violence.

Look, the time has come for us boys to grow up, to take responsibility for our actions. A big step in that direction, if you're a batterer, is to get help. Now. Today. It won't be easy, even if you're highly motivated. But you *can* do it. (And, for God's sake, avoid batterers' treatment programs that try to "pathologize" you or "anger management" you out of your abusive ways. True, you may be nuts, and you may have a hell of a temper. But DV, like rape, is a crime of power and control. If I'm a controlling, self-centered abuser driven by an ingrained sense of entitlement, the last thing my partner needs is a calmer, "less angry" me. Something tells me David Brame was devoid of all anger when he put that .45 slug into his wife's head.)

Another suggestion? Look for a treatment program led by a *male-female* team, for reasons you'll understand when you get there. This bit of wisdom brought to you by my friends Don Drozd, a California attorney, and Anita Castle, executive director of the San Juan County, Washington, Domestic Violence and Sexual Assault program—who've teamed up to provide excellent batterers' treatment.

There's so much that needs to be done to make the American home a safe place for every member of the family. Research tells us that violence is learned behavior. As a society we do a depressingly superb job of teaching violence to our children, particularly our little boys. We need to *instruct* our kids in nonviolence, and gender equality, starting in grade school. Men in positions of power and/or celebrity—athletes and actors, pastors and principals, police officers and politicians—need to speak out. I'd love to see these guys use their positions to convey the message that real men don't hit women or kids.

Within the criminal justice system, police departments, prosecutors, and judges need to be held to a much higher standard of performance. For years it was the cops who sat in the cellar of learning and acumen about domestic violence; now it's mostly our judges, some of whom continue to make spectacularly stupid decisions when it comes to the protection of women and children.

Our communities at large need to insist on a vastly improved social and governmental response to prevention, enforcement, shelters, and other services, including batterers' treatment. I've never seen an instance of *sustained* community pressure that didn't exact significant changes in the priorities or performance of a public agency.

Every person convicted of domestic violence who has undergone batterers' treatment or who has been previously sentenced for domestic violence, and who re-offends (and is convicted a second time of stalking or felonious spousal assault or child abuse) *should be sent to prison for life.* Such a person is simply too dangerous to live in the free world. The victim/survivor needs to know that her assailant will never again harm or terrorize her or her children.

+ + +

To end on a positive note, a story of at least one exclusively male sports organization that did the right thing by women. In 1995 the Seattle Mariners came from thirteen games back in August to win their division. "Mariner fever" gripped the city, and a slogan—"Refuse to Lose"—was born. "Refuse" signs and T-shirts cropped up everywhere. My staff and I scurried down to Pioneer Square near the old King Dome and purchased armloads of the shirts. I set aside a day where all nonuniformed personnel could wear them and show off our Mariner spirit (it must have worked—we beat the Yankees in the playoffs). And all this has *what* to do with DV?

The next year, I joined a group of state and local DV advocates who presented a proposal to Mariners' management. They loved our idea, and soon thereafter launched the "Refuse to Abuse" campaign. The club dedicated a ball game at Safeco Field to the cause, and invited my Seattle colleague on the national advisory council, Dr. Marie Fortune (and rabid Mariners fan), to throw out the first pitch of the night. Throughout the game anti-DV messages were flashed on the scoreboard. Our new

"Refuse" T-shirts were all over the ballpark. But the strongest component of the campaign, which resonates to this day, was a series of TV ads, featuring Mariner stars (carefully vetted to make sure we weren't showcasing a batterer).

Here's Joey Cora's, a favorite of Seattle fans: "When I'm on the field I do everything in my power hit the ball. But I will . . . never . . . ever . . . hit . . . a . . . woman."

CHAPTER 2

WAGE WAR ON CRIME,
NOT DRUGS

I FLOATED INTO THE conference room and settled into a chair that seemed to have been constructed of warm air and goose down. A moment later my colleagues filtered in, in slow motion, the contours of their bodies blurring into gold and cerulean auras. These were the finest individuals in the universe. Worthy, noble, virtuous. It was a marvelous meeting, each person respectful, no one interrupting. Everyone agreeing with my point of view on every item on the agenda. It was a perfect Percodan day.

Alcohol had always been my drug of choice, but in the mid-eighties I went to work with my pockets full of painkillers. I popped them throughout the day, long after the misery of a failed kidney stone extraction had worn off. Administrative problems vanished, or lost their weight; organizational enemies became pals; dreaded bureaucratic meetings turned into pleasant, almost cosmic out-of-body experiences. After a couple of months, though, I stopped. Cold turkey. Why? Because I ran out of pills, and as a deputy chief of police I was afraid to ask for more.

+ + +

I wasn't the only doper in government. There were far more consequential personages into the drug scene. Richard Nixon, depressed over the public's reaction to Vietnam and Watergate, scored a dealer-volume supply of Dilantin and wolfed down hundreds if not thousands of the mood-altering caps from 1970 through the end of his presidency in 1974.* Bill Clinton

---

* Anthony Summers with Robbyn Swann. *The Arrogance of Power: The Secret World of Richard Nixon.* Viking, 1992.

denied inhaling but confessed to puffing. Al Gore copped to being a heavy weed smoker in college. George W. Bush refuses to refute accounts he was a cokester in school. And Marion Barry? Please.

Where does it end? It doesn't, and it's not just politicians, of course, or the occasional police official. It's *everybody*—every demographic, every occupation in the country is well represented, including shock-talk radio hosts like Rush Limbaugh whose housekeeper kept him supplied with cigar boxes full of OxyContin and other narcotics. We do like our drugs.

And so what? If I want to inject, ingest, or inhale a mood- or mind-altering substance—whether to find God, flee personal problems, or just feel good—that's my business. Not the government's. Unless . . . well, exceptions to follow.

I say it's time to withdraw the troops in the war on drugs.

For a jaw-dropping illustration of drug enforcement's financial costs, take a look at drugsense.org's "Drug War Clock." To the tune of $600 a second, taxpayers are financing this war. For the year 2004 the figure will have added up to over $20 billion, and that's just for *federal* enforcement alone. You can add another $22 to $24 billion for state and local drug law enforcement, and even more billions for U.S. drug interdiction work on the international scene. We're talking well over $50 billion a year to finance America's war on drugs.

Think of this war's *real* casualties: tens of thousands of otherwise inno-cent Americans incarcerated, many for twenty years or more, some for life; families ripped apart; drug traffickers and blameless bystanders shot dead on city streets; narcotics officers assassinated here and abroad, with prose-cutors, judges, and elected officials in Latin America gunned down for their courageous stands against the cartels; and all those dollars spent on federal, state, and local cops, courts, prosecutors, prisons, probation, parole, and pee-in-the-bottle programs. Even federal aid to bribe distant nations to stop feeding *our* habit.

"Plan Colombia" was hatched under the last year of the Clinton administration to wage America's drug war on Colombian soil. Costing over $1.3 billion ($800 million going to the military), the plan sought to "eradicate" that nation's coca and heroin poppy plants (Colombia supplied 95 percent of this nation's cocaine). The chemical used was the herbicide glyphosate which, sprayed on crops, does untold damage to the environment; when sprayed on water supplies or unprotected people it causes a host of serious to fatal medical problems. Similar efforts in Peru and Bolivia have reduced production only temporarily, and always at high cost: recall that the Peruvian air force, on the strength of mistaken U.S. drug intelligence, shot down a civilian aircraft carrying an American missionary and her infant daughter in April 2001.

In Afghanistan, the Bush administration supported the Taliban, to the tune of $125 million in foreign aid, plus another $43 million for enforcing its ostensible ban on poppy production—right up until September 10, 2001. (As Robert Scheer makes clear in his May 22, 2001, column in *The Los Angeles Times*—"Bush's Faustian Deal with the Taliban"—the president knew all along that the Taliban was hiding Osama bin Laden.)

Today Afghanistan's drug lords give the country's warlords (when they're not one and the same) a run for their money. The Government Accountability Office (GAO) in the summer of 2004 issued a scathing report citing the phenomenal growth in Afghan poppy production—and the Bush administration's failure to monitor its own anti-drug aid. The United Nations estimates the value of the 2004 crop at $2.2 billion, with production up 40 percent, breaking all records for a single year. According to Peter Rodman of the Pentagon, "profits from the production of illegal narcotics flow into coffers of warlord militias, corrupt government officials, and extremist forces" (BBC News, September 24, 2004).

The United States has, through its war on drugs, fostered political instability, official corruption, and health and environmental disasters around the globe. In truth, the U.S.-sponsored international war on drugs is a war on poor people, most of them subsistence farmers caught in a dangerous no-win situation.

+ + +

Another casualty of the drug war: the reputation of individual police officers, individual departments, and the entire system of American law enforcement. If you aspire to be a crooked cop, drugs are clearly the way to go. The availability, street value, and illegality of drugs form a sweet temptation to character-challenged cops, many of whom wind up shaking down street dealers, converting drugs to their own use, or selling them. Almost all the major police corruption scandals of the last several decades have had their roots in drug enforcement. We've seen robbery, extortion, drug dealing, drug stealing, drug use, false arrests, perjury, throw-down guns, and murder. And these are the good guys?

There isn't an unscathed police department in the country. New York, Los Angeles, Chicago, Philadelphia, Detroit, Washington, D.C., Memphis, Miami, Oakland, Dallas, Kansas City—all have recently suffered stunning police drug scandals. You won't find a single major city in the country that has not fired and/or arrested at least one of its own for some drug-related offense in the past few years, including San Diego and Seattle. Smaller cities have not been spared. The cities of Irvington and West New York, New Jersey, and Ford Heights, Illinois, saw cops transporting, peddling, using, protecting drug shipments, and/or extorting dealers. In Ford Heights, it was former police chief Jack Davis. A twenty-five-year veteran, he was convicted of extorting heroin and crack cocaine dealers, allowing them to operate on the streets of his own city as he pocketed their dirty money.

Tulia, Texas, offers another example of a cop—and a *system*—gone bad. Tom Coleman, an ex-police officer, was hired by the federally-funded Texas Panhandle Regional Narcotics Trafficking Taskforce to conduct undercover narcotics operations in Tulia in 1998. In 1999 Coleman arrested 46 people, 39 of them black. He put dozens of "drug peddlers" behind bars—for 60, 90, 434 years (we're talking Texas, here). The only problem? Coleman made up the charges. He manufactured evidence. Working alone, he never wore a wire, never taped a conversation, never dusted the plastic bags he "scored" for fingerprints. He testified in court that he wrote his notes of drug transactions on his leg. Who *was* this Tom Coleman?

A 1997 background investigation revealed that he'd been disciplined in a previous law enforcement job, that he had "disciplinary" and "possible mental problems," that he "needed constant supervision, had a bad temper and would tend to run to his mother for help." According to *New York Times* reporter Adam Liptak, Coleman had "run up bad debts in another law enforcement job before leaving town abruptly in the middle of a shift. . . . Eight months into the undercover investigation, Coleman's supervisors received a warrant calling for his arrest for stealing gasoline. They arrested him, let him out on bond and allowed him to make restitution for the gas and other debts of $7,000. The undercover investigation then continued."

In August 2003, Governor Rick Perry pardoned thirty-five of the people Coleman sent to prison, thirty-one of them black.

Thousands of drug cases have been dismissed throughout the country in just the past few years because of similar police malfeasance. Spurred on by federal financial incentives, departments exert tremendous pressure on narcotics units and individual narcs to make a lot of busts, impound a lot of dope, and seize as much of a drug trafficker's assets as possible.

+ + +

On June 17, 1971, President Nixon declared drugs "public enemy number one in the United States." Just how prevalent is drug use in America? In 1975, according to the Monitoring the Future survey, 87 percent of high school seniors reported that it was "easy" or "fairly easy" to buy marijuana. At the dawn of the new century, and millions of arrests later, the figure is at 90.4 percent. The National Center on Addiction and Substance Abuse reported in 1998 that high school students found it a lot easier to score pot than to purchase beer. In 1988 Congress set a goal of a "drug-free America by 1995." Yet, according to research of the Drug Policy Foundation in Washington, D.C. (which in 2000 merged with the George Soros–funded Lindesmith/Drug Policy Research Institute to form the widely respected Drug Policy Institute), the number of Americans who have used illegal drugs stands at 77 million and counting. That's a lot of enemies.

Not that the war on drugs hasn't taken prisoners. The Department of Justice reports that of the huge increases in federal and state prison populations during the eighties and nineties (from 139 per 100,000 residents in 1980 to 476 per 100,000 in 2002), the vast majority are for drug convictions. The FBI reports that 580,900 Americans were arrested on drug charges in 1980. By 1999 that annual figure had ballooned to 1,532,200. Today there are more arrests for drug offenses than for murder, manslaughter, forcible rape, and aggravated assault combined.

Nowhere is this misguided campaign waged more mindlessly than in New York. The "Rockefeller Drug Laws" call for life in prison for first-time offenders convicted of possessing four ounces, or selling two ounces, of a controlled substance. The result? The state's prison system is filled to the gills, with drug offenders, most of them convicted of minor offenses, most of them nonviolent, taking up 18,300 of its beds.

+ + +

By any standard, the United States has lost its war on drugs. Criminalizing drug use—for which there is, was, and always will be an insatiable appetite—has been a colossal mistake, wasting vast sums of money, and adding to the misery of millions of Americans.

The solution? *Regulated legalization.* "Decriminalization," the controlled legalization of drugs, means you take the crime out of the use of drugs but preserve government's right—and responsibility—to regulate the field.

How would it work? If I were the new (and literal) Drug Czar I would have private companies compete for licenses to cultivate, harvest, manufacture, package, and peddle drugs. I'd create a new federal regulatory agency (with no apologies to libertarians and neo-cons) to: (1) set and enforce standards of sanitation, potency, and purity; (2) ban advertising; (3) impose taxes, fees, and fines to be used for drug abuse prevention and treatment, and to cover the costs of administering the new regulatory agency; and (4) police the industry much as alcoholic beverage control agencies operate in the states.

But I wouldn't stop there. I would put all those truly frightening, explosion-prone, toxic meth labs out of business—today; make sure that no one was deprived of methadone or other medical treatment for addiction or abuse; establish free needle exchange programs and permit pharmacy sales of sterile, nonprescription needles in every city; and require random, mandatory drug testing (of the type that would have nailed me) for those workers whose judgment and mental alertness are essential to public safety—cops, firefighters, soldiers, airline pilots, bus drivers, ferry boat operators, train engineers, et al. (Not part of the et al. are brain surgeons, mental health counselors, and countless others whose sensitive work, if botched, would generally not jeopardize *public* safety.)

And, in my spare time, I'd mandate effective drug prevention education in all elementary, middle, and secondary schools. But what about DARE, you say? All those black and red bumper stickers, T-shirts, coffee mugs, dump trucks—surely it's the best "drug abuse resistance and education" going? Not according to the Triangle Research Institute out of North Carolina. Their comprehensive mid-1990s study, commissioned by the Department of Justice (which then refused to publish the damning results, showing that DARE grads were just as likely as non-grads to use drugs), convinced me to get rid of the popular program in Seattle. I replaced it with—nothing. We were fortunate in that city to have a public school system teaching a comprehensive "healthy living" curriculum in the elementary grades, which included a superb drug prevention/education component. Based on the work of J. David Hawkins and Richard F. Catalano at the University of Washington, it remains a model for the nation.

I would insist on the enforcement of existing criminal laws and policies against street dealing, furnishing to minors, driving under the influence, or invoking drug influence as a criminal defense. Consequently, if someone chose to take a drug, anything they did under its effects would be 100 percent their responsibility, which would make them 100 percent accountable for any and all results. If they rob a bank, drive high (or low), furnish drugs (including alcohol) to a minor, smack their neighbor upside the head, slip Ecstasy into their date's drink, they should be arrested, charged, and prosecuted. If convicted, they should be forced to pay a fair but painful price for their *criminal* irresponsibility. Moreover, if they've injured or killed someone in the process, they should be slapped with civil damages. I've never understood defense attorneys who argue, "Gee, your honor, my client was so loaded she didn't know what she was doing."

+ + +

But what of the undeniable harm caused by drugs? Wouldn't legalization make things worse? Who knows? We're too scared to approach the subject in a calm, open, levelheaded manner. But, I'll tell you what I *think* would happen: there would be a slight increase in drug use, and no measurable increase in drug abuse. Experiences in Portugal and the Netherlands suggest that decriminalization does not unleash a mad rush for drugs among the currently abstemious.

In the 1970s, at the time New York governor Nelson Rockefeller was crafting his eponymous drug laws, Amsterdam, not unlike New York City, was witnessing huge increases in heroin use. And in socially upsetting, often violent incidents as hypes fought to obtain and keep their dope. Unlike New York's officials, however, the Dutch set about a rational, compassionate civic dialogue on what to do about the country's drug problem.

Recently, I met in Seattle with about a dozen police and prosecutorial officials from The Hague. They told me that while Dutch law enforcement continues to zealously pursue drug-related organized crime, it treats *all* drug-dependency as an illness, not a criminal offense. Today, marijuana may be cultivated, sold in cafes (in small quantities), and used (responsibly). Methadone is available on demand, heroin by prescription. Bottom line, according to both my foreign colleagues and the research of this nation's Drug Policy Alliance? Drug use, in every single category, is lower in the Netherlands than in the U.S.

Handled properly, legalization would improve the overall health—physical, emotional, and financial—of our society and our neighborhoods.

How? For starters, it would put illicit traffickers out of business, and their obscene, untaxed profits would evaporate overnight. Dealers and runners and mules and nine-year-old lookouts would be off street corners, and out of the line of fire. It would take much of the fun out of being a gang member (gang-banging being synonymous these days with drug dealing, "markets" synonymous with "turf"). Firearms, big, rapid-fire firearms, employed in the expansion and protection of drug markets would go quiet—a welcome change for peace-loving citizens, and the nation's cops. Drug raids on the wrong house would be a thing of the past.*

---

* In the late 1980s I showed up shortly after my narcs had shot and killed the utterly innocent father of a suspected drug dealer; I stared in disbelief at the body of a fifty-eight-year-old man who'd made the mistake of answering his door with a TV remote in hand.

And since most junkies finance their addiction by breaking into your home, stealing or prowling your car, or mugging you on the street, crimes like burglary, robbery, auto theft, and car prowl would drop. A *lot.* Justice Department studies linking patterns of property crime and drug use suggest a reduction of *35 to 50 percent* in those crimes alone.

Legalization would arguably wipe out at least one variety of structural racism, as well as class discrimination. A sad but safe generalization: poor blacks smoke cheap crack, upscale whites snort the spendy powdered version of cocaine. And who goes to jail? For longer periods of time? Blacks, of course. Nowhere is this more evident than in Texas where, according to the Justice Policy Institute, blacks are incarcerated at a rate 63 percent higher than the national rate . . . for blacks! (Nationally, according to the Bureau of Justice statistics, 12 percent of all African-American men between the ages of 20 and 34 are in prison versus 1.6 percent of white men). More than half of these African-Americans are in prison for nonviolent offenses, mostly drug-related. Needless to say, this same group is grossly underrepresented in drug treatment programs.

+ + +

Before I became a cop I didn't think about any of this. I'd seen *Reefer Madness*, and a detective once brought marijuana to school to show us what it looked like—so we wouldn't accidentally smoke it and rot the membranes of our noses. (*Pot*, he'd said, would do that.) But, except for underage alcohol bingeing, I wasn't interested in illegal drugs so the scare tactics were wasted on me.

Then I became a cop. In my first year I kicked in a dozen or so doors, charged into people's homes, scooped up their weeds, seeds, and pot pipes, and carted these "felons" off to jail in handcuffs. It was fun for a while. But it got old.

Patrolman "Mike Jones," who worked a beat near mine, lived to pinch druggies. He wasn't a narc, just a uniformed patrolman like me. But for some reason he had a hard-on for anyone holding. He'd twist and bend the U.S. Constitution left and right to get a "consent" search on everything from traffic stops to loud-party calls. Then he'd rip out back seats, rifle through drawers, and stuff his hands into people's pockets until he'd come up with half a baggie, or a seed. A *seed!* Since Jones drove the police ambulance, I usually wound up transporting his prisoners—older teens and young adults mostly, not likely to make anyone's "most wanted" list. They'd sit in the back seat of my cage car, mumbling, "Oh wow, man. Oh wow." Or, "This cage is *weird*, man." Or, "Hey, you got any Fritos?" I had plenty of other things I could—and should—have been doing. Like arresting wife beaters and child abusers, giving rides to real criminals.

By then I was convinced that drug abuse was a medical problem. I found myself debating fellow cops, arguing that society ought to help abusers get off drugs. I won few converts. Most of my colleagues thought drug users should rot in hell and traffickers lined up and shot. But a few showed compassion, and some actually tried to get medical assistance for the strung-out junkies on their beats. The best we could do for them was to haul them to County Hospital for a stomach pump, or attempt to sneak them into the East Wing, known in those days as the "psycho ward."

+ + +

Today, in these more "enlightened" times, the most caring cop would still be hard-pressed to find adequate services for those in need. Ethan Nadelmann, director of the Drug Policy Institute, says he does not favor broad legalization of drugs. But he does advocate, forcefully, "harm-reduction." Writing in the January/February 1998 issue of *Foreign Affairs*, he defines the strategy:

> Harm-reduction innovations include efforts to stem the spread of HIV by making sterile syringes readily available and collecting used syringes; allowing doctors to prescribe oral methadone for heroin addiction treatment, as well as heroin and other drugs for addicts who would otherwise buy them on the black market; establishing "safe injection rooms" so addicts do not congregate in public places or dangerous "shooting galleries"; employing drug analysis units at the large dance parties called raves to test the quality and potency of MDMA, known as

Ecstasy, and other drugs that patrons buy and consume there;
decriminalizing (but not legalizing) possession and retail sale of
cannabis and, in some cases, possession of small amounts of
"hard" drugs; and integrating harm-reduction policies and principles into community policing strategies.

Sound sensible? Of course it does, at least to those not under the influence
of shortsightedness. Yet many cities refuse to adopt or even allow needle
exchanges. They're thinking, among other things, "There goes the neighborhood." Doctors and other professionals have been known to use
heroin, but more often the user resembles your worst stereotype of a drug
fiend. Moreover, many communities cannot afford to staff an exchange—
particularly late at night when an IV user is searching for a clean needle.
Still, it's in everyone's best interest, for public health reasons alone, to have
sufficient numbers of needle exchange programs, or better (as California
has done), to allow nonprescription sales of clean needles in every city in the
country. Thirty-five percent of all AIDS patients have been infected by
contaminated needles, or through sex with an IV user.

Methadone clinics, in those few communities willing to tolerate them,
have long waiting lists—and that's for people who *want* to wean themselves
off heroin, who are willing to work at it.

Where do we find the money to treat addiction and other drug abuse
problems when tens of millions of Americans can't even get basic health
insurance, or insulin or heart meds or cancer drugs at affordable prices?
Law enforcement officials at every level—federal, state, and local—know
the answer, and it scares them to death: take it from them, the cops.

Use the money now being squandered on drug enforcement, domesti-
cally and internationally, to finance a fresh, new public policy that educates,
regulates, medicates, and rehabilitates.

+ + +

But shouldn't certain drugs, certain *really* dangerous drugs be outlawed?
Possibly, but only one comes to mind: the animal tranquilizer, PCP (see
sidebar).

PHENCYCLIDINE (PCP)

Phencyclidine, a synthetic drug manufactured originally as a human anesthetic (and quickly abandoned when people under its influence turned violent or suicidal), wasn't around—or at least being used by humans—when I was a beat cop. Along about the time I became a lieutenant it started showing up under its various colorful street names: Angel Dust, Hog, Peace Pills, Rocket Fuel, Wack, Ozone, and, my personal favorites, DOA and Embalming Fluid. PCP wasn't pretty, and it took us a good while to learn how to handle it on the streets.

Let me illustrate with a hypothetical, drawn from experiences both in San Diego and Seattle, replete with the obligatory racial and political overtones.

You're a white cop. You get a call about a young black man acting strange at a grocery store. You show up, find him sweeping items off the shelves. He's incoherent but unambiguously threatening. He's got a wild look in his eyes, he's sweating buckets. You try to calm him, speaking softly, murmuring soothing words. He acts like you're not there. You know that you need reinforcements, at least three, preferably twice that many additional cops. You understand that you and your colleagues will be criticized for "ganging up" on the young, black, unarmed man, but you've been here before. This is not your first PCP case. You know that the best way to get him into custody and into a secure medical facility (the jail won't, and shouldn't, take him in that condition) is to swarm him, literally overwhelm him. No guns, no sticks, no fists, no feet. Just a good old-fashioned eight-arm bearhug. It's what they taught you in the academy.

As your backup units stream into the parking lot, your suspect starts flinging canned comestibles your way. You and your fellow officers keep your guns holstered, likewise your mace and batons—an act of remarkable (and legally unnecessary) restraint. Slowly, no sudden movements, you inch toward him. As a tin of green beans sails past your head you and your mates lunge, grab the guy, take him to the floor. Even with all that weight on him he puts up a hell of fight, flailing savagely and kicking you in the cojones. Through your pain, you attempt to wrestle a pair of plastic flexcuffs on him. The fight lasts three minutes which seems like three hours. Finally, he's subdued.

As you start to lift him you notice he's not breathing. Nobody's choked him, nobody's hit him. But, there he lies, limp, motionless, his eyeballs rolled up into his head, drool running down his chin. You immediately cut the flexcuffs off, and you and a second cop begin CPR. Another gets on the radio and summons an aid car, Code 3. You lay him out on the gurney, get him into the ambulance. You follow the medics to the ER. But your man's DOA.

You're devastated. And, as members of the black community rally and march and demand your dismissal and prosecution for murder, you wonder what you could have done differently. An autopsy reveals the probable cause of death: acute PCP intoxication combined with intense physical exertion and "positional asphyxiation" leading to sudden, irreversible cardiac arrest. Maybe he had a preexisting condition—heart disease, arteriosclerosis, high blood pressure, asthma. Maybe not. Whatever. He's dead. At the hands of the police.

Who killed him? He killed himself! (See "100 percent responsible, 100 percent accountable.") But that will not satisfy the ignorant throngs calling for your badge. And, it probably won't satisfy you, as you continue to grieve and to speculate. What if . . . If only . . . Apart from not showing up that day, or pretending not to hear the call, what could you have done differently? How might you have been able to get that guy into the hospital—alive?

You'll ask yourself that question for the rest of your life.

So maybe we ought not to legalize PCP. But are there others? Police officers will chime in with crack cocaine; they do fight a lot of crazy-acting crackheads. Crankheads too, for that matter. And what about gamma hydroxybutyrate, also known as GHB? Ecstasy has been abused, unconscionably, especially on the clubbing/dating scene. But, realistically, *any* drug can be scapegoated. In fact, people under the influence of booze, or anger, or jealousy, can be just as dangerous as those who've smoked crack. Hell, even a pot smoker can occasionally get in touch with his or her inner demon and come out swinging.

If decriminalization makes sense, why is there such virulent opposition to permitting and regulating drug use and "medicalizing" drug abuse? Well, many parents have witnessed firsthand the harmful effects of drug abuse in their own children. They've seen their families damaged or destroyed. To them, decriminalization makes as much sense as letting a three-year-old play with a loaded .38. To others, drug use is a sin, a moral transgression—and what is government for if not to enforce morality? Then there are those like former attorney general John Ashcroft, who argue that in addition to its moral deficiencies, drug legalization would aid terrorism.* And, let's not forget the drug dealers: at last count *they* were overwhelmingly opposed to legalization.

But the greatest resistance is embedded in the culture of the "drug enforcement industry." Generations of lawmakers and law enforcers have invested, psychically as well as financially, in our current system.

Thousands of local PDs, for example, rely on "seized assets" from narcotics suspects to fund a significant slice of their budgetary pies. Lest there be any misunderstanding about my position on nailing drug traffickers and sticking it to them, let me just say I remember the day SDPD took delivery of a pair of matching Bell Jet Ranger helicopters. They'd been "donated" by a couple of dealers who wouldn't be using them for, say, twenty years to life, their trafficking means and proceeds having been forfeited to the cops who'd captured them. I harbor no love for dealers; they're a despicable lot, on the whole. But I've grown serious doubts about the asset seizure philosophy, as well as the seizure and forfeiture practices of most police agencies.**

Opposition to legalization runs so deep among law enforcers that many refuse even to talk about it. And they'll do their best to shut you up if you so much as mention it.

+ + +

At three different drug conferences in Washington, D.C, through the eighties and early nineties, I heard then-LAPD chief Daryl Gates, followed by high-ranking Justice officials from both the Reagan and Bush-the-Elder administrations, introduce sessions with this admonition, *Don't even* think *about decriminalization—it's not on the agenda.* Gates went so far as to say,

---

* This genuinely laughable notion comes from the same hypocritical "states rights" reactionary who tried to gut perfectly sound state laws on medical marijuana.

** Many local PDs make a bundle by converting drug dealers' seized assets to their own. They pad annual or biennial budgets with everything from bulging briefcases of cash to stocks, bonds, laundered bank accounts, homes, businesses and other real estate, cigarette boats, Jaguars, Harleys, weaponry, even fine art. These departments have developed a dependency, an *addiction* you might say, on this extra revenue stream. They're supposed to put the proceeds to use in drug prevention and enforcement only, but any muckraker with a follow-the-money nose for "misappropriation" could easily uncover multiple violations of federal and/or state laws in all but the most squeaky-clean agencies.

"If someone brings it up, shut him off!" He glared right at me. Under Clinton's Department of Justice the message was no different.

Not everyone is frightened of the First Amendment. Many Americans are speaking up, demanding a new, *workable* approach to the drug problem. An October 2002 *Time*/CNN poll showed that 72 percent of Americans already believe there should be no jail time for possessing small amounts of pot, and 80 percent support medical marijuana programs (maybe that's because 47 percent of them had used the weed). When, as chief of the Seattle Police Department, I made my views on drugs known at a conference of mayors from Washington, Oregon, and British Columbia, the response was overwhelmingly positive. In presentations I made to business groups throughout southern California in the early nineties, the typical reaction was, *Why can't our government see the folly of the drug war? It's just plain* bad business, *a gigantic waste of taxpayer money.*

A handful of politicians and even a police chief or two do favor decriminalization. I know this because they whisper endorsements in the privacy of their offices or over an adult beverage after a drug conference. Why don't they speak up? They're *scared*. They think they'll be voted out of office or forced to turn in their badges. But they "misunderestimate" the wisdom, the common sense of their constituencies.

Americans want to see their tax dollars spent on prevention and enforcement of *predatory* crimes, crimes that frighten them, take money out of their pockets, restrict their freedoms and cause them to change the way they live: domestic violence, child abuse, rape, robbery, burglary, auto theft, workplace and school violence, white collar, political, and environmental crimes.

Right now, the only people actively campaigning for sanity on the drug scene are hempheads, political mavericks, and career *decriminalistas*. If a small collection of thoughtful, currently closeted law enforcers were to make their views known they'd have influence far beyond their numbers. At the very least they might encourage a dialogue with their colleagues who remain under a culture-imposed gag order. It's time to talk about this, my brothers and sisters in law enforcement. It really is.

In the Netherlands, in England, in Canada it's been the cops leading the way. In the early nineties I keynoted an annual conference of the Canadian

Association of Chiefs of Police. I was struck by the candor and wisdom of several of its members as we chatted about the drug problem in our respective countries. In 1999, CACP passed a resolution calling for the decriminalization of small amounts of marijuana. Soon after, the Royal Canadian Mounted Police offered a statement in "full support" of the police chiefs' resolution.

Much to the dismay of the Bush administration, Canada is now earnestly debating the decriminalization of marijuana possession and use. At least one North American country has the strength and the sobriety to look at adult drug use as a basic human right. And to treat drug *abuse*, including my own near-addiction, as a medical not a criminal problem.

CHAPTER 3

PROSTITUTION: GET A ROOM!

"I'LL BET YOU CAN'T guess what my eight-year-old boy took to show-and-tell yesterday." The woman had been taking in her trashcans when she spotted my car and flagged us over. I'd been driving at patrol speed down her street, chatting with a *Seattle Times* columnist who was along for an earful of community-policing philosophy.

"What's that?"

"You won't believe it," said the woman. "Let me go in and get it." We got out of the car and waited on the sidewalk. She came back out carrying one of those small boxes your checks come in. "Here, take a look for yourself." We gazed down at a used condom in the corner of the box. I knew where this story was going. I'd heard it before at a community meeting in San Diego, except that version involved a nine-year-old girl who'd scooped up a used syringe to go with the condom.

"Where did he find it?"

"Right where you're standing." She called her husband out of the house to confirm the story. "And this isn't the first one," said the woman. "We find these things all the time. Plus needles and wadded up Kleenex and . . . I don't know *what* possessed that child to do such a thing!" Her husband explained that they'd tried to shield the boy from these findings. It was his job to police the area before the kid went to school. But, "Sometimes you miss one."

"Look down our street, Chief," said the woman. "What do you see?"

"For Sale signs." Every other yard sported one.

"Ours is going up next." The family lived on a busy residential arterial in a low-income neighborhood, perfect sales territory for hookers and their pimps.

The couple was forced to contend with prostitutes who work the morning commute: businessmen, professionals, blue-collar workers on their way to their jobs (or just getting off the graveyard shift). The hooker stands on the sidewalk, usually at the corner. The john pulls up, rolls his window down. The two of them play the language game, settle on a specific service and a price. She hops in, they drive off. But not far. If there's an alley with off-street parking they may go there, pulling into an empty apartment space. Or they may drive a block, pull over, and do the deed at the curb. It's usually over in five to fifteen minutes, the detritus of the trade often left behind for homeowners to clean up. Or for their kids to take to school.

It's a dirty business, practiced that way. And a dangerous one.

Dr. Stig Larsson, professor of social medicine at Lund University in Sweden, reports, "Historically, one finds the worst conditions in street prostitution." This is borne out by the numbers of serial killings of street hookers over the years.

In Vancouver, B.C., we have Robert William Pickton, a pig farmer charged with twenty-two murders but likely responsible for many more (over sixty women disappeared from the streets of Vancouver between 1978 and 2001). There's John Eric Armstrong, an aircraft refueler, who has killed all around the world—Detroit, Seattle, Virginia, Thailand, Singapore, Korea, Israel, Hong Kong. He claims thirty victims but, again, the number is probably much higher. Then there's the "Spokane Serial Killer," Robert Lee Yates, Jr., who's serving 408 years in prison on ten counts of murder, though it's anybody's guess how many prostitutes he's actually killed (by uncommon means, incidentally: he shot most of his victims, a loud way to take a life). The beginning of his spree is traceable back to two murders in Walla Walla in 1975. Then we have truck driver Gary Ridgway, the "Green River Killer," who may have killed as many as ninety street prostitutes in Washington. It's hard to imagine a medium-size or large city in America that has not experienced serial killings of street prostitutes.

San Diego had its own major series back in the eighties and nineties, but with a minor twist: for a long time people close to the investigations were sure police officers were involved.

+ + +

In 1992 I received a call from San Diego district attorney Ed Miller. We exchanged pleasantries then he said, "We need to talk. In person."

"When?"

"Now."

"Where?"

"The Task Force office."

"You'll have to give me the address." The San Diego Metropolitan Homicide Task Force, investigating the deaths of more than forty prostitutes, operated in virtual secrecy, even though my department helped with their funding and gave them four cops. Its detectives and attorneys worked out of a nondescript office complex on the south side of Mission Valley. Only its members—and a handful of prostitutes and potential witnesses—knew of its exact location.

Miller gave me the address. "I'm on my way," I said.

"And, Norm . . ."

"Yes."

"Don't tell anyone, not even Bobby."

"Bobby" was Chief of Police Bob Burgreen. I looked out my glass-walled office and across a reception area into my boss's corner office. Burgreen and I had worked together since 1966. Like yours truly, he was not exactly a cop's cop. Back when everyone smoked cigarettes he puffed a pipe. He quoted Shakespeare, recited from memory "The Love Song of J. Alfred Prufrock," lapsed from time to time into Old English, or Swedish, and would entertain me on graveyard shifts with weird metaphysical musings ("What if we, the whole known universe, were floating around in the testicle of a giant? Did you ever think about that?"). The chief was seated at his desk, phone to his ear.

"All right, I'm on my way." I strapped my off-duty gun to my ankle, put on my coat, and walked to the elevators.

Miller met me in the parking lot outside the office. "Come on. Let's take a walk." He put his arm around my shoulder and nudged me along a semi-exposed corridor under the building's second floor. Formerly the region's U.S. attorney, Miller was a big, earnest, amiable man. He'd made his bones prosecuting government and corporate corruption, and had sent some of the city's biggest names, including a couple of "Mr. San Diego's" to prison. He was in the middle of his sixth four-year term.

"We'll head upstairs in a moment," he said, keeping his arm around my shoulder. "What we're going to show you is extremely sensitive, and very troubling. I should tell you, the guys are wary about this visit, especially your four people. But we need help, so we took a little poll. The guys trust you."

The implication was obvious: They didn't trust Burgreen.

"What's this all about, Ed?"

"Let's go on upstairs. It's easier to show you than tell you."

We walked up a flight of stairs and down a couple of doors. Miller punched in a code and we entered. With its warren of rooms, the place didn't look like any detective offices I'd seen. Except for the paperwork. There were files everywhere, case and forensic reports and photos stacked on desks, chairs, and on the floor. It seemed deserted—no clicking keyboards, no bantering across desks, no phones ringing off the hook. Not even a box of doughnuts. A moment later Brian Michaels, Miller's chief deputy, walked out of an inner room to greet us. Miller had assigned him to the task force. We followed him into the room he had just left. Inside, sitting and standing in silence, were most members of the task force, including my four cops—two from Vice, two from Homicide. Laid out on a large conference table were two "link charts," each diagrammed neatly, their broken and unbroken lines connected to boxes, each box containing a single name.

On the first chart: prostitutes who'd been killed, or who had disappeared and were presumed dead, along with suspects and witnesses. It contained the names and "linkages" of several vice cops and patrol officers, each of whom I knew personally. On the second chart? People well known to most San Diegans: Chargers football stars, prominent businessmen, political figures. And Karen Wilkening, a notorious madam who'd provided services to, among others, Don Dixon, former head of failed Vernon Savings and Loan. Dixon had hosted lavish yacht and beach house parties for his pals, furnishing sex, gratis, to guests who chose to partake. Dixon had socialized with and contributed to the campaigns of local and national politicos. Several of those names were on the chart. I was surprised at many of the entries on Chart No. 2, but shocked at two: Bill Kolender, former chief of police. And Bob Burgreen. I felt ill.

Kolender had been my rabbi. If it weren't for him I'd never have been promoted through the ranks. I'd been his speechwriter, and confidant. A Jew, he used to joke that while crime may be up in the city, "We're the only police department in the country showing a profit." He had a self-deprecating sense of humor, an infectious, uncontrollable laugh. People, myself included, gravitated toward him, loved being in his company. For a Republican, he was one of the most progressive police executives around. And Burgreen? He could have picked anyone to be his assistant chief, including an able deputy, Manny Guaderrama, who was being pushed by prominent members of the Latino community. But he'd picked me, and had shown that he meant it when he said he would *lead* the department. And that I would *run* it.

Michaels seated me at the head of the table then slid the charts under my nose. "What you see in front of you is evidence not only of serial killings but of an especially disturbing pattern of official misconduct, behavior that may or may not be linked to prostitution activity."

I shouldn't have been surprised. It's not uncommon, working prostitute killings, to hear from women on the streets that a certain victim seemed to have been a little *too* cozy with a certain cop. Or that a certain cop seemed to have it in for hookers.

It's also common to find in a prostitute's little black book the names of prominent locals—businessmen, elected officials, judges, athletes. Cops.

Michaels spent five minutes on the prostitute killings, two and a half hours on the "official misconduct." Kolender, it turned out, was on the list because someone thought they'd seen him, or someone who "looks an awful lot like him," dining in some upscale Tijuana restaurant in the company of nefarious characters who'd been linked to other names on Chart No. 2. Also, a "source" had intimated that the former chief had a personal if not intimate relationship with Karen Wilkening. Burgreen? He was on the list because, well, "It's well known that he and Kolender are 'tight.'" I wasn't sure about Kolender—I didn't believe it, but Michaels seemed so confident. I *knew* Burgreen's name did not belong on that sheet.

"We've thrown a lot at you," said Michaels when he finished tracing events, personal bios, rap sheets, relationships. Links. "It's got to be a little mind-boggling. Do you have any questions at this point?" Everyone in the room was poised to hear the interloper's reaction to what they'd been secretly working on for years.

"Yeah. You're talking about a man I used to work for, another I'm now working for. What makes you think I'm not 'tight' with them?"

"We've checked," said Michaels. "You've got a reputation for putting integrity first." I wasn't flattered.

Miller said, "You can see why we're careful to keep this information absolutely confidential." I understood, but what did they want from me? Miller answered before I could ask. "We need more investigators from the PD, Norm. We figured if you knew *why* they're needed you'd be more willing to cough them up."

"What kind of people, Internal Affairs?" It had occurred to me that the task force had become hopelessly entangled in the "misconduct" cases, with their real or imagined "linkages." This would account for the lack of tangible progress in solving the serial murders. Burgreen and I had discussed the subject several times. My deputy chiefs were agitating to take our guys out of Mission Valley. They wanted them back in Homicide and Vice. Now it was clear: several of the task force cops, under-equipped by training and experience, had wound up handling high-level Internal Affairs cases—at the expense of the prostitute murder cases.

Michaels answered. "Well, IA types would help. And we do need more detectives to work the homicides."

"Let me think about it." I was responsible for allocating and distributing cops throughout the department. I needed a lot more information about the structure and operating methods of the task force to even consider adding more people at that point.

Sitting in the corner this whole time was Bonnie Dumanis, a deputy DA who, I learned that morning, was preparing to take over the day-to-day lead from Michaels (who would soon be presenting information from Chart No. 2 to the county grand jury—either as criminal matters or in keeping with the grand jury's role in California as protector of "good government"). Dumanis approached me as soon as the meeting adjourned. "Let's go to lunch."

"Well, I'm really . . ."

"We *have* to talk. Today. Before you make any decisions."

We took separate cars, met at a downtown restaurant. "The guys may trust you," she said, as soon as the waiter walked off with our order. "But I don't. Not as far as I can toss you."

"Why not?" As the PD's second in command, I wasn't used to being addressed so bluntly.

"Because I don't know you. Simple as that. You've got to earn my trust."

As soon as I got back to my office I called Miller. "I can't justify adding a single body until I'm satisfied the task force is properly and efficiently organized. And staffed with the right people. I just don't have that feeling at the moment."

"I'm glad to hear you say that. I've got similar concerns."

"How about I go down there, spend some time looking at the operation?" We were being eaten alive in the press. We had to get to the bottom of things, find out whether our cops were killing hookers. And whether police officials, past or present, were involved in shady practices. "I'll read the cases, interview the detectives, your lawyers, see what kind of changes are needed." I especially wanted to talk with Chuck Rogers, who was by then a municipal court judge. As a deputy DA he'd preceded Michaels on the task force.

"Sounds like a plan," said Miller. I pictured Dumanis, smiled at her reaction to my presence in the thick of her task force's clandestine operations.

"Good. But I need to talk to Burgreen. Today, Ed. Right now." It was absurd that his name was on that chart. "Unless you have an official objection, I'm going to tell him everything. Everything."

He paused. "Yeah, do it. Please do."

The afternoon of the day I'd been instructed to talk to no one about my visit to Mission Valley, "not even Bobby," I walked into Burgreen's office and talked. If it had been *me* on the receiving end of the news I would have been apoplectic. But if my boss was the slightest bit upset, he didn't let on. He blessed my "management audit" of the San Diego Metropolitan Homicide Task Force.

Within a week, I'd interviewed about a quarter of the task force personnel, and had read through maybe a tenth of the case files. This initial examination confirmed that the task force was indeed poorly organized, especially in light of its "mission creep" into official misconduct, and badly understaffed.

We made a decision to call on the attorney general for help with the "misconduct" cases, effectively taking them out of the hands of local government. California's AG dispatched a crackerjack attorney, Gary Schons, to oversee these investigations—including any bleed-over onto Chart No. 1.

Next, we needed to select additional bona fide homicide pros to complement those already working the serial killings. I interviewed a dozen or so current and former members of SDPD Homicide, including some aces who had retired in recent years. Known for their expertise in scene reconstruction, forensic trace-evidence (especially blood, DNA, and fibers), suspect interrogation, and analytical reasoning, these experts provided names of individuals who'd be able to help our overworked charges in Mission Valley. In vetting potential new members, I realized that a couple of the experts I had consulted would, themselves, make excellent additions to the task force, even though they were now ranking officers. I assigned them to detective work. A total of six new people.

At that point in the investigation we were pretty sure we had several, separate series. The most common modus operandi: Suspects would hook up with a prostitute on El Cajon Boulevard, a six-lane artery stretching from north of Balboa Park east to the La Mesa city limits. They'd drive their unsuspecting prey to an outlying area, have sex, or not, strangle them to death (the most common method of prostitute killings), then dump their bodies in the mountains or foothills of East County.

It was the case of Donna Gentile, seven years earlier, that had aroused suspicions of police officer involvement. Gentile, an attractive, well-spoken twenty-two-year-old who worked the Boulevard, had spoken to the press in 1985. Her picture had appeared on the front page of the newspaper, she'd been interviewed on TV. Michaels had presented her to the grand jury where she testified that certain vice cops and patrol officers were "overly friendly" with several of the "girls," and that some of them had extorted prostitutes for sex. At least one of those prostitutes had turned up dead, and another had gone missing.

With an internal investigation of Gentile's assertions underway, a nude body was found at dawn, June 23, 1985, just off the Sunrise Highway east of Pine Valley. The victim had been beaten and strangled. Pea gravel had been shoved down her throat while she was still alive (her lungs contained aspirated gravel). A warning, perhaps by a police officer to other prostitutes to keep their mouths shut? The body was that of Donna Gentile.

Even though cops were eventually cleared of that murder, several officers, the result of IA findings, had been disciplined or constructively terminated (meaning they quit before they could be fired) for "inappropriate" behavior with prostitutes. Still, the original task force members couldn't shake the feeling that police officers might be involved in other cases. Murder cases.

It was not an unreasonable assumption, given the rabid anti-prostitute attitudes of a few twisted cops.

+ + +

I've heard some police officers refer to prostitute slayings (or to the slayings of blacks) as "misdemeanor murders," employing an unofficial code for them: NHI, no humans involved.

"Sex workers," as many in the trade prefer to be called, are vilified, stigmatized, and written off. They're immoral. They engage in sinful, illegal activity. They have no self-esteem, no self-discipline. They don't really "work," yet they haul in tax-free dollars. They're dirty. They use drugs (wouldn't you?).

Dehumanizing or demonizing sex workers makes it easier to ignore them when they go missing or are found dead. I wonder how these officers of the law would respond to the murders of forty teachers? Forty homemakers? Forty ER nurses?

+ + +

Judge Rogers told me in his chambers that the original task force members felt their own PD "just didn't care about the deaths of hookers." Kolender had been chief when Ed Miller approached him with a proposal to put together the prostitute-killer task force. (It was, in fact, the DA who first discerned, or at least acted upon, a pattern of serial homicides in our city.)

Kolender, urged by his deputy chiefs to reject Miller's proposal, stalled the DA for some time.* When he finally agreed to assign people, he limited the commitment to the four detectives.

I spent two months in the hermetically sealed headquarters of the task force. Not once did I hear an "NHI" reference or an anti–sex worker sentiment. These officers genuinely cared about the victims, and their anguished friends and family members. From conversations with true crime writer Ann Rule, the same can be said for those detectives who worked the Green River killings. (Rule's book on the subject, *Green River, Running Red* [2004] has been praised, aptly so, for rendering the stories of each and every one of Gary Ridgway's known victims with respect and sensitivity.)

Whatever might have been their original motives and attitudes, the detectives had developed extraordinary empathy and compassion for "their" victims. To watch those detectives at work in Mission Valley was to conclude that Donna Gentile might just as well have been a wife, a sister, a daughter. Catching her killer, and the murderers of the other victims, had become an obsession.

Society at large should feel such concern.

+ + +

Task force members determined that Ronald Elliot Porter, ex-Marine and Escondido automobile mechanic, killed Donna Gentile. Although convicted of a single second-degree murder charge (and serving twenty-seven to life), fibers, blood samples, and witnesses linked Porter to as many as fourteen additional cases.

This development, the fingering of Porter, astonished a lot of people—especially when it was learned that Gentile had been in the employ of Karen Wilkening. In fact, she had gone to one of Don Dixon's three-day

---

* I was one of those foot-dragging deputy chiefs, assigned at the time to Field Ops. My argument? Officer safety. We were severely understaffed in patrol, being "nickled and dimed" by Investigations: If four detectives went off to some nebulous task force, I'd have to give up four patrol cops to replace them. I regret my initial opposition to the DA's proposal. In fact, I'm ashamed of it.

blowouts in Del Mar—and had returned to the Boulevard only one day before her death.

Brian Maurice Jones was tied to four prostitute killings, and sentenced to death on two of them.

Richard Allen Sanders was posthumously tied to several of the other cases. And fourteen more suspects were arrested in ten additional cases.

Schons, with help from SDPD personnel, cleared all police officers of any involvement in the deaths or disappearances of sex workers. Almost as important to me, personally, was that Bill Kolender was cleared completely of any wrongdoing. Today, he's the sheriff of San Diego County. And Bonnie Dumanis, deeply devoted to safe streets and justice for all, is the new district attorney.

+ + +

I'd never worked vice, and had made only a handful of prostitution arrests. But I'd hassled large numbers of hookers, pimps, and johns during my days as a rookie beat cop—most of them right there on the Boulevard. I knew that prostitution was common, that it was frustrating and infuriating to homeowners and businesspeople, and to church and school and park officials. But with my task force involvement, I got a much broader and deeper education into the habits, patterns, and complexities associated with street prostitution.

The experience deepened my conviction that prostitution, like drug use, should be decriminalized.

+ + +

For years, I'd predicated my decriminalization argument on familiar grounds: oldest occupation, still around, always will be . . . consenting adults . . . government out of the bedroom . . . the right of adult women to make a living of their choice . . .

I'd also argued, though with less confidence (and no empirical data), that prostitution was a "healthy outlet" for *potentially* violent men. Not the Gary Ridgways of the world, of course. But "normal" men, unlucky in love, possessed of a normal sex drive but unable to attract women without paying for them. I figured prostitution might serve to reduce the incidence of rape and other sexual assaults among these men. Now, I'm not so sure. The task force revealed that some of the suspects, having had their performance or their equipment ridiculed, responded by murdering the woman.

But rather than outlawing a risky form of commerce that will always find a way to operate, I believe we have a moral imperative to do everything we can to make prostitution as *safe* as possible. Serial murder expert Robert Keppel has established that true serial killers keep killing until they're caught, or they die.

+ + +

"Morality" seems to be the biggest sticking point between "harm reduction" public policy on the one hand, and a reckless disregard for the safety of sex industry workers (and their clients, for that matter) on the other. The issue is fraught with contradictions and controversy. Many of the arguments against decriminalization are compelling:

- Prostitution, as it's commonly (but by no means exclusively) framed, i.e., males buying sex from females, is degrading and demeaning to women.
- Beyond the most talked about health risks—violence, HIV, and other STDs—women who engage in high-volume vaginal sex risk major structural damage to their sexual and other organs.
- Many women don't *choose* prostitution so much as have it chosen for them.
- While many prostitutes don't work for pimps, those who do are exploited and otherwise mistreated, physically, emotionally, financially.
- Significant numbers of young girls, including the occasional preteen, find their way into the trade.

Research findings are mixed. Sweden, for example, "recriminalized" prostitution in 1999, largely on political and social, not scientific grounds. Its parliament, which has reached gender parity and is committed to ending patriarchal domination of Swedish life, has officially defined prostitution as "violence against women and children." The new law allows for the selling but not the buying or the attempted purchase of sex. Men who get, or offer to get, sex for money can be fined between one and two thousand (American) dollars or jailed for up to six months. A prostitute who provides sex is guilty of no crime. As the Swedes conceive it, the law is designed to tip the scales of gender power, to reverse the age-old pattern of penalizing women who have been forced into or otherwise victimized by the occupation of prostitution.

How is the Swedish model working? If there's a research-based answer I haven't found it. What we do know is that very few arrests have been made under the law since it became effective on January 1, 1999. Further, there is evidence that while street prostitution has been reduced significantly (in Stockholm the numbers of street hookers have gone from three hundred to one hundred) there's been a dramatic *increase* in apartment and hotel room coupling for dollars. Still, illegal. For the man.

Other countries, such as England, Canada, New Zealand, and the Netherlands, have decriminalized indoor prostitution, citing the safety of sex workers as the primary reason. In Canada, it remains illegal to engage, on either end of the transaction, in street prostitution. It is also unlawful to operate a "bawdy house." But a sex worker may legally provide sex for money in a private dwelling.

Trading street for indoor prostitution does not answer the moral or political objections of sex industry opponents. Nor does it mean that sex workers are completely safe from misogynists or sociopaths. But when one considers the M.O. of serial killers like Pickton, Armstrong, Yates, Ridgway, and many others, each of whom abducted his victims from the streets, sex in a room offers far greater safety for sex workers.

One approach for lawmakers: decriminalize home, apartment, and hotel room prostitution. License and tax third-party owners and managers (*aka* pimps and madams), as well as sex workers. Collect business and license fees, using the revenue to offset the costs of (1) inspection and enforcement, (2) health examinations for all sex workers, and (3) outreach services to assist those who want to leave the trade, or to resist pandering (the encouragement of another to become a prostitute) in the first place. And maintain laws against soliciting or purchasing sex on the streets.

It's not as if we don't know how a transition from streets to indoor prostitution would work. It's all around us. Do you have an alternative weekly newspaper? Check its last pages. Scantily clad women (and more than a few men in G-strings) offering themselves, body and, well, body—for a price. And don't think sex for dollars is not going on in all those adult nightclubs. As the new chief in town, I dressed in my grubbies one night, pulled a baseball cap down low, and accompanied one of my Seattle vice cops into a neighborhood club that featured table dancing (more aptly called chair humping). My partner bought a dance and demonstrated the "challenges" of proper law enforcement. A moment later another dancer approached a patron (client?) seated next to me. Three dances later he zipped up, then lit up, and she ambled over to the next guy, sixty bucks richer.

Making indoor sex-for-sale legal would not eliminate street prostitution. But fewer kids would show up for show-and-tell with semen-filled rubbers. And far fewer of America's sisters and daughters would be beaten, abducted, murdered.

CHAPTER 4

CAPITAL PUNISHMENT: THE COWARD'S WAY OUT

OFFICER KIMBERLY TONAHILL, THE bottom third of her heart sheared off by a .9mm slug, is dead before she hits the ground. Officer Timothy Ruopp, shot in the legs and in the head, lies mortally wounded in Mercy Hospital. Patrol officers swarm the eucalyptus grove next to the parking lot of Grape Street Park. Police canines sniff their way through the damp brush. A black-and-white SDPD chopper hovers overhead, its blazing light helping in the search for the shooter.

Joselito Cinco, wanted for unlawful possession of a firearm, had bragged to friends, "I'm going to kill the next cop who stops me." That next cop was Ruopp, an ordained minister with four young children, a shy smile, and a slight lisp. He had stopped Cinco to write him a ticket (for furnishing alcohol to a couple of teenage girls) when the suspect pulled a semiautomatic pistol and opened fire. The cops never had a chance. Both officers' guns were still holstered when their backup arrived.

I ride with the police chief to Tonahill's mother's house to tell the woman she no longer has a daughter. Kim and Tim had worked for me; I was their deputy chief. I'm sick to my stomach, seething with anger, hoping our cops find Cinco soon. And praying he'll give them a reason to blow him away.

But, if he's caught, tried, convicted? What then? Should the state kill him? No.

When I read of yet another execution, most often these days in Texas, when I picture the actual occurrence—the frying, gassing, hanging, shooting, or lethal injection of a human being—my soul hurts for days. It's an emotional thing with me, but my opposition to capital punishment is multilayered.

Race and class discrimination are all too real in every phase of the criminal justice system, from arrest to sentencing. Impoverished black defendants are far more likely to wind up on death row than rich or middle-class whites. Of the 3,700 inmates now awaiting execution nationwide, 43 percent are African-American. Black defendants are not accorded the same due process rights as whites, their cases are not given the same scrutiny and consideration afforded white defendants. Not now, not ever, not in this country. Governor George Ryan first suspended then commuted the sentences of all death row inmates in Illinois because he was shown proof (most of it DNA driven) that several prisoners—as many as *twelve* of the eighteen—simply weren't guilty.

The Innocence Project, founded by Barry C. Scheck and Peter J. Neufield in 1992 at the Benjamin N. Cardozo School of Law at Yeshiva University, accepts only cases "where postconviction DNA testing can yield conclusive proof of innocence." Of their first 123 exonerations, 37 were for homicides. One of those cases involved Eddie Joe Lloyd, a black, mentally retarded man convicted of the brutal killing of a sixteen-year-old girl in 1984. Mr. Lloyd served seventeen years in a Michigan state prison before the Innocence Project, joined by the Wayne County Prosecutor and the Detroit Police Department, petitioned to have his sentence vacated. Evidence developed by the Project revealed that although the police had all kinds of physical evidence at the scene, including the killer's semen, they'd never had it analyzed. Further, they told Lloyd that if he played along with his arrest they might be able to flush out the real killer. Lloyd did "play along," signing a confession the cops had fed him. The judge in his case, barred from imposing a death sentence, had wanted to hang Lloyd, to face "termination by extreme con[striction]."

Mentally incompetent defendants—some with sub-50 IQs, some (like self-lobotomized Rickey Ray Rector, executed in Arkansas under Governor Bill Clinton) with the mentality of a *six-year-old*—are still put to death in this country. Those with mental retardation are incapable of informed participation in their own defense, and they are far more likely to make false confessions. The U.S. Supreme Court in November 2002 stayed the execution of James Colburn, forty-two, who had started seeing a psychiatrist when he was fourteen and who was diagnosed as a paranoid schizophrenic at seventeen. Colburn, a Texan who killed a woman he'd attempted to rape, was out of his mind on psychotropic drugs at his trial. It would have been "cruel and unusual punishment," said the court, to execute such a transparently incompetent person. They sent the case back to Texas where a state doctor, who agreed Colburn was mentally disturbed, opined that the man was sane enough to stand trial. Convicted and sentenced once again to death, the execution was carried out in March 2003. On death row Colburn was known as "Shaky" because of the tremors in his hands and body. He ate his own feces, drank his own urine. Even the warden was said to be distressed over the execution.

Prosecutions of capital cases, often waged against fundamentally unfit court-appointed defense attorneys, frequently rely on unreliable witnesses, shoddy police work, questionable forensics, and jailhouse snitches. Two federal court judges, an appeals court panel, and a Los Angeles superior court judge ruled recently that Lee Goldstein had been wrongly convicted of murder on the basis of testimony from a jailhouse snitch—twenty years ago. Goldstein is fifty-five now.

The death penalty is inefficient and extravagantly expensive: prosecuting and publicly defending a capital case—through up to eleven years of appeals—can cost taxpayers into the eight figures, plus an additional $2 million for the execution. The average cost of incarceration for one inmate on death row is $22,265 a year ($61 a day) at a maximum security facility. The average time an inmate spends on death row (before he or she is executed, released, or remanded for a new trial) is 10.43 years. That comes to a grand total of $233,000.

If these aren't reasons enough to do away with the death penalty, this ought to be persuasive: according to the Innocence Project, as of 2003, 132 people sentenced to death had been exonerated—in other words, *they didn't do it*. Experts aren't sure how many innocent people have actually been executed, but few would disagree that one is too many.

Some argue that the death penalty is wrong not because of what it does to the person we execute, whether guilty or innocent, but because of what it does to the rest of us. Bud Welch, who lost his daughter Julie Marie in the April 19, 1995, Oklahoma City bombing, told CNN News, "I'm not going to find any healing by taking Tim McVeigh out of his cage to kill him. It will not bring my little girl back." Welch became a board member of Murder Victims' Families for Reconciliation, an organization headed by Renny Cushing of Hampton, New Hampshire. Cushing's father had been killed by a police officer in 1988. He says that most loved ones of homicide victims have three basic needs: to learn the truth about what happened, to receive assurances that the killer will be held accountable, and to be allowed to heal in their own time, in their own way. Executions, he says, produce a "carnival-like" atmosphere and shift attention from the victim to the killer. "For those of us who know the pain of the graveyard, filling up another coffin does not bring any comfort."

A friend in San Diego called me with a remarkable story from my old hometown. Nineteen-year-old Tariq Khamisa, delivering pizzas one night in 1996, was gunned down by a gangbanger. His father, Azim Khamisa, reached out to the fourteen-year-old shooter's family. Together they formed a foundation in Tariq's name to try to prevent youth violence. Khamisa had been devastated by his son's death. He told a reporter, "I know the pain of losing a child. It's like having a nuclear bomb detonate inside your body, breaking you into millions of small pieces that can never be found. This violence scars the soul forever." But he also believes that "forgiveness is a surer way to peace than an eye for an eye. The more we role-model the death penalty, the more violence and revenge there will be."

These are all good arguments for opposing capital punishment but my main objection is this: It's the coward's way out. How can we justify killing someone whose threat has ended with incarceration? In my mind it's an extension of the mentality of child abusers who know their victims can't fight back. Or of a cop who beats a handcuffed prisoner. I've felt this way since my second year as a police officer, back in the mid-sixties.

+ + +

And before that? I was sixteen when Caryl Chessman was gassed to death at San Quentin. I remember reading about his crime spree: auto theft, kidnapping, robbery, rape (he was the notorious Los Angeles "Red Light Bandit," so named because he pretended to be a cop, stopping cars with a red light). I also remember newspaper accounts of his eight stays of execution during his twelve years on death row; his was the longest period any convict had spent on death row at that time. The governor, the warden, and a panel of judges were bombarded by appeals from general death penalty opponents as well as those who felt Chessman, in particular, did not deserve to die. Ray Bradbury, Pablo Casals, Robert Frost, Billy Graham, Aldous Huxley, Norman Mailer, Carey McWilliams, and Eleanor Roosevelt wrote letters urging that Chessman's life be spared. Steve Allen, Marlon Brando, and Shirley MacLaine were said to be among the protesters present on the day of his execution. I remember feeling strange that morning, like the whole thing was a little unreal.

For all his horrible crimes, Chessman did not murder anyone. In prison, he was clearly not a threat to others (at least in the free world; he once stuck a pencil into the cheek of a fellow inmate). Why did "they" have to kill him? Why had Governor Edmund G. "Pat" Brown, a death penalty opponent, not intervened—even after his Jesuit-trained son, Jerry Brown, called from Berkeley begging him to do so?

But the governor refused, and a bag of cyanide pellets was dropped into a vat of sulphuric acid under Chessman's death chair at 10:03 A.M. on May 2, 1960. Chessman took a deep breath when the pellets were released at 10:03. Seconds later his nose twitched, and his head dropped to his chest. He vomited up part of his ham and eggs breakfast. His bowels and bladder gave way. At 10:12 he was declared dead.

I guess you could say that when I was sworn in as a cop I was against the death penalty, sort of. I don't remember thinking about it a whole lot. But in my rookie year, sporting a blue "Reagan for Governor" bumper sticker on my Pontiac Tempest sedan and loving everything about police work and the cop culture, I became an ardent proponent of capital punishment. Just like my buddies in tan. My taste for state killings lasted as long as my love affair with Ronald Reagan. When I decided to think, and feel, for myself, I scraped off the bumper sticker. And returned, for good, to my roots as a death penalty opponent.

+ + +

I'm not a pacifist. I've killed a man and I would kill again, if I had to. But violence does beget violence, and state and federal executions have not kept the United States from becoming one of the most violent industrialized nations on the planet. Our retention of capital punishment (in most states) puts us in the company of China, North Korea, Rwanda, Iraq, and Iran. Half the nations of the world, including all fifteen members of the European Union, have outlawed capital punishment. So have a dozen of our own states—one, Michigan, from as far back as 1846.

I understand why my colleagues celebrate the same image I abhor, and why Americans support capital punishment.* They believe it acts as a deterrent. They believe in the biblical notion of "an eye for an eye" (although apparently not in the commandment, Thou shalt not kill). They believe a death sentence carried out brings "closure" to surviving loved ones; my cop colleagues *needed* Joselito Cinco to die in the gas chamber, if not in that canyon.

Over the years I've questioned my beliefs and assumptions about the death penalty. I confess to moments when my gut tells me, *This asshole's the exception—take him out and kill him.* The cases are not difficult to conjure— baby killers, wife killers, serial killers, terrorists, treasonous FBI or CIA agents. Cop killers. The unremorseful: stoic murderers, laughing killers with no trace of a conscience—like an impenitent Gary Ridgway here in Washington state, the most prolific serial killer in U.S. history.

Yet the rational case for capital punishment is flawed. True, the execution of a murderer means that he or she will never kill again. But a person bent on homicide— whether impassioned impulse or premeditated—is not likely to be dissuaded by what might await him or her at the end of a long, drawn-out criminal justice proceeding. If capital punishment were a deterrent you'd think our murder rate (between 15,000 and 20,000 killings a year) would be among the lowest in the civilized world. Instead of the sixth highest.

According to the *New York Times*, the twelve states that have abolished

---

* According to *The Hill*, Americans' support of capital punishment had been declining in the years prior to 9/11 (due, principally, to the wrongful convictions uncovered by "innocence" projects throughout the country); in May 2001, 65 percent of Americans supported the death penalty. Today 74 percent support it.

the death penalty boast average homicide rates consistently lower than in those states that execute their killers. A twenty-year, state-by-state analysis revealed that ten of those twelve states have homicide rates lower than the national average.

But what of "justice" and "closure"? Aren't they legitimate motives? Of course. But if we had the courage to question *why* they are so important to us, we might not like the answer.

Could it be that the same hunger for justice and closure that leads to a sanitized killing in a state penitentiary is no different from the motive that leads to unlawful violence on the streets, or in our homes? Domestic violence? Gang shootings? Child abuse? Even road rage? You cut me off on the freeway, hurt or insult one of my homeboys, irritate me while I'm watching the game, you gotta pay. An eye for an eye.

No one epitomizes the avenging angel better than George W. Bush. I'm not talking about his legitimate war in Afghanistan or his indefensible war in Iraq, I'm talking about his war against mercy and justice in Texas. During his reign as a "compassionate conservative" governor, Bush presided over the executions of 152 inmates.

Do you remember the case of Karla Faye Tucker? Convicted of two ax murders, she sought executive clemency, claiming to have undergone a spiritual transformation while incarcerated—understandable for a woman facing imminent death. She also exhibited profound remorse for her crimes (neither argument, if I were a death penalty advocate, would sway me). Bush screwed up his face like a pouty seventh-grader and whiningly mimicked Tucker: "*Please* don't kill me."

Texas did kill Karla Faye Tucker, on February 3, 1998, by lethal injection. She became the first woman executed in that state since the Civil War.*

Even more worrisome than Bush's callous and juvenile mockery was the governor's defense of Texas's killing record. Governor Ryan of Illinois had been haunted by capital punishment, particularly the specter of putting to

---

* Ron Carlson, brother of one of Karla Faye Tucker's victims, and the son of a man killed by a shotgun blast, had for years sought vengeance as he nursed a strong hatred for the people who'd killed his loved ones. He had hoped Tucker's execution would bring "closure." It did not. Carlson now speaks out against the death penalty, stressing the pain it causes both families.

death an innocent person. Bush had no such qualms, presiding over a state whose police, prosecutors, judges, and juries are certainly no more reliable than those of Illinois. "I'm confident that every person that's been put to death under our state has been guilty of the crime charged," he said.

And what was Bush's process of review before a death sentence was carried out? He would skim a three-page memo the morning of an execution, a memo written by Alberto R. Gonzales, White House counsel whom Bush has appointed as Attorney General for his second term—the man who wrote an internal memo in defense of torture, and a staunch supporter of the death penalty.

If Bush actually read newspapers he might have noticed that the day before his refusal to stop the execution of Gary Graham, the *New York Times* (June 23, 2000), had this to say: "There is powerful evidence that he did not commit the murder for which the state put him to death." The editorial continued:

> Mr. Graham, represented at trial by a court-appointed lawyer who failed to mount a meaningful defense, was convicted largely on the testimony of a single witness who said she saw him from 30 to 40 feet away through her car windshield. There was no physical evidence linking Mr. Graham to the crime. Tests showed that the gun he was carrying was not the murder weapon, and two other witnesses who were never called to testify at trial said they had seen the killer, and it was not Mr. Graham.

Even when faced with 100 percent "guilty as charged" defendants—criminals who have committed the most heinous crimes—it is still wrong to execute them. Capital punishment makes cowards of its executors. It turns Texas and Arkansas, George W. Bush and Bill Clinton, and the rest of us into a craven nation.

Michael Dukakis lost the 1988 presidential election in part because of his stilted, lawyerly response to Bernard Shaw's blunt question, "If Kitty Dukakis were raped and murdered, would you favor an irrevocable death penalty for the killer?"

Dukakis replied, "No, I don't, Bernard. And I think you know that I've opposed the death penalty during all of my life. I don't see any evidence that it's a deterrent, and I think there are better and more effective ways to deal with violent crime." A short man, Dukakis stood tall in my eyes when he answered that question.

Where are our national leaders today? Did you hear the death penalty mentioned, even once, in the 2004 presidential or vice presidential debates? Of course not. I wanted as much as anyone to see John Kerry defeat George Bush. But Kerry wasn't about to "pull a Dukakis," even though I suspect he harbors strong anti-death penalty sentiments.

+ + +

Matthew Shepard was pistol-whipped by two gay-hating goons, strapped to a fence, and left to die in a snowy field in Wyoming. After the guilty verdict but before sentencing, Aaron McKinney's attorney sought to convince the prosecutor that his client should serve two consecutive life sentences rather than face execution. The prosecutor had no intention of agreeing, but he took the offer to Dennis and Judy Shepard, Matthew's parents. Judy persuaded Dennis, who'd previously supported the death penalty under certain circumstances, to accept the proposal. (Russell Henderson, who'd previously pled guilty, was already serving two consecutive life terms.) The following day, Dennis Shepard stood up in court to explain to the jury why his son's killer had been spared. He looked right at McKinney:

> I would like nothing better than to see you die, Mr. McKinney. However, this is the time to begin the healing process. To show mercy to someone who refused to show any mercy. To use this as the first step in my own closure about losing Matt. Mr. McKinney, I am not doing this because of your family. I am definitely not doing this because of the crass and unwarranted pressures put on by the religious community. If anything, that hardens my resolve to see you die. Mr. McKinney, I'm going to grant you life, as hard as that is for me to do, because of Matthew. Every time you

celebrate Christmas, a birthday, or the Fourth of July, remember that Matt isn't. Every time that you wake up in that prison cell, remember that you had the opportunity and the ability to stop your actions that night. Every time that you see your cellmate, remember that you had a choice, and now you are living that choice. You robbed me of something very precious, and I will never forgive you for that. Mr. McKinney, I give you life in the memory of one who no longer lives. May you have a long life, and may you thank Matthew every day for it.

My own son is named Matthew. If, God forbid, he were murdered I'd hope to have Mr. Shepard's courage. The strength to stand up in court and say *enough*. To seek the same humble "closure" he sought: the comfort of knowing that Matthew's killers would have every day of the rest of their lives, behind bars, to ponder why they did what they did.

Life in prison, with no parole: it should be the toughest sentence on our books.

+ + +

Our cops captured Joselito Cinco at dawn. He'd burrowed into a small ravine and covered himself with brush. Surrendering meekly, he was later convicted on two counts of first-degree murder and sentenced to die in the gas chamber in San Quentin. He hung himself in his cell.

CHAPTER 5

CRIMINALS' RIGHTS: WORTH PROTECTING?

The following conversation takes place in a criminal justice class I'm teaching at San Diego State in the mid-seventies. The players are an upper-division student (who happens to be a veteran cop) and the head of the local defenders office, our guest speaker. The lawyer has just finished a rousing talk on what he goes through to get his clients off. The cop's hand shoots up. The lawyer calls on him.

COP: How can you look at yourself in the mirror? The pukes and assholes you defend are evil . . . guilty. Everyone knows they did it. How can you stand there and justify what you do for a living? It's . . . it's . . . immoral.

LAWYER: It's no more immoral for me to defend a client than it is for you to arrest him. My job is to give him the best defense I can. Why? Well, I could tell you that *every* American is entitled to constitutional protections; that our system of government demands no less. That the preservation of our republic as we know it requires no less. I could tell you that only a spirited, competent defense stands between an innocent defendant and prison—or worse. And I believe in all that. But there's another reason that people accused of even the most heinous crimes should get the best possible defense.

COP: What's that?

LAWYER: If I'm not effective at what I do, if defense attorneys are lazy, or dull, distracted, or just plain incompetent—do you really think that would make it easier for your side to win?

COP: I guess. Sure.

LAWYER: Wrong! What would happen is that *prosecutors* would become lazy, dull, inattentive, and incompetent. That's how systems work. If criminal defense attorneys are ineffectual, why would the DA have to hire sharp attorneys to go up against them? Why would he have to set high standards for his deputies' case reviews and research, their briefs and motions, their courtroom performance? If I don't do my job well it weakens the whole system of criminal justice.

COP: Yeah, but . . .

LAWYER: If criminal defendants were represented only by ambulance-chasing shysters how long do you think it would take for the effects to be felt on *your* work? You wouldn't have to work as hard to get a case charged. Convictions would be delivered on a silver platter and . . .

COP: Yeah, so?

LAWYER: Police work would become even sloppier and more unpro-fessional than it already is. Crime scene protection, the identification, col-lection, preservation, and analysis of trace evidence, witness interviews, scene reconstructions, suspect interrogations, report-writing, testimony on the stand—all that would suffer. You'd be a less skilled, a less proficient police department. And *you*, sir, wouldn't be the cop you are today.

COP: Hmm.

LAWYER: By the way, do you really think we believe all our clients are innocent? Hell, we know most of them are guilty.

COP: You do?

LAWYER: Of course. I'll tell you something. An honest defense attorney lives in fear of the day an innocent client walks through the door. We just want to force you guys, and the prosecutors, to take your best shot. To *prove* your case, not just phone it in.

COP: Are you saying, then, that Miranda and all those other Supreme Court cases have had the same effect on us? Like they've made us better cops?

LAWYER: What do you think?

COP: Well, I'll have to give that some thought . . .

What about "*Miranda* and all those other Supreme Court cases"? When you hear cops grumble and grouse about laws that "handcuff" them they're referring to one or more of the following landmark Bill of Rights cases.

MAPP v. *OHIO* (1961). Cleveland police officers broke into the residence of Dollree Mapp, discovered in the basement materials they deemed to be obscene, and arrested her. Her conviction was upheld by the Ohio state supreme court. The U.S. Supreme Court overturned the conviction, and extended a vital federal principle to all fifty states: Evidence seized in violation of a defendant's constitutional rights (in this case, to privacy, the Fourth Amendment) may not be used in court. Called the *exclusionary rule*, the majority opinion was written by Justice Tom C. Clark, father of one of my criminal justice heroes, Ramsey Clark. (The senior Clark retired from the bench in 1967 to avoid a conflict of interest when his son became Attorney General.) Clark wrote that *Mapp* v. *Ohio* may "appear as a technicality . . . but . . . tolerance of shortcut methods in law enforcement impairs its enduring effectiveness."

GIDEON v. *WAINWRIGHT* (1963). Clarence Earl Gideon was an impoverished ex-con who'd been in and out of prison most of his adult life. He broke into a pool hall in Florida, was arrested, tried, and convicted of burglary. At the time he was charged he asked the state to provide legal counsel. The state refused. Anthony Lewis's book *Gideon's Trumpet* (and a movie by the same name) tells the story of what happened next. Gideon appealed his conviction all the way to the Supreme Court where, represented by court-appointed counsel Abe Fortas (later to become a Supreme Court justice), the plaintiff prevailed. The Sixth Amendment provides that, "In all criminal prosecutions, the accused shall enjoy the right . . . to . . . the Assistance of Counsel for his defence."

ESCOBEDO v. *ILLINOIS* (1964). Arrested by Chicago cops in the shooting death of his brother-in-law, Danny Escobedo refused to talk to the police. Through his attorney he filed a writ of habeas corpus, Latin for "you have the body," asking a judge to release his body from jail. The judge granted the writ and Escobedo was freed. Eleven days later, following additional investigation, he was rearrested. Escobedo refused to answer questions without his lawyer present. The cops kept his attorney from him throughout the night, during which time Escobedo confessed to the killing. The Supreme Court ruled in this case that the right to counsel extends to those *detained*, as well as those charged with a crime.

MIRANDA v. *ARIZONA* (1966). Ernesto Miranda, a poor, mentally disturbed twenty-two-year-old, was arrested for kidnapping and raping an eighteen-year-old woman. The arrest and post-arrest fact pattern was not dissimilar from the preceding cases as it relates to a defendant's right to "lawyer up." But the Supreme Court's ruling on *Miranda* was the most sweeping and inclusive yet. It led to the police warning you've heard for years, as TV cops pull cards from their shirt pockets, or recite from memory: *You have the right to remain silent . . . anything you do or say can and will be used against you in a court of law . . . you have the right to be represented by an attorney . . . if you cannot afford an attorney one will be provided to you before any questioning.* Often not heard on the cop shows is what comes next: *Do you understand each of these rights as I have explained them to you? Keeping in mind these rights are you willing to answer my questions?* A "yes" response to each constitutes what's called an "intelligent waiver." If you don't have it, you can't interrogate.

These aren't the only landmark Bill of Rights cases (which cover everything from abortion to flag burning, pornography to the death penalty), but they *are* the ones that most often piss off the cops. Decided in almost every case in a five-to-four vote of the 1960s Earl Warren Supreme Court, they divided and continue to divide conservatives from civil libertarians. And lazy or incompetent police officers from conscientious, law-abiding police officers.

CHAPTER 6

GETTING A GRIP ON GUNS

ON A HOT FOURTH of July, 1967, I tried to arrest an assault suspect inside Belmont Park in Mission Beach. He pushed me and fled. I gave chase. He was awfully fast for a big man (six feet two, 240 pounds), and had no compunction about barreling into boys and girls of all ages on the jammed midway. I was losing him as he sprinted by the plunge and headed toward the water. When he reached the boardwalk he made the mistake of turning south instead of north (or vaulting the three-foot wall and continuing on into the Pacific). In his path, forty yards away were two San Diego police officers, Bob Manus and Oscar Tron, assigned to patrol the holiday festivities in plainclothes. The suspect was headed right for them. I saw Tron and Manus look at each other, nod, and, as old linebackers will do, get down into a three-point stance.

You could hear the collision above the roar of the surf, the rollercoaster, the barkers on the midway, the shrieking gulls overhead. We still had to fight him at the scene, and I had to mace him when he kicked out a back window of my police car on the way to jail, but to jail he went. I figured that was the last I'd seen of Wilburt Lowe.

Six months later I got a call of a shooting on Central Avenue in City Heights. A large man had broken into a house. I walked up to the porch and peered in through the open door. Lying on the floor was the body of Wilburt Lowe, dead of a shotgun blast to the chest. Knowing what I knew of Mr. Lowe, if he'd broken into my home I'd have shot him—*if* I'd had a gun in the house. And knew how to use it.

+ + +

I struggled with shooting in the academy. At the twenty-five-yard line I put as many rounds into adjoining targets as my own. One day, as I was on the verge of being fired for this particular problem, my classmates and I trooped down the concrete stairs into the target pit. We pulled our spring-loaded targets down and started scoring them. Sims, shooting next to me, looked from his target to mine, and laughed. His score was five points higher than possible. "Here," he said, handing me a pencil. "Poke a couple of '.38s' in the ten-ring." The donkey. Cheating was the fastest path to the unemployment line. I'd just have to work at it, and with the help of the rangemaster, come up with a passing score.

When that happened, it transformed a feared, onerous task into an almost enjoyable one. I never did come to love target shooting—even with ear protection the sound of a gun firing still makes me flinch. But I can see why a whole lot of Americans like nothing better than to spend a Sunday afternoon at the pistol range, pumping rounds into targets of concentric circles (or into images of Osama bin Laden).

Collecting guns? Why does anyone "accumulate" anything? Because they enjoy it. (I was grateful when in ninth-grade math, we could get Mr. Wynn, an avid stamp collector, to talk about his precious "first-day covers." He'd spend the whole period talking not about algebra but his latest philatelic acquisition.)

I once took a burglary report from an old man in Golden Hill who'd reported in tears that his collection of military handguns and antique percussion pistols had been stolen. I asked him in the course of the investigation whether he'd fired any of the antiques. "Oh *heavens* no! I'm a collector, not a shooter." He hadn't fired a weapon since the 1920s.

And hunting? As a boy I'd longed to have my own gun, and go hunting with my pal Gary and his father. I imagined cleaning my kill, eating it, and, as Gary's father put it (even back then), helping to control wildlife populations that threatened delicate ecological imbalances. I did make a couple of "hunting" trips—to Gary's grandfather's chicken ranch to shoot sparrows with a pellet gun at age ten, and to the backcountry with high school buddies to kill rabbits caught in the glare of our headlights. The experiences soured me on the sport, and I could never do it again. But I have no trouble understanding why people enjoy taking down elk or pheasant or duck (so long as *someone* eats the poor creatures).

+ + +

All these legitimate reasons for gun ownership notwithstanding, I am an unyielding proponent of gun control—because of what I saw and experienced as a cop.

For every armed home invasion robbery prevented by a firearm, there is at least one homeowner who has had his gun taken from him and used on him. Or who's shot his sixteen-year-old daughter or fourteen-year-old son trying to sneak back in to the house through a bedroom window. Or killed himself accidentally while cleaning the weapon. Or turned impulsively to a firearm to settle a domestic "dispute." Or picked up a gun when seized by a suicidal impulse.

Guns, with people attached to them, are responsible for roughly 30,000 deaths a year in this country. The Centers for Disease Control and Prevention (CDC)'s National Center for Injury Prevention and Control reports that of 29,537 gun deaths in 2001, 2,937 were of children between the ages of 15 and 19, 414 between 10 and 14, 160 between 5 and 9. And 81 between zero and four. Babies. Almost 17,000 of all annual gun deaths are suicides.

According to Arthur Kellerman in the *Journal of Trauma* (1998), a gun is eleven times more likely to be used to commit suicide than for self-defense. A home with a gun in it is five times more likely to experience the suicide of a household member than homes without guns (Kellerman in the *New England Journal of Medicine*, 1993; Peter Cummings, *American Journal of Public Health*, 1997).

Every year, according to the CDC, hospital ERs receive approximately 200,000 victims who've survived gunshot trauma. The average cost per patient? Fourteen thousand dollars. The cumulative lifetime cost of a year's worth of gunshot trauma is $911 million. Plus another $13.4 billion in lost productivity.

Who's getting shot? Young black men, disproportionately. African-

American males have a gunshot mortality rate of 41.6 per one hundred thousand people. White males? Less than half the rate, 16.2. The rate of gunshot deaths for women, of all races, is 3.3. The gunshot death rate in Western European countries is 0.1–0.5 per one hundred thousand citizens.

+ + +

It's personal with me, it always has been. I've seen the ravages of gun violence up close. I killed a man because I thought he had a gun. I wept for a colleague in San Diego whose five-year-old son shot himself to death with daddy's service weapon. I spent a night in Seattle's Harborview Medical Center, praying that one of my cops, shot by a stalled motorist he'd stopped to help, would make it. He didn't. A friend and colleague, an assistant U.S. attorney in Seattle and gutsy president of Washington CeaseFire, was assassinated as he sat at his computer one night. I'm sick to death of guns, of the needless pain and suffering they cause.

I've had it with the National Rifle Association—not its membership but its leadership. I've got even less use for the United States Congress, which consistently caves in to NRA lobbyists. The relatively few lawmakers who actually pay attention to the will of the people on this issue understand that *most* Americans are fed up with guns. Harris Polls in September 2004, conducted both before and after Congress permitted weapons banned in 1995 to once again be sold legally, produced these results (expressed in percentages):

QUESTION: A ban prohibiting the sales of assault rifles and high capacity ammunition magazines expires on September 14. Would you favor or oppose continuing this ban?

	FAVOR	OPPOSE	UNSURE
All	71	26	3
Republicans	72	25	3
Democrats	72	27	1
Independents	74	22	3

QUESTION: In general, would you say you favor stricter gun control, or less strict gun control?

	STRICTER	LESS STRICT	NEITHER	UNSURE
September 2004	60	32	4	3
May 2000	63	28	6	4
June 1999	63	25	10	2
April 1998	69	23	7	1

Bill Clinton, who as president championed the assault weapons ban and pushed for other modest but important gun control measures, makes clear the consequences of tangling with the NRA in his autobiography, *My Life* (2004). Some Democrats had urged the president to keep the assault weapons ban off the table during the run-up to the '94 congressional races. Clinton refused, and in his book writes that those who warned him the Democrats would lose a lot of seats "were right, and I was wrong."

In the 1994 election, an astounding fifty-four Democrats were voted out of office. This included Tom Foley, Speaker of the House, much beloved representative of my home state, and friend to lawmakers on both sides of the aisle (even Dick Cheney, in his 2004 vice presidential debate against John Edwards, referred to Foley as a pal), and Jack Brooks, the chair of the House Judiciary Committee. Of the twenty-four house members the NRA had targeted in that election, nineteen were defeated.

How does an organization of a mere three million members have such power over the U.S. Congress? The American Association of Retired People has *thirty-five million* members, yet the NRA wields far greater influence. Perhaps the answer lies in what Joan Esteban and Debraj Ray found in their research on political influence. Citing the "Olson Paradox," they point out how "larger groups may be less successful than smaller groups in furthering their interests." It has something to do with membership anonymity and inertia in the larger groups. And the fact that over 90 percent of NRA members consistently show up at the polls and vote—and that a lot of people who favor sensible gun control don't.

Tom Foley came from eastern Washington. He understood his constituents' love affair with hunting and firearms, yet he dared to support the assault rifle ban (which had the backing of the Major Cities Chiefs and the NRA to paint a target on his back. They pulled out all their big weapons and made a trophy of one of the most decent, principled men ever to serve in Congress.

+ + +

In pursuit of more and better anti–gun violence education, we developed in Seattle a program called "Options, Choices and Consequences." Cofounded by Dr. Roy G. Farrell, president of the Washington chapter of Physicians for Social Responsibility, we aimed the curriculum at kids but were confident it would capture the imagination of teachers and parents as well. We called it our "cops and docs" program: police officers, prosecutors, and ER doctors and nurses teaming up in the classroom at all middle schools in the city.

The cops' message? If you're packing, we're tracking. It doesn't matter that you took the gun to school for protection, or that you were "just keeping it for a friend." Zero tolerance was the message. And we enforced it.

A deputy prosecutor followed the cop into class and told the kids, "If the police arrest you we're going to charge you, aggressively prosecute you, and seek the stiffest sentence possible."

When an innocent sixteen-year-old Melissa Fernandez was struck by a bullet meant for a rival gang member outside Ballard High School, her death resulted in the arrest of every kid in the drive-by vehicle. The driver and two of the three passengers claimed that since they didn't do the shooting they ought not to be charged. Well, they were charged, and convicted, along with the shooter. All were sentenced to major jail or prison time. That sent an icy message to Seattle's banger community, as did my statement to the press and to my own detectives: "If there is a drive-by shooting in this city, there will *not* be a retaliatory drive-by."

Reporters and cops were incredulous: Given the pride and avenging compulsion of young people, how could this expectation possibly be met? My response: "We're smarter than the bangers, we're more organized, we have more resources. We're adults. We're going to 'adopt' every gun-toting, gangbanging kid in town, inform him of the new PD policy, and let him know the consequences of his actions." There were no retaliatory drive-by shootings on my watch. In fact gang-related shootings virtually disappeared from the radar screen.

But it was the "docs" who really captured the attention of the students: they explained to them what bullets do to bodies. Then showed them. The classroom exhibits—adult diapers, catheters, and the like—disabused the kids of their feelings of immortality, of invincibility. Recognizing the importance of vanity (and feelings of insecurity) in the lives of teenagers, they showed pictures of kids who'd taken one to the face. Or the spinal column.

Three years into the program, graduates of Options, Choices and Consequences were surveyed. The students were:

- 90 percent more likely to report a fellow student who carried a weapon to school
- 91 percent more aware of the serious medical consequences of weapons violence
- 94 percent more likely to believe that firearms are a poor way to resolve conflicts

Ninety-three percent said they would recommend the program to fellow eighth graders.

Clearly, the kids were impressed. But would they act on their feelings and change their behavior? Would they snitch off a fellow student who brought a gun to school?

In the year following the introduction of the program, reporting of school weapons declined, statewide, by thirty percent. In the Seattle school district, reporting went *up*, ninety percent. There was also a significant reduction in gun violence and school gun incidents during the first three years of the program—however, longitudinal studies, currently underway, are necessary to establish the link between OCC and these heartening reductions.

+ + +

When Americans get a deeper understanding of the scope, nature, and financial and emotional costs of gun violence, I believe they'll agitate and mobilize for change. Just as they did against the tobacco industry which, despite continuing to spend a hundred thousand dollars a day on Congressional lobbying, has taken some mighty hits in the past three decades.

I can be "for gun control," but if I don't vote what good is my opinion? If I don't help honorable lawmakers like Tom Foley stand up to the NRA, what good is my opinion? If I don't tell my elected representatives I'll not vote for them *unless* they support gun control, what good is my opinion? If I don't write letters to the editor and to my congressional delegation, what good is my opinion? If I don't join Washington Ceasefire, or the Center to Prevent Handgun Violence, or the Coalition to Stop Gun Violence, or the Million Mom March, or the Brady Campaign to Prevent Gun Violence (now united with MMM), what good is my opinion?

Nicholas D. Kristof, in his *New York Times* column of November 13, 2004 ("Lock and Load"), wrote, "Nothing kills Democratic candidates' prospects more than guns. If it weren't for guns, President-elect Kerry might now be conferring with incoming Senate Majority Leader Daschle." Maybe. But I couldn't disagree more with his assertion that ". . . nationally, gun control is dead." Citing the grisly statistics of gun murders, gun accidents, and gun suicides, Kristof argues that a "public health approach to try to make [guns] much safer" is the way to go. (That is what we did in Seattle with "Options," and in our work with Harborview Medical Center to promote gun safety, particularly through lockboxes.) But given the public's strong, albeit "latent," support for reasonable gun control laws, it's premature to declare the movement dead.

+ + +

It's long overdue: a persistent, durable grassroots campaign to counter the power and influence of the NRA. The legislative agenda of such a campaign?

- Reinstitute, immediately, a total ban on assault weapons and high-capacity magazines.

- Outlaw, or continue to outlaw, armor-piercing bullets, "plastic" guns that can defeat airport screening devices, and any other weapon or ammunition *designed to kill people.*
- Close the "gun show" loophole in the Brady Bill.*
- Require that all firearms be registered.
- License every gun owner—contingent upon his or her satisfying the requirements of a certified gun safety course.

We should continue—as politicians and the NRA regularly remind us—to aggressively enforce *existing* gun laws. We should continue the fight in the courts to hold gun manufacturers liable for the production of "unsafe" firearms. And we should push for the development of what Kristof calls a "smart gun," which can be fired only by a person authorized to possess it.

+ + +

Read what an al Qaeda training manual directs its inductees to do: *In countries like the United States it's perfectly legal for members of the public to own certain types of firearms. If you live in such a country obtain an assault rifle legally, preferably an AK-47 or variations.*

---

* The Brady Bill was named for James Brady, President Reagan's press secretary, who was permanently disabled when shot in an attempted assassination of the president by John Hinckley, Jr., on March 30, 1981. The bill called for a five-day waiting period before a weapon may be purchased, during which time a background check is made on the purchaser. President Clinton, speaking to Tom Brokaw on NBC on April 12, 2000, claimed that the Brady Bill was responsible for a "thirty-five percent drop in gun crime and a thirty-one-year low in the homicide rate, and [it has] kept a half a million people—felons, fugitives, stalkers—from getting handguns." The loophole? The five-day waiting period does not apply to those who purchase firearms at a gun show.

CHAPTER 7

MEN

WE WERE AT THIRTIETH and National in San Diego. "Units 16, 16-South, and 21 at 700 Thirty-fifth 415-Family. Psycho with a knife. Code 2." I was behind the wheel. My senior officer, Patrolman Frank Pernicano, was sitting in for "Andy Taggert" who was off nursing a sore everything, the result of one those "freak accidents" you read about (this particular one is described in chapter 12). I acknowledged the call and whipped the creaking modified* up to a respectable speed. Not as fast as Taggert would have gone but fast enough.

Code 2 to the brass meant get there quick but safe. It did not mean lights and siren—that's Code 3, a dispatch reserved for 11-99s ("officer needs help") and blood runs. The powers that be apparently found lights and sirens distasteful. To veteran cops it was more of that same old stuff: no shotguns, no dogs, no blue uniforms, no semiautos—no Code 3s, the brass trying their best to make us inconspicuous. Already at six weeks on the job I was developing a healthy case of cynicism about those gray suits in the corner pocket.

But to the cops, Code 2 meant haul ass. The night before, at Taggert's insistence, I'd gone balls to the wall—on a teenaged sailor in possession of a bottle of whiskey.

By the time I hit Wabash Boulevard, visions of a knife-wielding, family-threatening maniac spurring me on, the car was steaming, its alternator whining above the sound of the engine.

---

* An all-black sedan used during the day by detectives and at night by patrol officers who, before they begin their shift, reverse a placard, which reads SAN DIEGO POLICE, and is bracketed to both front doors.

Turning onto Wabash I nearly lost it. I recovered just in time, and prayed Pernicano hadn't noticed. But it had scared the hell out of me. To compensate, I did the logical male thing: I slammed the pedal to the metal. Nearing the intersection of Ocean View, I panicked: there was no way I was going to make that right turn. I jammed on the brakes, which responded by locking up on me. Two seconds later Pernicano and I sat in stunned silence as the engine sputtered and died in the middle of the intersection. I hadn't rolled us, but we'd done a complete 360.

I reached for the ignition key. Pernicano grabbed my wrist. "Wh . . . who . . . who you been working with kid?" I told him. He nodded. "Th . . . thought so. Well, you . . . you're working with Pe . . . Pe . . . Per . . . Pernicano now. So knock that shit off!"

"Yes, sir." He released my arm. I turned the key and the engine caught. We left Wabash and Ocean View, smelling of burnt rubber and rusty radiator water. I drove like a sane person the rest of the way there.

"Whatcha got?" said Pernicano as we walked up to the small stucco duplex.

"Well, it's a real 415," said one of the four cops standing on the porch. "See for yourself." He stood aside and let Pernicano take a look through the louvered windows, which ran the length of the front door. I took a peek myself. Inside was a petite black woman in a blood-drenched yellow robe, her face beaten to mush. She was hopping around, her wrists and ankles bound with belts. She spluttered blood as she screamed at some unseen person not to hurt her kids.

I was about to back away from the window when the unseen person walked into the living room. He was six-three, shirtless, his chiseled arms the size of my thighs. He was drunk. And had in his right hand a ten-inch kitchen knife. He screamed at the woman to get the fuck out of his life, and at us to get the fuck off his porch.

Pernicano nudged me aside, had another look. He turned to the other cops. "What the hell are you guys waiting for?"

"For the sarge," said the spokesman of the group, a cop with more time on than Pernicano. "He's en route, to authorize entry."

What? I shouted inside my head. *You silly fuck! Can't you see what's going on in there?* Was this what the corner pocket wanted? Marshal Dillon would have been all over this guy. Sure, Matt was a just a TV lawman. And he never seemed to raise his voice—I guess you could even call him "PR conscious," a term much venerated by SDPD brass. But my childhood hero would *never* let a man hit a lady. And he would *always* get his man.

"We're not waiting for any sergeant," said Pernicano. "You two guys? Take the south side." He turned to me. "Partner? See that window on the north? He's not likely to come out that way but if he does, you stop him." Oh yeah, I'll stop him. You bet I'll stop him, *partner.* "The rest of us will kick the door." He gave us thirty seconds to get into position.

I hustled through a gate and crept up to the window. It was to a bathroom. It had no curtains or blinds. A light was on but I couldn't see much—the bottom of the window was just above eye level. I stepped back a couple of paces and saw that there were two doors, one off the hall, the other leading back toward the kitchen which appeared to be just off the living room. As I scoped out the window itself, a crank-out job off its runner, the suspect walked into the bathroom. I could see his massive shoulders. I could see the knife. Which to my eyes now looked like a two-foot machete. I stood on tiptoe, drew my gun and jammed it through the window (where the guy could have wrenched it away with ease). Let's see. What would Taggert do now?

"Drop it, motherfucker!" I yelled, mustering all the command presence I could. The guy looked right through me and walked casually out the other door. I reholstered, blushing in the dark.

I pushed the window flush against the outside wall, grabbed the sill, and rappelled myself up and into the bathroom. (Maybe there *was* something to that six-foot wall you had to scale if you wanted to become a cop.) I slinked through the bathroom and glanced down the hall. The woman had retreated to the far end of it, trailing blood. Two or three wide-eyed children cowered behind her. All of our eyes met, a meeting that told me I was in the right place at the right time for the right reason. I stepped out into the hallway and spotted the suspect. What I didn't see—what I had fully expected to see—was a sea of tan uniforms. I glanced at the door—the unkicked, unshattered door—and wondered what the hell was going on behind it.

That's when I saw the hands of a cop, working to remove a louver from the window next to the door. I could picture the guy, the same cop who'd called for the supervisor, gently lifting each louvered pane, placing it gingerly on the porch so as not to break it. Doing his level best to be "PR conscious." When he'd cleared enough slats he would stick his arm through and unlock the door from the inside; that must be the new plan. But where did that leave me?

Two good things happened next. First, the suspect put the knife on the kitchen table—why, I didn't question. And, second, Pernicano's size 12 smashed through the front door just after his voice bellowed, "Jesus Christ, man! What are you doing?"

That ocean of tan finally gushed into the room. The suspect turned and started for the back of his apartment. Which was when he noticed me—standing between him and his family. His nostrils flared. His eyes bulged. He charged.

Now, I knew my limits. There was absolutely no way I could take this guy. But with five other cops on the scene and my adrenaline screaming, *Let's get the fucker!* I was up for it. As he charged I charged. A split second before the collision I stepped to his right, swung my right arm at his throat and snared him, stopping him dead in his tracks. It was just like on the mats in the gym, just as I'd practiced (half-speed) on Dottie. I lifted him onto my back, my right arm wrapped tightly around his neck, my left hand gripping my right wrist. I squeezed for all I was worth. My only purpose in life was to put this asshole out.

I'd applied it properly, I knew—the *standard police sleeper hold,* the *carotid restraint*, the *choke-out*—but the sonofabitch wasn't going under. Then I saw why.

Sticking out of the V of my bicep and forearm was a hand, trapped. I took stock. My hands were all present and accounted for. The ensnared hand was white, the suspect black—that ruled him out. It had to belong to one of the other cops, but I wasn't about to let go and figure it out.

I should have known it was Pernicano's. My senior officer had jumped on at the precise moment the suspect and I collided, and found himself in a one-armed fight.

The battle lasted two or three minutes, maybe four. Which, take my word, is a long, long fight. And during which I refused to let the man out of my grasp. When it was over, our suspect hooked up and marinating in the back seat of a police car, we surveyed the damage: half the furniture was broken, every knickknack knocked from the walls, the panel-ray heater destroyed. Black clip-on ties, including mine, littered the floor. A couple of tan shirts and trousers got torn. Pernicano's silver watchband got stretched and twisted out of shape. And there was a bloody nose or two. But the wife-beater/child-beater was on his way to jail where he belonged. The good guys had won.

Pernicano took me aside, for an ass-chewing I was certain. It was my first choke-out attempt and I'd failed. "You drive for shit, Stamper. But that was a hell of a job you did in there. I'd be proud to ride with you anytime." I flushed with embarrassment, and pride. I loved this job. I was a cop.

The patrol sergeant had pulled up as we were dragging the suspect out to the car. He divided up the investigating and reporting chores. A nice person, the sarge. But he seemed pretty much like the rest of the senior officers at the scene. I wondered, did those stripes on his sleeve make him any smarter? Why should we have to wait for him in order to do our jobs? If I ever made sergeant . . . Not that I wanted to. But if I ever became a supervisor I would make sure my cops understood: They'd better not raise their hands to get permission to do what they'd been hired to do.

The sergeant assigned me to talk to the kids. There were six of them, all under the age of ten. Five, all but the baby, spent their nights crammed into one of the apartment's two bedrooms. I'd heard the children sobbing, whimpering, wailing in the background during the fight, had heard their shouts of *Mommy-Daddy-Mommy-Daddy-Mommy-Daddy*. But in the heat of battle their cries hadn't really registered. Now I took a good look at them. What I saw had the look and feel of familiarity

+ + +

"Turn that goddamn thing off. *Now!*" He was in the dining room, playing pinochle with Mom and Aunt LaVella and Uncle Don. Another Saturday night episode of *Gunsmoke* had come to an end, but the mournful music was still playing. I couldn't turn it off, I hadn't said good-bye to Marshal Dillon, Miss Kitty, Chester, Doc.

He roared again. I got up off the floor, walked over to the set, punched the knob and watched as the white dot on the screen got smaller and smaller. I wouldn't budge until it had disappeared. That was the deal. "And stop jabbing at that goddamn thing. You'll break it."

It was brand-new, our black-and-white TV. Dad had finally won big at the track so Mom finally got her wish. Overnight, our fishing-cabin furnishings had been replaced by a houseful of blond veneer and turquoise plastic from Bay Furniture on National Avenue. "Winning big" being a relative term, they'd bought the furniture on time, just a few easy payments. I hated the stuff, every last stick of it.

"Get your butt into that bathroom right now!" he said. "I'm not telling you again, Norman." I walked by the foursome at the bright blond dining room table. They were slapping cards, smoking and cussing, cussing and smoking, the men accusing the women of cheating and vice versa. I was only too happy to get my butt into the bathroom.

I filled the tub with water as hot as I could stand and stepped in. As I sank down I imagined myself riding across wheat-colored hills with the marshal and Chester.

+ + +

We're off to an abandoned shack where the bank robber is holed up. He's wearing a black hat when he busts out and makes a run for it. I pull my rifle from its saddle holster and take cover behind a huge boulder. The bad guy is blasting away with a six-shooter in each hand. One of his rounds chips a chunk off the boulder, right next to my head.

I scowl, stand up, take a bead on him. *Blang!* One shot and he's down, writhing in the dirt. Matt walks over, picks him up with one hand, shoves him up on the extra horse we've brought along. He tells the crook to stop his bellyaching, tells him he's lucky to be alive. "My deputy only meant to wing you." He looks over at me and winks. "Nice shot, partner."

+ + +

I stuck my head under the cold faucet and kept it there for a long time. It was essential to get used to cold water, and to learn to hold one's breath underwater for as long as one could. One never knew.

Shivering, I turned off the tap and started to reach for the tattered blue towel on the rack when something stopped me. I froze. The room turned gray and everything went all muted and flatlike. Everything except the tweezers. They glistened up there on the glass shelf above the towel rack. *Pick me up*, they said, *and do something outrageous with me.* So I did. I stuck the tweezers in the electric wall socket. I guess I figured it would put an end to something, which it did. It knocked out every light in the house. And sent a jolt up my arm and into my head.

"Hey!" "What the . . ." Voices from the dining room. "Norman?" "Hey!" "Norman, are you okay?" Well, I was naked and quaking and a bit out of kilter from the dark and from the spooky feeling in my body, but I reckoned I was okay. I listened for *his* voice. It came soon enough, along with the thundering footsteps of his stocking feet. I squeezed into the far corner next to the toilet just as the door crashed open. He was one big shadow. He stood there for a second, then lunged. The belt slashed first across my face, and stung my eye. He brought it down again and again. And again. It felt like he was never going to stop. Someone, Uncle Don, produced a flashlight and that made it really awful, me naked in front of the grownups and all.

Everyone was yelling at him to stop. There was quite a crowd in the doorway, Dad, his sister, his brother-in-law, his wife. My brothers knew better, they stayed put in their bunk beds. Anyway, all the yelling didn't work. He just kept at it even when at one point Mom stepped between us and shouted some words I've forgotten, something unexpected. Dad pushed her. It was the only time I saw him lay an angry hand on her. Then Uncle Don stepped in. Dad turned on him like he was going to hit him. What a night. I'd never seen my father hit a grown-up. But he just said, "You stay out of this," and went back to work.

He hadn't done it this long, ever. I started to cry, then cried even harder when I realized I was crying. Finally, the belt caught a jar of cold cream on the glass shelf and both the jar and the shelf crashed to the tile floor, shattering. Shards sparkled in the beam of the flashlight. We kept dancing, though, my father and I.

It was weird. The only serious cut was to the *top* of my foot. But it was a bad one, gushing and spurting everywhere. Uncle Don jabbed the flashlight toward the wound, then to the pool of blood in front of the toilet. "Satisfied, Gene? Satisfied?" Dad stopped, then walked out of the bathroom. A second later he was back.

"Gimme that flashlight, will you, Don? I gotta go check the fuses." Dad and his brother-in-law, working together on a home improvement project.

After Uncle Don and Aunt LaVella left, Mom shrieked at Dad that I had to be taken to the emergency room, but he kept saying no. It was understood that Mom couldn't drive at night—she was unable to read the street signs, and she saw things jump out at her from the shadows. She kept yelling at Dad as she applied bandage after bandage to my right foot.

A little later I hobbled off to bed, my foot swaddled in layers of gauze, two or three pairs of sweat socks, and white adhesive tape over the whole works. It resembled a cast. "Look," I said to my brothers. "I have a broken foot."

"Wow," said Roy.

"Geezo," said Brian.

+ + +

I removed my helmet, a violation of department policy, and sat down on the bed. Five kids swarmed me, the youngest fighting for my lap. A couple of them were giggling, asking if my gun was real, if I'd ever shot anybody. I answered their questions, then asked some of my own, trying to remember what our criminal law instructor had told us about questioning kids. I was pretty sure you could "lead" young children, if necessary, to get the story out of them. But I tried not to need to, so I asked questions like: *What happened? Has something like this happened before? How did your mommy get tied up? Why was your mommy bleeding? How did you get that bump? Do you have any other 'owies'?"*

That last question triggered a lifting of shirts, blouses, PJs. There were large belt welts on all but the youngest, a crawler sitting in the corner with snot rolling out of her nose and over her lips. "See, see?" "Lookie here!" "No, no, policeman, lookitmine, lookitmine!" "He done these ones yesterday." "Oh yeah? He jes' whupped me jes' today."

"Who's 'he'?" I said.

"Daddy," they said in unison. "Daddy."

I'd noticed the number scrawled in crayon all over the crumbling plaster walls of the bedroom. It was impossible to miss: 232-6981. It looked familiar. When I figured it out I chuckled. I hadn't yet memorized it, the phone number of the San Diego Police Department. "What's this about?" I said, waving a hand at the walls. My own mother would never have called the cops, or given us the phone number. Cops were for writing traffic tickets, catching the bogeyman, bringing wayward boys home to their parents. But not for coming into your house.

"Momma said that's for when he does it the next time," said the oldest, a boy with mocha skin and velvet-painting eyes. His welts were the worst. "I tried to call it but . . ."

"You mean tonight?"

"Yeah, but there wasn't nobody on the phone." Daddy had ripped the instrument from the wall.

+ + +

Finally, I had a tale worth telling at the nightly critique. I picked up the story at our arrival on Thirty-fifth. I told the story of our 415 family dispassionately. Like it was nothing.

But it was not nothing. It was one of the most influential events of my police career. In that split second in the hallway, when I looked upon that mom and her kids, I knew I would never again question the "essentialness" of police work, or police officers.

+ + +

On Labor Day, days before his death in 1990, I wrote my father a letter. I hadn't really talked to him about it, so I spent a paragraph or two telling him, as an adult, what I thought of his racial intolerance, his physical violence, his endless pronouncements of my unworthiness. I wrote that I'd forgiven him all that.

But I also reflected on other things we'd never talked about: his grabbing a life-saving ring and jumping into the Pacific Ocean (he couldn't swim) to rescue a downed pilot, for which he was awarded the Navy Cross in World War II; his lifetime of backbreaking construction work to feed and house his wife and four boys; his voracious reading which made him as well-informed as any talking head on the tube; his taking us to Padres ball games at Lane Field, and on Sunday drives to Mission Valley after stops at Niederhoffer's for ice cream cones.

I told him how deeply moved I was when I recalled, as an adult, his tenderness in nursing me when I was hurting. Not always, of course. But he'd stayed up with me all night during many early childhood bouts with the croup, making a tent of my bedding, filling it with steam, rubbing my chest with Vicks. When I fell from a rope swing and severely sprained both my wrists he gave me two silver dollars he'd won in Vegas that weekend. And he rubbed bacon (bacon!) on my foot after I'd stepped on the tip of a pencil, driving its graphite tip deep into the bottom of my foot.

I played hooky from work the day after I'd finished the letter. I took Dad to see a Harrison Ford movie, the letter in my pocket. We sat in a mostly empty cavern of a theater. When an unmarked police car appeared on the screen, Dad said, loud enough for everyone to hear. "That's the kind of cop car you drive, isn't it, Norman?" I knew it was my father's way of saying he was proud of me. We were going to go to dinner but he was too tired so I took him home, to my brother's house in Santee, and put him to bed. I gave him his morphine, and left the letter on the nightstand.

The next day, I called the house. My son Matthew answered the phone. He told me he'd read the letter to Dad. My father had wept, and told Matt that he'd beaten me to toughen me up. He feared I was "too sensitive."

There were, of course, better ways to "toughen me up," if indeed that's what I needed. My father, like so many men, just didn't know how to raise a boy. One of Dad's brothers told me recently that their father, my "Pampa," whom I'd idolized, had raised his family (the girls as well as the boys) with sticks, fists, and belts. It hurt to hear Uncle Larry's accounts of my beloved

Pampa. But as a grown-up, as a cop, I would have been surprised to hear otherwise.

+ + +

Why, I asked Lieutenant Jay Helmick at the critique, had those cops just stood there on that porch?

"Because they *weren't* cops, Stamper. Whether they were afraid of the suspect, or afraid of the brass, they didn't act like cops, they didn't act like *men*."

COP
CULTURE

CHAPTER 8

WHY WHITE COPS KILL BLACK MEN

Momma and Daddy were lucky, they had girls. I had boys. My boys are eleven and nine now, and I'm scared to death for them. It's not that I'm afraid they're gonna get jumped into a gang, or wind up doing or dealing drugs. No sir. My big fear is they're gonna run into one of you people one night and they won't be coming home. It's like open season on young black men in our community, like they're walking around with targets on their backs. I have a recurring nightmare, Chief: I get this call in the middle of the night, "Come on down to the morgue, Mrs. Johnson. We got one of your boys here. Police shot him when he tried to run."

—An African-American mother at a community forum

It's open season on us in The Heights, Chief. If you're working the blacks you're wearing a target, plain and simple. For me it comes down to this: kill or be killed. I got a wife and two boys. My sons need their father. I'm gonna do whatever it takes to make it home at the end of shift.

—A white cop, and member of an
officer-safety task force, two weeks later

ANXIOUS ABOUT THE FUTURES of four young boys, a black mom and a white dad used identical metaphors in April 1985 to describe the "killing ground" that was, in their respective minds, the black community. There is no better case study of this issue than the Amadou Diallo incident in New York City.

Mr. Diallo was approached by four NYPD officers one night in February 1999. The cops thought he might be a rape suspect. Frightened, not understanding what was going on, Diallo reached for his wallet to show the officers his ID. One of the cops yelled, "Gun!" and in less time than it takes to read this sentence, forty-one shots were fired, nineteen of them striking Mr. Diallo. Diallo was not a rapist. In fact, he had no criminal record.

NYPD ruled it a "clean" shooting, meaning the killing of the twenty-two-year-old, non-English-speaking, unarmed immigrant was legally justified and within department policy. The Department of Justice found no civil rights violations. A state criminal trial ended in four acquittals.

But an innocent man was shot dead. Why? Because Mr. Diallo was black. I believe the cops were afraid of him for that reason, and that reason alone. So frightened they couldn't see straight, think straight, shoot straight. (If they'd been at their PD firearms range in the Bronx all forty-one of those shots, fired as they were at point blank range, would have found their target.)

But *why* were they so frightened?

President Clinton said at the time, "If it had been a young white man in a young all-white neighborhood, it probably wouldn't have happened." To determine whether the Diallo killing (or any other police action) was racially motivated you have to ask, *Would the cops have behaved the same way if the man had been white?*

No. Diallo was killed because of his dark skin. A white man reaching for his wallet, under identical circumstances, including a language barrier, would have been given the benefit of the doubt.

Simply put, white cops are afraid of black men. We don't talk about it, we pretend it doesn't exist, we claim "color blindness," we say white officers treat black men the same way they treat white men. But that's a lie. In fact, the bigger, the darker the black man the greater the fear. The African-American community knows this. Hell, most *whites* know it. Yet, even though it's a central, if not *the* defining ingredient in the makeup of police racism, white cops won't admit it to themselves, or to others.

I've studied fear for years. I've learned how it affects our bodies, our perception, judgment, and actions. Recently, I tried to dig up empirical evidence to support my particular theory that white cops are afraid of black men.

I researched the voluminous library of the National Institute of Justice (Bureau of Justice Statistics), scoured the reams of publications put out by the International Association of Chiefs of Police, consulted LexisNexis. I Googled till I was goggle-eyed. It's just not there. You can find all kinds of evidence of citizen fears *of* the police. There are studies on officer stress, some of which focus on cops' fears of being fired for doing the wrong thing (or not doing the right thing). There *are* studies showing that whites, in general, are likely to view blacks as more violent than whites. (One of those studies, recently completed by Dr. Anthony Greenwald and published in the July 2003 *Journal of Experimental Social Psychology*, actually went so far as to put computer "guns" in the hands of 106 undergraduate, mostly white, non-cop students. In 208 scenarios the students wrongly shot black "suspects" 35 percent of the time versus 26 percent wrongful shootings of whites.) But not until some brave soul conducts a valid, reliable study that focuses on actual white cops' actual *fears* of actual black men will we have actual scientific proof of my assertion.

So, why am I so certain that white cops are afraid of black men? Because I was a white cop. In a world of white cops. For thirty-four years.

At first I was afraid of everyone, white, black, old, young. I got over most of these fears pretty quickly (which is to say I sublimated or repressed them). But not, however, my fear of black men. Not for a long, long time. As a rookie, I felt a peculiar and particular fear every time I stopped or ticketed or arrested a black man, a fear I did not feel when confronting white men under similar circumstances.

From the earliest days of academy training it was made clear that black men and white cops don't mix, that of all the people we'd encounter on the streets, those most dangerous to our safety, to our survival, were black men.

One instructor began his presentation with: "Gentlemen, what you are about to learn may save your life." He was there to talk to us about a *particular* problem he said we would encounter with a *particular* slice of the black male population in Logan Heights. He directed us to his chapter in the academy manual:

> This information is designed to acquaint you with the NATION OF ISLAM OR THE "MUSLIM CULT." It should be noted at this time that your Police Department has always maintained a detachment from political, racial, and religious involvements. This policy has not changed as this is a sketch of a pseudo-religious organization whose creed is the anniliation [sic] of the white man . . .

We learned that this "pseudo-religious organization" was composed of twenty- to thirty-year-old men called the "fruit of Islam." That these men were "selected for their physical prowess and are adept at aggressive tactics and judo." That they were "almost psychotic in their hatred of Caucasians and are comparable to the Mau Mau or Kamikaze in their dedication and fanaticism." That "locally, members of this cult will kill any police officer when the opportunity presents itself, regardless of the circumstances or outcome."

Black men? "Almost psychotic" in their hatred of me? On the streets of my city. Dedicated to "anniliating" me? I wondered, but never asked, what the four African-American cops in that classroom thought of all this.

We soon learned it wasn't just the "Muslim Cult" we needed to worry about. It was all black men, something we were taught tacitly if not explicitly by other instructors who kept returning in their "real-world" tales to the streets of Logan Heights, to accounts of gunfights, fistfights, knife-fights—with black men. It got to the point where all they had to say was "The Heights" and you'd envision legions of black males who couldn't wait for the chance to kill a cop.

I was working The Heights one night as a rookie when my senior officer ordered me to pull up to the curb in front of a bar, aptly nicknamed the "Bucket o' Blood." "Get out of the vehicle," he said. "Take your nigger-knocker with you." I stepped out of the car, slipped my baton into its ring, and peered through the passenger window, awaiting instructions. "Go on inside," he said. "Pick out the biggest, blackest, meanest motherfucking nigger in the place and pinch him." I was halfway to the door of the tavern when he called me back to the car. It had been a test, a jest. He laughed his ass off. It took me five minutes to stop shaking.

What if he'd said, in front of the Kensington Inn, a white bar in a white neighborhood, "Go on inside. Pick out the biggest, whitest, meanest motherfucking honky in the place and pinch him"? I probably would have thought something like, *Dang, this guy's off his rocker. Why does he want me to go in there and bust some big white guy?* But I wouldn't have been afraid. I wasn't taught to fear white people.

A couple of nights later I rode The Heights with another white cop. This guy was different. Jack Pearson had grown up in an African-American neighborhood, had attended Lincoln High, a predominantly black school. We stopped a lot of black men that night, even put a couple of them in jail. Pearson's respectful, transparently fearless approach to them stood in contrast to the panicky, impulsive white cops I'd worked with. Watching him talk to black men (and women) and observing how he *listened* to them helped me recognize that I was a member of the panicky white-cop category.

This knowledge ultimately forced me to confront and to work (for years) on my own fears and racism. And to recognize that it was fear of black men (and no small amount of peer pressure) that, in part, drove me to behave during my rookie year as a thug, a brutal, overbearing, menace of a cop.

Good cops experience fear, to be sure. But they perform effectively by working through their fear. Ambrose Redmoon wrote, "Courage is not the absence of fear, but rather the judgment that something else is more important than fear." For fearless cops, that "something else" is getting a dangerous and delicate job done—properly, humanely and safely.

Fearless cops *perceive* their surroundings more accurately, and they make more informed judgments when the work does turn tense or dangerous. It's not that they don't register hues of black or white or brown, they just don't impute *anything* to skin color. They size up Diallo-type situations—which happen *all the time* in police work—and recognize in the moment the inherent innocence of such persons. Because these cops are alert, not alarmed or paranoid, and because they assess behavior not pigmentation, they tend to produce routine rather than tragic outcomes. Cops like these, who make up maybe twenty to thirty percent of the force, are inspiring to watch in action.

Legitimate "kill or be killed" events do happen—far more often today than when I was a beat cop. A police officer would be a fool not to be ever vigilant. But I'm afraid this reality has licensed panicky white cops to shoot unarmed black men when they should be talking, or fighting, their way out of a sticky situation.

What to do about white cops who are afraid of black men? First, each "corner pocket" must understand the scope and the nature of racism within its own department. This means investigating the problem. My bosses in San Diego in the mid-seventies ordered the most exhaustive study of police racism in the history of the institution. Although the reports were never published, they produced for at least one agency a clear indication of needed reforms.

Academy and continuing education, focused on "undoing" racism, must be provided. Likewise, practical, theoretically sound courses on fear and how to manage it.

Psychological "trauma treatment" and debriefings should be mandatory for all officers involved in shootings or other harrowing incidents.

Most important, chiefs and other police leaders must set and communicate, systematically and regularly, nonnegotiable standards of nondiscriminatory performance and conduct. They must, themselves, model the same fearless and respectful behavior they expect from their cops. And they must fire any police officer who can't or won't refrain from "unprofessional" conduct, which includes those frightened, trigger-happy cops who are a special danger to unarmed black men. These kinds of cops *can* be located and removed from the force before they kill someone.

Over the years I observed that cops who are the most calm, the most courageous are invariably the most empathetic, and compassionate. Jack Pearson didn't act like he had a target on his back. He didn't live in mortal fear that he wouldn't make it home at the end of shift. He didn't view his work in the black community as a "kill or be killed" proposition. Pearson would have understood in a heartbeat that black mother's fears for her two boys—even as he would have been among the least likely to rob her of them.

+ + +

Finally, let me pass along some advice from Johnnie Cochran. The prominent attorney joined me one Saturday morning in the auditorium of Seattle's First AME Church to address a joint session of beat cops and hundreds of black youths from the community. "Listen up, young people!" he said. The din and murmur of the youthful audience ceased. "Hear and heed what I'm about to tell you. If you get stopped by the police do *exactly* as they say. If they tell you to put your hands on the dash, do it. If they tell you to get out of the car, do it. If they order you to step over to the sidewalk, or to spread-eagle yourself in the middle of the street, do it. If they ask for your ID, give it to them. Do *not* give them lip. Police officers have a hard enough job as it is. So, respect your city's police officers. Treat them the way you want to be treated. Got that?"

The din and murmur returned, the kids glaring back at Cochran, wondering if this was the real Johnnie—or some cop in disguise. "Now, if they don't have the right to stop you in the first place, if they disrespect you or violate your constitutional rights or mistreat you in any way, take a good look at their nametags. Get their car and badge numbers. Wait till they're gone, write it all down, along with the date, time, and location. Then give me a call." Words to live by.

CHAPTER 9

RACISM IN THE RANKS

IT WAS FIVE MINUTES after midnight. I poured myself a refill of scorched coffee, walked through the archway, down the hall, and into a tiny windowless room where I waited for "Tom," my first cop of the night. He showed up ten minutes late, rapped on the door, and called out in a voice that could be heard across town, "Captain?"

I let him in, extended my hand. "How you doing, Tom?" He rubbed his own hand on his uniform trousers but I noticed it was still clammy.

"Fine, sir," he said, almost shouting.

"Sit down, please."

"Sorry I'm late, sir. Last-minute arrest." I nodded and took the only other chair in the bare office, behind a gray metal desk. I hoped my expression—I was aiming for grim yet friendly, with just a hint of intimidation, a touch of coercion—would convey the seriousness of the occasion.

"You know what this is about, so I'm not going to play games with you." He stared at me, a bent smile on his face. "I'm going to ask you a lot of questions," I said. "I expect you to answer each one of them honestly, and fully." I paused. "You understand?" From my side of the desk I could tell his legs were bouncing up and down. He nodded. I waited.

"Yes, sir. I understand." His voice, now just above a whisper, cracked.

"Good." I picked up a blank legal pad, and told him his statement would be included with those of other officers but that his name would not appear anywhere in my report.

For the next hour and forty minutes Tom told me, in detail, what he thought of black people and other ethnic minorities. And how he and his colleagues treated them.

The "Southeast Investigation" was triggered by allegations of three probationary patrol officers who'd left the department in the spring of 1976. Each had resigned voluntarily, each had worked black and Latino neighborhoods, and each had witnessed stomach-turning events that led them to question SDPD's commitment to "professional" police work. Previous administrations would have round-filed the reports of these "exit interviews." But this was the Bill Kolender regime, an administration committed to openness and honesty, community policing, "humanistic" and "nondiscriminatory" police behavior. Between August 13 and October 1, it was my job to interview the thirty-one cops—twenty-seven patrol officers, three sergeants, one lieutenant—on my graveyard patrol squad in Southeast.

When we finished, I thanked Tom for his candor and asked him if there was anything he wanted to add. He'd gotten bolder, progressively more talkative over the course of the interview, and seemed to have been waiting for this moment. "Yes sir," he said. "Why are you doing this? You know nothing's going to change. It's always been like this. *Everybody* uses racial slurs. *Everybody* does this kind of shit. And we're not about to change." The guy had gall, I'll give him that. He'd just copped to being a practicing racist, in one of our uniforms. Now he was defying me and the rest of the brass to do something about it.

By that point in the investigation I was no longer surprised by such frankness; most of the other cops had been equally forthright. And self-damning: thirty of the thirty-one personnel (including my lieutenant and two of his sergeants) admitted to using racial and ethnic slurs. African-Americans were niggers, boys, splibs, toads, coons, garboons, groids (from "negroid"), Sambos, Buckwheats, Rastuses, Remuses, jigaboos, jungle bunnies, and spooks. Latinos were greasers, wets, wetbacks, beans, beaners, bean bandits, chickenos, spics.

Most cops said they used the terms among themselves, less often with the public, and then "only jokingly" or to "defuse a tense situation" or when they were "*really* pissed" at someone. I asked each man to tell me how many cops in Southeast talked this way. Answers ranged from "five percent" to "ninety-nine percent," but the mean was over ninety percent. "Everyone but the super-religious cops," was Tom's reply. "It's not that these 'Christians' lord it over you, they just don't talk the way the rest of us talk."

The quality of my officers' arrests? Not so good:

> "About twenty percent are attitude arrests, Captain. About fifteen percent don't have P.C. [probable cause]."

> "I've seen maybe ten to fifteen bum arrests."

> "A *lot* is overdone, overlooked. Search and seizure, you name it. I'm surprised officers haven't been impeached in court, and I'm only speaking from things I've seen."

> "With some it never happens; with others maybe fifty percent of their arrests are bad."

> "I've seen a few attitude arrests, maybe twenty percent."

> "I'd say maybe fifteen to twenty percent bum arrests . . . sober drunks, bad tickets."

> "I've seen some officers who've made arrests that leave me shaking my head. You wonder how they do it. You wind up with that feeling in your gut, you know? I see about two of those a week."

Tom said he'd witnessed many busts, and had made a several of his own, for what he called "BBN." *BBN?* "Busy being a nigger." (This was years before "driving while black" earned its popular name.)

Seventy-one percent of the officers admitted to using or witnessing excessive force. Frequency ranged from "three or four times in eleven months" to "two to three times a week." One cop told me that "twenty-five percent of the officers do it on a regular basis," and that "fifty percent do it on 'special occasions,' like when they've had a fight with their wife, they're emotionally upset, or maybe their last contact acted like an ass and they couldn't do anything about it, so they take it out on the next guy."

Most cops confessed to "minor" instances of excessive force: slamming people against a wall, ratcheting down on handcuffs until blood to the hands is cut off, twisting arms, kneeing a man in the nuts.

Tom told me he had that very evening choked out a handcuffed burglary suspect.

"Why?" I asked.

"Because I was in a hurry." Seems he had an interview with his captain, and the suspect wouldn't get into the car fast enough.

Only one of my interviewees said he'd witnessed an "out-and-out beating." It had followed a high-speed pursuit of a motorcyclist who, when finally stopped, was dragged off his machine and beaten to a paste by several officers. (Where was amateur cameraman George Holliday and his camcorder when we needed him?)

"What did you do?" I asked.

"I went 10-8 [code for 'back in service'], and got the hell out of there."

San Diego cops confessed to myriad other acts of discrimination, including additional dehumanizing references to blacks, such as "No humans involved" (on a radio call), "just an 11-13—nigger" (11-13 being code for an injured animal, followed on the air by a descriptor: "dog," "cat," "skunk," what have you). There was the cop who sang all the way to jail, "Mammy's little baby loves short'nin', short'nin' . . ." to his black prisoner in the back seat. The half-dozen officers who regularly goaded suspects into taking a swing at them. Cops who made fun of mentally ill people. The beat cop who told me he'd refused to give mouth-to-mouth resuscitation to a black woman. The hassling of white women in the company of black men. On and on and on.

One of the most poignant moments came toward the end, early one morning. I was interviewing the only black officer on my squad. When we got to the subject of racial and ethnic slurs and I asked if he used them, he fell into a silent weeping jag. "Yeah, I do," he said, finally, tears streaming down his cheeks. He went along to get along, he told me. It had shredded his insides for the five years he'd been a cop. How often did he trash blacks, use the language of white bigots? "All the time, really. It's kind of a defense. I know the white officers are testing me. Some of them won't say 'nigger' or any of those other terms to my face. But, I hear them anyway. Two bays over in the locker room, or out in the field when they're rousting some guy. Then they see me and get all embarrassed. So, I'll throw out a term or two myself, try to make them feel okay." He was sobbing now. "I . . . I'm ashamed of myself, Captain."

I can't pretend I was shocked at what my cops told me. I'd never called anyone a "nigger," but I laughed heartily at others' slurs and jokes, made my share of "slim" arrests in the black community, taunted prisoners, goaded individuals into taking a swing at me so I could bust them, choked out more than a few who'd "needed" it but whose actions didn't justify it. Still, I honestly thought we'd come further than that. It saddened me as much as it angered me. We'd been handing SDPD critics all the ammunition they needed to brand us, accurately, as a racist, brutal, uncaring police force.

Yet my cops had told the truth. That should count for something. It was a hopeful sign. Maybe the real progress of the Kolender administration up to that point had been to cultivate a deeper level of honesty—essential to combating racism. (True, the Southeast cops had been promised no discipline, that the investigation was less an inquisition than an inquiry, an effort to learn what was really going on in our police department.) In any event, we were now in possession of *facts*, not speculation. There would be no "King's X" for offending officers, no excuse or free pass in the future. The kind of behavior these cops described would, from that point on, land them in the unemployment line. Or in jail.

Tom was wrong. Our efforts would not be for nothing. We would root out racists, overhaul our policies and procedures, make systemic changes in training and supervision and accountability. The "Southeast Investigation" was, I thought, not the worst but the best thing to happen to our police department since the invention of the two-way radio.

The first order of business was to let the world know what we'd found. At the end of my 114-page report, I wrote:

> Having concluded its investigation, the department must now make a decision. Should the results be made public? I think that the circumstances argue for release. What will come as *news* to the public is not that problems exist (the minority community is acutely aware of them) but, rather, that we care that they exist and are doing something about them. We have nothing to be ashamed of, or defensive about. This is probably the only police department in the country that has undertaken such an exhaustive process of *self*-examination in the field of race relations.

I never thought the case for making our findings public would turn into a battle, but it did. And I lost it. Kolender ordered all copies of the investigation rounded up and all lips sealed. When I asked him why, he replied, "Because we'd look like fifteen cents if we put that information out."

"We'll look like a dime if we don't," I said. "And it's bound to get out."

+ + +

The article that appeared in the *Evening Tribune* a year later wasn't that bad. It was obvious the reporter, Ozzie Roberts, had gotten hold of someone's executive summary, not the whole fifteen-cent can of worms. What he wrote was hardly flattering, though certainly more benign than it might have been. It did not, for example, repeat the litany of racial epithets. And, he did give us credit for taking on the problem ourselves.

Of course, we would have gotten a lot more mileage out of it if we'd only been as forthcoming as our cops.

+ + +

The Southeast Investigation was conducted over thirty years ago. Three decades may sound like a long time, but in the parallel struggles for racial justice in America and for the "professionalization" of policing it's little more than the blink of an eye. The fight for racial equality has taken forever in this country, and the battle is far from won, especially in policing.

What would we find today if such an investigation were replicated in San Diego? Or New York, Philadelphia, Chicago, Omaha, Cincinnati, Miami, Houston, Los Angeles, Seattle? What have these and other agencies done to combat racism in the ranks? What makes chiefs and mayors believe today's police officers are all that different from those of the seventies? Do their cops provide equitable service in all communities? Do they respond rapidly and vigorously to crime in black neighborhoods? Do they follow proper procedures in stop-and-frisks, collecting evidence, making arrests? Do they refrain from excessive force? Have they dropped the unwritten law against "BBN"?

Not likely. The Neanderthal spirit is alive and well in America's police departments. Los Angeles cops, for example, used their MDTs (mobile data terminals) to send car-to-car messages about "gorillas in the mists" at the time of the Rodney King incident (1991). After O. J. Simpson was acquitted, one of my veteran cops in Seattle was inspired to use his own MDT to enlighten peers about the differences between white and black juries. (I took him off the streets and "constructively terminated" him, meaning he quit before I could fire him.) The King beating, the Diallo and Louima incidents in New York, the profiling cases on the New Jersey turnpike—all make it clear that racism continues to thrive in policing.

But what of the higher echelons of police leadership? Just two years before the Southeast Investigation, Kolender's predecessor, Chief Ray Hoobler, had this answer to a subordinate's sycophantic suggestion that he run for mayor: "Can't do it. I don't like the niggers and the Mexicans don't like me." A commander, years after that same investigation, sat a captain down in his office and told him he wanted something done about the "nigger whores" downtown.

I know several white police chiefs who are authentic, effective leaders in the effort to combat racism in their departments and within their local communities, but I know just as many who are either overt or closet racists. Or who are numbingly ignorant of their own insensitivity to racial issues. They give themselves away when they make Daryl Gates–type statements (who can forget his comparison between blacks and "normal" people?). They let slip a "good-natured" slur at an all-white Rotary meeting. They get defensive if not combative when one of their own shoots an unarmed black man and the community demands answers.

Most white chiefs fall in the middle, of course. They think things are fine, and they see no racial divide. To them, policing is "color-blind." To them, I say take off your blinkers and have a look around. If they're open to it these chiefs will see evidence of racism within their departments. If this troubles them they'll set nonnegotiable standards for performance and conduct—at all levels. They'll provide "diversity" training, "cross-cultural relations" training. But they'll also let it be known that they will *fire* cops, including ranking officers, who use racial and ethnic slurs or who engage in racist practices.

I'm proud of the actions my old department took on the heels of the

Southeast Investigation. The first thing Kolender did was reissue a statement he'd made when he became chief: "These walls have heard for the last time the 'N' word. You will treat *everyone* with dignity and respect. If you can't do that, Convair's hiring." *Most* people got the message.

+ + +

At that point in my career I'd been a cop for ten years. I decided to trade my captain's authority for greater influence within the broader institution of policing, thinking I'd wind up teaching and consulting. I resigned my police officer commission at the conclusion of the Southeast Investigation. But the city manager and the chief hired me back—as the PD's ombudsman, and it was in that capacity that Kolender assigned me to oversee and facilitate organizational changes designed to root out racism.

I headed up two groups, one of rank-and-filers, the other of department brass. We examined policies, procedures, training, equipment, supervision, discipline, performance evaluations, and promotions—and sought the kind of deep *systemic* changes required to give spine and muscle to our good intentions. Here's what we came up with.

- Modifications to the recruitment, testing, and screening of new officers to specifically target racial attitudes and behavior;
- All-new academy curricula on cross-cultural relations, interpersonal relations, and communications skills—much of it taught by teams of police, academic, and community experts;
- A program that put police recruits into social service agencies in the black community for two weeks at a time, *sans uniform*, to experience life through the eyes of the residents;
- Ongoing in-service training in performance expectations for supervisors and veteran cops;
- Debriefings for officers involved in traumatic incidents;
- Analysis and reporting of suspected individual and organizational patterns of racial discrimination;
- A "beat tenure" program that examined officers' ongoing fitness for duty in ethnic minority communities;

- Systematic and spot inspections of arrest quality, crime reporting, and courtroom testimony;
- A requirement that supervisors investigate all instances of rumored or suspected excessive force;
- A department-wide program of physical fitness, combined with a requirement that officers meet job-related standards of physical strength and agility;
- Training to help internal investigators distinguish between "discourtesy" and racial discrimination;
- Outfitting every patrol car with a shotgun; and, of course:
- The discharge of employees who used racial slurs, or who otherwise demonstrated contempt for the rule of law in policing ethnic minority communities.

Shotguns? How, you may ask, does providing cops with twelve-gauge shotguns foster improved relations between a predominantly white PD and a black community?

One of the things we had wanted to learn from the Southeast Investigation was whether our cops had the confidence needed to work effectively in a black community. So we asked questions about training, one-versus two-officer patrols, equipment, and so forth. When it came to the question of equipment the cops let me have it with both barrels: feeble police cars, too many miles on them; broken-down seats; bare retreads; filthy interiors; catalytic converters that produced excessive heat in the passenger compartment; an absence of light bars and handheld spots; not enough walkie-talkies to go around; no semiautomatic pistols, no canines, no saps, no tape recorders, no binoculars, no night-viewing devices, no photographic equipment, no print kits, no this, no that. But the biggest no was no shotguns.

There are good reasons in both urban and rural communities for cops to carry shotguns, locked and loaded, in their patrol cars—and no good reason not to. But my department had for years nurtured a list of pathetic excuses for not providing them: They were bad for our image; they were too costly; and, most telling: you couldn't trust the cops. Our officers had heard all these excuses for years. I figured the purchase of shotguns would buy much-needed credibility for an administration poised to come down hard on police racism and other misconduct. Besides, it was the right thing to do.

Throughout the Kolender administration and on into the next three, racial equality and nondiscriminatory policing inched closer to becoming a permanent way of life. We hadn't undone racism within the ranks, of course. But by the late 1980s the department had turned into a decidedly unfriendly place for anyone stupid enough to vent his or her bigotry. The "Toms" of the agency had been weeded out, or driven underground with the rest of the rodents.

If the "Southeast Investigation" were replicated today it would yield a picture of a far different police department. One that would make SDPD look not like fifteen cents but a million bucks.

CHAPTER 10

"SPLIT TAILS"

THE CONFERENCE ROOM AT Northern Division is a beehive of creativity, the buzz fueled by equal parts anger and bewilderment.

"They can make coffee at the command post during riots."

"Yeah, and rock concerts and parades. And they can sweep out the van when the events are over."

"What about missing juveniles? We can give them missing juvenile calls and . . ."

"Right. And death notifications. And found property calls. And . . ."

"Hey, wait a minute. I got it! They can handle *all* cold calls. You know, day-old burglaries. Things like that."

"Yeah! They could take *all* the reports in the field. They're *great* report writers."

It's 1973. I'm a lieutenant, attending a special supervisors' brainstorming session. Women will soon be hitting the streets, in uniform, and the department's captains have been instructed to coax ideas out of their sergeants and lieutenants about how to make the transition as smooth as possible. *But why?* the men want to know. Patrol is no place for a woman. It's unimaginable. How could Ray Hoobler, our own macho-cowboy-blood-and-guts-police chief—our hero, whose own publicly proclaimed hero is General George S. Patton, Jr.—let this happen?

+ + +

I remember Hoobler's position on the issue from just a year before. We were standing outside my Patrol Planning office when I suggested it was time to put women on the streets. He scowled, shook his head. "Over my dead body!" Then he gave me another lecture about my goddamn-bleeding-heart-social-worker-liberal attitude.

Later, I made the mistake of telling the chief about another police chief, one who'd dared to challenge the status quo.

Back when he was a sergeant at the Indianapolis police academy, Winston Churchill promised recruits Betty Blankenship and Elizabeth Coffal, then destined for "female seats" in the detective bureau, that if he ever made chief he'd put them out on patrol—something they'd lobbied for from the moment they signed on. In 1968 Churchill was named chief, and one of his first acts was to make good on his promise to the two women. Blankenship and Coffal were assigned to "Car 47," the first women in the U.S. to serve as uniformed patrol officers.

"You finished?" said Hoobler.

"Yeah."

"Good." He stuck his finger in my face and told me it would "never happen in San Diego." He punctuated the point with a not-so-soft poke to the chest. "Never!"

Hoobler saw it the same way most male cops saw it. Women on patrol would spell the end of police work as we knew it: the ladies fussing with their hair, leaving toilet seats down, "wearing" instead of carrying their guns, fainting at the sight of blood. Guys not allowed to say *fuck* or *shit* anymore.

Shortly before the brainstorming session I learned from one of Hoobler's assistants how our leader had suddenly become a champion of "women's lib." The feds had shown up one day, gunning for a police chief whose public defiance of the law had piqued Justice Department brass. The chief had been summoned to the city manager's office. I picture how the meeting went down:

Hoobler glares at the head fed, says, "Read my lips: It ain't gonna happen."

"But it's the *law*, Chief."

"Not where I come from, it ain't."

"Well, if you come from anywhere here in these United States of America it *is* the law, and even as we speak, you're breaking it."

"So sue me."

"Happy to oblige" says the fed, with the smile of a guy who holds the trump card. "But, first, we're going to take away all your federal money." Hoobler's fiscal minions have tallied up the department's federal law enforcement grants. The numbers in his hip pocket, the chief is unmoved.

"Fine," he says. "Take it."

"I don't think you understand," says the fed. "We're talking *all* your federal dollars."

"Take it, I said. I don't need your stinking money."

The city manager, Hoobler's boss, mum to this point, seeks clarification: "Whoa. What do you men by *all* our federal money, G-man?"

"Just what I said. We'll take every last federal nickel from your city treasury. That means *all* your transportation money, *all* your housing subsidies, *all* your . . ." The city manager grabbed Hoobler's cards and threw them on the table.

"We fold."

+ + +

I'm eight, standing across the street from the Boys Club on D Avenue, my nose in the air, sniffing. Whatever it is, it's close. I peer down the bank and into the shadows of the culvert. There it is, on the other side of the putrid creek. I scramble down the bank, my nostrils full of the ripeness of it. The bottom part of it is submerged in the green-black water, but the top half is reachable. I take off my shoes and sox, pick up a stick and wade across. Its head is bashed in. A bloody rock the size of a cantaloupe rests on the bank near the body of the gray striped creature. Catslaughter. I have to investigate. As I poke at it I hear a loud, pleasing sound: *potato, potato, potato.* I turn toward the sound and see an unforgettable sight. I rush home to tell Mom.

"Mom! Guess what I saw?"

"Where are your shoes, Norman?"

"I'll go get 'em, I promise. But guess what I saw?"

"What?"

"A motorcycle!"

"Yes?"

"A big one, with big handlebars!"

"So, it was a big motorcycle with big handlebars?"

"Yep!"

"And?"

"And, and, and . . . there was a *girl* driving it!" I picture the scene anew, the young woman motoring languidly, as in a parade, *potato, potato, potatoing* up D Avenue on a shiny black chopped Harley. She has long, flowing red hair. She's wearing jeans, engineer boots, and a sleeveless black leather vest with fringe on the back.

"Oh. A girl? Really?" My mother is duly astonished. "Well, now. That's something you don't see every day."

It's a major shaping incident in my young life, what sociologist Edgar Schein calls a "catalytic marker event." It shocks me, teaches me, makes a rudimentary little feminist of me. If that "girl" can ride a motorcycle—no training wheels, no big man's hairy arms around her to negotiate the beast—why can't girls and women do other things? Things that only boys and men are supposed to be able to do. Wasn't Mom the first girl at Sweetwater High to take wood shop, hadn't she—Beulah the Riveter—worked at Convair during the war? It isn't that I'd formed some fully realized understanding of and commitment to gender-based equal opportunity. I was only eight. And it *was* the fifties. But the image seared itself into my brain.

+ + +

When I became a cop in 1966, about 2 percent of police officers were women, "policewomen" to be exact, all them working as detectives. According to Dorothy Moses Schulz in *From Social Worker to Crimefighter: Women in United States Policing* (1995), the nation's first "policewoman" was Mary Owens, the widow of a Chicago cop in 1893. Because there were no pensions in the nineteenth century, the city had the grace and generosity to grant Owens the rank, title, pay, and even, symbolically, the powers of arrest enjoyed by her late husband. Although she served in the Chicago Police Department for thirty years, Owens never actually inherited her husband's work.

The next "real" policewoman to replace "matrons" (who began work in

1845 in New York, assisting with juveniles and jailed women) was Lola Baldwin of Portland, Oregon, in 1905. Baldwin was actually sworn in as a police officer. The first woman in the country with legitimate arrest powers, her job was to oversee the city's social workers. Later in her career she headed a program to protect the "moral safety" of young girls and women in the city.

Finally, we have Alice Stebbins Wells, who at a hair over five feet tall was hired by the 350-member LAPD in 1910. Wells never patrolled the streets of L.A.; she, too, was confined to working with women and children. But as the founder and first president of the International Association of Policewomen she would play a key role in the formation of "women's bureaus" that multiplied within American police forces from 1910 through the twenties. Thanks to her example, women did become involved in "real" police work, working mostly as detectives in vice and juvenile. During World War I, with men off fighting, large numbers of women joined police forces throughout the country. By the forties, there was good reason to believe women were on a path toward parity with their male counterparts.

Such hopes were dashed, however, by police chiefs August Vollmer (Berkeley) and O. W. Wilson (Chicago), veritable saints in this country's first wave of police reform. These guys decided that women were not "emotionally fit" to become crime fighters, much less police leaders. Lesser-known chiefs all over the country held the same opinion.

J. Edgar Hoover, despite his own penchant for nylons, heels, and tasteful navy frocks, had even less use for women in federal law enforcement. Before it became known as the Federal Bureau of Investigation, three women, Alaska P. Davidson, Jessie B. Duckstein, and Lenore Houston, served as Special Agents or Special Investigators for the "Bureau of Investigation." Shortly after he was named director of the new FBI in 1924, Hoover asked Davidson (hired in 1922) and Duckstein (1923) for their resignations, ostensibly because of budgetary reductions in the agency. When Houston resigned in 1928 she became the last woman to serve as an FBI agent for forty-four years. Hoover died in office in 1972. That year L. Patrick Gray, acting director of the FBI, citing new federal employment laws, appointed Susan Lynn Roley and Joanne E. Pierce as Special Agents. (Today, over 2,000 of the FBI's 12,500 agents are women, many of them serving as executives, overseeing field offices and occupying high ranks at headquarters.)

Employment discrimination against female officers in the fifties and sixties was sweeping, systemic, and deliberate. The American woman in policing was a subspecies within the classification structure of the civil service "merit" system. Since they were denied patrol experience, a prerequisite for promotion to supervisor, there were no women sergeants, lieutenants, captains, or chiefs. No women policymakers. The relegation of women to entry-level, women's bureau-type jobs denied them the take-home pay, and hefty pensions, of their male counterparts. And ensured that they would wield negligible political power.

+ + +

It was a pernicious form of discrimination, injected with a large dose of misogyny, that led to the labeling of the lone female officer in my academy class as a "split-tail." I didn't know what the term meant, and didn't ask, but I speculated it had something to do with a woman's vagina. One sergeant couldn't even bring himself to call Connie Borchers a gal or a girl. His every reference to her was as "the split-tail" in the Forty-ninth Academy class.

But Borchers was a woman of exceptional character, competence, and courage. She fought the system, and individual prejudice, even as she fought back tears. Borchers went on to amass a long list of "firsts" within the SDPD, including the first woman on patrol and the first to get promoted.

Connie Borchers wasn't the only target of the rampant sexism and sexual harassment of the day. The tiny cohort of outstanding women detectives had been hit on, leered at, and generally used and abused by men at various rungs of the hierarchical ladder. One friend tells me she spent as much time and energy fending off panting and pawing peers and superiors as she did working her cases. One of her colleagues had actually been raped by a high-ranking official. Others tell of strenuous physical fights to prevent the crime.

It wasn't just horny or vicious policemen of the late sixties and early seventies who objected to women on patrol. Most SDPD male officers (I'd put the figure at somewhere between 99.2 and 99.8 percent) were afraid *for* and afraid *of* women in uniform. Afraid they'd get hurt or killed wrestling a drunk. Afraid they'd get a male cop hurt or killed.

When Hoobler made his announcement, a palpable horror shot through the organization. One patrolman took to his soapbox in the coffee shop and delivered a soliloquy, paraphrased here.

Total political bullshit! What kind of a man puts the weaker sex at risk? Let's face it, girls are fragile. They're emotional, excitable, undisciplined, unstable. They can't hold their own with big, aggressive men—the pukes and assholes we fight every day. They can't run as fast or as far as we can. They can't wrench a body out of a burning car. They can't disarm a deranged suspect. They can't pull the trigger and take a life. They can't handle the hours, the cold, the heat. And what are they going to wear? It's certainly not going to be pants, I hope! Or a dress or a skirt? Come on. If they do put them in uniforms they won't fit. And, where are they going to change? They can't use the men's locker room, and that's all we got. And what about their hair? They'd have to cut it all off, basically. None of that eye stuff or lipstick or earrings either. The grooming standards don't make exceptions for girls. They won't be able to come to work once a month, most of them, and if they do show up just before "that" time of the month they'll be impossible to be around. I'm married, I know what I'm talking about. And what if they get knocked up? They won't be able to work at all. The manpower shortage will just get worse and worse, gals taking up slots that should be reserved for men. Furthermore, they're catty. Their gossip will get us in trouble, mark my words—if not with our bosses then with our wives or girlfriends, or both. How many of us can honestly say we can ride around with a chick all night, night after night, and not have "it" happen sooner or later? Even if it doesn't happen the sexual tension *will distract one or both of us—that's exactly when we'll get our lights punched out. And, what do I do with my partner when the squad goes drinking after work? Even if I'm innocent my old lady's going to* think *something's going on. I can't tell her they're all* lesbianese, *can I?*

The moron didn't mention one of the biggest reasons men bitched about women in uniform—that they would out-study and out-perform them in contests for promotions, and for plum assignments too. The women detectives of SDPD were smart, hardworking, self-confident. They'd kill the men on those civil service tests.

+ + +

Women have now been on the force for more than thirty years. How have they fared? Beautifully. The Police Foundation and the Urban Institute conducted the first major studies of women on patrol back in the mid-1970s. The Foundation's Catherine Milton examined the performance of eighty-six women against that of eighty-six men hired at the same time by the Metropolitan Police Department of the District of Columbia. Milton and her researchers studied data from supervisory ratings, the observations of trained observers (who rode around with the cops), citizen opinion surveys, and arrest statistics. Major findings:

- Women police officers "encountered the same number of dangerous, angry, upset, drunk, or violent citizens."
- Women as a group were more effective than their male peers in avoiding violence and in defusing potentially violent situations.
- Women made fewer arrests and wrote fewer traffic citations, which did not affect their performance ratings.
- Women were less likely than men to engage in "serious unbecoming conduct."
- Women were more likely to be assigned to light duty as a result of injuries, but these injuries did not cause them to be absent from work more often than men.
- Women scored the same level of "citizen satisfaction" as their male counterparts.

The Police Foundation did a follow-up study in the early eighties, and another in 1990. The results were essentially unchanged. More recent and extensive studies, including an exhaustive analysis by the National Center for Women and Policing, cast female officers in an even more positive light. They show that women cops build better relations with the community, work more collaboratively with all public safety "stakeholders," and respond more effectively to crimes against women, particularly domestic violence.

Despite overwhelming evidence that women do at least as well as men on most tasks, and better than men on some of the most critical of those tasks, the number of women in policing seems to have plateaued at around

14 percent. The legal barriers are gone (including the most insidious: height and weight minimums, which were cast aside by the courts in favor of job-related physical fitness testing). Why aren't there more women police officers?

The answer comes in two parts: (a) sufficient numbers of women simply aren't attracted to the job for a variety of reasons, which include (b) the Neanderthal attitudes of knuckle-dragging male cops and officials who persist in keeping a "NO GiЯLZ ALOWeD" sign up over the entrance to their boys' clubs.

One of the first women on the job in San Diego, a ten-year veteran but a rookie in patrol, once cleared from a call to find that someone had let the air out of her tires (the male cop who later confessed contended that women needed to be tested to see if they could change a tire—but all four tires?). Women officers have been the butt of endless jokes, sexual innuendos, and other stupid and crude remarks. Some women are ignored, their calls for backup met with silence. As recently as the eighties, LAPD had within its ranks an underground organization known as "Men Against Women." Katherine Spillar and Penny Harrington wrote in the *Los Angeles Times* (May 16, 1997) that the "male-only rogue group's purpose is to wage an orchestrated campaign of ritual harassment, intimidation and criminal activity against women officers with the ultimate objective of driving them from the force." They believe that "MAW" continues to be active, in spirit if not in name.

I figured that by the nineties, "split tails" would have been retired from the vocabulary of even the most backward male cops. Not so. Read Paula L. Woods's award-winning novel, *Inner City Blues* (1999). The term, mined from her research within LAPD, surfaces often enough during the era of the 1992 riots.

+ + +

The author Joseph Wambaugh, who left LAPD at a time when women were just starting to gain a foothold, believes that at least half a police department's sworn personnel should be women. So do I.

Look, I'm not blind to gender differences. I believe that men, *as a group*, are physically stronger than women. I believe the average male is more comfortable with violence. If the job consisted of pumping iron and sparring ten rounds a shift I'd go with men. But there's a lot more to police work than getting physical. Police work demands analytical reasoning, maturity, judgment, excellent interpersonal communication.

+ + +

For single mothers, the challenges of a police career can be staggering. Some single-mom cops (and single dads) work nights so they can be with their children during the day. That means trying to sleep while the kids are home, arranging for nighttime child care, getting someone to watch their children when they go to court, or to department-mandated training or firearms qualification shoots. Or when they find themselves working overtime on a last-minute pinch. For those working days, a more convenient schedule for most parents, the problems can be just as bad. I realize it's often hard for parents in other occupations to get out of work on time to pick up their kids at day care. But if mom (or pop) is in the middle of a homicide investigation or on the front lines of a barricaded-suspect incident she may be unable even to give caregivers a call to let them know she's going to be late. Or just *how* late.

+ + +

It's rare today for a male cop to intentionally refuse to back up a female cop; I believe we've turned that corner. But women officers continue to suffer men who "protect" them when they neither want nor need protecting. There's also the male cop who believes he can handle field situations better, who insists on providing his female colleague a tutorial in the finer points of police work.

For police work to become more attractive to women, basic changes must take place. Those chiefs who still live in the Dark Ages have got to go. Replace them with enlightened leaders, preferably women.

Make sure clear standards of equitable treatment are in place, and check often to see that those standards are being met—at every level of the organization.

Tailor recruiting campaigns to attract women candidates. Send women officers into every school in the city, starting with the elementary grades. Create opportunities for girls and young women to get acquainted with female police officers. Invite them to picture themselves as cops.

Conduct familiarization and training sessions for teens and young women. Let them know *everything* about the job. The inconveniences, the risks, the inevitable heartaches, as well as the extraordinary challenges, deep satisfactions, and the fun of being a cop.

Ensure that there are adequate restroom and locker room facilities for women officers.

Establish a child care program, replete with a department- or city-run 24/7 facility. Staff it with people who are sensitive to the schedules and other demands of police officers. Such a program could be open to others who work "odd" hours in order to help with financing. It might also be "privatized" in order to achieve similar economies. Progressive chiefs are family-friendly leaders. They understand how emotionally taxing it is for their cops, male and female, to concentrate on the demands of the job while worried about the safety and welfare of their kids.

Inoculate women recruits in the academy against the "conformity" pressures they'll surely face when they graduate. Let them know they're not alone. Help them understand, and give them skills to confront, those "traditional" officers who persist in inappropriate behavior. Make sure male recruits are included in this instruction—it helps them understand their own responsibilities. And be sure to hand all recruits a list of numbers they can call to report breaches of policy—or violations of federal law.

For the male who sits back, crosses his arms, rolls his eyes, and suggests that women should make the coffee or sweep out the command van? Bring out the two-by-four. If that doesn't work, show him the door. For the cop who thinks it's funny to call women "split tails"? Forget the two-by-four.

CHAPTER 11

SEXUAL PREDATORS
IN UNIFORM

SGT. HARRY PAUL HEATHERINGTON, SDPD's background investigator, settled into the one chair in our tiny living room. Dottie and I sat on the couch and listened to his lecture on the "Three Bs": booze, bills, and broads. A few drinks was all right, kind of expected, but get shitfaced and embarrass the chief? You're toast. And if the department received even a single letter from a creditor? "Well, you can kiss your shiny new badge goodbye," said Heatherington. Okay, okay. But what about the broads?

He waited until my nineteen-year-old wife went off to the kitchen for coffee refills and slabs of chocolate cake. Then he leaned forward, put his face up to mine, and said, "You a cockhound, Stamper?"

"A . . . a . . . what?"

"A cockhound. Do I have to spell it out for you?"

I'm afraid he did. I'd just embarked on the most exciting career imaginable, my thoughts riveted on helping people, busting bad guys, preventing mayhem. What did my *sexual* habits have to do with anything? It was beyond my comprehension that a policeman would even *think* about screwing himself out of a job.

My naïveté didn't last long.

In my first year I rode with a cop who spent half the shift trying to pick up nurses in the ER, carhops at Oscar's, or women who'd called the police to report a prowler. One summer night I drove into an elementary school parking lot and interrupted a veteran cop having his knob polished in the front seat of his police car. Over the years I would see it all: cops fingering and fondling prisoners, making bogus traffic stops of attractive women, trading freedom for a blow job with a hooker, making "love" with a fourteen-year-old police explorer scout, sodomizing children in a spouse's day care center.

And this: In 1986, on-duty California Highway Patrol officer Craig Peyer strangled a San Diego State University student named Cara Knott and threw her body off a seventy-foot bridge. Motive? She'd resisted his sexual advances.

Across the country cops continue to use their uniforms and their authority to pester and pounce on women. East Palo Alto cop Shawn Wildman lived up to his name when he fondled a domestic violence victim, then ordered her to expose herself; later, he stalked and harassed her. He was fired for that, and for groping a carload of young women. Frank Wright, a Suffolk County, New York, police officer gave female drunk-driving suspects on Long Island a choice: they could strip for him or go to jail. He pled guilty to two felony and two misdemeanor charges in federal court. A Texas cop, thirty-two-year-old Craig Ochoa, lost his job after he was found to have had sex with two teenage girls. Michael Benes was arrested for assault, aggravated rape, and aggravated sexual assault when he attacked a Nashville woman who'd called to report a vicious dog (he shot the dog). David Brame, Tacoma's police chief, had raped a woman he dated in 1988, using his service weapon to intimidate her (see chapter 1). Another Tacoma cop, thirty-nine-year-old Michael Torres, was recently charged with four counts of sexual assault on a minor—having won a staring contest with her, he claimed his spoils: oral sex from a seven-year-old.

Just how many cops are child molesters, sexual predators? Samuel Walker and Dawn Irlbeck, in their 2002 report "Driving While Female: A National Problem in Police Misconduct," present research they conducted by examining news media reports from 1990 to 2001. They found *hundreds* of such cases, but describe their estimates as "conservative." Why? Because (1) they examined only substantiated cases that had resulted in criminal sanctions; (2) many victims of this form of police abuse are reluctant to come forward, citing humiliation and/or fear of reprisals; and (3) too many police departments do a lousy job of accepting and investigating citizen complaints (this is especially true in those organizations whose bosses believe they "know" their cops: "That doesn't sound like Jim. Why he'd never do a thing like that . . .").

Every time a new case breaks, police chiefs and unions contend that the "overwhelming majority" of their officers would never abuse the badge in this fashion, a truism I'm delighted to confirm. But sexual predation by police officers happens far more often than people in the business are willing to admit. Governor Ed Rendell of Pennsylvania recently ordered an investigation into 163 incidents of sexual misconduct within the state police, dating back to 1995. Fourteen troopers have been fired (though four, thus far, have been rehired, the result of appeals to a labor arbiter).

My cautious guess is that about 5 percent of America's cops are on the prowl for women. In a department the size of Seattle's that's sixty-three police officers. In San Diego, 145. In New York City, 2,000. The average patrol cop makes anywhere from ten to twenty unsupervised contacts a shift. If he's on the make, chances are a predatory cop will find you. Or your wife, your partner, your daughter, your sister, your mother, your friend.

During my tenure as a police administrator, sustained allegations of sexual misconduct (a guilty finding) outnumbered proven allegations of racial discrimination on an order of fifty to one (only partly attributable to the unwillingness of police agencies to acknowledge their racists). "Racial profiling" is a ghastly problem in American policing, but sexual "mischief" is its nasty little secret.

Sexual predators in uniform are predominantly male, and over-whelmingly straight. Of the scores of disciplinary and criminal cases I saw in San Diego and in Seattle only two, one in each city, involved women or gay officers.*

+ + +

Heaven knows, there *are* temptations in police work, and I'd be lying if I say I hadn't been tempted. While still in the academy I stopped a fire-engine red TR-3 early one evening. It contained a luscious brunette whose lipstick and manicured nails matched her low-slung ride. I took her license, told her I was going to cite her for speeding.

* David Kalish, an openly gay, highly respected assistant chief of LAPD was recently relieved of duty for allegedly molesting six youngsters in that department's police explorer program back in the seventies. *Damn him!* Until the charges came to light I could honestly say I'd never heard of a gay cop molesting kids.

"Oh, officer," she purred. "Do you have to?"

"Yes, ma'am. I have to."

"Are you *sure*?" She parted her lips, licked them, batted her big brown eyes. "Can't we settle this out of court?"

I pursed my thin lips and shook my head. But she wasn't about to give up just because I wouldn't give in. She parted her legs and hiked her skirt to reveal panties in the familiar color, and she kept hiking . . . all the way up. I gawked, but took out my Bic and started writing. Over my ticket book I could see her long, tan fingers working the buttons of her silk blouse. I couldn't find the words to stop her—not that I would have necessarily used them. But when I handed her the ticket she clamped her legs shut and called me an asshole.

Author Ron Heifetz has an excellent suggestion for those of us whose power or position leads us to conclude we're irresistible to women we meet on the job: take a full-length photo of ourselves, blow it up, affix it to the inside of our office (or locker) door and take time to gaze upon it daily just to confirm how ugly we really are. Sgt. Heatherington was onto the same thing, "You're going to think you're Joe Cool out there, Stamper. You're actually going to believe the broads think you're hot shit. Well, let me tell you something, kid: *It's the uniform.*"

Every PD in the country has a Heatherington, not to mention a chief or a commissioner, who admonishes young cops in the academy about carnal temptations, who lays down the law on "inappropriate" behavior. Yet we still see the cases, ranging from unwanted sexual advances in the workplace to hardcore crimes of force and violence, sex with minors, stalking, and rape.

Why would a cop risk his career, reputation, and freedom by being a "cockhound"? For the same reason men everywhere, especially those wedded to their own sense of entitlement, force themselves on women. In police work, you can add the inescapable on-the-job enticements like "cop groupies," the not uncommon presence of misogyny within the male-dominated culture, and even the fear of getting caught which, as with other sex offenders, can quicken the pulse.

+ + +

You see these same conditions in other lines of work and play, celebrities from all walks of life using their positions to try to score with or force themselves upon women.

Some U.S. servicemen in Iraq, Kuwait, Afghanistan, sexually assault and rape servicewomen (in just a year and a half the Army recorded eighty-six incidents, the Navy twelve, the Air Force eight, and the Marine Corps six). And let's not forget studio bosses, other corporate and public CEOs, educators, athletes, shop foremen, priests. And elected officials who use the prestige of the highest offices in the land to woo a woman to her knees.

+ + +

What steps can a community take to protect itself from predatory cops? *Pay attention to your local PD*, for starters. Whom does it hire? Does it insist on rigorous background investigations and psychological screening of all candidates? Is every member of the agency made to understand, explicitly, that sexual misconduct will lead to disciplinary action, including the probability of dismissal and the possibility of criminal prosecution? *Are* cops fired when they're uncovered as sexual predators?

Citizens should ask whether an "inspection and control" or "professional responsibility" unit regularly and randomly monitors police behavior. Such units check for trends and patterns within the workforce, and in the conduct of *particular* officers. Say a certain traffic cop habitually stops nine female drivers to every male he pulls over, or hands out more citations (or, more telling, a greater number of nonpunitive warnings) to women than to men. Shouldn't we know a little more about this guy?

Sting operations make sense. A department that has cause to believe a cop is on the make should set him up. Arrange for him to cross paths with a woman dressed in tight skirt and fishnet stockings (or as Laura Bush, if that's what turns him on). Toss the bait, see if he bites. I once arrested a woman who was drunk out of her mind. Or was she? I put her in the back-seat of my police car but before I could shut the door she turned toward me, spread her legs and said (I'm not making this up), "Fuck me, fuck me now, fuck me hard." Had I succumbed—and had she been an Internal Affairs plant—I would have been cleaning out my locker that night.

Unfair? No. Effective supervision of cops demands a balance between trust and control. When it comes to the integrity of the force and public confidence in the local PD you've got to tip those scales toward control. My fellow chiefs and I did stings all the time when we suspected a cop was into dope, or stealing from local merchants. In terms of the sheer number of sexual offenders in blue, there's far greater justification for "sex stings."

It's also important, as it was during the aftermath of the Rodney King beating, to make sure that cops understand this: If they witness, or are aware of, sexual misconduct by another officer, including superiors, and they fail to blow the whistle they, too, will take the fall.

It's not enough for the PD to get tough on sexual misconduct. Local prosecutors have to be willing to file charges against cops who engage in criminal sexual conduct. Because they work with the police day in and day out, because they're afraid of the political fallout, and because they can't tolerate the migraines caused by vengeful police unions, some DAs look the other way in police crimes. More accurately, they look back to the PD for internal disciplinary action—leaving this ex-chief wondering if they'd do the same if the sexual predator were a shoe salesman or a construction worker.

The Los Angeles Police Department over a five-year period sent 350 cases (for all alleged crimes, including sexual offenses) involving five hundred police officer suspects to then-DA Gil Garcetti. How many did Garcetti prosecute? *Twenty-seven!* The guilt of many of those he declined to charge was overwhelming—some had been caught on tape, many had confessed. Prosecutor spinelessness has a chilling effect on the willingness of victims, and fellow police officers, to confront sexual abuse (or other criminal offenses) within the ranks.

Another step? Hire more women. Studies have shown that the feminization of police ranks over the past two decades has had many positive effects: fewer instances of brutality, fewer citizen complaints, improved problem-solving effectiveness, better relations with the community. One generally unexpressed benefit? A predatory male cop is at least somewhat less likely to try out his moves if his partner or backup is a female. (Unless, of course, he's got his sights on *her*.)

+ + +

Police emergency lights are meant to convey a strong message to citizens: *Stop and comply.* Twenty-year-old Cara Knott pulled over on that cold December night when CHP officer Peyer lit up her white '68 Beetle. But when she refused to "comply" she paid for it with her life. That a cop went to prison for murder is of small comfort to legions of women who've been hit on by lawmen. Women should not experience more than the normal apprehension when those blue and red lights flash in their rearview mirror.

CHAPTER 12

THE BLUE WALL
OF SILENCE

COPS LIE. MOST OF them lie a couple of times per shift, at least. In some cases lies are not only permissible but beneficial, perhaps even life-saving. Informing a murder suspect that his accomplice, who's actually been silent as a clam, has copped to the crime may offend a defense attorney but it's lawful, and sometimes effective. Lying to a stalker could save his victim. "Freeze or I'll shoot!" could very well be a lie but if it stops a fleeing suspect in his tracks then let's hear it for mendacity.

But there's another form of untruthfulness that has no place in police business: lying on a report, lying to an IA investigator, lying on the stand. As any defense attorney (or candid supervisor or chief) will attest, a good deal of "bad lying" goes on in police work, by cops who don't seem to know the meaning of *the truth, the whole truth, and nothing but the truth.*

Some police officers bring a lifelong tradition of bad lying to the job, but most seem to pick up the habit in the workplace. I remember vividly my first instruction in the fine art of bad lying.

+ + +

"Andy Taggart" was one of the first cops I worked with. I was still in the academy, and quite impressionable. Taggart was like a BB in a beer can, bouncing off the walls, darting in and out of alleys, stopping everything that moved on his beat—and on fellow officers' beats.

On our first night together Taggart cut his lights and started coasting down a long hill in a residential neighborhood two beats over from ours. The car picked up speed, going faster, faster. I puckered up. What the hell was he up to? How the hell could he see to drive? At the bottom of the hill he drove up over the curb and onto the front lawn of an old frame house. "Come on!" he said in an urgent whisper. "Come on!" I bailed out of the car and trailed him up to the front porch where he kicked in the door. I kept following him, past a family watching TV and down a hall to a back bedroom where he jerked open a closet door and pulled a man out of hiding. Taggert put the cuffs on the twenty-year-old murder suspect. We walked him past protesting family members out to our car. It was surrounded by six of San Diego's finest.

Taggart's colleagues had been sitting on the residence, whispering tactics over the radio, getting ready to take the house when this phantom car went zipping by their Code-5 locations. Taggart had bested them, like it was a sport. They were furious. "Fuck you," he told them, not bothering to stop and chat. "I didn't even know you guys were in the neighborhood." They knew better. He knew better. I knew better.

+ + +

Taggart worked The Heights, a predominantly black community in Southeast San Diego. But every shift, unless we caught a call right out of the barn, he would drive around the streets of downtown before heading east to his own beat. "The idea," he said, " is to get your numbers out of the way, right off. Keep the sergeant off your back. Then when you get out to your beat you can do some *real* police work." He was talking about the "numbers game," SDPD's quota system. Five shakedowns,* two "moving" citations (parking tickets didn't count), and one criminal arrest per shift: it was expected. "Working downtown," continued Taggart, "if you can't nail

---

* A "shakedown" (or a "shake," as it's referred to in Seattle) wasn't about cops extorting or blackmailing business owners. It was a "field interrogation," a "stop-and-frisk" contact. Its aim, sanctioned in the landmark *Terry* v. *Ohio* case (1968), was to establish the identity and the "occasion of purpose" of individuals in suspicious circumstances—short of probable cause for arrest. Taggart's definition of "suspicious circumstances" extended to anyone he wanted to talk to for any reason. "Shakedowns" were the primary source of community complaints against cops, especially among youth and people of color. Most cops had developed a stock answer, sarcastic and deceitful, to the question, "Why'd you stop me?"

a gaggle of swabbies from Bumfuck, Iowa, you shouldn't be a cop, you should be selling Kirbys door-to-door. With swabbies, you stop 'em, write 'em up, shake 'em down, maybe even haul one or two off to Shore Patrol. Presto! You got most of your numbers for the whole night."

To prove his point, he poached four sailors walking against the Wait sign at Fourth and Broadway. Taggart was a "hot pen" which meant that he could write out the four "coupons" in the time it would take me to complete one. Ten minutes later we were back in the car, the backseat crammed with four underage sailors, each with booze on his breath and a mover in his pocket. Four double-headers (four traffic citations, four arrests—you couldn't carry them as shakedowns if you pinched them), almost a full night's work for most cops. If you were lazy and ethically challenged you could complete the picture with a trip through Mt. Hope Cemetery, picking off names from gravestones and carrying them as shakedowns. Some used the phone book, a lot more convenient but it carried a risk since most people in it were still alive. In my first two years on the job there'd been major internal investigations into "daily padding." Two cops got fired for it.

Taggart's arrests that night were all the more efficient because all you had to do with hapless military personnel was deposit them at Shore Patrol headquarters and waltz out. No arrest reports required. No probable cause to justify.

The night after we'd pinched the homicide suspect, Taggart let me drive. "Aren't you forgetting something?" he said as I made my way out Market toward his beat.

"Sir?"

"I said, 'Aren't you forgetting something?' "

"What's that, sir?"

"Hey. Do me a favor, will you?"

"Yes, sir?"

"Stop calling me 'sir.' I'm not a ranking officer, okay? My parents were married."

I was sure it was a joke, but I didn't get it. "Yes, sir. I mean . . . okay."

"Now, let's get back to business. Do I have to spell it out for you? Turn around . . . go back . . . turn up Fifth. Will you?"

"Yes, si . . . right. Right." I dropped down to Island and worked my way back to Fifth Avenue where I began scanning the sidewalks for sailors from Bumfuck. Or an unlucky tourist, or a transvestite, or a . . .

"Aren't you going to answer that?"

"Wha . . . what?" How could I look for numbers, drive a police car, without wrecking it, and listen to the radio at the same time? It was an all-units. Shore Patrol chasing a suspect, on foot. Last seen in the vicinity of Sixth and G. We were now at Fifth and G, but I didn't know that. That's another thing: A cop is *always* supposed to know *exactly* where he is. Which would be fine if you were *walking* a beat, but . . .

"Are you planning to fucking *do* something about that?"

"Wha . . ."

"That!" He jabbed a thumb out his window. A hundred fifty feet away a shore patrolman was chasing a white male. "Get 'em! Get 'em! Get 'em!" screamed Taggart. I put my on turn signal, checked behind me, and prepared to make my turn. "What the *hell* are you doing! Get the bastard! Now!" He took out his baton. I thought he was going to hit me. Instead he rained down blows on the metal dash, screeching as he did, "Get 'em! Get 'em! Get 'em!" The inside of the car sounded like a brick tumbling in a dryer. I punched it, noticing out of the corner of my eye that Taggart had dented the dogshit out of the dash. What fib could possibly explain that? I swept east on G then south on Sixth, driving the wrong way on the one-way street. And cutting across three lanes of oncoming traffic. I made for the curb where the shore patrolman and his prey, a kid sailor in dungarees, white T-shirt with smokes rolled up in the sleeve, and a bottle of rotgut whisky in one hand, stood panting and heaving, staring at us.

At about 15 mph, Taggart attempted to "exit the vehicle," as we say in police work. He got tangled up in the seatbelt and fell to the pavement, his butt bouncing off the asphalt. Once, twice, three times. Like a cowboy thrown from a horse, his foot caught in the stirrup. I tried to stop, but not too suddenly—I didn't want to run him over. The whole time I'm thinking, *Oh shit. I've killed my senior officer. How am I going to explain this at critique tonight?*

I finally brought the car to a stop. My senior officer leaped from the pavement and sprinted to the sidewalk. The two men were standing side by side now, watching the show, still gasping for breath. Taggart went right for the kid's neck. He throttled him, pulled him up on his back, and shouted at me to get my cuffs out. The kid, his oxygen all but depleted, went out in a flash. I bent over and hooked him up. Taggart's pants were ripped to shreds, his black shoe laid open from heel to toe, his legs and hindquarters bearing the makings of some awesome strawberries and bruises to come. He looked into my eyes as he bent down to pull the groggy sailor to his feet. "You saw him start to hit me with that bottle, didn't you? Didn't you?"

+ + +

That was the first time I'd been asked to lie, but it was far from the last. Senior officers and peers were always making sure we "got our stories straight." *No, I didn't see Smith hit the guy, Sarge . . . No, Lieutenant, that dent in the fender was already there . . . I didn't hear Jones say a word to the complainant . . . Well, yeah, Martin choked him out, but the guy kicked him in the balls first . . . Yes, your honor, we saw the gun before we searched him . . .*

I don't remember actually lying on the stand. But I do remember composing some "creative" arrest reports. Every drunk I ever arrested, for example, whether hammered or sober, walked with a staggered gait, viewed the world through bloodshot eyes, and had about his breath and person an odor characteristic of an alcoholic beverage.

If I'd not undergone a near-religious conversion at the end of my rookie year, the result of that ethical prosecutor shocking me into a new habit of honesty, there's no telling how many of these bad lies I would have told. Before getting fired.

+ + +

From 1969 to 2000 I was a police supervisor, manager, or executive. In all that time I fired or influenced the firing of hundreds of cops for incompetence, major policy violations, or crimes. I'm guessing anywhere from 10 to 20 percent of the policy violators would have survived—if only they'd told the truth. To this day, I'm amazed at the numbers of police officers who, caught in an infraction, lie, and *cling* to their lies, until they get sacked—for dishonesty, not for backing their police car into a light pole.

Many chiefs, burned by bad-lying cops, have told their force: Tell a lie and you're history. This "zero tolerance" policy is intended to drive home the moral imperative of honesty in one's professional communication. It's a worthy goal, but zero tolerance often backfires, serving, paradoxically, to *institutionalize* deceit and dishonesty.

Most cops, especially rookies, are in love with the job. They can't imagine doing any other kind of work. It becomes their identity: what they live for, who they are. And because most police agencies embrace a chickenshit disciplinary process, their cops live in constant fear of being reprimanded, suspended, or *fired*, even for an honest mistake. It's important to understand that the first impulse of a lot of otherwise good and decent cops is to *lie* when called on the carpet.

As a captain, I once questioned one of my officers about his having witnessed an act of excessive force. The moment he answered I knew he was covering for a fellow cop. "I have a problem with your answer, John."

"What do you mean, Captain."

"I mean I don't think you're being truthful here."

"But I *am*. I'm *telling* the truth." I felt like his father, or his junior high school vice principal. And I'm sure he felt like a kid. But the truth was non-negotiable.

"Just so we're clear: If you're lying to me I'm going to see to it that you're fired."

"But, Cap . . ."

"Here's what I want you to do, John. Go home, now. Think about your answers. Come back tomorrow, same time. I'm going to ask the same question."

"But . . ."

"Leave. I'll see you tomorrow."

He came in to my office the next day. And told the truth. I ended up reprimanding him for failing to intervene in the excessive force incident (which, truth be told, was not an egregious case), and not being forthcoming initially. But he kept his job. And learned an important lesson.

+ + +

Peer pressure in every line of work is intense. In police work it can be all-consuming. You *have* to rely on your fellow officers to back you. A cop with a reputation as a snitch is one vulnerable police officer, likely to find his or her peers slow to respond to requests for backup—if they show up at all. A snitch is subject to social snubbing. Or malicious mischief, or sabotage (typically directed at his or her locker or his or her automobile). This peer pressure is childish and churlish, but it's real. Few cops can stand up to it.

That's why the second shot at truth-telling ("Is that your final answer?") makes sense. And zero tolerance does not. The exception to this second-chance rule? When an officer lies on a report or raises his or her right hand, swears to tell the truth, and then lies. When that happens its too late for a second chance. Dismissal from the force is the only option.

CHAPTER 13

THE POLICE IMAGE: SOMETIMES A GUN IS JUST A GUN

SOME BELIEVE MY ENDORSEMENT of social justice and my calls for police reform reflect a "soft" approach to law enforcement. They're wrong. In fact, if there's one thing I can't stand it's police agencies that act like PR agencies.

Yours might be such a department, its chief and the rest of the brass saturated in the ethic and the vocabulary of public relations. The impulse is understandable: These departments are attempting to sell a service most folks aren't interested in buying—such as a traffic ticket or a night in jail. Of course, the better agencies are also peddling prevention, community policing, the inclusion of citizens in advisory and review capacities, and other positive programs. Which is why chiefs (and other politicians) strive to "package" and "position" the local PD as a modern, "transparent," "user-friendly," "customer-driven" "partnership-based" institution.

But what good is a well-behaved, community-oriented police department if it can't catch a stickup man or stop a burglary series?

+ + +

Reacting to subtle symptoms of strains in community relations—such as police beatings, racial insurrections, and snipers firing at cruising cop cars—chiefs in the 1960s searched for ways to "soften" the police image. Many traditions needed to go, obviously. But some of those guys tinkered and tampered with *useful* traditions. They banned "harsh" cop lingo in favor of more neutral or even stately terms, and tried their best to make their cops look like anything but cops.

My predecessor in Seattle refused to call Intelligence "Intelligence" so he named it the "Criminal Information Section"—which made it sound like the place you go to get a report of your kid's stolen bike. The Gang Detail he labeled, I don't know, "Mischievous Youth" or something like that.

In San Diego in the early seventies Chief Ray Hoobler ordered politically correct name changes throughout the department. "Vice" sounded too hard-edged, so he changed it to the "Public Inspection Unit." He or his predecessor also had our cars painted, from black-and-whites to all-whites: we motored about in a fleet of ghostly cop car facsimiles, replete with a slogan of our suddenly enlightened chief's own choosing: *Your Safety / Our Business.**

At the same time, Hoobler rejected the plea of many, myself included, to change the color of our uniforms. We wore tan (SDPD blues having been abandoned in the late forties in a PR effort of *that* era to change the image of officers). Nor would Hoobler or his predecessors let us have K-9s, or shotguns, or semiautomatic pistols. Or patches on our sleeves, like every other police department in the country, to identify the city we served.

So there we were, generic beige cops looking like security guards for Sea World, and not a whole lot better equipped. It was all cosmetics, but, from where I stood, it marked the beginning of the end of *real* police work.

A confession: In my holy war to clean up policing, to eradicate all those embedded *isms* and put a halt to brutality and corruption, I lost sight for a time of why we were in business in the first place. In the early seventies it was more important that we "make nice" with our citizens than protect them. Defendants' rights took precedence over the pain and suffering of crime victims, even though the two goals were of equal importance. My biggest sin? I thought it would be cool to put our cops in blazers. *Blazers!* I wasn't a cop, I was more like a Fuller Brush salesman.

My drift into nonpolice police work didn't last long. It ended when I became an academy instructor, shortly after being promoted to sergeant. I'd been tapped to teach a class called "Patrol and Observation." Taught previously by Sgt. A. D. "Brownie" Brown, a bigger-than-life heroic cop figure,

---

* To show his sensitivity to the Hispanic community, Hoobler had the slogan translated into *español*. The only problem being that *Su Seguridad / Nuestro Negocio*, which he had affixed to all the cars, means, according to my Latino friends, something like, "We'll give you safety if you give us money."

it was your basic how-to course. It covered everything from the patrol mission to the inspection of your car before each shift to stop-and-frisk, ticket writing, arrests, and crime scene protection.

I spent months preparing for my first class. I read three or four police texts and a fistful of journals from the community college library. I researched press accounts of major police incidents from throughout the country, and interviewed some of the best cops in the department, including Brownie. I went to the lab and checked out an ancient 5x5 box camera. For the next couple of weeks, several of my cops and I posed shots of arrests, field interrogations, traffic stops. I also snapped photos of actual accidents and real crime scenes. Then I rewrote the Patrol and Observation chapter, sprinkling it with full-page captioned photos. Finally, I fashioned a brand-new lesson plan—with penciled cues, inspired by Brownie's suspenseful, hilarious presentations: *pause for effect . . . raise eyebrows . . . wait for laughter to subside . . .*

My voice broke as I introduced myself to the first class. I'd rehearsed an elegant opening but now couldn't remember a word of it. I stood there in flared Robert Hall polyester slacks, zip-up boots, print shirt, maroon knit tie, and tan corduroy sports coat with leather elbow patches. I'd intended to deliver a sermon on "social justice vis-à-vis the role of the police" as an introduction. When finally the words came tumbling forth they made little sense. Stage fright accounted for some of it. But mostly I'd walked into the classroom with an ill-conceived plan. I'd been a fool.

I went home to my apartment, poured myself a fool's portion of sour mash sippin' whiskey, and proceeded to get pickled. It was in the middle of the pickle that it occurred to me: The class I was teaching wasn't about *me*. Or how things *looked*, the "PR" of the presentation. It was about a roomful of anxious recruits, who, while they might appreciate a little entertainment, hungered most for *information*. They wanted, as I had when I was a recruit, a veteran's practical wisdom on how to catch crooks, solve problems, perform myriad other patrol tasks, and get home alive.

The next time I willed myself to reach out to the recruits with that in mind; to put myself in their spit-shined shoes. I brought entertainment, humor, a little pathos, but I stayed "on message." What a difference it made—in their education, and in mine. It was one of the most unselfish moments of my career, and it imbued in me a passion and a sense of duty to teach real-world cops real-world lessons.

It was at that time that I came to include in my definition of civil liberties the right of Americans to live free of crime, and of the fear of crime. I'd always taken it personally when a woman was beaten in her living room or raped in an alley or on a date. Or a child was thrown into a scalding tub. Or a home was burglarized, a car stolen, a school vandalized. My passion was to infect my students with a passion for social justice *and* effective crime-fighting, to mold them into the kind of cops who treated people decently but who also knew how to catch the bad guy.

+ + +

Really crafty bad guys are a bitch to catch. Every once in a while one of them is nabbed "accidentally" (think of Eric Rudolph, the bomber of the Atlanta Olympics, abortion clinics, and gay nightclubs, who eluded a massive FBI manhunt only to be pinched by a rookie patrol officer; or Timothy McVeigh, who fell on a routine traffic stop). But the really smart bad guys, from embezzlers to serial killers, often elude capture for years if not a lifetime. I blame this mostly on "PR PDs."

(And let's not overlook the feds: agents of the FBI, ATF, DEA, CIA, etc., and especially their brass, whose crime-fighting timidity is based on "PR" pressures borne of a new "professional class" of bureau leader—and of congressional oversight and strictures gone haywire. So haywire that we were caught sleeping on the morning of September 11, 2001.)

Even today, I make a point of observing the way modern police officers police their beats. It drives me bonkers. I watch them "patrol" at five miles over the speed limit, scanning neither left nor right, employing only a fraction of their peripheral vision, seeing nothing but the next latte stand, or traffic ticket. It's a conceit of mine that back in the seventies, coached by some of the best (Winston Yetta, Jack Mullen, Paul Ybarrondo, Ken O'Brien, and others), I taught at least one generation of cops *how* to police their beats—how to increase their chances of catching the bad guy. For evidence of deteriorating effectiveness in detecting and apprehending criminals, I invite you to compare your jurisdiction's burglary or auto theft or homicide clearance rates today against what they were thirty years ago. Unless they're clearing crimes with an eraser, they're probably off by 20 to 40 percent.

+ + +

In the classroom, we started with the act of *observation*—how to take in the physical world around you. To *train* yourself to focus your vision three to four blocks down the road; hone your peripheral eyesight; and to be alert for cues and clues that help distinguish suspicious from innocent activity, and safe situations from unsafe. We talked about the psychological "expectancies"—motivational, perceptual—that can cause a cop to see something that's *not* there.

We talked about driving with your windows down, no matter how cold it gets: If you're *patrolling and observing* you've got to employ all your senses. I once interrupted a stranger-on-stranger rape because I'd heard the muffled scream of a woman in the backseat of a parked car on a cold night in the 4100 block of Thirty-eighth Street. I wouldn't have heard it had the window been up, the heater pumping hot air in my face, an AM transistor radio blaring Led Zeppelin or the ball game. Or if I'd not been hypervigilant, *listening* as well as looking and smelling for evidence of crime. My partner, a recruit, hadn't heard a thing. He learned something that night.

I told my students the story of an L.A. area residential burglar who was good for over a thousand jobs (that's a lot of "B&Es," as they like to call them on the East Coast). I required my students to study everything about the pro's modus operandi, how he'd been able to outsmart and hoodwink dozens of cops for years. The crook's success came from his own disciplined course of study: the habits of Los Angeles police officers.

He was there, the whole time, right under their noses, hanging out near neighborhood station houses, diving their Dumpsters, picking up their "hot sheets" (stolen cars, wanted persons, etc.), and studying their shift-change times and habits. He was also, of course, an adept on-scene burglar. Among his other "policies": he wore a pair of shoes only once, buying them at thrift stores and purposely tramping around outside in the mud and leaving impressions everywhere he went. He'd burn the shoes after each job. Once inside a house, he'd trigger the thermostat (up or down), then use the resultant crackling noise to cover any sounds he'd make. He made friends with neighborhood dogs by tossing them raw hamburger.

Rarely did anyone call the cops—until the next day. But if someone did, he'd know it. He listened for and counted accelerations and decelerations of responding police units: Alternators on the police cars whined characteristically, and it wasn't uncommon for our burglar to detect steel-on-asphalt crunches as racing police vehicles bottomed out at intersections en route to the crime scene. If a cruiser got too close he'd cut through backyards (he understood that cops didn't particularly like running or going over jagged-top fences or facing Dobermans or pit bulls). Or, if the police were right on his tail, he'd shimmy up a tree or dive under a car knowing that cops tended to look straight ahead, not up, not down. Those poor police officers in L.A. didn't know any better; they hadn't been trained properly.

My cops would be *trained*. They'd act and look like cops—but they would know how to think like a crook.

+ + +

I believe citizens want their police officers to look like police officers. When they call to report a crime or a medical emergency they want a blue-uniformed cop to come running. They want to see him or her step out of a muscular black and white automobile. This traditional image is authoritative; it announces that professionals are on the scene, bringing aid and order desperately needed at a three-car fatality or a school shooting.

I don't like powder blue or baby-blue police cars. I don't like tan uniforms. I don't like police dogs named "Cuddles" or "Muffin." I like shotguns and sniper rifles and semiautomatic sidearms and ammunition (a cut above what the bad guys are packing). These things help police officers get the job done, safely, for you. The symbols foster a desirable image of authority, even respect. When that breaks down, or when a police officer violates your rights or otherwise mistreats you it is *not* because he or she is wearing a blue uniform and driving a black-and-white. Sometimes a gun is just a gun.

CHAPTER 14

IT'S NOT ALL COPS AND ROBBERS

THERE WERE HALF A million police officers in the country when I pushed a beat car. I'd be willing to bet your salary that not one of them ever had a chance to do what I did. In fact, I'd almost be willing to bet my own pension that it's never been done by any other police officer in history.

It all began with the radio operator's bored, professional voice. "Units 30 and 35-East, 11-40 OB." She sent us to a house in the 3800 block of Menlo in East San Diego. Unit 30 was the east end ambulance, 11-40 was notification that an ambulance was possibly needed, OB meant a woman was having a baby, and 35-East was me. Thirty was on the air immediately. "Unit thirty. I'm not ready to clear College Park yet. My gurney's still . . . messed up." He'd just delivered one of the victims of a ghastly accident down on I-8. "Better send forty-three," he said. Forty-three, however, was at that moment on the way to Hillside Hospital with a knifing victim. Radio wound up sending Unit 2 all the way from Balboa Park.

I acknowledged the call from Central and University, and arrived in less than two minutes. "Oh, thank God you're here, officer," said a woman who'd run out to the curb to greet me. The mother of the pregnant woman, she spoke with a heavy Italian accent. The mama-to-be was Gina. She was lying on the sofa, her legs spread but covered with a blanket. "Italiano?" I asked, mindless of the importance of gender to her language. She was wet with sweat and her face was contorted but she replied with a smile. "*Sí, sí.*" Another woman, an aunt, hovered nearby.

I didn't know what to do. We'd had a lesson on 11-40 OB calls but I figured the ambulance drivers—regular cops in black-and-white Ford station wagons outfitted with a first aid kit, a bottle of oxygen, and a flat gurney that didn't accordion up and down—would handle this kind of call ("11-41" meant an ambulance *is* needed). Gina let out a scream. The contractions were fixed and fast. I dashed out to the car, put out the 11-41, and zipped back inside where I shouted at the relatives to boil some water and get some sheets. Why? I have no idea. If I knew what to do I wouldn't have resorted to B-movie theatrics.

I nodded to Gina, telegraphing my intention to lift the blanket. A tiny head was pushing itself out of her. I say tiny, but it looked *massive*. I ran to the kitchen, washed my hands with Palmolive dish soap and near-scalding water, and dashed back into the living room, my hands held aloft like Dr. Kildare. I sat down between Gina's legs. She let out another scream and, just like that, delivered the precious cargo into my hands. I can't describe the feeling.

Gina, her two family members, and the newborn all wept. A bit teary myself, I wrapped the baby girl in a clean towel and put her on mama's chest. Then I began to fret.

What if I have to cut the umbilical cord? How far from the baby? How long are you supposed to wait? Suddenly I envisioned the apparition of Sgt. John Kennedy, standing before us in the classroom, announcing in his laconic Oklahoma twang, "Don't go getting any ideas about tying it off with your shoelaces and biting through it. No matter where you are in this city, you're close enough to an ER to get her there without having to cut the cord." Just then Unit 2 pulled up.

One week later, to the day, as I was driving by Gina's house, reminiscing, I got my next 11-40 OB call. I'd considered it a once-in-a-lifetime triumph to have experienced what less than a fraction of one percent of all cops will ever get to do. But *twice*? *A week* and *a block* apart, at the *same time of day*?

There was no greeting committee this time, only the now-familiar scream. I hustled up the walkway, surprised to hear a television blaring from the living room. Stretched out on the couch was a young man, barefoot and shirtless. The woman's screams could be heard halfway up the block. I knocked on the door. The guy looked up, annoyed. "Come on in," he said when he realized it was a cop.

"You call the police?"

"Nah, my old lady did."

"Where is she?"

"I don't know. Bedroom. Bathroom." He was maybe twenty-five. Tall, pasty white, prison-cut. I couldn't tell if he was drunk or high as he lay there, lids half closed, staring at the television.

"I'm going back there to check her out, okay?" It sounded like but wasn't a question. There'd be no winner if the two of us got into a fight. The woman let out another scream. "She pregnant?"

"Yeah. That's the problem." I wanted to hit him. Hard.

She was on her back on the bathroom floor. One hand was locked around the drainpipe under the sink. Her purple tie-dye maternity smock, homemade, was pulled up over her distended belly and her legs were in the customary position. "Oh, thank God!" she said when she saw me. God was getting thanked a lot that week.

"What do you think?" I said, bending down to her. "Are you ready?"

"Past ready," she said. "Jesusfuckingchrist, I'm *past* ready already!" I took the cigarette from her mouth, snubbed it out with the others in a saucer on the back of the toilet. A can of beer sat off to the side. I gave her a pat on the arm.

"I'll be right back." I ran through the house and out to the car—there were no walkie-talkies in those days—and got on the air. "Unit 35-East, have 30 expedite." That was code among street cops for *fuck-policy-put-your-freaking-lights-and-siren-on-and-get-your-ass-here. Now!* I rushed back inside, stopping in front of the jerk. "That your baby?"

"She says it is, but . . ." He mumbled his doubts, something about being in the joint when she got knocked up. I turned the tube off, checked to see if he'd jump me for it. The quiet was complete.

"Do me a favor, okay?" He looked at me dumbly. I sent him on the same fool's errand. "Boil us some water, get us clean towels." The towels I could use. He stood up, towering over me, even with my helmet on, and sauntered into the kitchen.

His woman was, indeed, past ready. I heard 30's siren shut down out front just as she pushed the baby into my hands. This one had outdoor plumbing.

+ + +

It was awfully sleepy out. We were working twelve-hour shifts on P3 (eight at night till eight in the morning), something we did every other week because of the riots in Southeast San Diego. Think Watts, Newark, Detroit— on a smaller scale. I'd seen some action earlier in the shift when, along with a hundred other cops, I attached a face shield to my helmet and waded in to the throngs of rock- and bottle-throwers at Mountain View Park. Things had calmed down at about two in the morning, which was when we east-end units got sent back to our beats. The Heights regulars would be held over another several hours to maintain the uneasy peace. You never knew when a smoldering ember could flame into another fireball.

The sun was just peeking around the side of Mount Helix. I was on the Boulevard, almost at the La Mesa border, having just cleared from a call. My eyelids felt like anvils but there was no way I'd park myself in some shaded glen to catch a few Z's. I had little use for peers who dozed on the job, even the ones who claimed they could hear the radio in their sleep. When you're needed you're needed. Besides, the thought of kids on the way to school standing next to a police car, eyeballing a drooling, snoring cop . . .

I started back to my beat, still congratulating myself for having delivered those two babies the week before. *Delivered*: a lousy term of art. It was the moms who'd made the deliveries, I'd merely accepted the packages. Still, it felt pretty special . . .

I was getting sleepier. I took my helmet off, smacked myself in the face a couple of times. Only half an hour to go. Maybe another call? Something to help me honor my vows, stay awake, stay alert? Dispatcher Betty Nulton obliged. Abandoning her half-dead tone, she put out the call: "Any unit for an 11-40. Infant not breathing." She broadcast it with the urgency of a mom. "Any unit" calls, as opposed to designating a specific car, came when there were few, or no, units showing green on the big board down at headquarters. Or when you needed the closest police car.

+ + +

Three calls cause cops to drop whatever they're doing and race to the scene. An 11-99 ("officer needs help"). The report of a naked woman. Or any situation involving a sick or injured kid.

+ + +

The cop world was no longer asleep. I was one of a chorus of units roused by the 11-40 call. At least two or three would beat me to the scene, I was sure. But I goosed it and dropped down to the interstate in order to avoid all the lights between Seventieth and my destination, the 4400 block of Marlborough. Commuter traffic was light on the freeway. I floored it, hitting speeds of ninety, ninety-five, my lights flashing and siren wailing, the ancient Ford shaking. I eased off the accelerator and pumped the brakes in time to make a harrowing turn off the freeway. Ninety seconds later, I pulled up to the house, my car smelling of rusty steam and burnt rubber. I was the first unit at the scene.

A man who looked too old to be the father ran out. He was dressed in pajamas, robe, and slippers. "Please, please! It's our baby! He's sick, we think. He's not breathing well." I sprinted into the house, ran down a hall and met a woman who looked at me in terror. Was it the helmet? Or what she'd woken to that morning? Her baby was dead.

Unit 43 was minutes away. Maybe I'd ask him to continue. What would be the harm of a "PR run"? We did them when angry crowds gathered at a fatal cutting or shooting. But I fought back the urge to go through with the charade. It didn't feel right, the "kiss of life" administered to a stiff little creature who'd been dead for hours, followed by a sham run to the hospital. "I'm sorry," I said. "Your . . . your baby died in his sleep." I pulled the baby-blue blanket up over the infant's head. *Michael* read the sign on the blue dresser, each shiny letter a different color. Her husband and I helped pull Michael's mother to her feet. She'd collapsed to the floor, wailing. She apologized.

"May I use your phone?"

"Yes, of course," said the father through his own tears. "Right in here." He pointed to the kitchen. Everything was neat, clean, polished. I called 232-6981, told the business office to call off 43. "It's an 11-44, civilian, natural. An infant," I choked. "I'll stand by for the coroner."

I sat with Michael's parents, discreetly asking for the information I needed to fill in every box of the death report. They brought me coffee.

+ + +

At the time, Dottie was pregnant with our first and only child. Delivering those two babies had brought joy, and optimism; their squealing, their wet squirming imparted confidence that our Matthew would be born healthy, with ten toes and ten fingers. The call to Marlborough Avenue left me numb, full of doubt and despair.

CHAPTER 15

DOUGHNUTS, TACOS,
AND FAT COPS

WHEN KRISPY KREME CAME to the Seattle area in the late 1990s, off-duty cops had to be called in to untangle the massive traffic jam and to control the hordes of pedestrians lined up around the block for the store's grand opening. I have no idea whether KK paid the cops in dollars or doughnuts, but I do know that the fatty little bombs have contributed to one of policing's most enduring traditions, a persistent cultural stereotype of fat cops and their love affair with the doughnut.

I don't like doughnuts, never have. I don't care for the stale jokes, the "all-you-cops-do-is-sit-around-and-eat-doughnuts" jabs at community meetings and parties. But, if my neighbors want to stuff themselves full of sugar and fried dough, more power to them, right? They're Americans, living in the land of the free and the morbidly obese.

Does that make it okay for police officers to make pigs of themselves? To create image problems for a department, to compromise the public's safety, their own safety, the safety of fellow officers?

When it came to Code 7 (meal break), graveyard cops in the forties and fifties had few choices. They could pack a lunch, pray for an all-night diner on their beat, or fill up on doughnuts. Doughnuts usually won out. They were, to most palates, tasty, and they were cheap and convenient. Thus was the legend born.

By the time I became a cop in the mid-sixties, 24/7 convenience stores and fast-food drive-thrus were everywhere. So my "doughnuts" were tacos and burritos from Azteca, "krautdogs" from Der Wienerschnitzel, burgers and fries from Jack-in-the-Box, and fish and chips from Arthur Treacher's. After only a year on the job I'd put on thirty-five pounds (see sidebar).

A DAY IN THE EATING LIFE OF A ROOKIE COP

My eating day started at midafternoon when Dottie and I would sit down to dinner of meatloaf and potatoes, or sandwiches and chips, or a little something from the Colonel's finest (which went the way of the doughnut for me the day our neighbors discovered maggots slithering around their lips as they lit into the familiar red and white bucket).

Even though my shift didn't begin until eight, I'd head for work before 4:00 P.M., telling Dottie I had to run records checks on the troublemakers on my beat, get my shoes shined by a trusty, and stake out a car that had fewer than a hundred thousand miles on it—all of which was true. But the larger truth was that I was desperate to get down to headquarters before Vi left work at the POA Coffee Shop. Nobody made a chili size like Vi: two giant hamburger patties, smothered in beans and cheese (hold the onions). And what's a chili size without fries and a chocolate shake?

Out on the beat, between 11 o'clock and bar closing, I'd stop at one of those fast-food joints that Eric Schlosser describes so lovingly in *Fast Food Nation* and order a sackful of fatmacs or hot dogs or cheesy burritos, and attempt to scarf them down before the next call.

When I got home from work at around seven or eight I'd dive into one of those plate-filling, old-fashioned, vein-clogging American breakfasts. (Cocktail hour for those of us working swings, and who "indulged," was around five in the morning. Six packs and tequila all around.) I'd finish breakfast, smoke a few cigarettes, down a second or third cup of coffee then hit the hay. When I awoke it was time to start the whole thing over again.

No one held me down and stuffed Mr. Treacher's deep-fat-fried cod down my gullet. I understood I was responsible for my weight gain. But the ubiquity of fast food outlets, the relentless advertising, the low cost and convenience (especially to a cop on the run), the "centralness" of high-fat outlets to our culture made those franchises a coconspirator. Don't you think?

In any case, with my new job came a new habit of eating (and drinking). Still, I was a slim panatela compared to some of the guys, the ones who got so stout they had to be taken off patrol.

When you reached the size of Divine or Andy Divine they'd assign you to the jail (where trusties served up huge, high-calorie meals daily, *gratis*) or they'd put you on a three-wheeler, writing parking tickets in La Jolla. Some cops were simply too fat to fit behind the wheel of a police car, or they'd crush the springs in the bench seats.

It took me twelve years, a hiatal hernia, two divorces, and a diet of grapefruit juice to shed those extra pounds. But I did it (and then some), and once I'd done it I had a hard time looking at an overweight cop without judging him. I went through a long period convinced that every police officer, regardless of age or gender or metabolic rate or body type or bone structure or thyroid or other medical condition or family history or life stresses should look like—me.

+ + +

Police work is physically demanding, in peculiar ways. To illustrate: It's early Sunday morning, your radio's dead quiet. It's all you can do to stay awake. Then, a hot crime, an armed robbery. The attendant at a gas station has been shot. The stickup man is headed your way. Before you can pick up the mike to let radio know you're joining the hunt, the suspect vehicle passes you going the other way. You notify radio, make a squealing U-turn, and the pursuit's on—at harrowing speeds. The suspect barrels down commercial streets, through residential neighborhoods, out onto the freeway, then back to surface streets. He's making hairpin turns, and bottoms out several times. Sparks fly, his and yours. Department policy says you should have backed off ten minutes ago, but you're determined to get the bastard.

A moment later, in testimony to the wisdom of the department's pursuit policy, you do catch up to the guy, only to find that he's T-boned a minister and her family who are traveling to church services in a distant city. Both cars are totaled, and it's obvious that death and/or serious injury has resulted.

Somehow your suspect has managed to extricate himself from the mangled mess and is now darting between houses. You stop your car, bail out, give chase. Two blocks later, sprinting the whole way, you corner him next to a kid's swing set in someone's backyard. Your heart is ready to burst through your chest and you're gasping so hard you can hardly bark orders—but your prey's not too pooped to put up a good fight. You thank God your backup is right on your tail because the bastard's got the upper hand and he's giving you a pretty good thrashing. Finally, with help of other cops you get him cuffed and haul him off to your car.

Forget that you've violated the law and half a dozen department policies, helped ruin a family, endangered innocent other lives, and ignored basic rules of self-preservation (where, for example, is the suspect's gun?)— you've done your job, you've gotten your man.

And your body knows it. At the peak of exertion your blood pressure spiked at 190/120. Your pulse rate almost tripled, jumping from a resting 65 at the time you were sleepily cruising your beat to 175 by the time you handcuffed your prisoner. ACTH (adrenalcorticotropic hormone, which floods the body when the mind is gripped by acute trauma) saturated your system, and stayed at dangerously high levels for several minutes following the arrest.

(Had you opted, instead of chasing the guy when he fled on foot, to stay at the scene and provide first aid your body would have been subjected to different but similarly taxing demands: prying dented metal, pulling bodies out of the wreckage, carrying dead weight, working feverishly to save lives.)

And that's how it goes in police work. From deadly boring to deadly physical, in a heartbeat. And back. Day after day, night after night. Add to that a diet rich in doughnuts and/or greaseburgers, frequently interrupted meals, a typical cop's drinking habits, smoking, sporadic or no exercise, shift work (with its corrupting metabolic effects), mandatory overtime, family commitments, court appearances, college classes, an off-duty job, perhaps the occasional extramarital affair—and you've got all the makings of a malnourished, sleep-deprived, cranky, and probably *fat* cop.

+ + +

Given the environmental, psychological, and biological pressures that produce obesity, shouldn't we let fat cops off the hook? No. Maybe. Yes. I'm not trying to sound like a consultant or a politician here—"no, maybe, yes" is not an unreasonable answer.

The answer is clearly no if we listen to U.S. surgeon general Richard

Carmona who told the National Sheriff's Association in March 2003 that "being overweight or obese directly impacts job performance when you're trying to defend the public safety. Remember, when you are called upon, you [must] be ready to back up a partner or a citizen. To me, failing at this calling when challenged would be a fate worse than death." It's rare that I agree with anyone from the Bush administration, but Carmona, who used to be both a cop and an ER surgeon, speaks to me with that "fate worse than death" remark.

An average of thirteen police officers die of on-the-job heart attacks every year. (Carmona also notes that my brothers and sisters in firefighting are felled far more often by heart attack than by flames, smoke, or falling roofs. Forty percent of all firefighter deaths are caused by heart attacks, resulting most commonly from overexertion.)

Also supporting the "zero tolerance" forces in the battle against fat cops is the Municipal Police Officers' Education and Training Commission. Citing the works of the world's foremost authority on police officer fitness, Dr. Kenneth Cooper of the Cooper Institute (whose test we used in Seattle to screen entry-level candidates), the commission found that:

- Fit officers use less sick time, and they recover quicker when they do get sick or injured.
- Fit officers go to the gym to work off their stress, while "unfit" cops are more likely to rip open a jumbo bag of garlic potato chips, pop open a brew, or light up a cigarette.
- Fit officers are less likely to resort to force (they don't need to because, in the [highly debatable] words of the commission, "bad guys don't want to go up against a fit enemy").

Given these benefits of a fit police force, wouldn't it make sense to mandate physical fitness? For years that was my official position. Several agencies at one point did demand fitness, or at least offered attractive financial incentives to encourage obese cops to lose weight. But police union politics and financial liability issues reared up and smote many of those programs.

Before I arrived in Seattle the city had traded away fitness testing at the behest of the union. This kind of thing happens often at the bargaining

153

table when cities lack, or claim they lack, enough money to satisfy the financial needs of the membership. Management throws labor a bone, labor picks it up, snarls about the lack of something more tangible, more *bankable*. But at least the members don't have to show up on their days off and run, jump, lift, and sweat their way through a fitness test. And that's how Seattle's fitness program went the way of the vibrating exercise belt. Shortsighted? You bet. I would have reinstalled the requirement, and the financial bennies, but was told fitness testing was a "nonstarter." I should have pushed it.*

Liability *is* a significant issue. Picture cops being tested in the gym: running, jumping, lifting, and—falling over dead. But also picture a police force trying to explain to irate citizens that 20 percent of its cops aren't available to answer calls for help because, having failed the fitness test, they're riding a desk. Or, imagine a city defending itself because a cop, officially determined to be unfit, was allowed on the streets—and failed to protect and/or serve.

Given that the whole country is in the middle of a full-blown, virulent outbreak of obesity (with Medicare likely in the near future to begin making payments for obesity treatments) we are unlikely to be filling our 900,000 police officer positions with Tom Cruise or Cameron Diaz body types. Besides, the "let it all hang out" argument deserves to be heard.

If, like certain professional football players, cops can carry an extra forty, sixty, or eighty pounds of body weight, and still get the job done, why not just leave them alone? (Have you seen the bellies on some of those NFL offensive linemen? Do *you* want to tell them they're out of shape?)

While my clear preference is that cops look fit, feel fit, and *be* fit, I can't shake the thought that at least some of my partiality is the product of pure prejudice. Since shedding my own surplus weight I've sized up obese cops as slothful, undisciplined.

But I'm also forced to admit that some of the best cops I've ever worked with, including two police chiefs, were overweight. Substantially, conspicuously overweight. But they were fully competent police officers

---

* SDPD continues to provide incentives. Its FIT ("Fitness, Image, Training") program tests body fat, cardiovascular recovery, strength, and flexibility.

who could (and did) pass job-related physical fitness tests—a standard and a practice I'm not wishy-washy about, at all. Plus, these cops were sensitive, compassionate, energetic, altogether decent people. So I guess what I'm saying is I'd take one of those fat cops over twenty slender, supercilious "recruitment poster" pretty boys and girls any day.

THE POLICE
DEPARTMENT

CHAPTER 16

DEMILITARIZING THE POLICE

Sgt. First Class "Arnold Davis" and his squad are on a mission to locate and take out a machine gunner who's pinned down half a platoon for the better part of a day. Darkness has descended. Night goggles in place, Davis and his men crawl through a desert dotted with darkened shacks and landmines. They flank the nest where the machine gunner is hiding. Davis signals for two of his men to leapfrog their way behind the nest, avoiding potential crossfire, and for the others to spread out and provide cover fire as necessary. The two soldiers work their way behind the nest, toss a hand grenade into it, and end the threat.

Police Officer "Dan Barry," while on routine patrol at three in the morning, spots a suspicious vehicle midway down an alley. The car, its lights off but its dome light on, is parked outside the back door of an electronics store. As Barry reaches for the mike to call for backup, a white male in his thirties rushes out of the store, a duffel bag in each hand. The suspect spots the police car, drops the bag in his right hand, and reaches for his waistband. Barry, gun drawn, aims at the suspect and orders him to freeze. The suspect complies, and Barry hooks him up. The officer collects and impounds evidence—including the .380 handgun the suspect had been reaching for—then writes extensive crime and arrest reports. Later that morning, he calls the shop owners on his beat, with whom he had been meeting for over a month, to give them the good news.

THE DIFFERENCES BETWEEN A soldier on the outskirts of Baghdad and a beat cop in Schenectady are noteworthy. The mission of soldiers is to win battles on foreign soil, the mission of police officers is to keep the peace in

America's cities. More to the point, *a soldier follows orders for a living, a police officer makes decisions for a living*. Therein resides the justification for a radical reconstruction of America's police agencies.

Many Americans view their local PD as an occupational force—repressive, distant, arrogant. It's no wonder: their police department operates within the framework of a *paramilitary bureaucracy*, a structure that fortifies that image and promotes the behavior. Your local PD takes raw material, the average police recruit drawn from your own community, and molds him or her into a soldier-bureaucrat, starting in the academy.

That rigid, top-down, highly centralized, militarily oriented "command and control" system simply does not work for policing—not in America, not in our multicultural, ostensibly pluralistic, democratic society. The paramilitary bureaucracy, or "PMB," as I've referred to it in my notes over the years, is a slow-footed, buck-passing, blame-laying, bullying, bigotry-fostering institutional arrangement, as constipated by tradition and as resistant to change as Mel Gibson's version of the Catholic Church. I cannot imagine other essential reforms in policing—improved crime-fighting, safety and morale of the force, the honoring of constitutional guarantees—without *significant structural transformation*.

The following is a rational and objective examination of the advantages and disadvantages of the police paramilitary bureaucracy.

A RATIONAL AND OBJECTIVE EXAMINATION OF THE ADVANTAGES AND DISADVANTAGES OF THE POLICE PARAMILITARY BUREAUCRACY (PMB)

ADVANTAGES	DISADVANTAGES
Gives cops a chance to play soldier	Reduces crime-fighting effectiveness
	Dampens enthusiasm for risk-taking
	Distances police from community
	Breeds ignorance and arrogance
	Discourages creativity and imagination
	Slows pace and quality of decision-making
	Encourages dishonesty
	Tolerates sloth
	Wastes time and money

ADVANTAGES	DISADVANTAGES
	Cultivates a culture of deceit
	Protects incompetence within the ranks
	Creates sinecures within management
	Rewards machismo
	Winks at abuses of civil liberties
	Invites the wrong kind of police candidates
	Promotes obsequious ass-kissers
	Teaches low tolerance of ambiguity
	Demands blind, often misplaced loyalty
	Supports heavy-handed conduct
	Hides mistakes
	Accepts excuses
	Institutionalizes mediocrity
	Laughs at bigotry
	Crushes differences in worldviews
	Homogenizes employee diversity
	Gags, censures, or exiles internal critics
	Installs barriers to effective communication
	Undermines officer safety
	Sniffs at "family-friendly" employee policies
	Fosters corruption
	Rejects accountability
	Snubs community activists
	Stonewalls the media
	Ignores excellent performance
	Disregards constructive employee advice
	Does violence to employee morale
	Safeguards the police "code of silence"

I think you have to agree that I've been *fair and balanced* in my presentation of the pros and cons of the PMB. It is a system I ran afoul of often, even as I railed against it during my thirty-four-year career. In the waning moments of my time in San Diego I decided to take one final, bloody stand against it.

+ + +

It was 1992. SDPD chief Bob Burgreen had asked me, as his number-two guy, to conduct a management audit of the department, and to "concentrate on our warts." To no one's surprise, a "lack of communication" surfaced as our biggest (internal) problem. Well, did I have an answer to that: *demilitarize* the place! And start by civilizing the titles of mid-ranking department bosses—which I theorized had a deleterious effect on communication.

I knew there'd be a shit-rain of opposition—military titles are a cultural icon in civilian policing, as much a part of the cop culture as mustaches, sidearms, and doughnuts. But, win or lose, I believed it was important to air the *rationale* behind "demilitarization." I hoped to encourage a departmentwide dialogue on the principles of a more "democratic," less militaristic police force. And since *language structures reality*, I was convinced that our military nomenclature stood between us and the community, between the brass and rank-and-file cops. I walked into Burgreen's office to let him know of my intentions.

"You're going to *what?*"

"Recommend a change in the titles of 'sergeant,' 'lieutenant,' and 'captain.' "

"What do you propose we call them?" Burgreen and I had been sergeants, lieutenants, captains. We knew what it meant to stitch stripes to our uniform sleeves, to pin the single bar, then the double bars to our collars. We could remember the pride we felt in having earned the insignia.

"I don't know yet. I was kind of looking at the federal model." The FBI calls its entry-level people "special agents." Its first-line supervisors are "supervising agents." The head of an office is a "special agent in charge." That might not be so bad. Maybe if the cops understood they were *special* . . .

I certainly wasn't going to recommend the "Lakewood Model."

+ + +

Incorporated in 1970, Lakewood, Colorado, had the rare opportunity to build its police department, and its vocabulary, from the ground up. Its officials, including Pierce Brooks, Lakewood PD's first chief, were driven to create a "user-friendly" agency whose members would be, in form as well as substance, part *of* and not *apart from* the community. Their beat cops would be "agents." Sergeants would be "field advisors," lieutenants "senior field advisors," and captains "agents in charge." They'd sport gray slacks, light blue shirts, and navy blazers.

It didn't last long. Patrol cops are still called agents, but as early as 1973 their bosses had been permanently rebranded: *sergeants, lieutenants, captains.* Seems other PDs didn't know what the hell an "advisor" was. Their blazers wound up at the Goodwill, replaced by sharp, traditional police blues. Score one for common sense on that last one.

+ + +

"The feds? Hmm." Burgreen conjured the gathering clouds. "Why risk what's left of your credibility with the troops? Why recommend something you know is not going to fly? Why allow your critics to . . . *Ah ha!* You sly bastard. It's a *stalking horse*, right? Get everybody in a lather over 'demilitarization' so your other recommendations won't seem so 'extreme.' " I laughed. It was a plausible theory—I *had* decided to recommend the "flattening" of SDPD's tortuously long chain of command by eliminating two ranks. And to impose "quality assurance audits" of the work of top-ranking personnel. You could see where these ideas *might* be a little threatening.

"No. I'm serious," I said. "Look, I know you're not going to buy it, but let's just put it out there for two or three months." Until now, my advocacy of the idea had been confined to classrooms and conferences. "Let's see what our cops have to say."

Burgreen laughed.

"You know damn well what they're going to say." But my chief always did love a spirited debate. "Two months. That's it."

That week we announced all my recommendations, injecting "demilitarization" directly into the bloodstream of the department. Would the body reject it, or, miracle of miracles, accept it?

We wanted more communication? Well, we got it. People throughout the department, and beyond, couldn't wait to express themselves. Critics of demilitarization shrieked, howled, chortled, guffawed. They penned hate mail—from down the hall and from across the country. They wrote derisive editorials, sketched mocking cartoons. The *San Diego Union-Tribune*, while lauding the other twenty-one recommendations of my audit, suggested that "Normanclature" be deep-sixed, posthaste.

One of my cops addressed a letter to me in my capacity as editor of *The Corner Pocket*, our in-house administrative rag:

> Dear Editor,
>
> If only Chief Stamper could hear the jokes and ridicule . . . from the working cop, he would really understand how out of touch he is with police work. While most of the recommendations are viable, changing names to fit the esoteric thoughts of Chief Stamper will do nothing in our effort to relate with the public. . . . We are a paramilitary unit at war with gang members who carry automatic weapons. Stamper, if you really want to be a CEO of a [corporation] then you take one of those "Golden Handshake" retirements and go work in the Silicon Valley. I aspire to be a Police Captain not a Division Director . . .

That was cool, but my favorite less-than-enthusiastic commentary came from a sergeant who wrote an article for *The Corner Pocket*. In it she offered a new lexicon for just about every noun used in police work. My position, for example, she labeled "One Who Oversees Division Directors, Assistant Directors, Assistant Division Directors, Supervising Agents, and Agents." She put it on a nameplate and sent it to me. I kept it on my desk throughout our "dialogue" on demilitarization.

I wasn't without supporters. Former U.S. Attorney General Ed Meese called to offer solace and, to my surprise, an endorsement of the plan. He always thought frontline police officers deserved more respect—from their bosses, mostly. And Joe Wambaugh phoned in his encouragement: "What the hell were you thinking, Norm?"

"What, you don't like the idea?"

"I didn't say that. I think it's a terrific idea, I really do. But you want to model things after *federal* law enforcement? You know the locals never get along with the feds." He suggested the British system (constables, chief constables, and so forth). With the origins of American policing traceable to the U.K., he was probably on to something. The British titles had a more, what did he call it, *historic*, *romantic* ring.

After the initial shock, many of our employees settled down and actually started talking about the substance and the symbolism of the proposal. But I still couldn't walk ten feet without running into another explanation of why it was such a bad idea.

When Burgreen ripped the life-support needle out, true to his word, sixty days later, it was time for a last check of vital signs. How had the cop culture taken to this transfusion of "new blood"? Was the lieutenant who'd come to see me a week before the drop-dead date typical? A bright, up-and-coming individual, he told me, "When you first raised the issue I thought, 'Man, the cheese has finally slipped off Stamper's cracker.' I thought it was the goofiest idea I'd ever heard. But the more I thought about it the more I realized, hey, we're *not* the military, we're cops. We're *community* cops. We ought to have titles that make sense to the community. What does 'lieutenant' or 'sergeant' mean to the average citizen?"

The lieutenant's change of heart brought the number of converts up to approximately eleven. Given that we had 2,800 employees, I guess you could say it was an idea whose time had not yet come.

+ + +

"Demilitarization" may be fine in theory, said the cops. But what of the real-world challenges of barricaded suspects and riots and other emergencies that crop up in police work? These incidents require military-like tactics, communication, and compliance. And what about esprit de corps and discipline? Don't these matters cry out for retention of the paramilitary system? No, they do not. They represent issues that must be resolved in the construction of what I'll call a "PPO," or Progressive Police Organization.

We underestimate the intelligence, creativity, and adaptability of our communities, and of our police officers and their leaders, if we assume they can't get together and build a new system. The PPO would retain and strengthen SWAT (special weapons and tactics) units. It would continue to provide (improved) first-responder training to all emergencies, including terrorist attacks. It would continue to field better equipped cops in *police* uniforms, driving *police* cars. Officers and all other employees at all levels would continue to be held to (even higher) standards of performance and conduct. These real-world demands—as well as the need for the coercive powers of government to be both conspicuous and authoritative—require that certain critical traditions be preserved.

What, then, would change under the new and improved PPO? Just about everything else:

- The steep hierarchy would be dramatically flattened to improve the timeliness of communication and the speed and quality of decision making. Generous severance packages (handed out in both San Diego and Seattle) ensure a safe landing for those losing their management jobs. The costs are more than offset by long-term savings.
- Decision-making authority would be reduced to the lowest possible level, not merely in theory but in policy-driven practice.
- Rank-and-file police officers and civilian employees would participate freely in policymaking, program development, priority setting, and other issues, including "oversight" activities, that affect them—and about which they often have more firsthand knowledge than others in the department, including top brass.
- Citizens would be involved in the same arenas as rank-and-file officers. They, too, would sit on oversight boards that investigate and/or review citizen complaints, monitor intelligence gathering, and render judgments on police shootings.
- The creation of effective communication vehicles would be mandated (sessions with the chief, cross-bureau meetings, community forums, and teleconferencing), and the timely exchange of relevant information would, instead of being left to chance, become nonnegotiable.
- Standards of performance and conduct would be required for all employees at all levels. Individuals who exceed those standards would be recognized, tangibly if not financially (time off with pay is a terrific reward for today's overworked, often underpaid aces). Individuals falling shy of these standards would be required, within a given period of time (say 30,

45, or 60 days), and with proffered assistance, to improve their performance and/or conduct. Or be fired.

- Police officers would be treated like adults. Discipline would be two-pronged: punishment for misconduct, nonpunitive assistance for honest mistakes or performance problems. "Progressive" discipline would be used except in cases of broomstick rectal exams, sex with teenage explorer scouts, or other such egregious behavior—in such instances the officer would be fired, prosecuted, and a photo, suitable for framing, provided to all media outlets.

- Police officers would be given everything they need to get the job done properly and safely. Their equipment and working conditions would be monitored constantly, with deficiencies attended to promptly. They would be compensated at a level commensurate with the danger and sensitivity of their roles in society—in today's market, a hundred thousand dollars is not unreasonable.

But *can* a police officer working in a "demilitarized" police force *spring into military-like action* as needed? Is it possible, psychologically, for that officer to make a smooth, rapid transition from a "democratic" cop to a compliant member of, say, an assault team headed into a public school to take out a shooter?

Absolutely. Good cops do it all the time, morphing from discretionary social problem-solver to armed tactician. The sad thing is they do it with little, if any, help from their rigid, myopic organizations. Imagine the improvements, across the board, if the *system* itself expected and facilitated such progressive police behavior?

+ + +

A word of caution. If you're a reformer bent on rearranging the way your PD's molecules are organized, best keep this in mind: *If you push a system, it will push back—with equal or greater force.* The status quo has powerful defenders who can get downright vicious when cornered. Proceed slowly, build support, and be as respectful as you are tough. And forget about calling sergeants "advisors."

CHAPTER 17

PICKING GOOD COPS

WE'D BEEN AT IT for weeks. Most of the candidates had long before started looking and sounding alike. *Why do you want to be a police officer?* "To help people." *What makes you think you'd be a good cop?* "I like people." *What's your strongest quality?* "I'd have to say my people skills." *Your weakest?* "Well, my friends say I work too hard." We needed some comic relief, Jon Murphy and I. Murphy was a personnel analyst. I was, as a lieutenant, SDPD's representative on the civil service oral board. We'd heard the same mind-numbing themes from over two hundred people.

Our salvation came in the form of a recently discharged Marine, currently working as a rent-a-cop. Murphy was asking the questions. Why had the candidate left the Marines? "Too lax, sir," he said. Murphy and I exchanged glances. His current job? How did he like working for a security company? "It's okay, but my mission in life is to be a policeman." Could he tell us a little something about his current job we might find interesting? "Yes, sir. Just last week I was working the sports arena, the Rolling Stones concert? A big fight broke out on my side of the parking lot." What did you do? "Well, I caught this punk who was getting ready to chuck a bottle at the policemen." What did you do with him? "Nothing, sir," he said, snarling and nodding in my direction. "One of *your* people came along. He made me turn the punk over to him." Ah, but what would you have liked to do? "*Liked* to do?" Be honest now. "Sir, I would like to have knocked him on his ass." Yes, yes. Then what?

Our candidate stood up, the look in his eyes causing me to pat my right side to make sure my weapon was where it was supposed to be. The guy put his hands on the table and lifted his right leg. "Then I would've *kicked* him in the face!" He brought his foot down so hard the thud echoed off the metal walls. He lifted the foot again and brought it down, harder. "I'd kick that commie hippie's face over and over and over!" His foot came down, over and over and over, his eyes bulging from their sockets, beet-red cheeks puffed up like a blowfish. "Over and over and . . ."

When he left the room, Murphy and I took out our rating sheets. We agreed, straight down the line. Today that man is a police chief in . . . just kidding. We did get our comic relief, but the candidate's over-the-top performance made me stop and think: about the slicker aspirants, the glib sadists and smooth sociopaths who are drawn to the work.

Of course, we saw candidates at the *other* end of the spectrum: people who spoke barely above a whisper, still lived at home, taught Sunday school, had never been employed, never been in a fight, never fired a gun, never had sex or tasted whiskey. People who'd faint dead away at the sight of blood.

Some people, *most* people, are not cut out to be a cop. If honest and otherwise morally upright, they're either too aggressive or not aggressive enough; insensitive or overly sensitive; rigid as rebar or lacking a spine altogether. I think back to my own candidacy, and give thanks that SDPD was hard up for cops at the moment—and that there was no psychological screening in those days.

+ + +

I'd grown up a frightened, neurotic kid, afraid of just about everything. Dad's fists, his belt. Women's screams. Sirens. Gunfire. Schoolyard fights. I'd played sports, desperate to prove to myself I wasn't afraid, but it didn't work—I lived in terror of being crushed by a linebacker, elbowed by a power forward, beaned by a fastball.

For years I had a major preoccupation with death, *my* death. I don't mean I'd planned to kill myself. But there were ways it could just *happen* to you. You could, for example, accidentally hang yourself from the pepper tree in the backyard, or take a sip from a vial whose skull and crossbones you'd not seen until too late. Or step on a rusty nail and get lockjaw. Or get shot by a bullet on the way to the Boys Club, run over by a speeding car, stabbed by a knife, slashed with a straight razor, run through with a samurai sword. You could slip from the roof of the El Cortez on prom night, get trapped in a blazing elevator, or tossed into a fire ring at the beach in Coronado. A burglar could cover your face with a pillow and suffocate you. Your brother Roy could drop the radio into your bath water. You could get ripped apart by a grizzly in the Rockies or bitten by a rabid Rottweiler. "Happy," the crazy guy who hung around Kimball Park, he could whack your head off with an ax.

See what I mean? I was hardly your ideal cop candidate. Like many other screwed up kids who go on to become police officers, I used the job, or it used me, to work out all kinds of developmental and emotional challenges. I figure upwards of a hundred San Diegans paid a price for my on-the-job "therapy" during my rookie year alone.

Ultimately, I *did* grow on the job, evolving into a pretty good, if somewhat controversial, cop.

But I wouldn't have hired me.

So, how did it happen? Well, I passed through all the "gates" the civil service system and department placed in my path: written exam, oral interview, medical, physical fitness, polygraph, background investigation. Also, I was a warm body with a pulse. And, as I said, SDPD was hurting at the time.

+ + +

Nowhere in the country is police experience necessary to apply for and pass a civil service test for the entry-level position: patrol officer. Just basic communication skills, decent medical and physical condition, a level head, and a moral compass that points north.

More and more cities are having their candidates complete a behaviorally anchored, empirically validated paper-and-pencil test, provide a sample of writing skills, and watch a video of realistically staged police incidents after which they answer questions about how they'd handle each. Not a bad way to go. Certainly an improvement over the "general intelligence" test I took in 1965. Culturally biased against ethnic minorities and not even close to being job-related, it got bounced years later for those very reasons.

Candidates who survive the written test are interviewed, typically by a police supervisor or manager, a community rep, and a civil service analyst.

They're asked many of the same questions I was asked: motivation for the position; background experiences; self-perceived strengths and weaknesses; and what he or she would do if he or she witnessed another cop steal a candy bar. Or a Rolex.

After the written and the oral comes the medical exam. Today's are more rigorous than in my day.

+ + +

"Jump up and down fifteen times on your left foot," said Dr. Brown. "Good, good. Now fifteen times on your right foot. Good, good." He took my pulse, which he'd done just before all the jumping, then wrote down a number. I remember that part well, because I failed it. *Tachycardia* they called it, "unsatisfactory exercise tolerance." I worked out daily for a month, laid off the beer, ordered no pizzas or subs at Mike & Joe's, came back and passed on my second attempt.

Most of us in the applicant pool had known exactly what to expect from the medical. Dr. Brown, a kindly man, was a creature of routine. He tested our hearing, for example, by standing behind us and whispering "66 . . . 99"—same numbers, same order, every candidate. In addition to checking our hearing and having us jump up and down, he drew blood, took our blood pressure, and had us turn our heads and cough. That was it. Still, his exam was a lot more thorough than that of the "police surgeon," three weeks later.

An archaic position even then, the police surgeon's main job was to conduct forensic medical examinations of rape and other assault victims (it's contracted out today). Working out of a tiny office next to the jail, Doc Williams was also responsible for the PD's in-house applicant "medicals." His signature was required before you could move on to the next step.

Doc Williams was a gruff, impatient bastard. I was in and out of his office in under a minute, and never took my clothes off. "You flatfooted?" he said.

"No."

"What color's that green box?"

"Green?"

"Next!"

+ + +

Today's physical fitness testing has been reduced to a science (with the "Cooper Test" out of Texas setting the national standard). On the whole, it's an easier test—but more job-related. In most cities, you do eighteen pushups within a minute, twenty-seven sit-ups within a minute, and a mile and a half run within fifteen minutes and twenty seconds. I'm no Jack Palance, but I can double those standards, even today.

+ + +

The polygraph? By far the most controversial step in the process. The reliability of "lie detection" has been questioned by experts. Its results are not admissible in court, it has been discontinued by many agencies, and its use in preemployment screening has actually been outlawed in a number of states.

I remember my visit to "the box" in late 1965. Word had spread throughout the applicant pool: *No matter what you've done, no matter how humiliating, for chrissakes cop to it: It's all over if they catch you in a lie.* The conventional wisdom was that you *might* be able to fool the detective who ran the machine but you couldn't fool the box.

I walked into an office on the second floor of the detective bureau, having no knowledge of how the machine worked. I didn't know it measured blood pressure, pulse rate, respiration, muscle movements, and "galvanic skin response" (sweating). For all I knew a loud buzzer would go off if I fibbed. I wasn't aware that the polygraph occasionally produces a "false positive," that it might, in other words, catch me lying when I was telling the truth. Or vice versa. Civil service and PD personnel had convinced me that the lie detector was 100 percent accurate.

A detective in a white short-sleeve shirt motioned me into a chair next to the box. He asked a lot of time-consuming questions about my application, simple stuff: the spelling of my name, my address, work history, and so on. Then he hooked me up. He asked the same questions all over again. I couldn't see the lines on the graph but I didn't hear any buzzers or bells. "Okay," he said. "That's it." *That's it? I'm out of here?* "Now," he said with some enthusiasm. "Let's get to the *good* stuff."

For the next half hour he asked every kind of personal question you can imagine. Sex. Drugs. Alcohol. Family. Finances. How I spent or misspent my youth. Crimes I may have committed, my driving record, medical history. Relations with friends, coworkers, neighbors. He went over my application in detail, my body doing its thing, signifying on his graph. Finally, he unhooked me.

"So, how'd I do?" I said. Despite all the dire warnings, I'd decided to fudge the truth a bit about my trick knee. I guess I'd figured it was worth the crapshoot: the injury was definitely a disqualifier. Maybe I could put one over on the machine just this once . . .

"I'll never tell," he said. And he never did. Polygraph operators were sworn to secrecy, the results of their examinations confidential. Only the chief's office, he told me, would get the results.* I never heard a word, good or bad, about how I did.

Forty years later, cities like San Diego still use the polygraph. But what do we know about its accuracy, it usefulness in screening police candidates? The 245-page report of the National Research Council, a branch of the National Academy of Sciences, reports that the polygraph "error" rate in standard employment screening is terribly high: about thirty percent false positives or false negatives. But the American Polygraph Association asserts, self-servingly, that in over 250 studies during the past twenty-five years, the accuracy rate of polygraph examinations hovers around perfection, give or take zero percent. In fairness to the APA, they do not consider an "inconclusive" finding to be an error—while critics of the polygraph do. I'm siding with the APA on this one. How can inconclusive (or "I don't know") be construed as an error? Inconclusive is inconclusive.

Sociopaths believe their lies, professional spies have been taught to lie. For everybody else? The polygraph's greatest value just might be psychological. It scares candidates into telling the truth.

+ + +

---

* A couple of years later I'd sit with polygraph operators in the Coffee Shop where'd they'd regale the booth with tales of torrid affairs between cop wannabes and the Golden Retrievers who loved them, of sexual liaisons with members of the melon family, of *Playboys*, nooses, masturbation, and . . .

The very best assessment of a police applicant's fitness comes from incumbent police officers, in the form of competent, well-trained background investigators. The kind of cops you'd want to show up at your door if your car's been ripped off, or your kid molested.

Many cities are grossly negligent when it comes to background investigations. They don't assign enough investigators. They fail to provide critical training. They don't furnish computers, software, office space, and/or other essential tools. They won't foot the bill to put a backgrounder on a plane so that the core of the investigation can be carried out on the candidate's home turf.

Scrimp on background investigations, you'll wind up hiring check artists, dope dealers, gang members, and other assorted fugitives from justice. The Mellon Commission (1994) found that an incredible 88 percent of 413 officers fired or suspended for corruption in New York had entered the NYPD academy before completion of their background checks. (I don't know why that statistic surprises me: *I* wasn't backgrounded until weeks after I'd been hired. But least I was still in the classroom when it was finally accomplished.) In New York, a third of those new hires were *on the streets* before they'd had their background investigations completed. Such investigations would have revealed that 24 percent of those cops had a criminal arrest record.

New York, Washington, D.C., Chicago, Houston, Philadelphia, Detroit, Los Angeles, Atlanta, San Diego, Seattle, and countless other cities have at one time or another tried to hire too many people too fast.

You pay a price when you sacrifice quality for speed. Every single time, guaranteed.

It's not all that hard to keep crooks out of a police department. A simple check of names, dates of birth, social security numbers, and fingerprints against local, regional, and the National Crime Information Center databases will do the trick. But only if you take the time to do it. (*And* if the crooked candidate has a police record. Bulletin: Not all crooks get caught.)

There's no substitute for a shoe-leather investigation that brings you face-to-face with former employers, coworkers, spouses, ex-spouses, other intimate partners, former teachers, neighbors, people who've had close contact with the candidate. A competent background investigation turns up all kinds of juicy information that otherwise would have not made it to the desk of the appointing authority. For example: a candidate with no criminal record who routinely beat his live-in girlfriend and threatened to kill her if she reported him (she never did, but our background investigator, going door to door, pried the history from a neighbor); a woman who'd been embezzling from her employer (a trusting individual who'd ignored his suspicions until the cops came knocking on his door); a man whose "paper trail"—employment, education, other biographical data—was stellar but whose interpersonal skills, as described by coworkers, would make Don Rickles seem like Mister Rogers; a California man who, using the address of a brother-in-law, did all his major shopping (household appliances, boats, campers, automobiles) in Oregon, thereby avoiding state sales tax—and committing fraud; and a man who would get drunk, pin his wife to the bed, and rape her at least once a week.

Background investigations are also how one learns whether the candidate has met the most basic requirements of the job: age, citizenship, education, possession of a valid driver's license, the absence of felony or domestic violence convictions, an honorable discharge from the military.

+ + +

Psychological testing is critical, indispensable in fact. Dr. David Corey, a renowned police psychologist based in Oregon and an expert on applicant selection methods, is part of a panel looking at "patrol officer psychological screening dimensions" for the state of California. Working to help police agencies "screen in" the best applicants, the panel has identified ten "dimensions" essential to professional police work:

- Social competence
- Teamwork
- Adaptability/flexibility
- Conscientiousness/dependability
- Impulse control/attention to safety
- Integrity/ethics
- Emotional regulation and stress tolerance

- Decision making and judgment
- Assertiveness/persuasiveness
- Avoiding substance abuse and other risk-taking behavior

The panel is also developing a long list of "*counterproductive* behaviors," and expressing each in ways that make it easier to test for walking landmines. You really don't want a cop in your neighborhood who:

> Baits people . . . takes personal offense at comments, insults, criticism . . . provokes suspects by officious bearing, gratuitous verbal exchange, or through physical contact . . . antagonizes community members and others . . . gossips, criticizes, and backstabs colleagues and coworkers . . . is paralyzed by uncertainty or ambiguity . . . sneaks out before shift is over . . . brandishes [or] is otherwise careless with firearms . . . gets in off-duty altercations . . . lies, misrepresents and commits perjury . . . steals . . . engages in inappropriate sexual activity (e.g., prostitutes, sex with minors, etc.) . . . is *overly* suspicious and distrusting in dealing with others . . . comes "unglued," freezes, or otherwise performs ineffectively when feeling overloaded or stressed . . . is naïve, overly trusting, easily duped . . . displays submissiveness and insecurity when confronting challenging or threatening situations . . . commits domestic violence . . ."

By framing these traits in *behavioral* terms, and by developing new measures and instruments to test for them, screeners can do a much better job of keeping both the goons and the "naïve, overly trusting, easily duped" out of a police uniform.

+ + +

There are four basic issues on which the law enforcement community is divided when it comes to picking new cops. How old is old enough? How much education is necessary? Is military experience an advantage? And, how much dope-smoking is too much?

The typical minimum age requirement is twenty-one, with a few agencies, like Chicago, setting it at twenty-three. But a handful of cities allow eighteen-year-olds to become cops. Now, that's just plain stupid. Developmentally, your average teenager is simply not ready to exercise life-and-death decision-making authority. If your city's officials are putting children in police uniforms, please tell them to stop. If they refuse, recall them.

+ + +

Most agencies require a high school diploma or GED equivalent. According to the Bureau of Justice Statistics, only 15 percent of local PDs require some form of higher education, with sixty semester units the norm.

In 1979, I proposed that the city require all SDPD candidates to have an associate degree or sixty semester units or more of higher education from an accredited college or university. I believed then and still do that higher education, preferably in the liberal arts, gives a candidate an edge over a non-college-educated applicant. It's not so much the *product* of the learning but the *process* of matriculation that produces the advantage: setting out a program, declaring a major, picking courses, enduring the registration nightmare, getting up in the morning for classes or attending at night after work, reading dense texts, writing term papers, questioning professors, associating with people and ideas that force you to think, taking midterms and finals. The *politics* of higher education, the discipline of learning *how* to learn—that was the most useful thing about higher ed. Not the degree, not the units.

The city accepted the proposal. But two years later we had to abandon the requirement when the pool of eligible ethnic minorities all but dried up. (The number of women candidates was unaffected.) For college-educated ethnic minorities, police work simply couldn't compete with the pay or the cachet of the private sector. Or was it because of the "blue-collarness" of police work, or the image of policing in the black community? Or the dangers and strains of life as a cop? We dropped the requirement, the pool filled back up.

It's a tough call, but unless a department in a multicultural community is able to reflect that community's diversity within its ranks, I'd oppose a post–high school educational requirement. And look for ways to "incentivize" a career in policing.

I said earlier that tenured cops in big cities ought to be bringing home $100K a year. But what do they make? According to the U.S. Department of Labor, the average salary of a police officer in 2002 was $42,270. The middle 50 percent earned between $32,300 and $53,500. The highest 10 percent earned more than $65,330 and the lowest 10 percent less than $25,220. An NYPD officer makes $54,048. (Elsewhere in the state, in Suffolk and Nassau Counties, top pay has reached almost $85,000—with some Suffolk County cops bringing home over $100,000 when you throw in longevity pay, shift differentials, and other add-ons. This, of course, has made NYPD a choice training ground for those other agencies.)

+ + +

A lot of people think being a cop and being a soldier are *interchangeable*, that honorably discharged military personnel would make super cops. Just because they've served in the *armed* forces and worn a *uniform*. This is nonsense, of course.

There are huge differences in the everyday existence of a soldier vis-à-vis a cop (not to mention profound variances in the geography and political systems against which each occupation is set). Also, being a soldier in wartime is a hell of a lot more dangerous than being a city cop. Military personnel are trained to kill, to inflict pain, and some can't seem to turn it off. Those four or five soldiers who killed their wives at Ft. Bragg are a case in point, the soldiers at Abu Ghraib another. While it would be both morally wrong and shortsighted to generalize based on these horrors, it does suggest the need for a rigorous check for such tendencies during the selection process.

My position is simple: judge each candidate, with or without military experience, against the standards set for the job. Some of the best cops I worked with were military veterans who brought to the work a maturity, self-discipline, and loyalty to the principles of ethical policing that some nonservice personnel lacked.

+ + +

Drugs? I remember the day we learned SDPD was going to start accepting candidates who'd smoked pot. It was scandalous! Of course, it was also the late sixties: if the department refused to hire ex-pot smokers we'd have three people sitting in the academy classroom instead of forty.

A few years later, the doors were opened to cokesters. The test was whether you were a user or an "experimenter." Those who'd tried cocaine had to have been clean and sober for three years. Potheads? Twelve months.

Those standards fluctuated a bit over time, in San Diego and elsewhere, as we coped with the cultural reality that millions of young folk had at least dabbled in a variety of banned substances. We stuck to our guns on certain drugs: no hallucinogens (the literature was full of tales of years-after LSD flashbacks) and no "injectibles."

Despite my "relaxed" attitude about social drug use I'm rigid on the topic of cops who use. I say just say no: Cities must reject candidates who went far beyond youthful experimentation, or who've used recently. They're not worth the risk.

+ + +

Bill Kolender used to tell his recruiters, "Bring me *good* people, damn it! I can't make chicken soup out of chicken shit." Picking the right people starts with rounding them up in the first place, and "role model" cops of all colors, both genders, straight and gay do it best.

Critical to the success of police recruitment is specialized training for the recruiters, as well as a modern, well-crafted, adequately financed recruitment or "marketing" strategy. Not to be overlooked in the campaign: officers out on the beat. They are an *excellent* source of new blood. I gave my cops a day off with pay when they recruited a successful candidate.

+ + +

Today's rookies are tomorrow's sergeants, lieutenants, chiefs. Within four to six years of their hiring, police officers become eligible for promotion to sergeant. Which means, if they make it, they'll move from *doing* the work to *leading* it—the most demanding transition in any upwardly mobile police career. Just as not everyone is cut out to be a cop, not every police officer is supervisory material. As a chief, I saw the picking of a new leader as one of the most important decisions I made.

Similar to most systems, Seattle's public safety civil service commission gives its police chief and fire chief the authority to pick any promotional candidate who, at the time of an opening, is in the top 5 or top 25 percent of an eligibility list. My predecessor, like most chiefs, found it expedient to go right down the list. It made life easier for him, passing only those candidates widely known to be dipsticks. The Seattle Police Officers Guild certainly favored that approach.

They were most unhappy, by contrast, with my method. I picked, to the best of my ability, the *best* candidate certified—no matter his or her standing on the certification list. In other words I "collapsed" the vertical list of those certified, making of it a *pool* of equally eligible (though certainly not equally qualified) candidates. To the union (and to my own top staff, at least at the beginning) this was heresy, a violation of the spirit if not the letter of the civil service *merit* system.

Let's examine that "merit" business. Say Mary and Betty take the civil service test for sergeant. It starts with a straightforward paper-and-pencil exam: department policies and procedures, law, hypothetical questions designed to assess knowledge and judgment on crime fighting, field tactics, cultural diversity, interpersonal relations, officer safety, ethical issues, personnel problems, and the like. Mary scores 85.34, Betty 85.35. Next they go before an oral board comprised of a couple of outside agency captains and a representative of the local community. Each of the candidates spends forty minutes alone with the panel. Mary collects a 90.66. Betty opens her envelope to find a score of 91.

In Seattle, there's one other element to the process: seniority, or "service credits." (There's no justification for this provision. Seniority ought to count for *nothing* when it comes to the selection of department leaders; it's a terrific tie-breaker when, say, two candidates are otherwise evenly matched—but how often does that happen in the real world?) Since Betty's been around long enough, she gets a service point. Mary doesn't.

Even if these three elements—written, oral, service credits—are "weighted" (more points for the written, for example), Betty has clearly beaten Mary on the test. But does her sliver of a 1.35-point edge make her a better candidate than Mary? Is she more *meritorious?*

Of course not! Where are their scores, Betty's and Mary's, for *on-the-job performance?* Their respective track records, their relative worth to the community, to the organization? *There is no better indication of a person's future behavior than his or her past behavior.* Yet, the exalted, century-old civil service focus on "merit" gives exactly *zero* points for that.

Let's compare their track records. Betty is a slob, a nose-picking, ass-scratching, knuckle-dragging ne'er-do-well with lousy work habits, major body odor, and Jack's secret sauce all over her tie. She walks into roll call at the last nanosecond. Her reports look like they've been written with a spoon. She doesn't speak, she mumbles. She's a lead-foot on patrol. Her favorite hobbies are washing out crimes in the black community, grousing about department policies and priorities, and working crosswords during SWAT missions. She takes more than the average number of sick days, which invariably fall just before or after her scheduled days off. She consistently pisses off her peers, and is a magnet for citizen complaints. Crime runs rampant on her beat but she has no interest in "partnering" with the community to prevent or solve it.

Mary is sharp, enthusiastic, demonstrably committed to professional police work. She gets to work early, reads up on suspects and incidents on and around her beat. She's an excellent communicator, on paper and in person. She gets along with, and appreciates, all sorts of people. She's a strong team player, collaborating with fellow patrol officers, detectives, and citizens. She's an idea person, always coming up with better ways to get the job done. When she disagrees with the brass she expresses her dissent forcefully but with class, respect. She seizes the initiative, analyzes problems thoughtfully—and solves them. Whether fighting crime or rendering aid, Mary gets the job done. Unlike Betty, she is experienced throughout the organization—and on her beat—as a fine, natural leader.

Alas, none of that stuff counts—Betty's stuff, Mary's stuff. There's not even a nod to this *true* test of one's "merit" in Seattle's Public Safety Civil Service Commission rules or procedures.

Shortly after I got to Seattle I assembled my staff and told them I wanted a report on each candidate certified for promotion. I then required our commanding officers to come in and present to my senior staff the strengths and limitations of each candidate who worked for them. Finally, I harvested the opinions of my senior leaders, asking each of them in turn: *If this were* your *call, whom would you promote?* And, *why?* Then I made my decision.

Not objective! shouted the union. *Political!* they howled. *Unfair!* they bellowed.

Bullshit! I countered, in calm, measured terms. I used my system (also used in San Diego and a few other cities) for the entire six years I was chief, the union fighting it all the way.

Funny, the guild was quiescent when I promoted one of their own, Don MacMillan. A white male member of the guild's board of directors, MacMillan was clearly one of the good guys: smart, seasoned, hard-working, and an outstanding coach of younger officers. He happened to be fourth or fifth on that "vertical" list of "certifieds." But he was clearly the best *leader* of the bunch so I made him a sergeant. The president of the guild had the temerity to whisper, unsarcastically, at a meeting, "Good choice, Chief." Yeah? Where were you when I promoted a more competent woman or ethnic minority ahead of a less competent white male who happened to have a higher civil service score? I'll tell you where you were. You were clinging to the ceiling of your office, nails planted in the tiles, screaming like a banshee and vowing to haul my ass into to court.

Which you did. In June 2004, the Washington State Supreme Court handed down a ruling against the guild saying, "Chief Stamper always had the discretion to select" from within the pool of certified candidates. An attorney for one of your clients had the extreme poor taste to question my right to promote MacMillan. Don, who'd performed superbly as a sergeant and who'd won the hearts of his squad and many others, died of cancer shortly before I retired. Call me sentimental, but I feel good about having given the man the job, and the recognition, he deserved.

Police unions complain that an assessment of an individual's on-the-job performance is "subjective." My response? You bet it is, and I wouldn't have it any other way.

You're not assessing a lawnmower or a computer. You're evaluating human beings, men and women engaged in sensitive work that involves other people. Look at men and women in other lines of work: No matter what the field (if it's not *too* esoteric), you can usually pick them out, the ones who are really good at what they do.

+ + +

Police departments *must* be representative of the communities they serve, and their leaders representative of the PD workforce. The black community, for example, needs to see similar faces, hear familiar voices in order to believe that the local law enforcement agency belongs to them as well as the white community. Black faces in leadership convey the message that the higher echelons are not the exclusive province of white leaders. That means women and ethnic minorities and gay cops on the front lines, women and ethnic minorities and gay cops all the way up to the executive suite. It does not mean promoting a candidate who's not up to the task.

As much as I fought for women and ethnic minorities and gays and lesbians to make it in our straight, white male–dominated police culture, I would never, ever promote a person I thought would fail.

It's this philosophy that led the city of Chicago to call me as an expert witness in defending against an anti–affirmative action suit filed by white detectives and supervisors. Unlike California and Washington State, Illinois, to its credit, still allows affirmative action in order to achieve true equal employment opportunity. The city won its case.

+ + +

Picking and promoting the right person has implications far beyond the moment. An individual cop, an individual supervisor has the power to crush or to affirm life, to tarnish or add luster to the reputation of a police force—for up to twenty-five or thirty years.

That is why I make no apologies for approaching the picking and promoting of people in a fundamentally *political* way. When would-be cops and would-be leaders ask how they can make themselves more hirable or more "promotable" I tell them: Study the qualifications and requirements first, and work to meet or exceed those requirements. Then study the *politics* of hiring, the *politics* of promotion. And master the political as well as the technical aspects of the job.

SDPD's decision to take a chance on me in 1965 was political. Mayor Norm Rice's decision to hire me as his police chief in 1994 was political. *Everything* about policing is ultimately political. Who gets which office: political. Which services are cut when there's a budget freeze: political. Who's going to fill the next homicide vacancy: political. Who gets hired, fired, promoted: political, political, political. The challenge for the honest police administrator is to make sure the politics of picking and promoting people is as fair as possible. And as mindful of the *greater good* of the organization and of the community as possible.

I hire my brother-in-law's cousin, a certifiable doofus, because he's got a bass boat I wouldn't mind borrowing—bad politics. I promote a drinking buddy because he's a kick in the ass, or because he's got something on me—bad politics. I pick an individual because he or she will add value to the organization and will serve the community honorably—good politics. It's the kind of politics I tried to play—even if the best person sat fourth not first on the list.

CHAPTER 18

STAYING ALIVE
IN A WORLD OF SUDDEN,
VIOLENT DEATH

LOGGING IS MORE DANGEROUS. So is fishing (if you value your life *do not* go crabbing on the Bering Sea in the dead of winter). Meatpacking is more perilous, as is piloting or navigating a plane, constructing or roofing a building, installing electrical power, plowing a field or harvesting crops or driving a truck. All of these occupations, and others, are less safe than police work. In fact, policing doesn't come close to cracking the Top Ten List of the country's most dangerous jobs. There are even two other municipal civil service jobs, fire fighting and refuse collection, that experience higher mortality rates than police. With over a million federal, state, and local law enforcement officers, the annual average for cops slain in the line of duty from 1990 to 2000? Sixty-four. Not a bad safety record.

But those numbers don't tell the real story. Police work is a very risky business. One that records over 57,000 assaults on police officers each year, resulting in thousands of injuries. It is also *the* most "emotionally dangerous" occupation in the country. Air traffic controllers might mount a good case, but when's the last time you heard of one of them getting shot on duty? Tree cutting may produce a higher death rate, but mortality on the job is less "personal"—like falling from seventy feet up (and hitting the ground at forty-six miles an hour) versus being shot to death.

Police officers live with the possibility of sudden, violent death every moment of their working lives.

+ + +

On a Sunday afternoon, six and a half months after slain police officers Timothy Ruopp and Kimberly Tonahill were buried (see chapter 4), a San Diego patrol officer stopped several young black men in Encanto, a neighborhood in southeast San Diego. A scuffle broke out between Officer Donovan Jacobs and twenty-three-year-old Sagon Penn, a martial arts expert. The two fell to the ground. Jacobs jumped on the suspect's chest. Moments later, SDPD agent Tom Riggs, in the company of a civilian ride-along, Sarah Peña Ruiz, showed up to help. Penn, flat on his back, wrestled Jacobs's pistol from its holster, knocked the officer back, and fired at Riggs who was approaching from several feet away. Riggs fell to the ground. Penn then turned and shot Jacobs. As both officers lay wounded, Penn walked to Riggs's car where he saw Peña Ruiz seated on the passenger side. He reached into the car and shot her. He then got into Jacobs's police car, drove over Jacobs's wounded body, and sped to his grandfather's house.

I was having dinner with a friend in North Park when I got the page. Twenty minutes later I was at the scene. The life-flight helicopter had just landed, its blades still rotating. Firefighters and medics hovered over Riggs. They gave him CPR, bandaged him, filled him full of tubes, lifted him onto a gurney. As they made their way past me, I brushed my hand over his head. "Tommy" was the son of Charlie Riggs, one of my sergeants at the academy back in the seventies. Charlie's boy did not look good.

Appearances can be deceiving, I told myself. But years of observing near-dead bodies offered little hope. Still, I prayed and prayed for him to pull through.

I was about halfway to the hospital when I got word that Riggs was DOA. I changed direction and headed toward the east county hospital where Jacobs lay in critical condition. One officer was already gone, there seemed to be little hope the other would make it. I stood by Jacobs's bed for hours, making somber small talk with the cops who penetrated, one or two at a time, the hospital's protocol. Sometime after midnight the officer's condition improved. Doctors were guardedly hopeful.

I drove home to Solana Beach, heartsick once again. The day's toll: one cop deceased, another in critical condition, run over by his own car and left for dead, an innocent observer who, while she would survive her flesh wound, would never be the same.*

Three days later I met with my captains in a sun-drenched conference room in Qualcom Stadium. I hadn't slept much in the past seventy-two hours. I was anxious, afraid that Tommy's death would not be the last, that the next was just around the corner.

The city was in the middle of a long run of officer fatalities: ten killed in the line of duty in eight years, the highest mortality rate for any police department in the country. Privately, I'd come to the conclusion that too many of our cops were simply unfit for the job. That's not a judgment you announce to your officers, but deep in my heart I knew it to be true. And I felt personally responsible. I was the patrol chief during the time that three of those cops went down. And I'd taught all ten at the academy.

In truth, several of the officers hadn't stood a chance. Ron Ebeltoft and Keith Tiffany were ambushed in 1981 when they responded to a neighborhood dispute. They'd just gotten out of their cars when they were dropped in their tracks by a mentally disturbed man with a high-powered rifle (who'd been warring with a neighbor over a rosebush and a property line). Kirk Johnson had pulled up next to a parked San Diego sheriff's vehicle for a friendly, cross-jurisdictional chat when without warning he was shot in the face. Behind the wheel of the sheriff's car: the joyriding seventeen-year-old stepson of a sheriff's sergeant who'd dressed up in his stepdaddy's uniform, including a .357 magnum revolver. The kid had panicked when the PD unit pulled up alongside him.

But what of the others? Patrol Officer Dennis Allen had been fooled into thinking a suspect was armed with only a knife when the man pulled

---

* Jacobs survived, though he was permanently disabled. His justification for the traffic stop and his conduct at the scene were challenged at two separate murder trials. According to eyewitnesses, he had screamed at Penn as he straddled him, raining down blows, "You think you're bad, nigger? I'm gonna beat your black ass." (Jacobs acknowledged on the stand using a racial epithet, and it was shown that he'd been counseled for racial insensitivity back in the academy.) Penn's lawyer claimed his client's actions were in self-defense, and said of Jacobs that he was an "ideal candidate for the Ku Klux Klan," a "Doberman pinscher of a cop" whose conduct had sullied the good name of the San Diego Police Department. Jacobs went on to study law during a six-year run of light-duty assignments after the incident. He became an attorney representing police officers in personal injury, wrongful termination, defamation, and discrimination suits.

a handgun from the back of his waistband and shot him dead.* And Ruopp and Tonahill in Grape Street Park? Had those two officers been adequately trained? Were they guided by sound policies and procedures? Were they equipped properly? Were they sufficiently alert? Had they practiced sound safety procedures that awful night? *No.* No to each question. Their deaths could easily have been prevented. I was certain of it. I took it out on my captains.

"Look, goddamn it, these officers work for you! Are they *trained* and *equipped* and *able* to do the job? Do you *know* them? Do you know their strengths, their weaknesses? Do you have confidence in them?" Their blank expressions only made me angrier. "Consider this an order: Every cop who works for you *will* have the street smarts, the mental toughness, the physical fitness and upper-body strength for this job. *Your* job is to see to it that each and every one of your cops makes it home at end of shift. Understood?"

Upper-body strength? What else was that but a reference to women officers? It was, in fact, an implicit reference to Kimberly Tonahill. (A lot of our people never knew what the chief and I had learned the night we went to the Tonahill residence to give her mom the news. Kimberly had been to two funerals within a week's time, the second on the day of her own death, two of her dearest friends having committed suicide. Don't let anyone tell you a cop can just "shake off" something like that and hit the streets fully alert. Cops are human, like everyone else.) Was Tonahill strong enough and tough enough to be on duty that night? Was she strong enough and tough enough to be a cop? I had my doubts.

I bow to no one in my support for women police officers. But I wanted my captains to understand that under no circumstances was it okay to put a cop out there who couldn't pull his—or her—own weight.

After the meeting Winston Yetta, my central division captain, approached me. Yetta was one of my favorite people. We'd worked the same beat on overlapping watches when I was a rookie. He'd taught me a

---

* The suspect had been released on bail earlier that same day. The charge: attempted murder of a police officer.

lot about *good* police work, especially how to talk to people. He evidently thought it was time for remedial training.

"You're not the only one hurting, you know."

"What?"

"We're *all* hurting."

I apologized to Yetta, and later to my other captains. But, this was no time for a pity party—or a guilt fest. It was time to stop our cops from getting killed.

+ + +

Bill Kolender accepted my proposal for an officer safety task force. A big one, with dozens of police officers, defensive tactics and firearms instructors, civilian analysts, legal experts—a total of eighty-five members. We would break down into groups and examine in detail every facet of officer safety and survival: the department's philosophy of policing; policies and procedures; whom we were hiring, and why and how; staffing levels and scheduling; safety equipment; training; safety inspections and controls; and critical incident critiques. We all took the pledge in our search for truth: no sacred cows; no getting defensive; egos and ranks checked at the door.

Every subject was critical, but none raised more hackles than "department philosophy."

+ + +

Shortly after Kolender became chief in the mid-1970s, the senior staff went off for a retreat. They affirmed, with varying degrees of enthusiasm, their commitment to a "humanistic" approach to policing, to "community-oriented" and "participatory" management of the department, to an "open" style of communication and decision making.

Even though as a captain I hadn't been invited to the Big Boys' retreat, I'd worked closely with Bob Burgreen, a deputy chief at the time, and with Kolender. Kolender was my "patron." I was his unofficial speechwriter, composing eulogies for fallen officers, and his not very secret confidant. We three were among the most "liberal" cops in the country. Our enlightened philosophy had found its way into training syllabi, department policies and procedures, just about everything official. And our open, humanistic, progressive worldview had become the "company line." What did the rank and file think of all this? They thought it was all a bunch of happy horseshit.

+ + +

It was no surprise when the first meeting of the philosophy committee exploded into angry denunciations of department policies—and of those of us who wrote or promoted them: We were more interested in "PR" than officer safety; we automatically took the side of citizens who beefed cops for aggressive crime fighting; we bent over backward to protect the civil liberties of pukes, assholes, hairballs, and assorted other lowlifes—even as we would sell out a cop in a heartbeat; we handcuffed our officers with restrictions on use of force, and on force-reporting requirements; we deadened their enthusiasm with nitpicking discipline; we mortified them in the eyes of their peers in other agencies with all our non-cop fancy talk of "community" this and "humanistic" that. Daryl Gates—now there was a *real* police chief. And LAPD—there was a *real* police department.

I'd written myself a one-word note before the meeting and stuffed it in my pocket. *Listen!* it said. Throughout the meeting I fingered the scrap of paper nonstop, willing the word to travel up my arm and into my brain. I did listen. Empathetically, if not always sympathetically. I heard cops making complete sense, from their point of view. They were bone honest. They were "open" in their communication.

Until the very end I was doing fine, honoring my pocketed admonition, gaining insights into certain policy changes we *might* need to make. But when "Larry Johnston," a patrol officer, informed the group that SDPD was inferior to the National City Police Department, I almost lost it. I knew the cops in my old hometown. I knew, as did everyone else in the room, that their chief had recently boasted of hiring San Diego's rejects—cops we'd fired for documented cases of racism and brutality! This was just too much.

"That's a crock of shit, Johnston, and you know it. You can't really believe National City's a better police department."

"Let's just say their chief's got balls."

"Oh?"

"Yeah. The man lets his cops be cops. He backs them when they take action. He doesn't apologize when they generate a little heat."

"Such as?"

"You know, when they have to get a little rough out there. He doesn't get all bent out of shape about people's 'civil rights.' "

"So he looks the other way when his cops break the law?"

"*No!* Well . . . yeah. Maybe. I don't mean *break* the law. I'm just saying sometimes you have to *bend* it out there in the real world. Get creative. Let the pukes know who's boss. We shouldn't have to live in fear that if some asshole beefs us for doing our jobs the chief won't back us. That's all I'm saying."

I gave him a short, faintly condescending lecture on the Bill of Rights. He shot right back, "That's all fine and dandy, Chief. But you're not out there getting your ass shot at. Are you?"

"Touché." In fact, I'd never had my ass shot at (neither had he, for that matter) but his statement did bring us back to the subject: namely, cops dropping like flies in our town, and how to put a stop to it.

I remembered a conversation we'd had in the chief's office just weeks before the Ruopp-Tonahill killings. Another deputy chief mentioned he'd been a cop for over thirty years and couldn't remember the last time he'd pulled his gun, if in fact he'd *ever* pulled it. The damn thing might as well have been superglued inside his holster. "You'd probably be dead today," I'd said, reflecting on all the guns I'd seen and heard about in recent years.

+ + +

By the mid-seventies it seemed that every other car our officers stopped had a gun in it. And every other family beef, too. And every interaction with bangers and drug dealers. But I understood where my colleague was coming from. Hell, when I went through the academy it had been thirty-seven years since a San Diego cop had been slain in the line of duty. No wonder we were "out of touch." Our world had been different, certainly far less deadly, from the world of today's beat cops.

+ + +

"Look," I told Johnston. "There's no way we're going to ignore the Constitution. And we're not about to stop taking citizen complaints, or investigating them. That said, what *can* we do to back you, to help you make it home safely?"

"Easy," he said. "Make safety a goddamn priority around here. Make it as important as PR. You guys are always talking about 'professional conduct,' and 'treating people with dignity and respect,' and, like you said, 'encouraging community feedback.' Hell, you even cooperate with the *media*." He spat out the word. "You tell *them* more than you tell us. Well, how about talking to *us* more? How about *thinking* and *talking* and *doing something about* officer safety? And when it comes to training and equipment, how about putting your money where your mouth is?"

He couldn't have been more correct in his analysis. We'd created an appalling imbalance in our administrative philosophy, and in our priorities. In our noble, concerted effort to "humanize" both the workplace and relations between cops and citizens, we'd paid criminally insufficient attention to the most primitive imperative of our cops: the need to survive. We had taken officer safety for granted.

+ + +

Part of my personal failure on this front was borne of a belief that we had too many paranoid cops (in the popular, not the clinical meaning of the term)—police officers who failed to do the job because they were *excessively* fearful. Obsessed with personal safety, they put their own well-being above that of the citizenry. My thoughts on the topic have not changed.

One unavoidable aspect of the job, no matter how much attention the agency pays to safety, is *risk*. It galls me to hear of a police officer who observes, say, a man beating a woman—and who refuses to drive forty feet down the block and stop the guy unless he's got backup. By the time backup arrives that woman could be dead. A police officer who lets that happen is a lousy, yellow-bellied, chickenshit excuse of a cop.

(Years later, one of my staunchest Seattle detractors, a grizzled detective, seemed to agree with me on this point. During a brief lull in the World Trade Organization [WTO] riots we passed each other in the police garage.

With a look of genuine disgust on his face, he told me he was sick and tired of cops pissing and moaning about taking rocks and bottles on the streets downtown. "Hell, we faced a lot worse in my day [a time when antiwar riots occurred regularly in Seattle, when banks were being bombed to smithereens, when violent demonstrators were taking it out on cops]. It was just us against them. We didn't have all this ninja shit—ballistic helmets, shields, vests. *Shin guards*, for chrissakes . . ." I reminded him how bad it was out there on the streets. "Ah, they're still a bunch a pussies," he said as got into his car and drove off. As usual, he'd overstated his case. As usual, he couldn't resist a sexist allusion. As usual, there was a kernel of truth to his rant.)

+ + +

Our safety task force, under the skillful direction of Commander Mike Rice, researched *everything* that had to do with officer safety. Members traveled to numerous other police agencies, including those in Los Angeles and L.A. County, Oakland, Sacramento, San Francisco, San Jose, Phoenix, Oklahoma City, and most other San Diego County departments including, yes, National City. They visited the California Commission on Peace Officer Standards and Training and returned with several officer-safety nuggets.

They also spent time in San Quentin. As executive director of the mayor's crime commission a few years earlier, I'd witnessed prison inmates buffing up physically, as they do in most prisons. But these guys were also drilling one another endlessly on how to disarm and kill cops. (I couldn't believe it when prison officials told us they'd been ordered by the courts to allow it. It was the inmates exercising their First Amendment rights.)

When we were finished, some twenty-two weeks and 235 committee and subcommittee meetings later, we had produced 119 recommendations for improving officer safety. One hundred and two were quickly approved. Within a year all but thirteen had been fully implemented. Not bad for a large, sluggish, political, paramilitary bureaucracy like ours.

+ + +

Indirectly related to the task force effort, I'd assigned John Morrison, a bright, sharp-tongued lieutenant, to reenact on video the Grape Street Park shootings. Using police employees (including in the "starring" role a beat cop who looked uncannily like Joselito Cinco), Morrison and his crew made a remarkable film. Hard to watch for its graphic reminder of the tragedy, it showed clearly what went wrong that foggy night in September 1984. Out of the project came a new department policy, new training, and a new method for handling such "routine" interactions. We called it "Contact & Cover," and insisted that every officer follow its dictates. Law enforcement agencies all over the country requested and received a copy of the video. I would bet my own life that "Contact & Cover"* has saved the lives of police officers and citizens.

Three other task force–inspired improvements stand out: (1) the development of an intensive eighty-hour block of officer survival training at the academy—realistic "experiential" instruction that far surpassed the traditional "defensive tactics" and "arrest and control techniques" taught previously; (2) the burial of the "low-bid" mentality that had characterized city purchasing to that point, and the naming of a new safety officer whose sole responsibility was to search for, purchase, and oversee the maintenance of the finest possible safety equipment—without regard to cost; and (3) the adoption of a four-day workweek.

If police work isn't the most stressful job on the planet, it comes close. Creating a schedule that gave our cops an extra day off each week (in exchange for extending the workday an additional two hours) had become a personal crusade with me. I agreed with my cops who said they needed an extra day to decompress, to come down from the demands of the job. The "10-Plan" was a family-friendly step that could only help in building *morale*, a factor often overlooked in the search for causes of a department's poor safety record. A demoralized force is an unsafe force—risky for the cops, and risky for the citizens they serve.

---

* The task force talked a lot about the need to keep safety procedures confidential, for fear of compromising them. I think a lot of cops go overboard on this issue, but not in this case. Which is why you won't find an explanation of the actual procedures here.

+ + +

Taking that last point into account, soon after the task force had completed its work the command staff met in a daylong workshop to consider other ways to boost department morale. Ours was a force of men and women who clearly believed, with ample reason, that they were underappreciated—and understaffed.

I'd been saying for months that San Diego was a "dangerously under-policed city," that we had too few cops to get the job done effectively, and safely. My statement won nods from the cops, of course, and from most in the community. But when I made it to a reporter I got a call the next day from the city manager. "Did he quote you accurately?" said Jack McGrory.

"Yep."

"Do me a favor," he said.

"What's that?

"Don't say it again."

"10-4." It was okay, he said, for me to tell folks we were "understaffed." Euphemisms in politics are not only ubiquitous, they're actually under-standable. But they sure suck sometimes.

+ + +

One of the outcomes of the command staff workshop was a decision to assert San Diego's commitment to all things excellent, in officer safety and in service to the community. How? Ken Moller and Dick Toneck, a couple of veteran captains, suggested we announce to the world that we were the *best* police department in the country. A short time later the entire fleet sported *America's Finest* signs.

Much more administrative work was needed, of course, in order to keep the phrase from being turned into a source of derision rather than pride: We had to sell our sweeping, costly changes in officer safety to the city council.

It was Bill Kolender's finest hour. He and Burgreen pored over the officer-safety task force report. Burgreen put his number-crunchers to work, then had a series of sit-downs with Kolender, helping the super-chief polish his presentation to the city council. At the meeting in council chambers Kolender gained and held the attention of the elected officials from start to finish. Not that they weren't already motivated—San Diego police officer mortality had become a hot political issue. One council member in particular, Mike Gotch, a liberal Democrat, had made officer safety his top priority. The result? Not a blank check, but damn near. From a notoriously stingy city council.

Within months we had painted our insipid all-white police cars black-and-white, and purchased a slew of other equipment. There was even money (though not nearly enough) in the budget for new police officer positions. With 1.6 officers per thousand citizens versus NYPD's six per thousand or LAPD's 2.6 or Seattle's 2.5, San Diego remains to this day a *dangerously under-policed* city.

Edward Conlon in *Blue Blood*, a riveting first-person account of life in the NYPD, paints a sharply contrasting picture of workplace pressures and demands of patrol officers. In patrol, Conlon would get three or four calls a shift. I remember shagging twenty-four calls in a single eight-hour shift, and averaging twelve or thirteen. Conlon had time to read the paper or a book on the job. His backup, which when summoned would show up in droves, was usually half a minute to a minute away. In San Diego, a city of four hundred square miles, you were lucky, working any of its outlying beats, if your backup arrived within fifteen minutes. Comparing officer mortality rates, which adjusts for department population, it's far more dangerous being a cop in sunny San Diego than in New York City.

+ + +

Even with a woefully understaffed force, those improvements in officer safety really paid off. The number of officers slain in the line of duty since 1985? Three, including one killed, deliberately, in a traffic incident. (Several other San Diego officers have been killed in traffic accidents both on- and off-duty.)

That's three too many, of course, but it does show that a police administration that cares about its cops can have a powerful, positive effect on officer mortality rates. And given San Diego's enviable record of steady crime reductions since that era, I think we can infer a positive relationship between officer safety and crime fighting (not to mention the effects of authentic versus "PR" versions of community policing). So, it's not just the cops and their families who benefit when police officers' health, safety, and morale are scrupulously attended to. Everybody wins.

+ + +

Having been for years too laid back and ignorant about the issue, I vowed that the safety of my officers would be forevermore my number-one internal priority. (I took this attitude to Seattle where I found cops still packing .38 revolvers, an administrative laxity quickly remedied with .40-caliber Glock semiautos.)

I forbade myself from ever again uttering something you hear all too often from police brass, as if it's a cost of doing business: "It's not a question of *if* but *when* another officer gets killed in the line of duty." That's a fatalistic, passive way of thinking. It feeds rank-and-file fears of the "inevitability" of on-the-job mortality.

Most police officer deaths can be prevented, but it's got to start with excellent training—and a confident attitude. Cops who believe they're going to get shot, or who believe they're going to die if they do get shot, need reprogramming. Their outlook should be: *Somebody takes a shot at me, I'm going to drop, roll, and fire back.* And: *If someone is lucky enough to put a bullet in me, I will not die of it.* That's not an expression of "hope." It's a *survivor's mentality.*

+ + +

Officer Johnston, the task force cop who instructed me on the need to *think* safety, *talk* safety, *deliver* safety, was absolutely right. But he was wrong on one important point: He assumed it wasn't possible to fight crime, be safe, *and* honor civil liberties.

I ended that first session of the philosophy committee with an "ethos statement," that would quickly reverberate throughout the department. I could have put it more delicately, I suppose, but it seemed to work magic with the cops:

I am a police officer. I'm not here to hurt you, or to embarrass or demean you. Or to violate your rights. I'm here to help. Whether I'm returning your lost child or arresting you for harming a child, I'll treat you with dignity and respect.

But know this: I was not placed on this earth to be your victim. I don't care if you're the police chief or the mayor or the biggest shot in town, I am not your victim. I don't care if you "know the chief personally," I am not your victim. I don't care how big you are, how menacing you are, I am not your victim. I don't care if you file a complaint with Internal Affairs, I am not your victim. I am *nobody's* victim. So don't even *think* about pulling that gun, or that knife.

I will do you harm only in my own defense or the defense of another. But if it comes to a physical or armed confrontation I will not lose to you.

In other words, I am not to be fucked with.

CHAPTER 19

UNDERCOVER

WHAT DO YOU PICTURE when you think of police undercover work? Narcs, right? Long-haired, unshaven dudes in foul-smelling Harley T-shirts who talk the talk of the streets, work informants, sidle up to dealers, score drugs, and pop the sellers. Indeed, most undercover cops *are* narcs. But there's a different breed out there, one that became virtually extinct during the seventies: the police spy who infiltrates political groups, befriends social activists, and reports his findings back to HQ. That's the kind of spy I was in the late sixties, at the height of antiwar protests, campus uprisings, and civil rights demonstrations.

Shame being an effective muzzle, I've never made this story public until now. But now is an important time to tell it. With antiwar, antiglobalization, antigovernment sentiments and demonstrations nearing a fever pitch, pressures are building to put "narcs" back into the political mix.

+ + +

Having resolved in 1967 to mend my evil ways, and having accepted exclusive personal responsibility for transforming American policing, I expanded my crusade to include the rectification of the way my colleagues saw the *world*—not just their work. They were wrong about Vietnam, gun control, capital punishment. They upheld imperialism, ethnocentrism, fascism, racism, classism, sexism, elitism—and every other flaw I could attach an *ism* to. They were, *I* was, part of an occupational army, the oppressive arm of a repressive establishment. We, the police, were "running dogs" of corporate Amerika, defenders of an insidious military-industrial complex, foot soldiers in the war against minorities, the poor, the disenfranchised.

Reading is a dangerous thing, and I'd been doing a lot of it. When I'd started my studies at Southwestern Community College I didn't know Schopenhauer from Eisenhower, Aesop from Alsop. But now I was reading everything I could get my hands on, not just sociology, psychology, politics, and criminology but literature: Barth, Grass, O'Connor, Bellow, Hesse, Kafka, and the Russians Tolstoy, Dostoevsky, and Yevtushenko. I was making up for lost time. Early on, I'd not been a good student. My elementary school report cards spoke of my "potential"—and how I was in no immediate danger of realizing it. My reading, writing, and arithmetic skills were all "below standard." But my biggest problem was behavioral. "Norman continues to be a disruptive influence in class," wrote Miss Weir, my sixth-grade teacher. She could have saved herself a lot of time if she'd bought a stamp. Every other day, it seemed, she handed me a note to take home to my parents.

Years later, I was a disruptive influence in the workplace. I remember laying my newfound political consciousness, in all its manifest glory, on a dazed rookie as we drank coffee and he feasted on a chocolate doughnut with sprinkles at the Winchell's at Fortieth and Meade. I was halfway through my lecture when he got a routine call. "Well, back to work," he said. "Thanks for the information." He dumped his coffee and took off.

"Don't forget what I said," I yelled after him.

The next morning I got a call at home. I was to meet my C.O., Lieutenant Jay Helmick, at Louie's drive-in in National City. So this is how they do it, I remember thinking. They believe I'm a communist. They're going to fire me. After only two years on the job. At *Louie's*.

The new Louie's had just opened at the north end of town. It was indistinguishable from a Denny's. The old one, a hangout during the days of our R&B band, had looked like a 1930s national park lodge—except for the giant neon faces of a cow and a pig, one pink, the other blue, atop its sweeping dormers. It was open 24/7, served breakfast around the clock, and played host to our countless philosophical / political / musical raps.

I walked into Louie's and saw the back of Helmick's shaved head in a corner booth. Seated in the cop's spot, facing the entrance, was Ken O'Brien. I'd met O'Brien when he flitted in and out of the Sex Crimes office during my Pink Beret days in Balboa Park (see chapter 26). He was the chief of

Intelligence. One look at him and you knew O'Brien didn't follow orders, he gave them. His passions, known to all, served a view of the world jarringly out of alignment with mine. What was he doing here? What was *I* doing here? It had all the makings of some kind of an IA investigation.

"Sit down, Stamper." Helmick nodded toward the empty space next to him. I slid in. "Here's the deal," said O'Brien. "I'm putting you in a deep cover assignment." His leg was aquiver under the table; he was one of those compulsive leg bouncers who made you think *earthquake!* if you sat next to him at a poker game. "This isn't about busting fags. Or sucking up martinis in Mission Valley." O'Brien had done his homework. (Three other patrol officers and I had just finished a week of undercover at the Hanalei Hotel, dining high on the hog, guzzling upscale booze, smoking Cohibas in the hot tub, and getting careless with our room keys and the "flash rolls" the department had given us. We were looking to bust a prolific room prowler, but all we'd been able to nab was a sixteen-year-old panty burglar who'd fled security from the Motel Six next door.) "You're going to infiltrate the commies and pinkos at UCSD, and wherever else you find them." He tried to take me out in a stare-down. Surely he knew my politics, was testing me. I held his stare. "We need to know what they're up to, their every move."

Did he make a distinction between that fringe of lefties who bombed buildings or derailed trains, and those of us who opposed the war, who thought America could do better by its poor and its minorities? Apparently not. "They're *thugs*," he said. "Two-bit thugs hiding behind their goddam 'ideology.' Or, they're daddy's little rich kids, bored and spoiled rotten. Either way, you're going learn what they're up to, whether it's the Panthers or the long-haired pukes out in La Jolla." He was particularly scornful of "that commie creep, Marcuse," which he pronounced Marcoosey.

+ + +

Herbert Marcuse, author of *One-Dimensional Man* and *Eros and Civilization*, among other works, was born in Berlin in 1898. He left Germany soon after Hitler's rise to power and lived briefly in Switzerland before coming to the U.S. He became a citizen in 1940, and worked for a time in the government's Office of Strategic Services, precursor to the CIA. He taught at Columbia, Harvard, and Brandeis before joining the faculty at the University of California at San Diego in the mid-sixties.

I'd never heard of the guy. I didn't know he was widely regarded as the Father of the New Left, that his writings had influenced generations of Marxists, and that Angela Davis, also at UCSD, was a protégé.

+ + +

The meeting over, Helmick told me I would report to Patrol/third watch (P3) that night, my last shift before disappearing from the department. The "official" word was that I had, indeed, been fired from SDPD.

+ + +

Truth is layered, I think. There are the cheap surface truths, an extrinsic layer of declarations we make to others and to ourselves that are accurate—but incomplete, or irrelevant or unimportant. Below these surface truths are other truths, more meaningful but sometimes painful to acknowledge. Below them, buried deep in the unconscious, is the final layer of truth. Real Truth. That's how I see it, anyway.

Real Truth still scares me, sometimes. I like to pretend it doesn't but it does. Especially if it hits me at a bad time, leaving me stuck with more information than I want.

How could I possibly infiltrate the radical left in San Diego? How could I spy on my ideological allies? As I drove home I considered ways to get out of it. O'Brien would be pissed, Helmick embarrassed. But that would be their problem. By the time I pulled into our driveway, though, I'd found enough in the surface truths to justify the assignment. Some of these "idealists" were, as O'Brien had put it, ruthless, single-minded zealots bent on criminal violence as a means of political expression. Some were wingnuts along for the ride, happy to pitch Molotov cocktails for the sheer fun of it. And hadn't Deputy Chief Gore's son, Lieutenant Larry Gore, almost been taken out by a sniper's bullet during our last riot? Terrorism in the name of "the Movement" was morally reprehensible, and stupid. *Someone* needed to sneak in there and disrupt those bastards.

But had the Real Truth revealed itself in '68? Would I have turned in my badge before taking the assignment? I think so.

This is what the Real Truth would have announced to me as I prepared to tell Dottie about the big change coming up in our lives: *O'Brien's like your old man, isn't he? When you were a kid he beat feelings of unworthiness into your flesh. But now? He respects you, has confidence in you. He's entrusting you with a job that's never been done before, a dangerous, sensitive job. You want to take the assignment because it represents another nail in the coffin of doubts you've had about your adequacy as a human being.*

The next morning I drove out of the POA parking lot in a "cool car," a ten-year-old Ford station wagon that had been chopped or raked or whatever it's called when you drop the front end a foot and raise the back three. It had been painted a deep metallic green and fitted out with moon caps. Not exactly befitting a campus radical but it was the best of the seized stock on hand.

I'd just been briefed, exhaustively, by O'Brien. Again, an assignment with no gun, no radio. And this time, unlike my work as a "Pink Beret" there would be no badge. There would be no visits to the station. I would not be wired unless absolutely necessary, and O'Brien would see to it that it would never become absolutely necessary. This was *deep* cover, pure intelligence gathering. I'd make no arrests, or do anything that would make me as a cop. For at least a year.

My previous undercover work was merely sneaky—I'd disguised but not replaced myself. This assignment called for more drastic measures. All of my records at the PD had been sealed and removed from Personnel. I held my own records-sealing ritual at home, wrapping a rubber band around my driver's license, credit cards, a picture of Dottie and Matt. I stuffed the bundle in the bottom of my sock drawer. When my hair had grown a bit shaggy and my face showed the makings of a beard I drove the cool car down to the DMV in Chula Vista.

"Yep, tha's right," I told the woman behind the counter. "Hit was *turrible.*" I winced for her, recalling the tragedy. "Lost ever'thang. The whole trailer up in smoke. *Woosh!*" It had been caused by faulty wiring, I told her. The fire back home in Corpus Christi. "Ever last thang I owned, burnt to a crisp. My wallet, birth certificate. I got nothin' left. Not a single worldly possession." Did I have a local address? "Nope, I just pulled into town two days ago. That's why the P.O. box. I'm livin' out of my friend's car at the moment." I was in search of a job, maybe she knew of something?

I passed the written, then the driving—no "California stops," parallel-parked with reasonable precision, didn't hit anyone. I went to window three to have my eyesight checked and my picture taken. Three weeks later my official fake ID arrived at the P.O. box.

I'd decided to keep my first name. O'Brien was right: anyone, someone I'd arrested, an old high school buddy, even a naïve or malicious cop, could shout it out in a sensitive situation and blow my cover. Cops, I would soon learn, were the worst. A few weeks after my trip to the DMV a beat cop in Old Town yelled out my name from the front seat of his patrol car. "Hey, Norm! What are you working? You dirty or something?" *Idiot! Don't you remember what they told you in the academy?* You *never* acknowledge an undercover. Thank God, I was alone. Still, I copped an attitude and shot him a withering glare. He cringed, apparently in recognition of his faux pas. I wondered what he'd think when he learned I'd been fired.

The cool car had been registered in my new name, through contacts in Sacramento, and I'd been licensed to drive. Beyond that I was a man with no history. I concocted a cover story (one that didn't require me to affect a Texas accent).

I spent hours in the downtown library and at SDSU and UCSD reading up on the Students for a Democratic Society, the Black Panther Party, and other lefty political organizations. I took a crash course on Marx, Lenin, Hegel, Trotsky, Marcuse. And on Malcolm X, Stokely Carmichael, Eldridge Cleaver, Che Guevara, Fidel Castro. I bought, read, and carried around Mao's little red book. The cool car was littered with back issues of campus and underground newspapers.

I'd made a decision to interrupt my own studies at SDSU. I'd be too busy, for one thing. But also I wasn't sure I could pull it off: a maniacal-looking, red-bearded, afro-haired honky in a peacoat festooned with the distinctive red-and-gold Mao pin. How would I fit in with a bunch of criminal justice majors who looked like Dobie Gillis and Gidget?

Within a month I had infiltrated the UCSD chapter of SDS. I attended meetings, ran the mimeo machine, leafleted, did other did shit work, marched in antiwar protests, participated in sit-ins, and demonstrated against ROTC and Dow Chemical recruiters at the university. As my face became better known, and trusted, I was invited to social events off campus (dopeless parties where people talked the same talk they talked on campus). In time I penetrated the inner circle of La Jolla's "radical chic," meeting black militants and later some of the "old left" forces, similar to the marvelous, romantic communists seen in Warren Beatty's movie *Reds*. I was in on strategy planning sessions. I wrote for and had articles published in one of the underground papers. My 35mm camera had become as trusted and as ubiquitous as I was.

Every week I met with my contact, Bud Bennett, SDPD Intelligence. We'd meet in a different place each time, a busy coffee shop usually, somewhere in the vastness of San Diego County. I handed him a five- to fifteen-page report, documenting what I'd seen and heard. Who was planning what? Where? When? How? Why? As I stood at my makeshift stand-up desk puffing away on my pipe and hammering at the keys of the antique Royal, I felt like a reporter. An investigative reporter.

When moral anxiety cropped up from time to time, which it did often enough, I stuck its head under water and held it there. I'd heard enough rumors and direct threats to know that a small minority of crazies and dyed-in-the-wool anti-Amerikan forces were capable of following through on their threats: to bomb a troop train, or take down Richard Nixon (or Hubert Humphrey) on a campaign swing through San Diego, or turn in a phony call for the police and then "off the pigs" when they showed up (none of the above, incidentally, was suggested by SDS members but by off-campus, loudmouthed "agitators"). Because I was often present when threats were made and demonstrations planned, I was able to sort them out, weigh them on a scale of potential violence. Rarely did I have our patrol cops called in; most often my intelligence was used to keep my fellow cops at bay. But there was this one time . . .

+ + +

"They say they gonna off the sister. *Tomorrow!*" It was "David," my source. He sounded like a sassy black woman on the phone. In truth, he was a skinny white guy. Short, intense, with Trotsky's beard and glasses. He spouted Marxist theory nonstop. He was on record, my record, on the need for the violent overthrow of the government.

David showed up, Zelig-like, everywhere (something that could have been said of me), but I did notice that, like me, he never took the mike at rallies or demonstrations to demand that we bomb the admiral's home over in Coronado or torch police headquarters down on Market. He did do a lot of ranting, though, in our small-cell conversations. Others mostly dismissed him. I took him for an FBI snitch with a loose circuit. But he was in the know on a lot of stuff.

"They mean business, Norm. It'll be bad for the Movement and, I'm telling you, she's as good as dead even as we speak." I put the phone down, tugged at my bushy beard and peered through rimless glasses at the rain and lights of Rosecrans. It was a Sunday, just before midnight. I'd been working sixteen-hour days, six or seven days a week for months. Throughout that day I'd been sniffing out the same rumors David had apparently picked up: that a contingent of black men from UC Santa Barbara was headed for San Diego to "silence" Angela Davis.

What did that mean? Were they going to caucus with her, get her to agree to lower her profile in the Movement? Davis, tall, eloquent, charismatic, had garnered a great deal of national and international media attention. One rumor was that her clout was undermining the role and status of indigenous black male leaders, and inspiring people like Daniel Patrick Moynihan to write, in "The Negro Family: The Case for National Action," of the power of the "black matriarchy" in America. Black women, he'd written, had a disproportionate influence over both family and community life because of the absence of strong men. Such men being absent owing to their rates of incarceration—and death by homicide. Another possibility: Certain black militants were unhappy with Davis's ideology, her political priorities. They wanted her to rearrange those priorities so that she would be less a New Left Marxist, more a black nationalist or liberationist.*

---

* Davis was, in fact, a member of the Black Panther Party, the Student Nonviolent Coordinating Committee, and the American Communist Party.

Whatever its reasons, was the Santa Barbara crowd's unhappiness with Davis enough to want her whacked? I didn't know, which was why I'd had my ear to the ground that Sunday. My conversation with David, however loopy, clinched it. I had to call in the troops.

+ + +

In police work you get all kinds of chances to choose between two wrongs: do something when you should do nothing, or do nothing when you should do something.

+ + +

It was now after midnight. I slipped two dimes into the slot and waited for Bud to pick up. It was a short conversation, ended by Bud with, "I gotta call the boss right away. If you're right about this thing we don't have any time to use."

"You mean if *David* is right." I wanted as much distance between me and loony tunes as possible.

And yet, I wanted loony tunes to be right.

I may have been a "liberal" cop but I was still a cop. I was hardwired for action and hadn't gotten any for several months. Don't let any police officer tell you otherwise: We talk crime prevention, and some of us even mean it, but we live for the moment the bank gets robbed or the murder fugitive is spotted on our beat.

It's not that I wanted anyone to get hurt, especially Dr. Davis. I admired her for her courage—she was taking a lot of heat from people who, I thought, should have been on her side—and her ability to calmly, forcefully present the case against racism, classism, imperialism, the war in Vietnam. The ideal scenario? The dudes from Santa Barbara show up on campus, pull all manner of artillery out of knapsacks and duffel bags, and get taken down by a small army of my (armed) undercover colleagues. No shots fired, the day saved.

As much as I wanted to be involved in the arrests it was out of the question. My cover had taken months to establish and was too important to blow. If we were going to go with undercover operatives the best choice would be narcs, *real* narcs. Even if they got burned they'd have no trouble going right back to their buy-busts on the streets of City Heights or Barrio Logan.

Throughout the night detective supervisors were on the phone, scaring up dirties. In the end they rounded up only four, three from Narcotics, one from Fencing. Plus a number of plainclothes detectives and their supervisors.

Foregoing sleep altogether for what seemed like the hundredth time in two years, I took a quick predawn tour of the campus at UCSD. Nothing. No doors propped open, nobody lurking on the balcony of the big central library that overlooked the free-speech square. I hit the parking lots, getting out once to palm the hoods of a small pickup and a van parked side by side near a grove of bluegum eucalyptuses. Both were cold.

Back in the car, I drove down I-5 for my first and only headquarters visit during the undercover stint. I parked three blocks away and walked up to the Pacific Highway entrance. It was still dark out. Bud let me in. We walked up the stairs and into the Intelligence office. "He don't smell as bad as he looks, boys," he announced to a room full of cops, most of them dirties or detectives, slurping from styrofoam cups. O'Brien, standing just outside his office, was the only one in coat and tie. The cops eyed me warily. It occurred to me that most of them had never seen me. I didn't look like other dirties, didn't look like a Haight hippie either. I looked . . . *political.*

It felt weird being in that room, like I'd entered enemy territory. Just weeks before, I'd called the man who would soon become our new chief a pig. Inspector Ray Hoobler had stepped on my foot at a Hubert Humphrey campaign rally. David had noticed it, I had to say something.

"Okay, listen up, guys," said O'Brien. "Most of you don't know Stamper." He nodded at me. "Hell, you wouldn't want to cop to it if you did." Laughter, some of it a little too robust for that time of the morning. "Seriously, Stamper's been working the reds and pinks at UCSD. Quite a bit with the Panthers too, if you can believe that."

Yeah, right. The Panthers.

+ + +

Usually it was Bud who called me: *We heard something might be going down in Ocean Beach. Can you swing by and check it out? We got word that some shit's going down at the love-in in Balboa Park. How about . . .* I was like a Dirty for All Seasons. This call, however, had come directly from O'Brien. He wanted me to go to a meeting on Imperial Avenue. Intelligence had gotten word that the Panthers were planning "something heavy" in response to perceived (and no doubt actual) police harassment. "Sure," I said. "I'll check it out." It was the last time O'Brien would send me somewhere on the strength of the FBI's say-so.

I walked into the building, a nondescript storefront. The front office was empty so I walked through it and down a dark hall that fed an equally dark, windowless room. Four black men were seated around a table under a low-watt bare bulb. They'd been talking quietly but went stone silent when I walked in. I recognized one of them, not the others.

"Who are you?" said one of the strangers. He shoved his chair back and stood up. "What are you doing here?"

"Is this where the meeting's at, man?"

"What meeting? What you talking about?"

"The *meeting*," I said, impatient. "You know."

"No, man, I *don't* know. You tell me."

"You know, the meeting to plan the demonstration."

"What demonstration?"

"Against the war, man." I let my frustration show. "You've heard about it, maybe? A little skirmish in Southeast Asia?"

"Look, my friend . . ."

"No. You look. If I got the wrong place all you gotta do is tell me. I got better things to do with . . ."

"All right, all right. Just cool it. This happens to be a *private* meeting, catch my drift? It's not about the fucking war, okay? Now why don't you just tell me how it is you've come to this place?"

"What? You gonna act like the Man now? You gonna fucking *interrogate* me? I told you, man. There's supposed to be a meeting to plan the demonstration. Today. Right now." I jabbed my finger at the floor. "Right here. A brother at the university told me about it. He . . ."

"What's the brother's name?"

"James."

"His *last* name, fool."

"Okay, that's it. I'm out of here." I turned to leave. "But I'll tell you his last name. It's McCory." One of the men at the table wrote it down. "And don't think I'm not going to tell him about the reception I got here. Seems to me we got enough shit going down these days without . . ."

"Look, you honky motherfucker . . ." He caught himself. "Look, we . . ." He caught himself again, I could see it. "What's *your* name, my friend?"

I was already headed for the hall to make my exit. I formed the words "fuck you" but I'm pretty sure they never left my throat. "I told you I'm out of here." I refused to run, but I scurried out the door, praying these guys wouldn't locate a James McCory anywhere in San Diego.

+ + +

O'Brien turned to me to explain what was going down on campus. It was the first time since high school that I'd stood in front of an audience. I liked it. So much that I droned on and on. A glance at O'Brien cleared things up. These men, all with eight or ten or twenty years on me, had been awakened in the middle of the night for a reason. It wasn't to witness a rookie cop's emergent love affair with the center of the stage. I cut to the chase. O'Brien finished up, handing out assignments and offering cautions. He stressed that I was not to be burned, under any circumstances. "You get your tit in the wringer, don't even think about approaching Stamper. You don't know him, got it?"

For the rest of the guys there was time for a refill and a doughnut from the box that had remained untouched during the briefing. I had to hustle back out to the university.

The sun was up. A few dozen cars had materialized on the lots. I circulated among them, finding nothing suspicious. I parked the cool car near the Revelle campus and walked up the stairs to the library balcony which gave me a bird's-eye view of the square. I'd be able to monitor almost every potential ambush site *and* keep on eye on my fellow spies.

As I stood at the railing, a cup of machine coffee in hand, the realization of what I'd set in motion shot through me, a fleeting high-octane rush.

Which quickly gave way to dread and foreboding. There'd been a lot of shouting down on that square over the past several months, a lot of obscenities and threats, but no physical violence. And no guns. Until today, and we were the ones who'd be importing them.

I knew my brethren had to be packing; the intelligence left us no choice. But what if something went wrong? What if innocent kids got caught in the crossfire? Kent State hadn't happened yet (that was May 4, 1970) but I had visions of young innocents lying in pools of blood.

The first dirty got burned the moment he walked on the square. An angry ex-girlfriend. "Narc! Narc! Narc!" she bellowed. Loud enough to be heard over the bullhorned incendiary comments of the first speaker. Loud enough to be heard in Bakersfield. "Narc" didn't stick around to protest. I watched as he pivoted and split, with deliberate haste—cops don't *run* unless they have to—toward the north where he'd come from.

Moments later, not knowing at the time what had caused the first cop's exit, I spotted a second one powerwalking *his* way back to the lot on the east side of the campus. I chalked this one up, erroneously it turned out, to his attire: Hawaiian shirt, Bermuda shorts, a Panama hat (a *Panama hat*, for chrissakes!). What was he thinking? It's a wonder he wasn't sporting black socks and black leather shoes. (He'd also been burned by an ex, an ex-wife who was putting herself through school and who'd been trying to collect child support from the cop, a deadbeat dad. If he wouldn't cooperate with her she saw no reason to cooperate with him.)

Two down. I'm leaking confidence. I could see what was happening below but had no way of knowing why, until later. If those dudes from Santa Barbara showed up now we'd be at half strength. Even as I was lamenting the odds they got worse. Forty-five minutes into the detail, a *third* cop got burned. This was beyond bizarre. Had members of the crowd swept the square with some magic narc-detector device? The third guy fell when an old pal recognized him. "Jimmy!" he'd yelled. "Jimmy, you old fucker, you! What's it been? Three, four years? You still with the PD? What's with the beard? Oh, I'll bet they *fired* your ass, didn't they?" A vocal subset of the crowd started pointing and chanting, "Pig! Pig! Pig!" Jimmy quickly walked to his vehicle, a few diehards escorting him the whole way.

Terrific. This was just dandy. We're down to a lone cop, packing a two-inch Chief's Special in a shoulder holster under his windbreaker. I'm packing nothing. We've got no way to communicate. And Angela Davis has just been introduced to a thundering ovation. I abandoned my post and walked down the concrete steps to mingle with the masses. I checked the crowd, scanned the surrounding buildings. Nothing suspicious. But where the hell was David?

+ + +

The UC Santa Barbara "assassins" were a no-show—if in fact they had ever existed. Had they shown up, locked and loaded, they would have found SDPD hopelessly ill-prepared. This was during the pre-SWAT era of policing. It was before PDs wised up and started meeting, doing joint planning with those affected by threats such as these. It was a time when kids didn't get shot on a college campus, or at a high school or a day care center.

I was happy that the only damage done that day was to the pride of a handful of cops. To this day, I can still hear a spindly little white guy in a Trotsky beard cackling about the one he pulled on some goofy undercover cop.

+ + +

Toward the end of my assignment the People's Park issue exploded in Berkeley, largely the product of Governor Reagan's impatience and intransigence. The effects of the street rioting reverberated up and down the state and, like the free speech movement before it, all across the country.

At UCSD, weary of marathon teach-ins, SDS and like spirits were preparing to take over the university's administrative offices. There was no way I could not be a part of it.

About a hundred of us entered the provost's complex. Leaders of the takeover had done their intelligence gathering. They'd passed out copies of the floor plan of the warren of offices and corridors, and they knew the provost would be present at that moment. We charged into his inner office. The leaders of the pack penned him in. They jacked him around for several hours, haranguing him for the university's role in everything from the war in Vietnam to apartheid in South Africa. The university's secretaries and other staffers were by turns intimidated and entertained by the radical proselytizers. But nobody got hurt.

Then again, nobody's worldview got changed either. Certainly not mine. I was still more philosophically aligned with the protestors than with my fellow cops. But the way my "comrades" treated the provost and his staff left me nauseated. A couple of them got in his face, spittle flying, doing their best to browbeat and filibuster their ideology into the guy. Michael Moore would have been much more respectful. One student pushed the provost because he'd asked them to "cool your language." Who did they think they were, this minority of protesters? Who gave them the right to bully others?

It was wrong, and inaccurate, however, for my police colleagues to write off all antiwar protestors and civil rights demonstrators as rich spoiled brats or social misfits. As individuals, some of them may have been just that, but most of the people I befriended and spied upon were among the most dedicated, hardworking, and morally upstanding I've ever met. They applied themselves to a study of our world: what was wrong with it, what needed to be done to put it right. And they acted.

+ + +

Somebody in one of the dorms was playing, for all the world to hear, Steppenwolf's "Magic Carpet Ride." I applauded the selection, as well as the fog that had crept up the hill and through the pines from the shores of La Jolla. It was a Friday, late in the afternoon. The square was empty but for a small knot of laughing nerds and preppies near the fountain. No demonstrations, no screaming speeches or chanting to drown out Steppenwolf.

The quarter was over, library books turned in, grades handed out. The dorm dwellers—those not already headed home to New York or San Francisco, or India, Lebanon, Mexico, Germany, Japan—had the place to themselves and they were in a party mood. I was probably the only commuter on campus that afternoon, and I had no real purpose there. My undercover assignment was over, my own magic carpet ride ended. The results of the sergeants' exam had just been posted. My name sat at the top of the list. Soon, I'd be debriefed, write a manual on this different kind of undercover work, shave off my beard, trim my hair, and sew on the stripes.

+ + +

For most of my thirty-four years as a cop I kept a journal. I saved photos, newspaper clippings, commendations, evaluations, disciplinary actions, major-event reports, notes and memoranda, calendars, audiotapes, videos of key events. I was driven to do this, in part, because I'm a packrat but mostly because of a vague notion that at some point in my life I might want to write of my experiences. As I assembled those materials for this book I came face to face with a large crater in my recorded history.

Two months into my new job as a sergeant, recently divorced and crying myself to sleep over having left my three-year-old son, I came home to my apartment and pulled from the closet a big cardboard box, its contents overflowing. I slung it onto the sagging bed. One by one I removed every item: weekly reports; campus and underground newspapers; stacks of photographs. One photo is of me. It had appeared in *The Triton*, UCSD's student paper. I had no idea it had been taken, and was shocked when it showed up on page one. I'm at my hairiest, sitting on a concrete bench next to the square, smoking a Schimmelpennick cigar, peering forlornly through my granny glasses, and waiting on a cold morning for the demonstration *du jour*. The caption contained words like *dwelling . . . gut . . . soul*. I was probably thinking I'd like another cup of coffee right about now but then I'd have to piss and the demonstration is just getting under way so if I drink another cup now I'll *really* have to pee and I might miss something and it could be important, so, all things considered, I'd better pass on the coffee. David, the "Trotskyite Marxist," had seen the paper, called it to my attention. "Lookin' *très* artistic there, my man."

Also in the box was the manual I'd written to help guide the work of future undercover agents. It contained a brief history of criminal violence that had stemmed from radical political movements in the city, the most violent of which dated back to the early part of the twentieth century when city fathers directed San Diego cops to wade into IWW (Industrial Workers of the World) demonstrators; I forget how many were killed. I offered tips for infiltrating radical groups: how to position and insinuate oneself into a trusting relationship with a variety of personalities, how to carry out the work artfully.

I put the manual down and picked up other memorabilia: political flyers, programs for "radical" plays in local theaters, pins and buttons . . . Staring down at the mound on the bed I was mortified. I had lived a lie for a year.

I stuffed everything back into the box and headed for the kitchen where I layered aluminum foil into the bottom of the sink and burned everything that could be burned. I trashed the rest. It was only mildly cleansing.

I resolved to keep my own counsel about that year, volunteer nothing about it, furnish deceitful answers to the inevitable questions. At least there would be no physical evidence of my spying.

+ + +

For years I lied to people like Larry Remer, publisher of one of the underground papers and contributor to *San Diego Magazine*. And friend. "Tell the truth Norm," he said, some seven years after the assignment. "You worked the Red Squad that year, didn't you?" He knew. Of course he knew. He was a freaking journalist. But I lied, hiding behind a technicality. "Nope. I worked O.C. that year." Organized crime. Hey, if students decide to block a recruiter, take over a building, trespass on private property, well then, they're "organized criminals." Aren't they? Besides, why should I tell a *journalist*, friend or foe, about what I really did? Isn't the idea to keep undercover work . . . under cover?

This is my first public telling of the story. I spied. I lied. There you have it.

+ + +

In light of violence at recent antiglobalization and antiwar demonstrations, shouldn't local police departments, and the FBI, for that matter, get back into spying on political activists? No. Absolutely not.

Although I was never burned as an undercover operative, one of my successors was, and he was soon implicated in a variety of nefarious activities, such as pouring glue into university locks, and other conduct of "agents provocateurs." His exposure produced San Diego's "Red Squad" scandal. Similar such scandals broke out all across the country in the seventies as local officials learned of the scope and nature of police spying in their own backyards.

In Portland, Oregon, Winfield Falk, a former police intelligence detective, sneaked into his own agency and "stole" thirty-six boxes of materials, the product of police spying during the sixties and seventies. The materials had been earmarked for the shredder under that city's restrictions on police spying. In the boxes were dossiers on city council members, a grape-boycotter who would go on to become Portland's mayor, and even an Oregon governor. There were intelligence reports on food banks, voter registration organizations, a rape crisis agency. In Denver, as recently as 1999, files were discovered on 3,200 Colorado citizens representing 208 organizations, ranging from the League of Women Voters to American Friends Service Committee to Amnesty International.

San Diego, Seattle, and most other big cities now have local "intelligence ordinances" designed to halt police spying abuses. Preambles to these laws state more or less the same thing: Police intelligence on criminal and terrorist activity is invaluable, in fact essential to the mission of public safety. But spying on *noncriminal* activists is abhorrent—and illegal.

How to prevent abuses? Seattle's ordinance, the first in the nation, passed in 1979, has, among other provisions, three that make sense—and one that I question. The ordinance (1) bans spying (absent evidence of criminality) on political, social, or religious activities or affiliations; (2) requires the signature of the chief of police authorizing any investigation into "private sexual information" as well as inquiries into political or religious organizations; (3) employs a civilian auditor, nominated by the mayor and confirmed by the city council, with complete access to all intelligence files and a mandate to conduct random inspections, review the chief's authorizations, and enforce all provisions of the ordinance. It's a strong ordinance, and I support it.

The provision that creates heartburn for me? The one that allows the auditor (a position held by a succession of experienced, respected local attorneys with unimpeachable integrity) to inform the subject of intelligence gathering that he, she, or it (in the case of an organization) has been (1) spied upon, (2) unlawfully. Damages for "substantial" violations of this provision may be assessed against the spy and his or her supervisor, and paid to the unwitting victim of the abuse. My concern is over the chilling effect the provision *can* create. Detectives afraid to do their jobs. Snitches afraid to come forward. Other agencies reluctant to share information. The feds, for example, withheld important information from my department for three days, pondering whether it would get anyone in trouble in the lead-up to the protests surrounding the meeting of the WTO in Seattle, November 29–December 4, 1999.

The challenge is to achieve a balance between appropriately aggressive crime fighting (including the prevention of crimes and acts of terrorism) and rigorous protection of citizens' rights to privacy (the Fourth Amendment) and free speech and assembly (the First). It's a delicate balance and, all things considered, I guess I can live with my mild case of heartburn.

On February 18, 2003, Seattle joined hundreds of other U.S. cities condemning certain provisions of the USA Patriot Act (October 2001). The resolution, passed unanimously, is an eloquent statement on the need to combat terrorism *and* to curb the impulses of law enforcement that, however understandable in times of war and terrorism (and noisy protests), would make America a country less worth defending.

POLICING
THE POLICE

CHAPTER 20

TREATING COPS LIKE KIDS: POLICE DISCIPLINE

You're the chief. What do you do with a cop who:

1. Uses profanity while ordering a suspect to the ground?
2. Sideswipes a fixed object, causing major damage to a brand-new police car?
3. Smashes his heavy flashlight into the skull of a suspect?
4. Runs a records check on the new boyfriend of his ex-wife?
5. Fires a warning shot, in direct violation of department policy?
6. Drives her police car into the back of a semi?
7. Shoots and kills an unarmed man?

IN SCENARIO ONE, OFFICER Dana Jackson is attempting to arrest an auto thief. Ignoring her warnings, the suspect advances, threatening to knock her on her ass. The man is not armed but Jackson has no doubt about his intentions, and his ability to carry them out. She shouts, "I told you to get your fucking ass on the ground! *Now!*" Not exactly proper language, and you've made it clear to your cops that that kind of talk is unacceptable. But the man drops to the ground, spread-eagles himself, and presents his wrists for cuffing.

In *Scenario Two,* it's one in the morning, foggy, quiet, not another car on the road. Officer Rob Brown has been out shaking doors, flashing his light around some of Balboa Park's most popular attractions: the Old Globe, the Aerospace Museum, the Museum of Modern Art. A nighttime arsonist has been torching combustibles in the vestibules of these civic treasures and Brown is eager to nab the guy before he burns one to the ground. The officer returns to his car and glides out onto El Prado. A second later he hears a loud explosion—followed immediately by the sound of glass shattering. Thinking he's been shot at, he ducks down in the seat, cuts the wheel sharply to the left, and hits the accelerator. His car sideswipes one of those aggregate-stone, concrete-encased trashcans. His shiny black-and-white Crown Vic, delivered just that day, has a long, ugly crease in its side. It's going to cost a thousand bucks to repair it. (The shot? Turns out Brown ran over a pop bottle.)

The man Officer David Ruiz has just arrested in *Scenario Three*—a fugitive with several out-of-state warrants, is sitting atop the officer's chest. He's already knocked Ruiz to the ground and pummeled him with his fists. Now he reaches for the cop's gun. Ruiz gets a hand free, grabs his weighted flashlight, and smashes it against the guy's skull. The suspect slumps, dazed. Ruiz handcuffs him and hauls him off to jail via County Hospital.

Scenario Four: Officer Jonathan Davies uses the mobile data terminal in his car to run a check on his ex-wife's boyfriend. He discovers the man has been convicted in the past of theft and disturbing the peace. He provides this information to his ex-wife.

Surrounded by a hostile crowd bent on lynching his prisoner,* Officer Kevin Stuart in *Scenario Five* pulls his gun and cranks off a round into the air. Insupportable, states your policy: Warning shots are dangerous (bullets that go up tend to come down). The crowd scatters long enough for Stuart to shove his prisoner into his police car and fishtail it out of the area.

In *Scenario Six,* Officer Deborah Clancy drives out of the Eastern substation at dawn to begin her shift. She turns east onto Aero Drive. As she crests a hill, traveling well under the posted speed limit, she's met by a big orange orb, bright enough to temporarily but completely blind her—and an eighteen-wheeler, stalled in the middle of the traffic lane. The collision puts Clancy in the hospital for weeks.

Edward Anderson had been beating his girlfriend off and on throughout the day. Now, in *Scenario Seven,* he's threatening to kill her and their baby. Officer Bill Edwards shows up at the house in response to

---

* Lynching, as defined in the penal code, refers not to a hanging but to the unlawful seizing, or release of, a prisoner in police custody.

a 911 call, just after midnight. It's cold and blustery, the rain coming down in horizontal sheets. Edwards sees Anderson jump from a first-floor window of a house and flee across a rubble-strewn backyard. The officer bails out of his car and gives chase. Aware of the suspect's threat to kill, and not knowing whether the man is armed, Edwards pulls his .40 Glock. He gains ground on Anderson, and is only a second or two behind when the suspect suddenly trips and falls. Edwards reaches for Anderson to lift him to his feet. The officer's gun "goes off." Accidentally. The bullet enters the suspect's throat, exits the back of his head. He's DOA at Harborview Medical Center. (Edwards is white, Anderson, black. The suspect had no gun. It's Martin Luther King Day, and you're scheduled to speak to a thousand people at Garfield High later that day.)

These are not hypothetical cases. They all happened on my watch as a patrol chief in San Diego or as chief of the Seattle Police Department. With the exception of the last incident, a well-publicized Seattle case, I've used fictitious names. So, if they were *your* cops, what would you do? Should they all be disciplined?

Only one of these cops deserved to be punished. If you picked Jonathan Davies in Scenario Four you picked right. Without official justification for prying into the lives of private citizens, Davies is hanging out a mile. He should be (and was) fired. The rest of the cops were doing their jobs, under trying if not dangerous circumstances. A couple of them could have wound up dead but for their quick thinking and decisive action.

+ + +

Sadly, most chiefs would have punished the cops you just read about. They regularly and systematically penalize police officers based not on the cops' intentions, or their state of mind, or even their actions, but on the *impact*—the unhappy or tragic or politically embarrassing effect of their actions.*

---

* In each of the foregoing cases, I received recommendations from supervisors—and from some in the community—that the individual be punished. Severely in the case of Edwards in Scenario Seven. And in Scenario Six? If not for Commander Mike Rice intercepting a supervisor en route, Officer Clancy would have been served disciplinary papers in her hospital bed!

I've seen it in police departments across the country, large and small: police administrators acting like bad parents when it comes to internal discipline. They treat their cops like dependent or misbehaving children— then puzzle themselves silly trying to figure out why some cops *act* like juvenile delinquents.

One of the major reasons police misconduct is so common and so predictable is because of *administrative* misconduct. Inappropriate, overly harsh discipline creates a paranoid, angry, childish police force. And it's the community that pays the stiffest price.

The theory that leads to such hypercritical, draconian discipline is seductive: If you punish cops who screw up, you'll (1) prevent bigger problems; (2) hold officers "accountable" for their mistakes; (3) send a message to other cops that policy violations will not be tolerated; and (4) satisfy the public (and your boss, the mayor or the city manager) that you're the kind of chief who "takes care of business." It's a pretty theory, one that animates the philosophy of many "accountability-oriented" chiefs, but it's hogwash.

If you want to build trust in your officers and help them get their dangerous and demanding jobs done safely and effectively, you don't *punish* them when they make an honest mistake—or a conscious, defensible choice to violate policy in order to save a life.

Punitive discipline for inadvertent (or transparently excusable) violations of SOPs triggers a passive-aggressive response from affected officers, and that includes every cop who learns of the discipline. Cops stop working as hard; they refuse to take risks; they lie about or cover up future transgressions. This is especially true if said "discipline" is handed down in an insulting, paternalistic, regimented fashion that is all too common in most agencies. Treating cops like kids tends to produce childish behavior. It's not rocket science, even though it took me a good while to figure it out.

+ + +

I'm a patrol sergeant in 1970. "Cal Peters," one of my young cops, a white male, has stopped a black youth to issue him a traffic citation. It starts badly and goes downhill from there, culminating with the young man tossing a lit cigarette at Peters who pulls the young man out of his car—through the window—prompting the young man to file a complaint. I investigate the complaint, sustain it, and secure, with approvals up the chain of command, a four-day suspension for my officer along with a transfer out of the black community.

Looking back, I made a *huge* mistake.

I'm not saying the cop was right, far from it. The discipline on the face of it was appropriate, if not too light. But what lesson did Peters come away with? I acted throughout the process like a nasty drill sergeant, scolding the cop, rubbing his face in it, not listening to his belief that his actions were justified. I took four days' earnings out of his paycheck, and shooed him off to some other part of the city—where he seethed at the injustice of it all. And likely took it out on the unsuspecting citizens of his new beat.

I should have listened to the guy. Peters's rationale for his actions was that being hit with a lit cigarette (which landed on his heavy jacket and fell harmlessly to the ground) constituted an assault on a police officer. True, his method of extracting the kid from the car was . . . unorthodox. Yet this was a terrific learning moment at this early stage of his career, and I blew it. I could have reprimanded him, kept him in the squad, and worked with him. I could sense all along that he was far from a lost cause, that he had potential to become an excellent police officer. But he'd acted like a kid, so I treated him like one.

One thing I certainly should not have done? The suspension. Those four docked days came right out of his family's budget, hurt his wife and children and only added to his resentment toward me, and toward the brass in general. If a cop has earned that level of punishment why not go all the way and fire him? Which is exactly what I'd do today, *if* I thought the officer was beyond redemption.

+ + +

Thirty-four years of intimate experience with police discipline, combined with research into principles of individual accountability (heavily influenced by Richard C. Grote's *Discipline Without Punishment: The Proven*

Strategy That Turns Problem Employees into Superior Performers, 1995), make it clear that putting an employee on the beach without pay almost always has precisely the opposite effect of that intended.

If you want your cops to actually *think* about their transgressions and mend their wayward ways, send them home for a day or two, *with pay*—and instructions to reflect on what they've done. (This is assuming their transgression is not a terminable offense.)

Maybe police work isn't for them. Maybe they don't have the patience or the courage or the maturity. By listening to them, leveling with them, and encouraging them to really think about whether their chosen career is a good fit, you've taken a dignified, effective path. And you've put the onus squarely on the shoulders of the one person responsible for the screw-up.

None of this should be taken to mean that you can't or shouldn't fire incompetent or willfully disobedient police officers. Police work is no place for amateurs, for individuals who lack the tools—emotional, moral, physical, or behavioral—to get the job done.

+ + +

As field operations chief in San Diego, and with Chief Bob Burgreen's blessings, I drew a new line in the sand. We would continue to discipline our cops for policy violations. But our system would be "bifurcated": *punitive* disciplinary action for acts of willful misconduct or gross negligence, *corrective* disciplinary action for honest mistakes or performance problems.

The discipline, whether punitive or corrective, would be administered "progressively," meaning each new violation of an identical or similar nature would result in progressively more stringent or assertive action.

To illustrate: For years in California, I taught a statewide police personnel management course. One morning, I asked my students (supervisors, middle managers, a sprinkling of chiefs): "What action do you take when one of your subordinates commits a minor infraction of department policy?" From around the room came, "counseling," "verbal warning," "written warning."

"*Really?*" I said. "Is it possible that you might simply note it, mentally, but do nothing at all?" A few nodded in agreement. "Could it be that you don't say a thing unless they do it a second time?" More nods. In other words, their cops got a free ride, perhaps a frown or a raised eyebrow on the first violation, with something a little more "official" the second time around. And a tougher response the third time out. That's progressive discipline.

+ + +

What disciplinary actions are available to police supervisors? Many. On the punitive side: warnings, reprimands, suspensions, demotions, terminations (with the possibility of prosecution). On the corrective side: coaching, counseling, additional schooling including remedial education or training, and—termination. If a cop is struggling with report writing, for example, he or she could be required to take a community college course, or to work with a peer or supervisor in a tutorial relationship. An officer who lacks assertiveness could be sent to a class or a counselor to gain those skills and strengthen his or her self-confidence.

The governing philosophy is to *help* police officers perform to the best of their ability, and to behave professionally. To build them up, not tear them down. (Even when you have to fire them: A lot of decent human beings, trying their best, simply can't cut it as a cop. There's no need to rub their noses in it before you send them packing.)

+ + +

As a deputy chief in San Diego, I made it a habit to spend a day from time to time with each of my captains, riding around with them, chatting informally about crime and crime fighting, strategic and tactical planning, personnel issues, and so forth. I called Captain Mike Tyler on a Wednesday to confirm my visit to Western Division the next morning.

"Great," he said. "I'm looking forward to it. But could you come a little later? I've got to suspend one of my graveyard cops." I knew all about it. He was going to suspend a patrol officer for recklessness in a high-speed pursuit.

"Do you mind if I sit in? Do you think 'Mitchell' would mind?"

"No problem here. It'll give me chance to teach you how the pros do it." Modesty was not one of Tyler's failings. "I'll have someone check with Mitchell this afternoon and get back to you."* Mitchell, it turned out, was cool with it.

At six the next morning, greetings accomplished, Mitchell took a seat across the desk from his captain. I sat in a corner. Mitchell had waived his right to representation.

TYLER: "We've already talked about your actions on the chase, Mitch, and my disapproval. I don't have anything more to say about it. You know the discipline: four days on the beach. Do you have any questions or comments?"

MITCHELL: "No, sir. Guilty as charged. It won't happen again."

TYLER: "Good, glad to hear it. Sign here."

Mitchell signed the form. Tyler gave him a copy. Mitchell started to leave. "Hold on second," Tyler said. "When you get back to work next week I want to see you here in my office before you hit the field, okay?" Mitchell nodded. Handshakes all around. Out the door.

I complimented Tyler on the brevity of the meeting. During my early years as a supervisor and middle manager I'd felt it my duty to launch into a long, repetitive, moralizing lecture on the offending officer's transgression(s), to inform him where he went wrong, to explicitly condemn the behavior, to explain what steps he must take in the future in order to stay out of trouble, to lay out the consequences he'd face if he became a repeat offender, and on and on . . .

Tyler knew better. He knew "Guilty as charged" meant Mitchell had accepted responsibility for his actions. The officer did wrong. He got punished. Case closed.

But what's with the meeting next week? I asked Tyler about it as we headed out for breakfast.

"I do that with everyone I suspend." (I had let my captains and commanders know that I wasn't prepared to outlaw suspensions . . . yet.)

---

* Checking with a *beat cop*? To see if it's okay for a *deputy chief* to sit in? Even though traditional managers gag on such gestures, and I could have ordered my way into the meeting, what does it cost to show a little respect for your cops, pay some attention to their wishes, treat them like grown-ups?

"Why?"

"To welcome them back."

"Yeah?"

"I let them know they've served their sentence, and I welcome them back into the fold. I tell them the reason they didn't get fired was because they're good cops. I tell them I'm glad they're working for me. Then I tell them to get their ass out in the field and do the job the way it's supposed to be done." Sentence served. The offense not forgotten (some never will be), but forgiven. Grown-up discipline. Tyler did, indeed, teach me how the pros do it. He was in charge of that meeting because it was his division. Mitchell and all the other officers and detectives and supervisors and civilian employees who worked out of the Friars Road station reported to Mike Tyler. Not Norm Stamper, not Bob Burgreen.

Tyler's "ownership" of the disciplinary proceeding was crucial to my campaign to push police decision-making down the chain of command to its logical locus. In decentralized, geographically based policing—in *community* policing—you need the precinct commander to both be and *feel* responsible for what goes on, 24/7, in his or her command. You want police officers, as well as citizens, to appreciate the decision-making authority of their captain.

In Seattle I took heat from my critics, internal and external, for allowing captains to make disciplinary decisions that were formerly reserved for the chief of police. But over my six years as chief I saw captains become more and more responsible (and accountable) as they grew into their expanded roles.

The biggest beef about delegating discipline authority to precinct commanders? "Inconsistency." What if Mitchell had worked not for Mike Tyler but for Joe Schwalbach at Northeastern who would have, hypothetically, slapped the guy with a ten-day suspension? Or for Paul Ybarrondo at Central who would have handed him a reprimand? Consistency is a valid and serious concern.

We addressed it in San Diego on two levels, the first of which was philosophical: Did we want a "bail schedule" approach to discipline in which *everyone* who, for example, backed a police car into another car, or left a knife on a prisoner, or used excessive force, or missed court, or got rude with a citizen, would pay the exact same price? Consistency freaks said yes. Thinkers said no.* As Emerson wrote, "A foolish consistency is the hobgoblin of little minds." The second level dealt with something I'll call the "Yes, but" issue.

Yes, but shouldn't two cops with identical records, time on the department, and discipline history pay the same price for identical violations of policy? Yes. In the unlikely event that that state of affairs exists, Officer B should get exactly what Officer A has coming. If nothing else, it facilitates a healthy organizational *predictability*, and brings more justice to the administration of police discipline.

So with no fixed, published penalties for policy violations, how did my captains and I achieve this kind of "smart" consistency?

Recall that I knew in advance that Tyler was going to be suspending Mitchell. How did I know? Because each of my captains was required to present at our weekly Field Ops meetings an outline of all pending discipline. Listening to one another, asking one another for information and advice, getting a feel for what's fair and appropriate became an institutionalized ethic in our administration of discipline. And there was this: Although it was the captain's call, he or she had to inform me before sticking a disciplinary package under the nose of his or her officer. Why? Because, in the interest of citywide consistency and fairness, I retained veto power (and did not want the captains to lose standing in the eyes of their officers if I chose to overturn a decision).

Of course, if I'd vetoed more decisions than I'd accepted (or even as few as, say, 10 to 15 percent of them), I couldn't say with a straight face that I'd truly delegated discipline responsibility to my captains. But in two or three years I vetoed only two of approximately a hundred decisions (both from the same captain, once for being too lenient, once for being too harsh). I knew in San Diego and in Seattle that I was accountable for all discipline but my captains were responsible for it.

---

* Return to the scenarios that open this chapter for an illustration of what's wrong with that "bail schedule" approach.

+ + +

An entirely different, and appallingly neglected, facet of police discipline comes down to this: How do you discipline your *boss?* The incompetence or misbehavior of one's superior is a *huge* problem in police work. Before pointing fingers at some of the bosses I've worked for, let me confess to my own shortcomings.

In 1992, my third wife, Lisa, and I went on a delayed honeymoon, to Kauai. I was now the assistant chief. When I returned to work two weeks later my senior deputy chief walked in and asked for a meeting. We set it up for later that morning. He didn't show up alone: All four of my chiefs filed in and took a seat in my office.

"What's up?" I asked.

"We don't see enough of you," said the senior chief. "There are a lot of decisions we can't make without you. It's nice you get asked to speak. It's great that you teach those classes at the Training Center and at San Diego State. But you're just gone too much." Gone too much? True, I was in demand as a trainer and a speaker, and I loved standing in front of audiences throughout the country. I was proud of my (often controversial) contribution to the field, and felt it was important. But gone *too* much? Hell, when Burgreen picked me to run the organization I'd cut back, a *lot.*

"Everyone feel this way?" Four heads nodded. I felt betrayed. It took me a day or two to come down. But when I did, I knew I'd been busted. I *was* spending too much time away from my desk, my day job. I cut out *everything*—no more classes, no more keynotes, no nothing that wasn't directly related to the job.

In Seattle, I listened as a roomful of journalists bitched about supervisors denying them access to rank-and-file officers, especially in Investigations. I can't remember exactly what I said but it was along the lines of, "Look, we've got a department to run but I understand your need for information. We'll see what we can do about standardizing access. In the meantime, I know you know how to cultivate sources, and I would encourage you to do just that."

My chief of staff, an assistant chief who'd spent a lot of time in Investigations (much of it cleaning up messes caused by loose-lipped dicks) was livid. After the meeting he walked into my office, sat down, and unloaded. "I can't remember when I've been more pissed! We're trying to *stop* leaks in the department, trying to avoid compromising investigations and jeopardizing prosecutions. And what do you do? You invite the press to camp out in the offices and hallways, to 'chat up' every cop they see! You were wrong to say what you said, and we're all going to pay for it in the future."

My rationale had been that there had been a failure to communicate, and we needed to correct that. As long as our cops followed our press policy I was prepared to live with the consequences of a more "open" approach to media relations. But whether I was right, wrong, or simply misunderstood, my immediate subordinate felt free to "discipline" his boss. And that's a good thing.

I'd learned in my days as a subordinate in San Diego that there are times when you have to exercise leadership *up* the chain of command, as well as down.

+ + +

I was a lieutenant. My boss, "Frank Stanton," was a deputy chief. He drank his lunch. He put moves on everything in a skirt. He didn't show up for critical meetings (on one such occasion, taking one of our key attendees, an attractive consultant, to Tijuana for the day). He lied, daily. I confronted him. He laughed, told me not to take life so seriously. The pattern continued, unchanged. I told him I was going to snitch him off if he didn't knock it off. No change. I snitched, to the assistant chief. He'd take care of it, he said. He didn't. I went to the super chief. He'd take care of it, he said. He didn't. I asked for a meeting with the two of them, the super chief, the assistant chief. I told them that if they didn't take care of the lying, womanizing sot down the hall I'd run to the city manager. They took care of it.

A few months later, Commander Cal Krosch must have felt the same way when he came forward to suggest that we knock off our *own* high-level, on-duty boozing. It had been a not very well-kept secret for years, a tradition among the senior staff.

Every Wednesday at five o'clock, the Big Boys would parade into the assistant chief's office where we'd open the liquor cabinet, pour generous portions of bourbon, or scotch, or gin and drink ourselves silly.* Krosch's conscience got to him, and he had the guts to "discipline" not only his superiors but his peers—leadership at its toughest, leadership when it counts. He brought up the subject at a senior staff meeting. "I think we're being a little hypocritical here, guys," he said. He looked around the room, then at the chief. "Not very long ago you forced one of us to resign, partly for his drinking. I have to wonder if we weren't all enabling Stanton. Regardless, what we're doing is wrong. I can't justify it any longer." Neither could any of the rest of us. That was the day the San Diego Police Department went dry.

+ + +

Sometimes the distinction between willful misconduct (and/or gross negligence) and an honest mistake can be difficult to discern. The Edward Anderson shooting (the last scenario) is a prime example.

Officer Bill Edwards had eighteen months on at the time of the shooting. A more experienced cop probably would not have reached down, gun in hand, to lift a suspect to his feet. A more experienced cop would have had his trigger finger "indexed" as he chased the suspect.

Officers are taught in the academy to extend their index finger *alongside the slide* of the weapon and not inside the trigger guard (when not planning to immediately pull the trigger, that is). But this was the first time Edwards had ever chased anyone with firearm in hand. Put simply, he lacked "muscle memory," built through a repetitive process that must be refreshed periodically on its way to becoming second nature. Which brings up training and retraining (an *administrative* responsibility). And experience. Which Edwards didn't have.

Had Edwards purposely shot Anderson I would have fired him—and urged prosecution on at least a manslaughter charge. Had he been reckless (or grossly negligent) I would have fired him. Had he established a performance

* I'd been on the scene for months before noticing that each of the bottles carried a set of initials and a badge number. That's right: impounded as contraband by our officers on the streets. We would have fired them for doing what we did on a weekly basis.

record of carelessness (as opposed to the exemplary record he'd compiled as a rookie) I would have fired him.

So, I had a decision to make. What to do with a police officer whose actions led directly to the death of an unarmed man? Many in the community were demanding his badge. Three hundred and fifty irate African-Americans let me have it with both barrels at a community meeting a week after the incident. I listened to the crescendo of boos and catcalls at that meeting, and I witnessed in the months that followed a concerted campaign to drive Edwards from the force. Several of my colleagues in the Major Cities Chiefs organization, to whom I'd explained the situation in one of our regular "roundtables," believed the man should be fired—not because they thought the shooting was reckless but because it would pacify the black community. Canning the rookie would certainly have been the politically expedient thing to do. His fellow cops fully expected it.

I studied the investigation, talked to the officer and his supervisors, called firearms training experts to my office, and drove down to the academy to observe the firearms training (which I'd previously taken). When my review was finished I knew exactly what to do with Edwards.

I walked across the street and informed the mayor of my plans. An African-American with deep roots and enormous popularity in Seattle's black community, Norm Rice disagreed with my decision. But he understood it, and the principles that shaped it. (He backed me, publicly, without equivocation.)

Next, I drove to Mt. Zion Baptist Church, the scene of the angry meeting, and told the Rev. Dr. Samuel B. McKinney what I'd decided. He also disagreed with my decision.

The decision? I would (1) retain Edwards; (2) not punish him; (3) have him undergo psychological fitness-for-duty screening; (4) put him through two days of one-on-one firearms retraining with the department's reigning semiautomatics ace; (5) get a sign-off from the instructor that Edwards had, in fact, developed that muscle memory; (6) condition the officer's return to the streets on his passing a rigorous test of both his emotional fitness and his retraining; and (7) assign him to a different area of town for at least eighteen months.

"I hear you, Chief," said Dr. McKinney after I'd explained the rationale.

"You've made a responsible decision, from your point of view. And I respect that. But, answer me this: How can you possibly condone this young policeman sprinting through a field, in a driving rain, with his gun out? Chasing after a man he does not *know* to be armed? Wouldn't that qualify as 'gross negligence' under your definition?" It was an excellent question, one local reporters hadn't thought to ask. My answer to McKinney's question was, in fact, central to my thinking on the Edwards case.

I told him the following story, which explains why, as chief I would never, ever prohibit a cop from running, gun in hand, in a foot chase. Even though I think it's a recipe for disaster.

+ + +

A San Diego cop for less than a year, Jerry Hartless was riding shotgun one night in 1988 when he spotted gang member Stacy Butler standing on a corner. Hartless knew Butler was wanted on warrants. He got out of the car and started to approach him. Butler rabbitted. Hartless, winner of his academy's award for physical fitness, gave chase and quickly closed the gap. Butler, sensing he was about to be nabbed, stopped suddenly, pulled a 9mm semiautomatic from his waistband, spun around and fired. The bullet caught Hartless between the eyes. The officer hit the ground with his pistol still holstered. He died twenty-three days later without regaining consciousness.

Hartless's chance of survival if he'd had his gun is drawn? At least fifty-fifty. Holstered? Zero.

+ + +

"That's why," I told Rev. Dr. McKinney, "I can't fault Bill Edwards for running through that field with his weapon in hand."

"I see," said McKinney, "I see." Then he said something I'll never forget. "You did the right thing, Chief. You showed up for our meeting. You took heat for the killing. You struggled to make the right decision. Now that I understand how you reached it, I think you're doing the right thing by your young officer. But I'm not sure you're doing the right thing by our community, you understand? I hope you understand I cannot and will not agree with you publicly."

He reminded me that the Edward Anderson shooting was only the last in a long string of black men killed by the police—many of those killings questionable, if not unjustified. Edwards (and I, and the department) paid a price for that sorry history. But I believe Rev. McKinney did understand, a lot better by the end of our conversation, what it was like for the cop that night—and what goes through a chief's mind when deciding the appropriate course of action.

CHAPTER 21

A DARK TAKE ON
FINANCIAL LIABILITY

IT WAS NEW YEAR'S Day 1988, ten o'clock at night. San Diego police officer Michael Scott was responding to a nonemergency call for backup on a routine stop when at seventy to seventy-three mph he struck Frances Maday's '83 Honda Sedan broadside. The accident left the thirty-one-year-old marketing analyst and avid tennis player a paraplegic, speechless (from a permanent tracheotomy), brain damaged, and requiring twenty-four-hour care, which included feeding her through a hole in her abdomen. Eighteen months after the accident Officer Scott told a reporter, "I'm still dealing with the whole situation. I'm just as sorry as I can be, for the family, and about the whole thing."

The city was sorry too. It paid Ms. Maday $9.6 million, and bought her a house equipped for a wheelchair. And an annuity: If she lives to a then-normal life expectancy of seventy-nine, total payments will reach $72 million. Since the city is self-insured, most of that money has been and will continue to be borne by San Diego taxpayers.

I've checked taxpayer-financed payoffs for traffic accidents caused by police around the country: $2.3 million here, $7.5 million there. According to the *San Diego Union-Tribune*, city and county police are at fault in roughly sixty percent of their accidents. The City of San Diego, between 1996 and 2002, paid out $4.1 million for accidents caused by its officers. The County paid out $4.9 million (between 1997 and 2002) for accidents in which its deputies were at fault. Those are the kind of numbers that fuel Republicans' demands for tort reform.

Most of the big-ticket financial judgments and pretrial settlements in police liability cases originate from traffic accidents—high-speed pursuits, responding to calls for backup, lead-footed patrolling, driving with your head up your ass. But excessive force and false arrests also give rise to set-tlements in the Monopoly-money range. The citizens of Los Angeles paid Rodney King $3.8 million for absorbing all those kicks and baton blows. Also in Los Angeles, in 1996 Javier Ovando was shot then framed by LAPD officers Ray Perez and Nino Durden. The nineteen-year-old gang member was sprung from prison and given $15 million by the city. And Abner Louima received $8.7 million ($7.1 from residents of New York City and $1.6 from the New York City Patrolmen's Benevolent Association) for suffering a broomstick shoved up his behind and then inserted into his mouth.

There's one thing that the preceding cases, from accidents to willful mis-conduct, have in common: Almost all the victims survived. What if they had died, wrongfully, at the hands of police? Those multimillion-dollar settlements would have been pared down to the hundreds of thousands or the tens of thousands. Or to nothing. Financially speaking, in cold accounting terms, the city of San Diego would have been better off had Frances Maday perished in that accident.

And Rodney King? Let's say everything happened exactly the way the cops said it did that night—up to the point that they laid hands, feet, and clubs on him: King takes the cops on a long chase, endangering everyone around him before he's finally stopped. He steps out of the car. But instead of being pummeled he is immediately shot dead by a bullet from a police service weapon. The police report reads that Mr. King leapt from the car, crouched and turned toward the officers, reaching for what the shooter thought was a pistol. *Bang!* King's out of the picture—no subsequent, "Can't we all just get along?" statements. Amateur cameraman George Holliday doesn't even have time to take the lens cap off his camcorder. What do you want to bet that (1) no cop gets disciplined; (2) there is no trial in Simi Valley, or anywhere else; (3) the city is spared fifty-five lives and a billion dollars in damages for four days of rioting; (4) truck driver Reginald Denny doesn't get his skull caved in; and (5) the City of Angels pays King's survivors not one thin dime?

That's how it works in police work. Lawyers and police chiefs will tell you: From a purely pecuniary point of view it's better to kill than to vegetize.

But, what of the moral questions? What of the *truth* of what happened out there on the streets? Unfortunately, morality and truthfulness are often victims in police liability cases. It was one of the few things I hated about being a police chief. Year after year, in both cities, San Diego and Seattle, I listened to the steady drumbeat of "risk managers" and city attorneys: *Keep your mouth shut on this one, Chief. We're hanging out a mile.*

To keep it from costing the city *too* much, we were advised, if not ordered, to suck it up and admit no wrongdoing. "Exposure" they call it. As in, *Just how guilty are we on this crash?* The greater the exposure, the stonier the silence of city officials. (Shortly after the Tacoma police chief shot and killed his wife in April 2003 [see chapter 1], a city council member told a reporter that the city had made "all kinds of errors in judgment" in hiring, retaining, and promoting the woman-hater, and in failing to respond to "all kinds of signs" that he was a vicious, controlling, emotionally disturbed individual. The council member was spot on, of course. But when informed of what she'd said, the mayor replied, "She *what?* You mean she admitted *guilt?*")

+ + +

A hypothetical situation: You're the police chief in your city. One of your officers, responding to an urgent call for backup and driving twenty-five mph over the speed limit, slams into a car containing a young father and his three preteen kids. Two of the children die in the crash. The father survives but will never walk again, or feed himself, or wipe himself. The surviving child, oldest at eleven, has brain damage and major internal injuries but is expected to recover. Physically. Your cop is in the hospital, being held for observation and nursing minor injuries. He's beside himself, understands he did wrong, feels wretched. He doesn't know it yet but he will find himself crying uncontrollably every time a tiny cue penetrates his consciousness. He may wind up drinking himself to sleep each night. He may decide to eat his gun.

You're furious at the cop even as your heart goes out to him. You don't have all the facts yet. Your traffic investigators will be at the scene for hours, recording conditions, measuring skid marks, calculating centrifugal force, doing all manner of science and arithmetic you don't pretend to understand, but which will confirm what you already know: Your cop was wrong, dead wrong. Your city is "exposed."

Because you preside over the most sensitive department in the city; because you are responsible for *everything* that goes on in your agency; and because you owe it to your employees, the community, the officer, city government, and that poor, suffering family to conduct yourself like a leader— you don't know what the hell to do.

You want to reach out to the family but you're not supposed to say anything (such as the truth) that could come back to bite you and the town's treasury in a trial four years down the road. You want to fire the cop but the police union will fight it, key members of the city council are in bed with the union, the city attorney intimates that a termination will weaken the city's defense, the county prosecutor won't file manslaughter charges, and the civil service commission would probably just overturn your decision. You want to send a crystal-clear message to your officers about reckless driving but you know they'll dismiss it as the politically-correct, holier-than-thou sentiment of a *chief*, someone who's been off the streets for a hundred years and doesn't remember what it was like out there in the real world. They'll label you an ivory tower bureaucrat who cares more about PR than police work—or the safety of his officers. They'll say things like, "What if it was *his* ass getting whupped?" and "How fast would *he* drive if he knew a fellow officer was being held at gunpoint?"

So what do you do? If you're a principled leader, blessed with a spine, *you tell the truth*, as you know it. You hold your cop accountable. If that means firing him you fire him. You tell the rest of your officers what you will and will not permit. You go see that grieving family and tell them how sorry you are.

You also check to see whether your *exposure* is even greater than you might have thought: Did you do a thorough background investigation on the cop before you hired him? Did you provide proper academy and ongoing training? Was he supervised effectively? Had he been disciplined before for similar transgressions?

Employment law is full of examples of negligent policies, procedures, and practices: negligent hiring, negligent training, negligent supervision, negligent retention, negligent equipment maintenance. Hell, there's probably even a law on negligent negligence. The important thing is for you to satisfy yourself that it was the guy behind the wheel, and only that guy, who was responsible for the crash. Not his academy instructor, not his supervisor, not the car he was driving, not his mother, not . . .

+ + +

One of the strengths, and drawbacks, of public employment law is that individual employees, from the cop on the beat to the police chief, are rarely held personally liable, financially. (That's *if* their actions spring from the "course and scope" of their duties.) The provision is a strength because having the city pick up the tab for damages means beat cops and police chiefs don't have *that* excuse for not taking bold action when they should. It's a problem because it licenses some cops to drive like maniacs, shoot people for no cause, or ram a broom handle up a man's rectum with impunity.*

Whether victims of police wrongdoing die or live out the rest of their lives physically disabled or brain-damaged, you've got to call it the way you see it. Police liability cases are horrible enough—the pain, the suffering, the money. It only makes matters worse when the chief of police gets timid and fails to do the right thing.

It's a horrible cross to bear, keeping your mouth shut when your heart tells you to speak up. Looking back, I believe I did speak up—most of the time. But there's one thing I never did, and it haunts me to this day. I never went to the home of a person we wrongfully injured or killed to accept responsibility and to apologize to his or her family. I would have been given hell by my cops, and by a battery of city lawyers and risk managers. But it would have been the right thing to do.

---

* If you want to call a thirty-year prison term impunity, which is what NYPD officer Justin Volpe paid for his *criminal* actions in the Louima case.

CHAPTER 22

UP WITH LABOR,
(NOT SO FAST,
POLICE UNIONS)

I WAS PART OF "management" for twenty-nine of my thirty-four years as a cop, but I'm a labor man at heart. No matter how often I listen to them, I get chills when I hear Woody Guthrie's "Union Maid" or Joan Baez's version of "Joe Hill" ("From San Diego up to Maine / in every mine and mill / where working men defend their rights / it's there you'll find Joe Hill . . ."). Upton Sinclair's *The Jungle*, which I read as a teenager, filled me with a passion for social justice that developed during my twenties. And Barbara Koppel's 1976 film *Harlan County USA* gave me a glimpse into the ancestral home of my father, reminding me of how greed and power corrupt, and why it's imperative that workers everywhere unite in the cause of economic and social justice. Whatever its modern-day faults, American labor comes from a proud history. But there's one sector of "working men" that cannot lay claim to anything remotely resembling a glorious history, certainly not in modern times: the nation's cops. Or, more accurately, their labor unions.

Police unions are, with noteworthy exceptions, a pernicious embarrassment to law enforcement. They've fought ferociously against equal employment opportunity for women, people of color, gays and lesbians. They've opposed citizen review initiatives, and undermined existing accountability measures. They've whined their way to a second set of "due process" protections for brutal or dirty cops. They've done public fundraising for corrupt, violent, criminal police officers. They've even engaged in systematic exploitation of, and theft from, their own members—and lied about it. And they've resisted even the most rudimentary reforms in community policing, promotions, internal discipline, and other efforts to professionalize the service.

All of which would be tolerable if they lacked clout.

But police unions pack big heat. How they established that power is a fascinating case study. Ironically, they owe a good deal of their political muscle to police management and to citizen critics with whom they waged acrimonious battles throughout the second half of the twentieth century. In San Diego, for example, the union resisted for decades the mere mention of a citizen review board. But in the mid-eighties, learning that some of us in management were researching citizen review possibilities, and spurred on by a ballot initiative, the union pulled a neat trick: They put their *own* civilian review scheme on the ballot. They spent a lot of money, politicked hard for it, and got it passed—the only police union–sponsored citizen review initiative in the country.*

Police unions fought, and continue to fight, management- or community-pressured reforms such as citizen review boards, the inclusion of citizens on internal shooting review panels, citizen participation in policy councils, the creation of "early warning" systems designed to curb abuses among individual officers. But where they've come to pass, these reforms have improved the public's image of rank-and-file cops— improvements that the unions then convert into constituent pressures on elected officials for higher pay and enhanced benefits.

Union leaders exploit this *unearned* political capital to woo (or frighten) state and local politicians. In the sway of police union power, many politicians, mostly Democrats, have accorded the unions unprecedented access and influence.

One example of the muscle of police unions, cited in an op-ed piece by Anndel Llano of ACLU Texas in the *American-Statesman* (February 4, 2004): "The Austin Police Association operates a political machine that . . . can single-handedly elect or defeat any city council member. The *Statesman* editorial board rightly concluded that the APA's power needs weakening."

And there's little doubt that police unions in Detroit and Los Angeles, unhappy with their reform-minded chiefs, used their considerable clout to

---

* In 2000, facing the greatest scandal in LAPD history, and seeking to send a message of no confidence in their chief, the 9,500-member union called for an independent panel of citizens to provide oversight to internal investigations into police corruption and brutality.

force two prominent African-American chiefs (Jerry Oliver and Bernard Parks, respectively) out of the business.

+ + +

I'm not against police unions. On the contrary. Working cops unquestionably need their own labor organization. Before the emergence of true unions in the early years of the twentieth century (as opposed to purely social or fraternal associations—which lasted on the West Coast well into the 1950s and 1960s), cops were systematically used and abused by elected and appointed officials (see sidebar).

A new Boston police officer in 1917 was paid two dollars a day, a salary that had not been raised in over sixty years. He worked seven days a week, putting in an average of eighty-five hours. Every other week he got a day off, but he couldn't leave the city without authorization. He slept in a dilapidated, bug-infested station house.

For two years, unofficial leaders of the rank and file pressed for basic reforms. They were ignored. In 1919 they applied for membership in the American Federation of Labor (AFL). Their commissioner, Edwin U. Curtis (appointed not by the mayor but by the governor of Massachusetts), reacted angrily, contending that police officers were not "an employee, but a state officer." The AFL came through for the cops, however, granting them a union charter in August of that year.

Attorney General Albert Pillsbury immediately introduced legislation that would make union membership illegal for all public employees. He railed that the "organized work man has taken us by the throat and has us at his mercy." The attention of both local and state officials was focused not on the grievances of the cops but on their right to unionize.

Curtis suspended unionization leaders. Talk within the rank and file turned to possible job actions. On September 9, 1919, Boston's cops went on strike, the nation's first police walkout. Senator Henry Cabot Lodge called the action the "first step to sovietizing the country."

Although 25 percent of the force remained on the job, it was apparent that volunteers would be necessary to keep the peace. Lawrence Lowell, president of Harvard, encouraged his student athletes to cross the strike officers' picket lines and volunteer for duty. Many did, but it wasn't enough. Capitalizing on the inadequacy of police presence, many residents engaged first in petty crimes, then in full-scale rioting. Inspired by the riots, the *Los Angeles Times* editorialized that "no man's house, no man's wife, no man's children will be safe if the police force is unionized and made subject to the orders of Red Unionite bosses."

The political, ideological context for these sentiments was obvious. In February 1919, a general strike in Seattle had closed the entire city for six days. Bombs had shown up in the mayor's morning mail. And some forty other mail bombs were intercepted on their way to public leaders throughout the country. It appeared to the power elites that a communist workers' revolution was under way.

But the striking cops in Boston weren't part of some grand international conspiracy to bury capitalism. They just wanted living wages and livable working conditions.

Every one of the strikers was fired, reflecting Governor Calvin Coolidge's resolve that "There is no right to strike against the public safety by anybody, anywhere, any time." The fired cops were quickly replaced by hundreds of unemployed or underemployed members of a labor force bulging with recently returned veterans of World War I. These new employees received handsome pay raises, reduced hours, and improved working conditions.

Police officers through the 1960s were grossly underpaid (they still are, for my money), and their working conditions were abysmal, and more dangerous (owing to a lack of training and equipment) than necessary. Their bosses often treated them like third-class citizens.

Some chiefs and commanders went out of their way to make life a living hell for their cops: middle-of-the-night transfers for no reason, and with no explanation; involuntary overtime, at no additional compensation; endless, illegal interrogations in internal investigations; nitpicking, demeaning discipline; promotional systems that advanced the chief's cronies; arbitrary assignments to detectives; and on and on. Police unions emerged for the same reason the AFL-CIO, the NEA, and the Teamsters were formed: to redress legitimate grievances, and to demand fair pay and fair play for their members.

As an SDPD sergeant in 1969 I wore a black armband with the number "22" on the left sleeve of my uniform, to signify our pay standing in the state. While I'd taken a firm stand against "blue flu" or other job actions that would jeopardize public safety—I supported Coolidge's dictum that public safety must not be compromised, ever—I had no such scruples when it came to symbolizing, conspicuously, the miserable salaries allocated to the policemen of the second-largest city in California.

But there remain many unattended problems with America's police unions. Let's start with money. Coincident to their rise in power in local and PD politics, many police union leaders developed a pattern of financial abuse. A few recent examples:

- In 2003 the former president and treasurer of the Dallas Police Patrolmen's Union was indicted on two counts of stealing from his fellow members. Seems he never left home without his union-issued American Express card, which he used to make the down payment of $2,420 on his new Ford F-150 pickup.
- In Hackensack, New Jersey, the treasurer all but gutted his union's benefit fund for the families of deceased officers when he ripped off $180,000.
- In Miami, a crooked accountant bilked the Miami Police Relief and Pension Fund, diverting monies to the "Florida Fund." It was your classic Ponzi scheme, the kind detectives work all the time. When a U.S. judge found out that the cops, who'd learned early about the scheme, had failed—criminally— to report the crime to the FBI for two months (thus recovering their own money at the expense of other bilked investors), he ordered them to repay the other twenty-seven creditors of the bankrupt estate of the Fund, along with $137,243 in back interest. The MPRPF recovery strategy had been orchestrated by its president, who has since been convicted of an unrelated charge of stealing from a police children's charity.
- Crooked union officials do seem to like going after funds earmarked for underprivileged kids and families of deceased police officers. Witness the Harris County (Houston area) Deputies Organization. Union officials there pocketed money they'd raised for the Marine Corps' Toys for Tots drive. They wound up repaying the fund a total of $274,756 (including attorneys' fees).

- A former Santa Clara County (California) Sheriff's lieutenant and ex-union president has been indicted for grand theft, tax evasion, and money laundering—money he'd raised for, you guessed it, police widows. The tab on this one: $1.4 million.
- A past treasurer of the Denver Sheriff's Union skimmed and embezzled from fellow members, and pled guilty to two misdemeanors. Then he ran for the Denver city council (he lost).

George F. Will, a columnist I read only when my blood pressure dips too low, made rare common sense in his May 12, 2003, *Newsweek* column ("The Stiletto's Sharp Idea"). He took on the duplicity of union leaders who demand "transparency" in management practices, including particular budgets and other fiscal matters, but who themselves behave like cabals, withholding critical information from their own members. He quotes Richard Trumka, secretary-treasurer of the AFL-CIO, cautioning big business not to " 'look like you don't want to disclose because you have something to hide.' Said the kettle, calling the pot black." (Question: How were the police union crooks cited above able to steal so freely from their members? Answer: They hid the dough before they stole it.)

There are many other examples of union leaders (presidents and treasurers lead the pack) who steal from their brothers and sisters in blue, or from the families of fallen officers. But there are other reasons, nearer and dearer to my heart as a former police chief, to question the principles, priorities, and values of police unions throughout the land.

- In 1993 the FBI informed the police commissioner in Buffalo, New York, that one of his narcotics officers was passing confidential information to drug dealers. Apart from the obvious moral and criminal indiscretions, this guy was endangering the lives of fellow cops. You'd think that on any of these grounds the Police Benevolent Association would support the commissioner's decision to transfer the narc (you'd also wonder why the hell the commish didn't fire the bastard). But, no. The PBA fought the decision—and won. The cop was reinstated to narcotics and awarded $18,438 in overtime he would have earned had he been allowed to remain a narc. Seven years later the cop was busted and charged with taking bribes, passing on information on upcoming police raids, investing his own "hard-earned" cash in dope deals, stealing drugs, and setting up his son in the drug biz.

- In the early 2000s in Boston, union leaders decided to play hardball—with their own members. In a recent round of contract negotiations they imposed a requirement on their members to picket the mayor's public appearances: five to seven hours every other month or face the loss of union-covered life insurance and dental plans, as well as scholarships, legal services, and voting rights.

- In Los Angeles, the Oscar Joel Bryant Foundation, a five hundred-member African-American officers' group, filed suit against the Police Protective League, calling the union a "bastion of white supremacy" and alleging discrimination in training and promotions. That same union supported Mark Fuhrman, financially and emotionally, even with his virulent racism firmly established.

- In New York City, twenty-three African-American cops have been shot and eighteen others assaulted by white officers in cases of "mistaken identity." Not one white cop has ever been shot by a black cop. The PBA, while bemoaning these "tragic incidents," has done nothing to help remedy the problem.

- Pat Frantz, president of the Tacoma police officers' guild, blamed a reporter for pushing his boss (and former guild president), Chief David Brame, over the edge. Days before Brame shot and killed his wife and then himself, John Hathaway, the muckraking publisher of *The New Takhoman*, had exposed Brame's abuses. Frantz sent Hathaway an e-mail: "If you want to throw stones you had better live in a bulletproof glass house." (He later apologized.) (See chapter 1.)

- Throughout the country, including Seattle, police unions have fought citizen review panels—in any form. Where they have been established, several unions (Philadelphia, Oakland, New York, and others) have instructed their members not to cooperate, or have otherwise dragged their feet.

The river of police union duplicity and hypocrisy runs deep. Police unions rail nonstop about laws and court decisions that afford criminal defendants their constitutional guarantees of due process; yet they lobbied for, and now enjoy (throughout most of the country), various versions of the "Police Officers Bill of Rights," a supplementary collection of due process privileges exclusively for cops, some provisions of which have seriously handcuffed internal investigations of alleged police misconduct. State and local laws, the direct product of police union influence, bar the release of names of officers involved in misconduct and/or the outcome of internal police discipline.

I support full due process rights for all public employees, including police officers. But I can't help but choke on certain *extra* privileges: A cop suspected of wrongdoing may not be required to give IA investigators a statement for up to a week after an incident (Delaware); he or she may have the right not to be interviewed at all but instead to supply a written statement to written questions (Seattle); he or she must be informed in writing of the nature of an internal investigation prior to being questioned (almost everywhere). Try conducting a garden-variety *criminal* investigation under these procedural burdens.

The Mollen Commission, the latest in a long series of blue-ribbon groups empowered to investigate and study police corruption in New York City, noted that "police unions and fraternal organizations can do much to increase professionalism of our police officers. . . . Unfortunately, based on our observations and on information received from prosecutors, corruption investigators, and high-ranking police officials, police unions sometimes fuel the insularity that characterizes police culture."

In order to understand how police unions foster such insularity, thus defeating organizational effectiveness and accountability to the public, it's useful to understand the unique features of the police culture itself.*

+ + +

Jerome Skolnick, author of the classic *Justice Without Trial* (1966), argues that cops become insulated from the communities they serve because of

---

* If I were still Seattle's chief and Mike Edwards still its union president, I'd get an earful from him on this particular topic. Questioning my use of the term, he claimed, preposterously, that there was no such thing as a "cop culture." Which made me think of that remark by Hanns Johst, often attributed to Hermann Goering, "When I hear the word 'culture' . . . I reach for my pistol." Hmm.

their unique work, which consists of exercising *authority* in the face of *danger* against a backdrop of organizational *"efficiency"* (i.e., demands for the production of traffic citations, field interrogations, and arrests, and the prompt handling of 911 calls). These conditions inevitably produce *social isolation* and *in-group solidarity*. Which gives rise to a powerful, insular culture of policing. A world of *us* versus *them*.

In a sense, police unions become the surrogate family for their members, with union leaders acting as Daddy. (I've never met, or even heard of, a female president of a police union, although I understand a woman constable filled in for her president while he was on annual leave from his job—in Wollongong, New South Wales.)

Insulation, isolation, alienation. It's no wonder most union leaders can't stand being questioned. They develop a pattern of brittle defensiveness, and snarky offensiveness against their "enemies," attacking honest efforts, internal or external, to make policing more accountable to the citizens it serves. It doesn't have to be that way.

+ + +

It's 1998. I've just finished fielding questions at a roll call at Seattle's South Precinct. One of the patrol officers intercepts me as I head for my car. "I don't know how you stand it, Chief."

"What's that?"

"All that bitching and whining back there." I have to smile.

"Have you ever known cops not to bitch and whine?"

"Yeah, yeah. But don't you get *tired* of it? And all that garbage in *The Guardian?*" I tell him I stopped reading the union's newspaper long ago. Month after month of articles and editorials about my positions on discipline, promotions, affirmative action, community policing, internal investigations—full of factual errors, mind-reading assertions about my "motives," and endless innuendos. I used to read it as entertainment, some of it being so over-the-top malicious or juvenile it was downright funny. But the "humor" wore thin.

"Tell me, how many of the officers agree with those articles in *The Guardian?*"

"Honestly? I'd say maybe twenty percent. Depends on the issue, of course. If you're talking promotions, where a white male gets passed over?" He shakes his head, grimaces. "I'd say just about everybody is with the Guild on that one. Hell, I'm with the Guild on that one."

"What about community policing?"

"We're with you there, Chief. We need to be better partners with the community, more open and so forth. And community policing really works. I think the majority of the cops are with you on just about everything you do. I really do."

"What about discipline?"

"Sore subject with me. The Guild bends over backwards to protect assholes who should not even be wearing this uniform."

"Aren't they just trying to protect the rights of *all* officers, you included?"

"Yeah, sure. But they carry it too far. They don't appreciate what it's like to work around a thief or even someone who's just basically a moron, you know, rude—the guys that are always picking fights. They . . . Look, you want to know why these guys get elected to the Guild board in the first place?"

"Sure."

"To do our dirty work. We all want more money, right? More this, more that? So who do we look to, to get it for us? Guys that'll stick it to the city, that won't back down. They may be obnoxious but they'll get in there and scrap for better pay, better benefits. I'll tell you, if it looks like we're fixing to get screwed by the city on medical benefits you don't want some Mr. Goody Two Shoes on your side of the table. I mean we're talking about my family here." He raises his eyebrows, and exhales audibly. "Shit. I guess *I'm* one of those guys that want these obnoxious assholes bargaining for us. Trouble is, it's these same guys who are dissing you and your programs."

+ + +

Trouble is? The trouble is that my ally in blue was unable to picture union leaders who could be tough, persistent, effective—and respectful. They had to be "obnoxious" to get the job done. And I, as their chief, according to his theory, had to bear the brunt of any "spillover" effect of their take-no-prisoners belligerence.

I worked with a union president in Seattle who spent his days marinating in a stew of mistrust. He pouted, he sued, he wrote nasty columns in the union rag, he refused to meet with my African-American community advisory panel, and he resisted numerous collaborative overtures, including an open invitation for him—or any member of his board—to actually *join* my senior leadership team. I guess he was afraid of being co-opted.

If I were representing the rank and file on labor issues I'd have *jumped* at the chance to meet every morning with senior members of the department, participate in discussions of issues of mutual interest—and for the benefit of the working cop. (If nothing else, I'd have seized the opportunity to gather intelligence about what the brass was thinking, and the actions it might be contemplating.)

It's not hard to understand why so many police union officials view "labor relations" as a struggle for supremacy, why every disagreement feels to them like a fight to the death. It can be an awfully lonely and thankless job—rank-and-file cops are quick to attack their union leaders for selling them out, for sleeping with the brass if they get the slightest whiff that their interests are not being protected by their union reps.

But when police unions refuse to join management in efforts to upgrade the force or improve its standing in the community, they give the impression they don't care about professionalism, that they'd rather protect than prevent dirty cops.

New York City's Mollen Commission took note of this trend, one I would argue is national in scope, and growing by the day: "[B]y advising its members against cooperating with law enforcement authorities [such as the FBI or one's own Internal Affairs bureau] the PBA often acts as a shelter and protector of the corrupt cop rather than as a guardian of the interests of the vast majority of its membership, who are honest police officers . . . *the [union] does a great disservice to the vast majority of its members who would be happy to see corrupt cops prosecuted for their crimes and removed from their jobs.*" [Emphasis added.]

So, how do we counter the power, the *misused* power of police unions? Through political and legal action. In Seattle, the American Civil Liberties

Union has filed suit to cause the city and the police guild to make transparent the union's push to gut the city's "civilian review" process, a process
so weak to begin with that it makes the whole drama somewhat laughable.
But, it is a start.

People who've been mistreated by cops only to see their complaints
whitewashed, and people who want their local police department to behave
competently, inclusively, and accountably need to become active. Find out
what kind of citizen review, if any, exists in your city. Determine how much
codified authority and political power your local police union wields. Insist
on transparency. Agitate for responsible collective bargaining (on both sides
of the table). Demand answers from the chief, the union president, the
mayor and city council. Police union leaders are, in one important respect,
no different from the managers they regularly do battle with—they're
political animals, subject to the pressures of the press and of the people.

Most important to reform are changes in labor law. Local and state officials must become emboldened if they're to curtail the excessive sanctioned
power of police unions—and of the bodies that oversee labor relations and
which issue judgments on individual "unfair labor practices" complaints.

Legislative and leadership failures are also endemic both within the
police unions and among the unions of different public emergency services.
In one example, the Seattle police guild has been at war with the firefighters' union for years over jurisdiction of their respective "dive teams."

+ + +

In August 2003, a boat overturned on Bitter Lake in the northern part of
the city. A fire department diver went into the water just as police divers
arrived. Moments later, firefighters on shore were instructed by a police
commander (adhering to protocols virtually written by the police guild):
"You do not have authorization to splash divers. You are not authorized to
splash divers. We are incident command on this situation." Thankfully, the
boat had been abandoned so the incident resulted in neither a rescue nor a
body recovery.

But police officers and firefighters fighting over who "splashes" into
which bodies of water to save a life? Unseemly, unspeakable. Picture it. A

witness spots a victim gasping for breath, going down for the third time. The witness calls 911. Cops and firefighters respond with lights and sirens. Witnesses, including family members, are greatly relieved to see emergency personnel pull up. But instead of rescuing the victim our public safety heroes stand on the shore, squabbling over jurisdiction, over who gets to claim this "body of work."*

The mayor ordered his police chief and fire chief to get their heads together and come up a new protocol, one that would sensibly allow whichever department arrived first to "splash" its divers. But, like the two mayors before him, he was talking to the wrong guys. He actually believed he and his department heads could make such decisions. He had not reckoned with the power, pettiness, and self-absorption of the police guild.

In his December 2003 column in *The Guardian*, guild president Ken Saucier had this to say about his firefighter brother in safety: "If the donkey from the movie *Shrek* and the Energizer bunny's crack-addicted little sister had a drunken but fruitful tryst, and then the offspring from that liaison was dropped on its head, you'd have a smarter, more subdued version of the President of Local 27, the fire union." (This is the same police union president who, grousing about the city's financial commitment to social programs, also wrote in *The Guardian*, "We still have the Sex Changes for Dwarf Junkies program and Internet access for the homeless. Never know when a good deal on a shopping cart is going to come up on eBay.")**

So the mayor, the city council, the police chief, and the fire chief are essentially powerless to make and enforce sensible public safety policies. And who's responsible for that sorry mess? Well, you can blame the unions, of course. But you can also finger those arbitrary and capricious government officials of yesteryear.

---

* The police guild contended that the fire union was making a grab for jobs reserved for police officers. "Body of work" is not an unimportant issue to unions, whether in the public or private sector. It means jobs. And it means strength in numbers at bargaining time.
** Ken Saucier was killed in an automobile crash in July 2004. He was returning to Seattle from Idaho, where, as one of the best shooters in SPD history, he'd participated in a pistol competition. Soft-spoken, always respectful in face-to-face communication, he was a fierce promoter and protector of officer safety and well-being. Something I greatly admired about him. I never understood the Jekyll-and-Hyde transformation that took place, however, when he put pen to paper.

In part to punish management Neanderthals, but mostly to set and enforce rules of fairness in management-labor relations, the state legislature in 1975 created "PERC," the Public Employment Relations Commission.

Every state has a PERC, whatever its name, whatever its powers. The Washington State commission is charged with providing "uniform and impartial . . . efficient and expert administration of state collective bargaining laws to ensure the public of quality public services." To carry out this mission, PERC engages in mediation, fact-finding, interest arbitration (for public safety employees in cities with populations over 10,000), and grievance hearings. PERC, headquartered in Olympia, is the eight hundred-pound gorilla at the center of local labor relations.

What did PERC decide when the police guild went crying to them about the firefighters' Local 27 "incursion" into their bailiwick? They declared the mayor's common-sense protocol null and void. He'd failed to bargain with the guild. Given that this jurisdictional battle has been going on for at least a decade, it's not hard to understand why the mayor would have little confidence that "bargaining" would resolve the issue.

Local 27, incidentally, is hardly a paragon of maturity and social responsibility. For years they've fought to keep the police department's harbor patrol boat from fighting boat and wharf fires—even though it's equipped to do so. Even when their own boats are miles away. Even when the freaking fire threatens to burn down half the town.

State and city legislators, in Seattle and in other cities, have got to end ridiculous incidents like these. If they don't, it's time for the taxpaying public to demand legislative changes.

+ + +

Exceptional police union leaders are worth recognizing, including former union president Mike Petchel of the Phoenix Police Department, former Police Officers' Association presidents Jack Pearson, Ron Newman, and current president Bill Farrar of SDPD, and Dr. Ted Hunt, president of the LAPD Protective League. These leaders, past and present, are obviously committed to improved "hours, wages, terms and conditions of employment" for their members. But they're also dedicated to the advancement of police professionalism, and to improved relations with the community.

Petchel, now retired, sponsored joint labor-management retreats that focused on trust-building. He was highly regarded throughout Arizona, and the country, for his political acumen, his inclusive, conciliatory approach to "the opposition"—from police brass to community critics. Farrar writes a monthly column for San Diego Police Officers' Association's newsletter, *The Informant.* While you'd never mistake its (justifiable) labor bias and its decidedly conservative bent, the message is consistently informative—and remarkably free of rancor and petulance. Hunt, with a Ph.D. in public administration, has been as assiduous as his department bosses in LAPD's struggle to understand and prevent another "Rampart scandal."* A senior fellow (on professional police practices) with the prestigious Institute for Developing Police Leaders (IDPL), Hunt believes, "Education is key to everything. It's the key to success, to understanding and tolerance."

Union leaders like these need to be supported and encouraged. They prove that police union leadership need not be corrupt or malicious or ill-tempered or defensive. They demonstrate that unions can actually help rather than hinder the cause of police professionalism and accountability.

---

* The scandal ignited in 1999 when officer Rafael Perez of the LAPD Rampart Station was caught stealing cocaine from an evidence locker, blew the whistle on widespread planting of guns and drugs, perjury, and the imprisoning and even shooting of innocent people. Ultimately dozens of officers were implicated and hundreds of convictions overturned.

CHAPTER 23

LIVING WITH
KILLING

Picture the end of your life. See it not as a natural death, the kind where your body slows down, its plumbing occluding, its vision dimming, its skin spotting and stippling, its frame shrinking and stooping. Imagine your death instead as something sudden, unexpected, and violent. One moment you're an emoting, interdependent being with obligations and aspirations, the next you're gone. No chance to make amends to your spouse, your kids, your parents, your lover, your friends. No time to finish reading or writing that novel, talk to your God, gas the car, pull up your pants. No opportunity to say good-bye.

That's how homicide is. I know this because of the hundreds of homicide scenes I visited as a cop. And because of the one I committed.

+ + +

It's a hazy Saturday afternoon, September 23, 1972. San Diego's version of fall is in the air. The beaches have thinned, the zoo is down to its post–Labor Day crowds, kids have gone back to school. Patricia, my second wife, is in her study working on her first collection of poems as I drive into the POA parking lot on West Market. I'm preoccupied with a dozen to-dos—budget, staffing, personnel evaluations, contingency plans for an upcoming antinuclear demonstration . . .

"Good, you're here," says Ken O'Brien. "Drop everything and come with me." He's more agitated than usual. I follow him into the patrol captain's office. "I need a lieutenant for this one." My boss hands me a note he's just scribbled. "We got a guy out in the east end threatening to kill his wife and kid." My adrenalin cranks up a notch. Cops live for these moments, even us midlevel managers who spend most of our shifts buried under mounds of paper. The note, in O'Brien's customary red ink, reads, *J. Carb. Threat to kill Baby. 2 1/2 yrs.* O'Brien has been rounding up as many plainclothes detectives as he can find on a late weekend afternoon. As they filter in, I bolt upstairs to the supervisors' locker room. I strip out of my uniform and get back into my civvies. I make a decision, and slip my service weapon into the waistband of my chinos: I realize the damage my off-duty gun can do but at the moment the snub-nosed Chief's Special feels like a toy. If this thing turns nasty I'd rather have the six shots, and the six-inch barrel.

When we're all present, O'Brien lays it out. Nancy Carberry, twenty, has filed for divorce from her estranged husband, Joseph Anthony Carberry, twenty-three. A records check reveals four or five arrests, for burglary and assault. There's a restraining order against him but he is allowed to visit their child, two-and-a-half-year-old Joey, once a week. Carberry is allowed no contact with Nancy, so earlier that day her mother dropped the kid off at his mother's house.

A couple of hours later Carberry starts calling people. His mother-in-law, his sister-in-law. He tells them he's going to kill the kid, any cop who intervenes, his wife, his mother-in-law, then himself. O'Brien has sent a sergeant out to pick up Nancy. We'll meet her in the field, get additional details.

I assign two-man teams: Sgt. Kenny Reson and Jim Sanders to Team 1, Ron Collins and Don Wright to Team 2, Dave Kelly and Joe Varley to Team 3. Hoyle and I are Team 4. We get word that Nancy Carberry is en route to Normal Heights. I send Team 1 to meet her at Thirtieth and Monroe.

Hoyle gets the keys to the armory, hands out binoculars, portable radios, shotguns. I send Teams 2 and 3 to Morley Field, east of the zoo. O'Brien activates SWAT, tells its commander to muster his team there, too. Hoyle and I hustle out to his Ford Torino in the POA lot and he drives us to Thirtieth and Monroe. We meet Nancy, and learn more about her husband.

Joseph Anthony Carberry, Jr. White male, 5'7", 150 pounds. Reddish auburn hair. Unemployed truck driver. Drives a '67 blue Ford Galaxie, driver's door smashed in. Father of two boys, Joey and one-year-old Jim. He's violent, unstable, Nancy tells us. Twice he's beaten up her brother as he tried to rescue her. He's thrashed her grandfather, sending him to the ER. He's slapped Joey repeatedly, beating him with a belt, intensifying his attacks as she pleads with him to stop. He's blackened both her eyes, tied her up with speaker wire, hung her upside down in a closet.

"Does he have a gun?"

"Yes."

"What kind?"

"A .32 pistol. It's his roommate's." Nancy sobs and shakes as she talks. "He's called back twice since Mom phoned you guys. He keeps saying he's going to kill Joey. He's really off the deep end, totally crazy. He hasn't been eating, or sleeping. He wants me back even if he has to kill me to get me."

It's nearing 5:30. Carberry is an hour and a half deep into a violation of a court order. He's out there somewhere, angry, confused, running scared. And acting cagey. He's been stopping, we theorize, at different pay phones, making his calls curt, untraceable. In his last one, he'd given instructions for Nancy to follow. She's to walk south on Texas from El Cajon, turn left at the next block, right at the next, left at the next. He'll be waiting for her there.

I assign the teams to north-south, east-west grids. We head out, leaving Nancy with the patrol sergeant. The last thing we want to do is use her for bait, but we have to consider it. Ideally, we spot Carberry before he gets to his next phone booth. He leaves Joey in the car, and gives us a shot at taking him down a distance from the kid.

"I keep thinking about that little boy," says Hoyle.

"Yeah, me too." I imagine him, from his mother's description. Tow-headed, thigh-high to a short adult. Wearing green pants, a green short-sleeve shirt, white socks, and one black shoe.* I picture Matthew, at Joey's age. He's in the backyard on R Avenue, running around on a hot summer day in a pair of Oshkosh B' Gosh overalls, no shirt, no shoes . . .

The radio crackles. Team 2 is on the air. They've spotted the Galaxie up ahead, though they can't tell whether there's a kid in the car. They tail

---

* We learn later from a friend of Carberry's that Joey had lost the other shoe as Carberry loaded him into the car that morning. He'd refused to go back for it.

Carberry for a while, then back off as Team 1 slides into place. Carberry takes a serpentine route through the residential streets south of El Cajon Boulevard. Team 1 sloughs off, replaced by Team 3. A few blocks later, Hoyle and I take over. I see Joey's blond mop on the passenger side. I get on the radio to the other teams, "The kid's definitely in the vehicle. Repeat. The kid is in the car." I switch over from tac to freq 3 and advise all patrol units to stay out of the area until notified. "We don't want to spook this guy."

Carberry turns north on Texas and crosses the boulevard for the first time since we've been tailing him. He's in commercial territory now. A promising sign. The Galaxie makes it through on the yellow at Meade but we catch the red. "Bust it, Freddie."

"You got it, Boss."

I switch back to tac. "Stay close, guys. But don't let him spot you." Hoyle rolls through the red light, slow, like a tourist with his head up his ass. "Nicely done, partner."

At Madison, Carberry signals a left. The gas station: He's headed for the Mobil station on the northwest corner to make his next call. It's only a hunch, of course, but strong enough for me to instruct all detective units to converge. When traffic clears the intersection, Carberry does indeed turn in to the station. He parks in front of a row of pumps, gets out of the car, chats for a second with the attendant, then heads for the phone located just inside the service bay. We pull onto the lot like we're going for gas. "Stay with Joey," I say to Hoyle. "I'm going after him."

I slide out of the car, letting Carberry get as far away from the kid as possible. He stops at the phone. As soon as he lifts the receiver I badge him. "San Diego Police." I don't shout it but say it in the firm, clear "command presence" voice I was taught in the academy. "Let's talk, Joseph." Joseph doesn't want to talk. He drops the phone, leaving it dangling on its coiled chrome snake, and rabbits across the service bay and out an open door on the other side. I pull the .38 from my waistband and give chase. This time, I do shout. At the top of my lungs: "Stop or I'll shoot!" I won't, I know. I'd never shoot the guy in the back, even with what I know about him. But talk's cheap: maybe it'll cause him to put on the brakes. Instead, he kicks on his afterburner and shoots past old tires and barrels of oil and solvent. He circles back to the car where Hoyle is trying to get into the locked passenger side to extract our little hostage.

Carberry beats me back to the car by three or four steps. It's at this point that the situation, not unlike dozens of similar incidents I've handled before, becomes dissimilar. I don't expect what comes next. All along, I'm thinking I'll use my mouth or my fists or my right arm to solve the problem—logically, I'd choke him out.

But Carberry takes away all but one option as he jumps into the car, grabs something from his waistband and, shielded from my view, jabs it hard and fast against Joey's head, then screams in an inhuman voice, "I'm gonna kill him! I'm gonna kill him!" He convinces me. I stick my gun into the car, point it at the back of his head, level the barrel so the slug won't follow a downward path, and pull the trigger.

A 125-grain bullet from a .38 S&W revolver leaves the muzzle at 1,025 feet per second. The bullet I put into Mr. Carberry's head traveled approximately six inches.

As I start to grab Carberry I hear a shot, and glass breaking. I jump back. *What the fuck?* Then another shot. I scream at Hoyle, "That's enough!" He'd seen Joey's head drenched in blood, was certain the kid had been shot. I pull Carberry's limp body by the back of his shirt and jerk him out of the car. He weighs no more than a pillow. I pitch him to the ground. He falls face first to the pavement. I reach in and extract the blood- and brain-soaked child. He's numb, silent. I bundle him in my arms for a moment and look into his eyes. I hold him aloft, check for holes. I stand him on his feet, long enough to see if he'll fall over. He looks down, sees his father, and begins to scream. As I lift him back into my arms I spot Kelly and Varley. They've sprung from their car and are charging toward me. Varley, a big, gregarious Portuguese from my academy class, gets there first. I pivot and lateral the kid into his arms. He hands him off to Kelly, darts back to their car, and jumps behind the wheel. The two detectives make a dash for Hillside, Joey on Kelly's lap. *This is good,* I think. Kelly, frog-voiced, gruff and cynical on the outside, is actually one of the department's most sensitive souls. And a first-aid instructor.

A few minutes later, with patrol cops and detectives swarming the lot, Kelly calls from the hospital. "The kid's okay, Norm. He's okay. No injuries." *No injuries . . . no injuries.*

Called from home, Homicide Team 1 shows up, most of them within the hour. Their sergeant is Jack Mullen, one of the best homicide dicks in SDPD history. He divides up the labor: witness interviews, scene reconstruction, measurements, diagrams, photos, identification, collection, and preservation of evidence. The gas station is closed down, taped off. Mullen sees to it that Hoyle and I are separated, our guns taken from us.

I'm standing alone, dispassionate, impressed by what I see. SDPD Homicide is doing its thing by the book.* They finish with us, at least at the scene. Hoyle and I, thirty feet apart, are about to be driven to headquarters, in separate cars. It's dark now. Most of the station's lights are off. Dew is collecting on Carberry's car. I feel—nothing. A patrol sergeant has been assigned to transport me to headquarters. Homicide detective Jim Sanders waves him off. "Come on over here for a second, Lieutenant." He takes my arm, moves me away from the others. "Take a look at this."

In the palm of his hand, wrapped in a mechanic's blue-colored rag is an invention of Sanders's creativity, and a product of his fealty to the brotherhood. It's a metal measuring tape with a black plastic-handled screwdriver jammed into its slot. "Look at it, sir. *Anybody'd* mistake this sucker for a gun. It was on the floor, right there where you pulled the body out."

"I didn't see it, Jim."

"You sure, sir? It was right there."

"I didn't see it."

"Oh. Oh, okay. Sure." I imagine the detective struggling with how *not* to mention this find in his exhaustive inventory of the car's contents.**

I started to walk toward my ride then turned around. "Jim?"

---

* Mullen, long since retired and living in Bandon, Oregon, writes police procedurals. If you're in the market for a good, authentic read on homicide investigations, and homicide detectives, I highly recommend his books.

** In preparation for this chapter, I opened, for the first time since the shooting, a file marked "J.A.C." Among the yellowing reports, their staples rusted to dust, is the Evidence Report for "Special Investigation CG-2123" by Detective J. L. Sanders. Item No. 3 is "(1) Plastic handle screwdriver wedged in steel tape, wrapped in blue cloth. Received by SANDERS, placed in Crime Lab."

"Yeah, Lieutenant?"

"Thanks."

There was no gun. The man I shot to death was unarmed.

+ + +

Back at headquarters, O'Brien tosses me the keys to the patrol chief's office. "There's a lot of press around," he says. "You won't get interrupted there." I walk down the long, dark corridor and unlock the double doors leading into the corner pocket. The place is like a tomb. I switch on the light in Chief Bob Jauregui's office, take a seat in his executive chair, and insert a blank 153 into the Olympia typewriter sitting on a credenza behind the desk. As I start to type I notice the blood. It hadn't registered. It's cakey, rust-colored, and splattered all over my shirt and pants, and my brand-new shoes. *I'll never get that out of these shoes. The bastard.* Then I remember. I call Patricia.

"Hi."

"Are you okay? You sound funny."

"I'm fine. I just wanted you to be aware of something. It'll be on the news tonight."

"What?"

"I shot a man."

"Oh, Norm. Is he . . . did you . . . is he . . . dead?"

"Yes."

I finish the report and walk it over to Sanders in Homicide. Then I call Patricia back. "Let's go have pizza, okay?"

"Pizza?"

"Yeah, Venice." Our favorite pizza joint, Thirty-third and El Cajon, just a few blocks from the shooting.

"Are you sure you . . ."

"Yeah, I'm sure. But I don't want to talk about it, okay? I need to do something normal." I pick Patricia up at our new home in Tierrasanta. At Venice we split a No. 3 with pepperoni and mushrooms and talk about Nixon and Vietnam and the hopelessness of McGovern's campaign.

+ + +

Four years after the shooting, Father's Day. My ten-year-old son is with us for the weekend. We're shooting hoops in the backyard. Matt wants to know why I always stare off into the canyon, why I'm always quiet, or mad at him, on Father's Day.

+ + +

Ten years after the shooting, divorced from Patricia, I'm dating a defense attorney in Santa Monica. We have an argument in her apartment. I walk to the beach, take my shoes off, and start running as fast as my legs and lungs permit, on the undulating dry sand. Off in the distance, rippling through waves of heat, I see the back of Carberry's auburn head. A second later it blows up, brains and blood exploding everywhere. Someone or something jerks my legs out from under me. I crash to the sand, and can't get back up. I can't catch a breath. I don't know what to do. I'm embarrassed.

+ + +

Thirteen years after the shooting, I'm sitting on a sofa, talking to a shrink. Under orders. Lisa, the new woman in my life has issued an ultimatum: Get help, or get lost. I don't understand. I'm fine. I'm happy. I'm not nuts. But I love her, so here I am. The shrink wants me to talk about the shooting. No problem. I've told the story, several times. To recruits, so they can learn about tactics. To citizen groups, so they can understand more about DV. But this is different. I relive that September afternoon. It hits me that I've never spoken to anyone about the *feelings*. That's because, until this moment, on this couch, I hadn't realized I had feelings about it. I cry, tears rolling down my face. I start shaking, and can't stop.

+ + +

It's better today. In the era of my shooting, police administrators were clueless. Nobody thought to replace the cop's firearm, sometimes for days. When the significance of that oversight dawned on police officials—a cop without a gun is like a CPA without a calculator—they adopted a policy of immediately replacing the firearm. Someone, I don't remember who, had loaned me a .38 the day after. I'd thanked him.

In the early seventies a cop who shot and killed someone was often subject to the worst possible response from his colleagues: praise. Not for his actions or his decision making or even the result but for the shooting act itself. We didn't know any better. We didn't have peer counseling or psychological services. We didn't know that a cop involved in a shooting, particularly one that ends in death, is a different person after he or she has pulled the trigger.

"Nice shooting, Lieutenant," said a patrolman who'd been giving me the cold shoulder ever since I'd gone public with my beefs about our business. "Guess I was wrong about you." *Nice shooting?* How could I have missed? *Wrong about me?* You asshole. You think I feel good about killing a man? But his was a common reaction around the station house. People who'd never done it saying "you done good," patting you on the back, like you'd scored the game-winning TD.

Almost as bad were those who acted like it hadn't happened. When O'Brien offered up the keys to the chief's office, it was the first and last thing he said to me about the shooting. Ever.

A cop who's involved in a killing (or any other traumatic event) needs to be handled with care—for his or her own well-being as well as the future safety of the community. The shooter must be taken off the streets, of course. (Permanently, if the incident is a terminable offense; manslaughter comes to mind, as does murder. Also terminable? A shooting that reflects a cop's incurable fear or impulsiveness or indecisiveness.) The officer should be given a desk job long enough for the investigation to establish the facts, and to determine whether the cop is fit for duty. How to make that determination? A session on the couch.

At the time of my shooting there was no requirement or expectation that cops involved in fatal shootings see a psychologist or psychiatrist. The only expectation was that you'd be back at work the next day, presumably with a borrowed gun. At the time that was fine with me: I didn't want my colleagues thinking I'd been *traumatized* by the event, for chrissakes.

In subsequent years, officers involved in fatal shootings were offered the *option* of seeing, at company expense, a psychologist or psychiatrist. But the problem with noncompulsory visits was that they tended, in our macho culture, to stigmatize those who elected to "talk it out," to get help for their flashbacks, their night sweats, their feelings of guilt (even in unassailably justified shootings). In time, we figured out that the best policy was to *mandate* psychological fitness-for-duty appraisals, conducted by competent professionals who are familiar with the police culture (and, of course, with the short- and long-term emotional effects of the use of lethal force). If everyone goes, no one gets stigmatized.

Even more helpful today is the assistance of "peer support" officers. We didn't pioneer it in San Diego, but SDPD was one of the first to recruit volunteer cops who'd been involved in fatal or serious-injury shootings. We gave these officers intensive training in "peer counseling" and made them available to every cop who shot someone. The counselors were on call, just like Homicide and IA and deputy district attorneys and a union rep, available to roll to the scene on a moment's notice. These cops had been there. They knew what to say and do—and what *not* to say and do. They knew how to help their fellow officers understand things about the shooting incident: department policies and procedures, the roles and responsibilities of Homicide, the DA, Internal Affairs, and what the shooter could reasonably expect from the department in the weeks and months ahead. Most important, they understood how the incident could affect officers psychologically, both in the moment and in the future.

+ + +

There are two critical accountability concerns about officers involved in fatal shootings who are allowed to return to the streets. First, will the officer be *trigger happy*, too quick to resort to fatal force when "less lethal" means are available and appropriate? Second, will he or she hesitate to pull the trigger again, in a situation that demands it? In either case, the lives of both citizens and police officers hang in the balance.

+ + +

EPILOGUE

Three months before I moved to Seattle I got on the elevator at SDPD headquarters and punched seven. The car stopped at the fifth floor and a DV detective got on. "Ah, Chief. I was just on my way up to see you. Got a minute?"

"You bet. What's up?"

We were alone but he said, "I'd rather wait till we get to your office."

"Okay." He had an incident report in his hand. *Shit*, I thought, a cop. One of our officers has gone and beaten up his spouse or girlfriend. We got off the elevator and walked into my office. The detective handed me the report. I looked at the name on it. My blood turned cold.

San Diego police officers had the night before been called to the 805 bridge over Interstate 8. A man was lying between the concrete abutment and the guardrail, threatening to jump. The California Highway Patrol had closed two southbound lanes, as well as the ramp below. Negotiators talked with the despondent man for an hour, before convincing him to surrender. In his hand he clutched a small photograph of his two-year-old daughter. His girlfriend, the child's mother, had just broken up with him after he'd beaten and threatened to kill her. On the way to County Mental Health, Joseph Alan Carberry blamed his problems on his mother, his girlfriend, and the police officer who'd shot his father twenty-one years earlier. He told the arresting officers he was going to track down and kill that cop.

I looked at the black-and-white DMV photo clipped to the arrest report. Joey was a man now, his chubby face topped by a mop of dishwater blond hair.

CHAPTER 24

CITIZEN OVERSIGHT

THE DEBATE HAS RAGED for decades, pitting citizen against citizen, political activist against government, police union against city administration. It's time to blow the whistle, end the agony, and do the right thing: Every city and county with a history of strained community-police relations should employ independent public oversight to investigate citizen complaints. No institution, including the police, can adequately police itself.

In 2001 the National Institute of Justice (NIJ) published "Citizen Review of Police: Approaches and Implementation," written by Peter Finn. While declining to promote a particular system, the report describes thoroughly the costs, advantages, and disadvantages of various systems of citizen oversight. It identifies four models:

Type 1: *Citizens investigate allegations* of police misconduct and *recommend findings* to the chief or sheriff.

Type 2: Police officers investigate allegations and develop findings; *citizens review and recommend* that the chief or sheriff approve or reject the findings.

Type 3: Complainants may *appeal findings* established by the police or sheriff's department *to citizens*, who review them and then recommend their own findings to the chief or sheriff.

Type 4: An auditor *investigates the process* by which the police or sheriff's department accepts and investigates complaints and reports on the thoroughness and fairness of the process to the department and the public.*

---

* Notice that none of the models calls for external panels to determine police *discipline*. That's a good thing. Remove disciplinary authority from the chief and you neutralize his or her power to set and enforce standards of performance and conduct.

The NIJ study, which examined nine representative citizen review jurisdictions across the country, analyzes each according to its: (1) openness to
public scrutiny, (2) mediation option, (3) subpoena power, and (4) right of
the officer to legal representation. The Berkeley (California) Police Review
Commission, for example, a Type 1 system, opens its hearings and commission decisions to the public and the media, holds general PRC meetings
for the public to express concerns, issues full public reports, including
interview transcripts, requires the city manager to make his or her response
public after review of PRC and Internal Affairs findings. (IA's findings and
the chief's discipline are not made public.) Berkeley's mediation option is
described as "dormant." Its model of citizen oversight includes subpoena
power. The officer has a right to legal representation both during the investigation and at the hearing.

By contrast, hearings are private under the Minneapolis Civilian Police
Review Authority, also a Type 1 system. The complainant is simply informed
whether his or her complaint was sustained. The general public is invited
to monthly meetings to express concerns. The chief's discipline is made
public. Mediation is an option. There is no subpoena power but officers are
required to cooperate. Officers are entitled to union representation during
the investigation, and legal representation during the hearing.

San Diego employs a Type 2 system, with a twenty-three-member Citizen Review Board. All Internal Affairs investigations are reviewed by a
rotating three-member panel of the board. In a collaborative, rather than
"adversarial," approach, the panel attempts to resolve disagreements
directly with Internal Affairs brass. The case is not closed until the panel
and the board agree with the IA finding. If the CRB disagrees with an IA
finding, it appeals to the city manager. If the board disagrees with the city
manager's decision, it is authorized to appeal directly to the district
attorney, the grand jury, or, in the case of alleged civil rights violations, the
Department of Justice. Since its inception in 1989, the board's "negotiations" with IA have resulted in several changes to the original department
finding (I recall one in which Homicide had failed to interview a crucial
witness in a fatal police shooting). Three cases have been referred to the
grand jury.

Seattle has a generally weak, hybrid form of citizen oversight, falling loosely into Type 2 and Type 3 categories. Established after I left (but responding to a mess created on my watch, a theft and attempted cover-up), the city created an Office of Professional Accountability. However, while the OPA is headed by a civilian employee who oversees internal investigations, she reports to the chief of police. A new three-person "citizen review" body is confined to reviewing *only* completed, redacted, randomly selected internal investigations, then reporting to the city council any "trends and patterns" it may find. Finally, there is a citizen auditor position, which was in place when I arrived in 1994. Held then by retired Superior Court Judge Terrence Carroll and now by former U.S. Attorney Kate Pflaumer, both highly respected in the community, the auditor's position is arguably the strongest of the constellation of "review" mechanisms. But, thanks to the uncompromising opposition of the police union, Seattle's approach to citizen oversight is scattered, inefficient, and unsatisfying to many.

New York City has a fully independent Civilian Complaint Review Board, a Type 1 model. Created in 1993 and staffed by 164 personnel (115 investigators), it receives, investigates, and holds hearings on citizen complaints about excessive or unnecessary force, abuse of authority, discourtesy, or offensive language. It has subpoena power, access to records, and the authority to make official findings on the 4,000 to 5,000 cases it receives each year.

At the end of 2004 there were only sixty-seven citizen review systems in place nationwide. With almost nineteen thousand local law enforcement agencies, it's safe to say most cities have rejected the notion of independent oversight of police practices. Even where there is little or no philosophical resistance, mayors, city managers, and city councils have decided the financial costs are too high.

Citizen oversight budgets vary greatly, predicated mostly on whether investigations are carried out by the department (then reviewed by the oversight body) or by the citizens themselves.* The "mean cost per complaint

---

* Using trained, professional investigators. Citizens serving on oversight commissions or boards have neither the time nor the expertise to conduct complex investigations into alleged misconduct.

filed and investigated" in 1997 for those nine agencies studied by the NIJ? It ranged from $20,000 a year for a one-fifth-time staffer in Orange County, California, to $4,864 per month in Berkeley. New York's CCRB costs the taxpayers $10.5 million annually (or $2,100 per investigation based on five thousand complaints per year).

+ + +

It's not just philosophical, or financial: Cops and their unions also *loathe* citizen review boards because of what they've seen in their own cities or heard about in others: untrained, unskilled, biased investigators; degrading treatment in public hearings; investigations that drag on for months, if not years; findings unsupported by the facts.

These were the kinds of issues on the minds of the PBA and its members who protested, violently, when in September 1992 New York Mayor David Dinkins expressed his support for the creation of the CCRB. Thousands of officers demonstrated in front of City Hall, blocking traffic to the Brooklyn Bridge and shouting racial epithets. (Rudolph Giuliani was there as an anti-CCRB protestor; he was elected mayor the following year.) It was ugly, from all accounts—not the best way to press a grievance about "public oversight." Yet, according to Human Rights Watch, the officers were prescient in their concerns.

HRW reports that the New York Civil Liberties Union, perhaps the strongest backer of the creation of the CCRB, soon became one of its most vociferous critics. Why? Lack of adequate funding, mismanagement, incompetence, shoddy investigations, a "guilty" finding in only .05 percent of the cases. And investigations that took forever to complete.

The CCRB says today that it completes the average investigation in nine months (which means, of course, many take far longer). If the *average* consumes three-quarters of a year, you can bet that many witnesses will have forgotten what they saw or heard, or will have moved away or died or developed a motive to tell the story differently from the way they witnessed it.

+ + +

You're a cop, out there in the elements, risking your life, delivering a service a lot of folks didn't ask for and don't want—some of whom let you know it by attacking you, verbally or physically. Whether you respond professionally or not, the last thing you want is to be hauled before a body of *civilians*, second-guessed, berated publicly, your reputation damaged, your career stalled or destroyed.

It should come as no surprise that some people who complain about police officers lie. They don't like cops. Or they don't like the fact that they got caught doing something they shouldn't have. Or they figure a complaint will bolster their defense in court. I believe that when a citizen willfully, provably lies, he or she should be prosecuted—and prepared to defend himself or herself against a civil action by the police officer. Citizen activists bemoan my position on this. They fear that taking action against a lying complainant (in all my years in the business, I met very few who fabricated complaints from whole cloth) puts a chill on the willingness of honest people to come forward. I don't see it that way.

If we want our frontline cops to accept, or at least not defy, citizen oversight (not a bad goal) we owe them an honest, credible system.

+ + +

One of the great frustrations arising out of citizen complaint investigations is that in a number of cases you'll never know who was right or wrong. These situations occur when, as is often the case, there is no physical evidence to tip the scales in an unwitnessed incident. You say X, the cop says Y. What does the investigator (or the investigator's boss) do? Labels your complaint "not sustained" (not saying it happened, not saying it *didn't* happen). It's a finding that satisfies no one. The best way to reduce the number of "not sustained" findings? Improve the quality of the investigation.

According to its web site, New York's CCRB investigators, all civilian, undergo "an intensive three-week training course that focuses on the CCRB's jurisdiction and rules, interviewing techniques, methods for acquiring documentary evidence, structure of the police department, and patrol guide procedures. They also receive instruction on legal principles governing the use of force, search and seizure, and discourtesy." They participate in simulations, critiquing one another's methods and skills. In addition, they must complete a two-day police academy class, go out on a ride-along, and view tactical field demonstrations. In 2003 fourteen of its investigators participated in a two-week Internal Affairs class for NYPD's IAB recruits. Once they're out of school, new CCRB investigators go to work with managers who have a minimum of fifteen years' investigative experience. These managers are drawn from such agencies as IRS (Criminal Investigative Division), DEA, Federal Defenders, and the U.S. Probation Department.

Which all sounds terrific. But what's the *quality* of the training? And *who are* these investigators? Are they rejects from other agencies? Who backgrounds the new investigators, and how thoroughly?

Shoddy investigations, by definition, lack credibility in the eyes of everyone, complainants and cops alike. Further, unskilled investigators produce a disproportionately high number of those unsatisfying not-sustained findings. They just can't figure out *what* happened.

+ + +

Other possible dispositions? *Founded:* It happened, just as the complainant said it did. *Unfounded:* It didn't happen. *Exonerated:* It happened, but that's life. The officer used precisely the type and amount of force you complained about but he or she was fully justified by law and policy in its use.

In San Diego, we developed two additional findings. The first, *misconduct noted*, meant that the officer was innocent of the accusation but not of other, uncharged misconduct that surfaced during the investigation. Cops don't like that one, but what are you going to do? The second was "retraining needed," a self-explanatory finding.

+ + +

In 1992 I studied SDPD's Internal Affairs investigations, and came away much impressed by the overall quality. I could see why the CRB had a few disagreements with our internal process, and its findings. The contrast between New York and San Diego couldn't have been more stark. We were sustaining fully 22 percent of all excessive force complaints and 31 percent of all discourtesy complaints. But there was one significant problem: The investigators were taking *way* too much time to complete their cases, an average of sixty-seven days! The office goal was forty-five. I dropped it to twenty-one, and added investigators, and more training.

I'd hate to be a cop in New York City, where my family and I would have to wait nine months to a year or more to learn what's going to happen to me. For that matter, I'd hate to be an aggrieved citizen who filed a complaint a year ago and still hasn't a clue about the outcome.

+ + +

As you can see, there are great variations in the types, costs, and quality of citizen reviews throughout the country. Personally, I favor a model that provides for (1) independent investigations by a paid staff of top-quality investigators; (2) subpoena power for the commission or board; (3) transparency throughout the process, including the publication of findings and the chief's disciplinary disposition; (4) full legal representation at all stages for the accused officers; and (5) an opportunity—through mediation—to avoid the whole adversarial process where possible.

Mediation? Let's say you're stopped by a police officer—the only *fact* not in dispute. You say the officer never told you why she stopped you; she says she did. You say she was abrasive; she claims she was polite. You say she threatened to take your kids to Child Protective Services; she asserts she said no such thing. You say . . . And on and on. Why tie up a citizen oversight panel with a case like this? Mediation should be a *front-end* option in all cases where the allegations do not involve excessive (physical) force, racial or other form of discrimination, sexual harassment, or criminal conduct (which would be handled as a criminal investigation anyway).

Regardless of the model employed by a particular jurisdiction, there are certain outcomes that a successful citizen oversight system will achieve.

The National Institute of Justice report does a nice job of identifying them.* Complainants report that they:

- Feel "validated" when the oversight body agrees with their allegations—or when they have an opportunity to be heard by an independent overseer, regardless of the outcome.
- Are satisfied at being able to express their concerns in person to the officer.
- Feel they are contributing to holding the department accountable for officers' behavior.

It's not just citizen-complainants who benefit from external oversight. The NIJ report cites law enforcement administrators who've found that their jurisdiction's program:

- Improves their relationship and image with the community.
- Has strengthened the quality of the department's internal investigations of alleged officer misconduct and reassured the public that the process is thorough and fair.
- Has made valuable policy and procedure recommendations.

And elected and appointed city officials report that public oversight:

- Enables them to demonstrate their concern to eliminate police misconduct.
- Reduces in some cases the number of civil lawsuits (or successful suits) against their cities or counties.

---

* As does Samuel Walker's *Police Accountability: The Role of Citizen Oversight* (2000), which goes beyond the NIJ report in detailing approaches to community outreach, evaluation of the work of citizen panels, and anticipating and overcoming the inevitable legal and political obstacles associated with creating healthy, sustainable citizen oversight. Also highly recommended: the International Association of Chiefs of Police report "Police Accountability and Citizen Review: A Leadership Opportunity for Police Chiefs," and the work of IACOLE and NACOLE, the International and National Associations for Civilian Oversight of Law Enforcement, respectively. I was privileged to address these citizen associations in San Diego and in Canada. As unwavering advocates of citizen oversight they can hardly be called "impartial," but they are overwhelmingly represented by people of strong principles and integrity. I was struck by their passion for fairness for all parties.

Still, rank-and-file officers really, really do *hate* citizen oversight, and often for good reason. But they must understand that they are *public* employees. An "occupational hazard" for those who do the public's work is that they are subject to the *opinions* of that public. As a police chief, I encouraged citizens to come forward with feedback, positive and negative, on all contacts with my officers (commendations, incidentally, outnumbered complaints by about ten to one).

I believe the type of oversight system a community chooses is critical to its success, and, as I've said, it ought to be one with teeth. But, in the end, the competence, fairness, flexibility, and integrity of the *people* involved— the chief, the panel and its investigators, the union, the rank and file—are of equal if not greater importance.

THE POLITICS
OF POLICING

CHAPTER 25

EGOS ON PATROL: GIULIANI vs. BRATTON

"MIRACLE IN MANHATTAN"
The Screenplay

FADE IN:

Over the strains of the Drifters' "On Broadway," a MONTAGE: Times Square, Broadway between Forty-sixth and Forty-seventh. DAY and NIGHT shots, FRIGID and SWELTERING moments, too. Squeegee men, panhandlers, numbers runners, hookers in miniskirts and halter tops, a man urinating against a wall, dope dealers, cops—all interspersed with scenes of yellow tape, chalked body outlines on the sidewalks, crime headlines from the newspapers, and the urgent voices of local TV's talking heads covering the latest murder against background sounds of boom boxes and sirens.

EXT. CITY STREET—NIGHT

Recently elected Mayor Rudolph W. Giuliani has just stepped from his chauffeur-driven SUV. Across the street, his police commissioner, William J. Bratton, has just stepped from his chauffeur-driven SUV. They're wearing identical Burberry trench coats. Neither expected to see the other.

Giuliani

Hey, Commish! Nice coat. What the hell are you doing out this late? Look at this shit. Can you believe it? You see why we gotta get my new crime plan up and running?

A TV truck shows up out of nowhere. A NEWSWOMAN steps out, approaches,
MICROPHONE in hand. The mayor turns to her, smiles. A bright light shines
in his face, a CAMERA rolls. Giuliani, his comb-over fluffing in the wind, looks
directly into the camera then back at the NEWSWOMAN.

> Hey, Julie. Nice to see you this evening. Just
> look at this mess. Hey, this is a good oppor-
> tunity to show your viewers I'm coming after
> every two-bit thug on these streets—the pan-
> handlers, the squeegee men, the dealers. If
> they won't behave like decent human beings I'm
> going to round 'em up, write 'em up, and clear
> 'em off the streets.

> ### Reporter
> Good evening, Mr. Mayor. We just finished a
> piece on homicides, a couple of blocks over. I'm
> glad we caught you. Any chance I can have a word
> with our new police commissioner?

The camera scans over to the commissioner.

> ### Giuliani
> Zero tolerance, my friend. That's our philos-
> ophy. Zero tolerance of lawbreakers, scofflaws,
> miscreants . . .

The camera switches back to the mayor. The reporter ignores him, addresses her-
self to the commissioner. The camera switches back to the commissioner.

> ### Reporter
> Mr. Commissioner, can you tell our viewers:
> What exactly is your strategy for dealing with
> crime and . . .

The mayor interrupts. The camera swings back to him.

Giuliani

Well, as I've explained, our strategy for dealing with crime is to tolerate *no* violations of the law. Tolerance of lawlessness, no matter how seemingly trivial, subtracts from our quality of life. It makes our streets fearsome and foreboding. We're going to *drastically* improve the quality of life of every law-abiding New Yorker by refusing to tolerate what you see here tonight. The prostitution, the illegal gambling, the urinating in public, the . . .

The reporter interrupts the mayor. The camera switches over to the commissioner.

Reporter

And, Mr. Commissioner, how do you propose to . . .

The mayor interrupts. The camera switches back to the mayor.

Giuliani

Did I mention zero tolerance? No law too small, no offense too petty. We're going to enforce all infractions. And I've got just the commissioner to do it. Best damn police commissioner in the country. Anyway, that's my crime plan. Right, Commissioner?

The mayor puts his arm around Bratton, pulls him into the picture. Bratton addresses Giuliani, the camera has them both in the picture for a moment then focuses on Bratton.

> **Bratton**
>
> That's right, your honor. "Broken windows." Take care of the small stuff, repair those broken windows, get those abandoned beaters off the road, pinch the misdemeanants, give the physical reality of the city a safe feeling. If the streets *look* safe and *feel* safe, New Yorkers will . . .

Giuliani, obviously agitated, interrupts. The camera swings back to him.

> **Giuliani**
>
> See why I picked Mr. Bratton, here? He's a thinker, a doer. What'd we have before I was elected, Commissioner? Twenty-five hundred, 3,000 killings a year? In a *single year*?

Camera switches rapidly from mayor to commissioner.

> **Bratton**
>
> Two thousand two hundred and ninety, your honor. In 1990.

Camera back on the mayor.

> **Giuliani**

Speaking directly into the camera.

> See what I mean? Unacceptable. Totally unacceptable. You watch. We're going to cut the murder rate in half. Better than that, actually. Mark my words. We're taking this city *back!* Now, if you'll excuse us. The commissioner and I have some crime-busting business

to discuss. Did I mention he's the best police commissioner this city has ever seen? First-rate. Doing a terrific job with my crime plan. Thanks for your time, Julie. Good to see you out here.

The TV reporter thanks the mayor and the commissioner, says a few words to the folks back in the studio. Lights and camera are cut. Reporter and cameraman head back to their truck. Giuliani and Bratton stroll down the block to a deserted ALCOVE.

Giuliani

Okay, Bratton. What the fuck was that all about?

The commissioner squints, shakes his head, obviously puzzled.

Bratton

What do you mean?

Giuliani

You know goddamn well what I mean. What the hell are you calling the press for?

Bratton

I didn't call any . . . Didn't she just say they were in the neighborhood?

Giuliani

Look. Let's get one thing straight. *I'm* the capo here. This is *my* city. No one elected you any-thing. Got that? *You* work for *me*. Capiche?

Bratton

Of course, your honor . . .

INT. MAYOR'S OFFICE—DAY

Sitting behind a massive DESK, U.S. and STATE OF NEW YORK FLAGS behind him, the mayor gets up, walks around the desk, shakes hands with his police commissioner who's just walked into the office, his trench coat draped over his left arm.

> Giuliani
>
> Bill, Bill, Bill. Good to see you. I just wanted to remind you why I selected you. You listen, and you take directions well. I like that. I like what you're doing with that Comstat thing, putting my program for precinct accountability into action. And hiring that guy, what's his name? The crazy guy with the crazy shoes. And that crazy hat. What kind of a hat is that, anyway?

> Bratton
>
> A homburg, I think.

> Giuliani
>
> Right, right. A homburg. What's the guy's name?

> Bratton
>
> Maple. Jack Maple.

> Giuliani
>
> Like the syrup?

> Bratton
>
> Like the syrup.

> Giuliani
>
> Well, he's a colorful one, he is. Seems to know his stuff, though. I'll give him that.

The mayor pauses, shakes his head, continues.

I don't know . . . Maybe he's a little too,
what, *too* colorful? If you catch my drift.

                    Bratton
Your drift?

                    Giuliani
Publicity, Commish, publicity. The press. Your
man Maple seems to need a lot of ink. A lot of
ink, indeed. I'm beginning to think maybe he's
even taking a little credit that might belong
to certain others. If you catch my drift.

                    Bratton
But, he . . .

INT. MAYOR'S OFFICE—DAY

*Nine months later. The press, academics, and voters have noticed a positive
change in the environment around Times Square. The mayor sits behind his
DESK, does not get up. The police commissioner walks into the mayor's office,
GLOVES in hand. Starts to remove his COAT. Giuliani waves him off.*

No. No need to sit down. I'll cut to the chase:
You, my friend, are skating on thin ice. You
know damn well that what's happening in this
city, this, this . . . transformation, is my
doing. Not yours, not your syrupy friend, not
your academic "broken windows" pals. This is
mine. *My* strategy. *My* tactics. *My* police
department. *My* success! You got that?

> **Bratton**
> But, sir, I . . . My commanders, and the men
> and women of the . . .

> **Giuliani**
> I said, you got that? Good. Then let's act
> accordingly, goddammit. And, what's this shit
> about you holding press conferences and enter-
> taining reporters in your office? What's with
> these late-night sessions at Elaine's, for
> chrissakes! What's that about?

> **Bratton**
> I don't have a big press office, like . . .

> **Giuliani**
> Hey, don't get smart-mouthed with me! I hear
> you're even planning a freaking "police parade"
> up Broadway? Right? On your freaking birthday!
> Is a pattern starting to emerge here for you?
> Or are you just a clueless fuck?

> **Bratton**
> I hear what you're . . .

Eighteen months later. Crime is down, dramatically. The streets are clean. Visitors are flocking back to New York. Giuliani has claimed credit for it. He's appeared on TV, on "Saturday Night Live" (in drag). He's become a celebrity. Bratton's had his share of publicity too. He's not been on SNL, he's not pulled the plug on artists' works, nor carried on a highly public affair with a woman not his wife. But he has energized his department, and he's talked about the success of NYPD's crime-fighting efforts. He tells the nation's chiefs that the police can cut crime, even as he cautions them to be ready for an increase in citizen complaints about "overly aggressive practices." Tensions have been escalating steadily between the mayor and the commissioner. Then Bratton appears on the cover of Time *magazine. The article attributes New York's turnaround to the new commissioner. Giuliani summons him.*

INT. MAYOR'S OFFICE—DAY

Bratton walks in to find Giuliani behind his desk, his jaw set, his eyes reduced to a reptilian slit.

> Giuliani
> Shut the door, asshole.

> Bratton
> Who you calling an asshole?

> Giuliani
> There's only two of us in this office.

> Bratton
> That doesn't clear up a thing.

> Giuliani
> Nice article in *Time*.

> Bratton
> Why, thank you, your honor. I was a little worried that you'd . . .

> Giuliani
> Get out. You're fired.

FADE TO BLACK

THE END

+ + +

Okay, so it's make-believe. But it can't be too far from the way it really happened. Much has been written about the relationship between New York City's former mayor and his police commissioner of 1994–96: Giuliani and Bratton's celebrated "he said/he said" battles, their struggle for media supremacy, their competing claims to the credit for the remarkable turnaround in the city's fortunes. Each man has written a book, each crowing about his success in office. I had drinks with Bratton toward the end of his all-too-brief tenure at a hotel bar in Albuquerque. We were attending the Major Cities Police Chiefs conference. I sensed that he believed the end was near, that neither he nor Giuliani was going to budge. Which meant the victory would by default go to the mayor. I was sad about that. I admired the "Commish," still do. He's cocky and brash, and he can be flippant at times. But he's the real deal, and he knows how to make cities safer.

+ + +

Bill Bratton had established a fine reputation as chief of Boston PD, and later as head of the New York City Transit Police, where he got rid of that all-too-familiar signature of New York, subway graffiti. (The New York City Transit Police Department was consolidated with the New York City Police Department to become a new Bureau within the NYPD on April 2, 1995.) Still, Bratton lasted a mere twenty-seven months before Giuliani sacked him. You have to wonder what more could have been accomplished were it not for the clash of those two publicity-thirsty, power-hungry egos. Bratton was, by all accounts, doing a hell of a job.

It wasn't on his watch that Louima, Diallo, and Dorismond were tortured or killed by cops of the NYPD. Nor was it on his watch that NYPD's finest, scores of them, stood by and watched several women being assaulted in Central Park during the Puerto Rican Day parade in 2000.*

---

* I happened to be in New York, to officiate at the wedding of friends. The incidents in Central Park were, if anything, even more disgusting than the media's accounts. I saw men in blue, riding around on a kid's motorized scooter, and laughing as sexist louts sprayed water on passing women, and called them names. Just yards away from their "post," which the cops told alarmed witnesses they couldn't leave, women's blouses were being torn off, their breasts fondled, their crotches groped.

It *was* on Bratton's watch that NYPD cops got naked in the lobby of a Washington, D.C., hotel.

+ + +

I was in what we in the Pacific Northwest call the "other Washington" for the annual police memorial service. One of my young officers, Antonio Terry, had been shot and killed in the line of duty. Most of the Terry family was also there, including his wife, Cheryl. A nurses' convention was being held in our hotel at the same time. When drunken, bare-ass naked NYPD (and other) cops weren't harassing the nurses, they were straddling the rails of the escalator and riding it up and down, pouring beer all over themselves, whooping and hollering into the night.

When finally someone got the drunks tucked in to bed, the rest of us hotel guests, many drained from a cross-country trip and the emotions of the occasion, settled in for a little shut-eye before the morning's service on the Mall.

In the middle of the night we were awakened and forced to parade out to the sidewalk in jammies and robes as the hotel's fire alarms shrieked— and the corridors filled with the acrid contents of fire extinguishers. Just another little prank by members of the biggest police department in the country.

The next day some of those same cops sat in the open trunks of antique police vehicles, firing rounds into the air as they raced about the streets of our nation's capital. Its humor was lost on Cheryl Terry and her family, including her young fatherless boys, Austin and Colton.

True to his nature, Bratton kicked major butt when his cops got back home to New York. He disciplined seven officers, firing two of them for the debauchery (including one known to his buddies as "Naked Man").

+ + +

More than most, Commissioner Bratton was willing to stick his face into the delinquent corners of the police culture, and capture the attention of both crooked and twisted cops. His strong commitment to integrity, and to corruption-free police practices, was much in evidence throughout his tenure. When he stormed the "Dirty Thirty," rounded up and arrested those corrupt cops, and melted down their tainted badges, honest police officers everywhere celebrated.

Bratton also addressed long-standing institutional problems of vague, unfixed responsibility and authority for crime fighting and problem solving. He put the onus squarely where it belongs, on *precinct commanders and field supervisors*. We police administrators like to think that we'd been holding our subordinates accountable for results long before Bratton came along. But we were bullshitting the public, and ourselves.

As police commissioner, Bratton put into practice a computerized mapping and statistics system that had been developed by his deputy and chief strategist Jack Maple, he of the homburg, when Maple and Bratton had worked on the Transit police force. "Comstat," also referred to by many as Compstat, was a rigorous, precedent-setting internal accountability program, with an improbably unimaginative label (it stands for "computer statistics"). Modeled after successful business practices in which individual departments and managers are held accountable for meeting specific performance standards, Comstat put precinct commanders under the gun, continuously, for *results* in the struggle to reclaim New York City.

Each week, commanders were called to a meeting at the command center to present and defend their crime-fighting strategies—and outcomes—in front of the brass. They were required to describe in concrete terms the statistical picture of crime in their precinct—and what they were doing about it. Behind them, on a huge screen, were arrayed the relevant numbers: crimes by type, time, place, frequency. And in front of them? Deputy Chief Jack Maple, grilling each commander mercilessly, questioning everything. Had the commanders reached their crime reduction targets? If not, why not? And what did they intend to do about it? The precinct commanders were not judged solely on their numbers of arrests or citations, but on their outcomes. Was the quality of life, as measured by crime and disorder, improving week by week, month by month?

Like hundreds of other chiefs from around the world, I sent representatives from SPD to New York to check it out. My people came back with glowing reports, and urged adoption of the Comstat model. We considered possible pitfalls: Comstat's potential to induce an unhealthy competition between and among precincts, fudging facts to generate additional resources, crime reduction "by eraser" (i.e, intentional underreporting). But even though there had occasionally been such problems in New York, they were immediately addressed. Some commanders quit under the pressure, some were shown the door.

We decided to create our own version of Comstat, which we tagged "SeattleWatch." Because of our size (four precincts versus New York's thirty-four), we held monthly instead of weekly meetings. And, because this was Seattle, after all, with its penchant for process and inclusion and honoring all points of view, ours was no doubt a kinder, gentler interrogation of precinct commanders. But the principle was the same: Devolve authority and responsibility to their rightful locus—geographically based, neighborhood-anchored precinct commanders, and hold those commanders accountable for getting the job done.

Bill Bratton did all that in New York, not Rudolph Giuliani.

+ + +

Bratton is now chief of LAPD, attempting to work a little Big Apple magic in the City of Angels. He's inherited a once-proud, badly understaffed, scandal-ridden, demoralized agency in a city plagued by increases in violent crime, particularly gang murders. If anyone can turn it around in L.A. it's Bill Bratton. But his experience in the East, being fired after only two years on the job, raises questions about mayoral–police chief politics—and the ability of city government to launch and *sustain* an effective, comprehensive crime-fighting strategy. Particularly one that builds improved relations with the community and fosters respect for civil liberties.

+ + +

Tension between elected mayors and the chiefs they appoint are all but inevitable. Why? Philosophical differences, power struggles, "personality" conflicts. But there are ways to work around these tensions.

When Norm Rice, Seattle's first African-American mayor, went looking for a new police chief he conducted a national search. Having recently lost out on the chief's job in San Diego, I mailed off my resume. It survived a "paper screen" that yielded eight candidates. Each of us was then interviewed by a twenty-three-member citizen panel. Next, I was grilled by the deputy mayor and other staff members. Then I was shrunk by an L.A. shrink, and backgrounded by mayoral staffers and police investigators (along with two junketeering city council members who, once the mayor had picked me, traveled to San Diego for their own investigation).

All of that time and effort would have been for naught if the mayor and I hadn't agreed on *how* to police the city of Seattle. Or if we had disagreed on our respective roles (i.e., the *decision-making jurisdiction* of the mayor vis-à-vis that of the police chief). Or if we couldn't stand each other.

I'd met with Rice several times during the selection process, but the most consequential of those meetings took place one brisk, sparkling evening in October 1993. We were on the seventy-sixth floor of the Columbia Tower in a private dining room that overlooked downtown and a huge expanse of Elliott Bay and the Puget Sound. By then, I'd fallen in love with the city. I thought I would just about die if I didn't get the job.

Norm Rice, a gregarious former TV reporter who could make his voice sound like he was talking under water, and who (privately) performed viciously accurate imitations of city council members, also had a serious love affair going with the city.

Like Giuliani, he craved safe, clean streets. But unlike Republican Giuliani, Rice, a lifelong Democrat, fiscal conservative and social progressive, insisted on *responsible* police practices to achieve those safe, clean streets. He was for gun control, against the war on drugs (or at least its excesses). He was for social justice, against racism, sexism, homophobia. He was the city's nominal and substantive leader in the creation of healthy communities, leading campaigns for libraries and literacy, low-income housing, parks, services for children, the elderly, and the homeless and other downtrodden members of society. Yet he was worshipped by the business community for his support of initiatives designed to ensure downtown redevelopment and economic vitality throughout the region.

You don't see mayors like this in San Diego, I thought. I really want to work for this guy. And *with* him. And move to Seattle.

Over halibut and chardonnay, Rice laid out his expectations for the person who would become his next chief, something he'd already done with the other finalists. "I want a chief who will take the initiative, solve problems, and get the job done," he said. "Without needing to have his hand held." I liked the sound of that. "But I also want a chief who understands who's boss."

"And that would be . . . *you?*"

He laughed. A big, honest laugh. Not a politician's laugh.

"You got it." He went on to talk about his need to be kept informed, not surprised by his chief, and a number of other commonsense boss-subordinate stuff. All of it sounded reasonable, not micromanagerial—or megalomaniacal. When he finished, I asked him if he wanted to hear *my* expectations. Of him.

He stared at me, eyebrows raised. But I figured if he didn't want to hear what I had to say, as much as I hungered to be Seattle's chief, it just wouldn't be worth the trouble. Every subordinate has expectations of his or her boss—it's just that these expectations are so rarely communicated, and when they are it's usually after a blowup, and in angry, passive-aggressive ways. I waited for his answer.

"Well, sure," he said. He sat back and listened.

I told him that if I were his chief I would expect him to: (1) keep his mitts off my vice, intelligence, and narcotics sections; (2) let me handle *all* internal discipline, no matter how hot it got for him (or for me); and (3) let my staff and me decide who got promoted and where they got assigned.

He nodded, then laughed again, something he would do often throughout our relationship. "I think I can meet those conditions, *boss.*"

It was my turn to laugh.

"I've got one more," I said.

He rolled his eyes. "Go for it."

"I'd prefer not to get blindsided by some policy from the twelfth floor of city hall, or some big decision that affects the PD."

He nodded. The look on his face suggested that he was able to picture himself in the role of police chief. "Agreed."

I was on a roll, but decided against asking him if I could turn in the retiring chief's baby blue Buick LeSabre for a new company car. "Your expectations make sense," I said. "If you make me your chief I'll meet or exceed every one of them. And I'll make you proud that you picked me."

Our relationship began inauspiciously. At a meeting with the editorial board of the *Seattle Times*, I was asked if I favored citizen review boards. I said yes. Seated to my right, the mayor said, "No, he doesn't." It was our first disagreement, but far from our last. We disagreed often on budget issues. I wanted more cops, he wouldn't give them to me. I wanted a new work schedule for my cops, he wouldn't hear of it—not without union concessions. But Rice was absolutely true to his word, right down the line.

He gave me feedback on the performance of my chiefs and precinct commanders, word he'd heard from the street. But he never "recommended" anyone for promotion. He never asked me to put this captain here or that one there. He monitored vice, narcotics, and intelligence operations but never once interfered.* He held his tongue on internal discipline.

While we warred over budgets and work schedules, Rice came through for me when he provided (unbudgeted) funds that allowed me to equip my cops with semiautomatic weapons, bulletproof vests, and, with council support, computers for detectives. Time and again he ended touchy conversations with, "You're the chief."

Put everyday mayor-chief tensions in the context of "differential" press attention (between egos like Giuliani's and Bratton's, for example) and you get a clear picture of the enormity of the challenge. Who gets the credit when things go well? Who gets the blame when they don't? With Rice, it was something I never thought about.

And he never blindsided me. I couldn't have asked for a better boss. We were a team, he and I. Seattle's public safety team.

It was not a happy day for me when Norm Rice decided not to run for a third term, but instead to throw his hat in the ring for governor (he lost in the primary to Gary Locke, the nation's first Chinese-American governor). To this day, my former boss and I get together for dinner a couple of times a year. It's always a treat, no matter who's buying.

---

* A smart move on his part. Politicians who intercede, for example, on behalf of pals or contributors whose names crop up in connection with a vice raid almost always get burned, sooner or later.

+ + +

Rice's decision to leave the mayor's office left me dangling. Who would be my new boss? How would we get along? One thing became clear during the primary: Jane Noland, a three-term city council member, saw herself as the next mayor, and she'd made it abundantly clear that, if elected, she'd replace me. Had she won, I'd have saved her the trouble.

The woman didn't care much for Rice, and for that reason alone had little use for me. It didn't look good. She had the strong backing of the police union, had raised a ton of money, and was considered the front-runner. But she came in fourth in the primary, with 15.8 percent of the vote.

Paul Schell, a wealthy developer-architect-attorney, became my new boss in January 1998. He was brilliant. A deep thinker, well-traveled, a true visionary with plans to upgrade the city's infrastructure, add amenities, and solve Seattle's horrendous traffic congestion. He was a likable sort. We'd crossed paths a few times when he was on the campaign trail. I think we had a good feel for each other, and a good feeling about each other.

Between his victory and his inauguration we met for an "expectations" conversation similar to the one I'd had with Rice. Our first year together went well, each of us abiding by the terms of our unofficial contract. But in his second year things began to happen that would damage our relationship.

It started when he created a citizens panel to examine department policies in the wake of that "unfortunate incident" I mentioned earlier (the $10,000 theft by a homicide detective). The mayor was already populating the panel when he bothered to inform his police chief. *Blindsided.*

In a nod to "bipartisanship," Schell appointed Mike McKay, George W. Bush's Washington State campaign chair, to head the panel. Although the panel's "investigation" produced several solid recommendations (including one that at least marginally strengthened citizen review), it was badly handled from the beginning. Confidences were breached, files lost, inaccurate information leaked to the press, reputations damaged.

We got through the "scandal" but in November of '99 Schell poured a bucket of salt into my healing wounds. The "Battle of Seattle" over the WTO meeting was brewing. Y2K was threatening to halt transportation, paralyze ATM machines, cut heat to homes and businesses, freeze public and private payrolls, and generally create massive chaos. It was a tough time for the two of us, but the mayor made it worse for everyone by publicly insulting my colleague, Sheriff Dave Reichert, and in the process damaging relations between the mayor's office and city and county law enforcement.

Schell became the first incumbent mayor since 1938 to lose a reelection bid in the primary. You don't have to be genius to conclude that he lost it because of WTO.

And "Mardi Gras."

A year after I retired, the city's annual Pioneer Square celebration turned violent. I read about it, almost dispassionately, as a citizen at large. As usual, the streets were clogged, youthful knuckleheads using the opportunity to ogle and grope bared breasts. But on the last of four nights of celebration, following steadily escalating troubles, "Fat Tuesday" erupted into a full-scale riot. Gil Kerlikowske, the city's new police chief, pulled his cops out—much to their dismay. Whether he made that decision because it was "too dangerous" for his officers or because the police would have "further inflamed" the crowd, both of which theories were tossed around in the aftermath, it was a fatal mistake. Twenty-year-old Kristopher Kime witnessed a young woman being trampled by the crowd. When he went to her assistance he was struck in the head with a bottle, then kicked and stomped to death. While the cops watched, and the mayor slept.

Despite our philosophical differences, power struggles, and personality conflict, I took no pleasure in Paul Schell's downfall. He always wanted what was best for the city, and he had an exciting vision for Seattle's future. But he learned the hard way that the shortest route to failure in the mayor's office is to mishandle—or to be perceived as mishandling—public safety.

+ + +

As Schell's experience proves, even mayors have bosses. Norm Rice and Paul Schell had 530,000 of them. Rudy Giuliani had eight million.

Prior to September 11, 2001, many New Yorkers entertained significant doubts about their mayor. Sure, he'd cleaned up the city, but at what cost to civil liberties? Crime was down, but citizen complaints were up. Giuliani used his clout, and the city's treasury, to censor art and needlessly antagonize liberals and civil libertarians. He fired a respected police commissioner who'd made tangible crime-fighting progress—and who'd shown firmness in curtailing unlawful police practices.

With Bratton gone, the mayor installed at One Police Plaza a safe, acquiescent commissioner. Former fire commissioner Howard Safir was blindly obedient to Giuliani, a puppet, according to many NYPD cops. When Safir stepped down Guiliani replaced him with his former *driver*. Bernard Kerik was a hell of narcotics detective in his day, and his life story is gripping, truly inspiring. But what organizational or administrative skills led Guiliani to believe that Bernie Kerik was qualified to become, first the mayor's chief of corrections, and five minutes later, the head of the NYPD, the largest law enforcement agency in the country? In light of the hugely embarrassing, near disastrous appointment of Kerik as President Bush's director of Homeland Security, quickly withdrawn for "character" reasons, it's apparent that the mayor had also failed to vet his pal for either job. The mayor, with compliant commissioners in place, continued to jump to the automatic defense of police officers during a run of "tragic" incidents involving people of color—Louima, Diallo, Dorismond, et al.*

Who knows? Had Giuliani been eligible to run for a third term, he very well may have lost. Remember, this was *before* 9/11.

+ + +

Like so many others throughout the world, I was extremely impressed and deeply moved by Rudolph Giuliani's leadership in the aftermath of the terrorist attacks in 2001. Giuliani earned his day in the sun, and his own picture on the cover of *Time*, as "Person of the Year." But we shouldn't lose sight of a painful, indisputable fact that speaks to Giuliani's failures in overseeing public safety in the years leading up to 9/11.

Had the mayor provided adequate budgetary support, particularly in radios and other communications equipment—and had he insisted that his

---

* New York currently has, in Raymond W. Kelly, a Michael Bloomberg appointee, a commissioner who is no one's lapdog. Serving for the second time as head of NYPD (Giuliani fired him in 1994 to make room for Bratton), Kelly is one of the most respected leaders in the field. He's as tough on police corruption and misconduct as he is on crime. One can only hope that the public's impression of the relationship between Kelly and Bloomberg, that of mutual respect, holds true in private.

police and fire departments develop reliable means of communicating with one another—it is likely that lives would have been spared on 9/11. The former mayor's livid response to criticism and questions of his handling of these issues is unseemly: Over four hundred firefighters, police officers, and other emergency service providers perished on 9/11.

In Giuliani's hubris, he believed he knew best how to *run* NYPD and FDNY. Only the most egotistical public official thinks he can be both mayor and police commissioner. Giuliani would have done himself a service by swallowing his pride and congratulating both himself *and* Bill Bratton for making New York glisten.

+ + +

I've been a chief-watcher for years, long before I joined their ranks in 1994. I've seen superb police executives, decent men and women, get chewed up and spit out by rank politicians, mayors who fail to understand their value. Some of these top cops, burned out and fed up, leave of their own accord. Some get the boot. Some, like James Jackson in Columbus, Ohio, sue their mayors. And some decide to run for mayor. Frank Rizzo (Philadelphia), Frank Jordan (San Francisco), Carlos Alvarez (Miami Dade), and Lee Brown (Houston) are just a few of the many police chiefs, good and not so good, who have morphed into big-city mayors—for better or worse. Tom Potter, former chief of the Portland Police Bureau, was just elected mayor in that city. He'll be a good one. (Potter's a fishing buddy, but I won't let that stand in the way of the truth: I'd have voted for him if I could.) Hell, even ex–middle managers have a shot, witness Tom Bradley, a former LAPD lieutenant who served three terms as mayor of Los Angeles. It's common among police chiefs to think they can do a better job of running the city than their bosses.

There is little that citizens can do to directly influence the relationship between a mayor and a police chief. The relationship is largely private, carried out by phone calls, e-mails, and office visits. Yet the public has a huge stake in the way these two officials behave. The best way to ensure that the relationship is not characterized by ego trips, bickering, and backstabbing but by mutual respect, is to elect self-confident mayors. Like Norm Rice.

CHAPTER 26

MARCHING FOR DYKES ON BIKES (AND AGAINST JESUS)

HOMOPHOBIA CAME NATURALLY TO me. At the time I hired on as a San Diego police officer, the only gays I assumed I'd met were the wheezing adolescent in engineer boots and leather jacket who'd unzipped my pants in the front row of the Bay Theater when I was six, and Johnny McGowen, a neighborhood boy who preferred to be called Suzy, wore poodle skirts, and twirled a baton after school.

In the seventh grade I asked Dad about Suzy. He mumbled something about odds and ends and queers and rears, and how guys in the navy took care of fairies like that. His explanation wasn't helpful, and I let it go.

Then I became a cop and was introduced to nonstop gay-trashing humor—in the classroom, the coffee shop, the locker room, everywhere cops gathered. I was also introduced to life on San Diego's lower Broadway, where everyplace you looked there were grown-up Suzies: she-he's strutting up and down neon-splashed streets, laughing in high-pitched voices, playfully slapping one another, picking up sailors and marines. When you'd arrest one—usually on the complaint of a serviceman who'd stuck his tongue down the throat of a hooker, reached for her pudendum and found something altogether unexpected—they'd tell you how they were only trying to earn money to swap out their sexual equipment for a new, improved model.

I was still a rookie, less than two years on the job, when Lt. Ed Stevens of Robbery–Sex Crimes called me into his office. "The chief wants the fags cleaned out of Balboa Park. That's a job for the Pink Berets. You're now officially a Pink Beret." Fags? Pink Berets? What did I know about that stuff? My patrol lieutenant had recommended me for the job, Stevens had picked me. Did they think I was one of *them*? I felt my face flush.

"Wear tight clothes," said Stevens. "You can smile but don't raise your eyebrows and don't lick your lips. That's entrapment. Just wait for them to start gobbling each other or go for your dick, then badge 'em." He handed me a typewritten list of relevant penal code sections: soliciting, indecent exposure, oral cop, sodomy. A conviction meant you had to register as a sex offender, for life.

That was it then, my mission. Hang around the toilets, grin at the degenerates, witness their abnormal sex acts, then bust them. "A word to the wise," said Stevens, shifting a toothpick from one side of his mouth to the other. "You'll be working alone out there. You won't be packing and you won't have a radio." The radio I could live without. "There's nothing more vicious than a cornered queer, so don't go doing anything stupid. Better to let one get away than get yourself hurt. Got that?" I gulped, nodded. "And try not to pinch too many at one time." Too many at one time? How many of these depraved, violent savages would I end up arresting?

Almost sixty, it turned out. But they didn't seem all *that* depraved, or even abnormal. In fact, they seemed like everyday people. And only one guy turned violent. It was late on a Friday afternoon.

+ + +

I'd told myself I'd make one last sweep through the head in Alcazar Gardens, across from the Old Globe Theatre. My "clientele" were always reaching through the metal cages to unscrew the bare bulbs, so it was pretty dark inside. And dank, reeking of piss. I spotted Willie Brown, a downtown cross-dresser by night, and shook my head: I'd already busted him once that week. Now he was paired off with a bruiser half again his size. Two stalls away a man was on his knees, swallowing another. A four-banger. I'd need the extra set of cuffs I had started carrying the day I'd been forced to bind a second pair with my belt, escorting all four of them down a tourist-clogged Presidents Way, past the statue of El Cid and the Organ Pavilion, to a waiting police car.

I shot Willie a keep-it-cool look and announced, "San Diego Police!" Willie grinned, gave me a here-we-go-again roll of the eyes. "You four are under arrest. You, you, you, and you." The announcement flushed another three men from the on-deck circle and out the door. You could see why the chief's office was getting all those complaints. I cuffed the ones closest to me and told them to stand by, then turned to Willie and the Bruiser. "Okay, you two: Turn around and put your hands against the wall." The command was a signal for Willie to resume beating off, and for Bruiser to jump me.

"Willie!" I yelled. "Put that thing away. Come over here and grab this guy." The guy wasn't trying to escape, he was trying to hurt me. My first clue? He told me he was going break every bone in my body and stuff my head down the toilet. He had me in a bear hug, never a good position for a cop to be in. Rookie mistake.

"Do I have to?" said Willie.

"Yes, goddammit! Right now!" He struggled to stuff his johnson back into his trousers. "Hurry up, Willie!" I glimpsed the other two, cuffed right wrist to right wrist, shuffling awkwardly toward the exit. I yelled at them over Bruiser's shoulder, "You two: You are hereby officially deputized. You too, Willie." Bruiser, my arms encircled by his, squeezed harder. "You (*gasp, gasp*) know (*gasp, gasp*) what that means?" I, myself, had no idea. Or whether I had the authority to deputize anyone.

"What do you want us to do?" asked one of the prisoners. It was odd. I could tell he was on *my* side. I took a risk.

"Move (*gasp*) over (*gasp*) to the (*gasp*) door. No matter what (*gasp, gasp, gasp*) don't let this guy out of here." It was personal now. Bruiser was going down, no matter what.

"Yes, sir," said both men. They planted themselves in the doorway. Willie, meanwhile, ran up and pushed himself against Bruiser's back.

"*Grab* him, Willie. Pull him off me." I needed to get my choking arm free, or at least get to my second pair of cuffs. This guy was *strong*. "Grab him, goddammit!" Willie hesitated a moment then jumped on Bruiser's back, throwing his arms around him. When he had him in a bear hug of his own I brought the heel of my right foot up, sharply, into my assailant's groin and slipped free. Bruiser let out a howl then chomped down on Willie's arm, causing Willie to emit a howl of his own.

"He's biting me! He's biting me! Stop it, mister. *Please* stop." He started to cry.

Something shifted inside. A confusing mix of gratitude and rage, and a sudden letting go of at least a fragment of the bigotry I'd carried for most of my twenty-two years. I *had* to protect the three men who were helping me, especially Willie. "You heard the man," I shouted. "Let him go." Bruiser showed no sign of unclenching his jaw so I doubled my fist and smacked him in the face as hard as I could. Nobody treats my deputy like that.

The fight was over, and my struggle with homophobia just begun. When someone keeps your head from being stuffed down a toilet you feel a certain warmth for them, maybe even a bit of a desire to get to know them better.

Until that moment I'd played a strong role in antigay locker-room performances, the lisping, swishing, faggot jokes. In the months ahead I continued to smile at the fun-making, even laughed a bit when I couldn't help myself. But something had definitely changed, and it wasn't only because of the efforts of my good Samaritans. The men I arrested in Balboa Park (except for Bruiser, for whom I could muster no sympathy at all) were decent, respectful, frightened human beings. It was wrong to call them degenerates. It was wrong to laugh at them.

+ + +

And it was wrong for Stevens to come to my patrol roll call, commendation in hand, a few days after I finished the detail.

He read from his report. "Officer N. Stamper set an SDPD record for the most arrests ever as a Pink Beret, fifty-six in fifteen days. Of course, the assignment was a bit . . . *distasteful.*" My peers, some fifty strong, tittered. I felt my face flush. ". . . And not without its problems. For example, Officer Stamper blew his first case." The crowd roared. "And another defendant got a sodomy charge reduced to following too close." Hoots and howls. "Later, we lost one in court because Stamper swallowed the evidence." Uncontained shrieking. I was bright red now. Stevens waited for the room to quiet. "In spite of these problems, Officer Stamper was able to take matters into his own hands." They were stomping on the floor, rolling in the aisles. "In fact, he bent over backwards to get the job done."

On and on it went. I pictured Stevens huddled that day with his Sex Crimes cronies, chortling over the nest of double entendres they'd hatched. I also pictured the men I arrested. Willie Brown being savaged by Bruiser. The sobbing Methodist minister, his hands cuffed behind his back, asking me to pray with him. My community college carpentry instructor who trembled uncontrollably as I put him in the backseat of a police car. The two or three terrified military personnel who knew exactly what their arrests meant.

Moments later, when Stevens read the chief's actual commendation, I couldn't hear him. I was mortified: God forbid, that roomful of uniformed peers should think my record-breaking performance was *remotely* attributable to the *possibility* that I *might* be gay. So I threw my head back and laughed harder than everyone else. I think they call that homophobia.

+ + +

At that early moment in my career as a cop, bigotry, mine and others', was starting to wear me out. It was easy to work on prejudice against blacks. Not so easy was confronting my attitudes about homosexuality. Then came Stonewall. June 28, 1969, New York.

Reacting to repeated police raids on the Stonewall Inn, a private club, gays fought back. There were thirteen arrests in the melee. Four officers were injured, one with a broken wrist. I pictured my brother cops, trapped inside a gay bar, being pelted with, according to the *New York Times*, "bricks, bottles, garbage, pennies, and a parking meter." Nine police officers against an army of angry, *violent* homosexuals. The riot on Christopher Street was no way for gays to achieve their rights.

But, as details of the incident became clear, I switched sides.

The cops had acted like pigs both before and during the Stonewall confrontation. I'd seen the same in San Diego, at the Brass Rail: vice cops demeaning and baiting gay men, arresting them on trumped up charges, pushing them around or beating them up. Those cops in New York had no justification for the way they behaved. They got what they asked for—an opinion I kept to myself.

By the end of my second year as a police officer I was railing against racism, confronting misogynist cops, making public my belief that policing was a tainted institution much in need of sweeping reforms. A few years and two badges later, when I was a lieutenant, the San Diego *Evening Tribune* carried a front-page profile by Steve Casey that labeled me a "new breed advocate of radical change in policing." It extolled my commitment to human rights. But there was no mention of gay rights. I was already, in the words of a senior officer, a "nigger lover." What would my peers think if I started speaking up for homosexuals?

I rationalized my fears. Unlike blacks and Latinos and women, homosexuals had made a "lifestyle" choice, or so I believed. I believed they had a right to that choice—live and let live. I believed in treating everyone fairly, and with respect. But deep down it bothered me that "gay liberation" had become part of the civil rights movement. All that lavender, all that flesh, all that gaudiness showing up at civil rights and even antiwar demonstrations.

+ + +

In the mid-seventies, Helen entered my life. Helen was a writer friend of my second wife, Patricia. She wore jeans, denim shirts, clunky boots, a single braid down her back, and occasionally a knife on her belt. She spent time at our old house on Adams Avenue, fixing toilets, clearing drains, and—from where I sat—pining over Patricia. Helen was cool toward me at first. Not icy, she just wouldn't make eye contact and she answered my home improvement questions with a word or two, or an unintelligible grunt. I was the enemy: man, husband, cop.

Gradually, she warmed up and started volunteering plumbing information and advice, even making small talk. Finally, she shared stories of run-ins she and her friends had had with the police. I pictured those run-ins, and was angry. I asked for names, times, locations. I followed up, and we became friends.

Spending time with Helen got me to thinking about what I'd read back in the early sixties about homosexuality, about weak or absent fathers, domineering mothers, social "explanations" of gayness. Helen was Helen. A lesbian. It was who she was; or, rather, a vital part of who she was. It wasn't at all about "preference" or "lifestyle." She could have been a suburban, tight-assed, Christian conservative, Donna Reed–dress-alike who voted for Nixon and held Tupperware parties. But she still would have been a lesbian.

Helen told me she'd never been erotically attracted to a man. "Well, that's two of us," I said. We laughed.

+ + +

What if I had been gay? What kind of a life would it have been? A life like Helen's? Gawked at, snubbed? Ridiculed, hassled, brutalized by the cops? Would I have been beaten—or worse—at the hands of homophobic bullies who didn't like the way I walked or talked, or the people I associated with, or what I did in my private life? What if I'd been one of the masses of closeted gay men who "passed"? What kind of a life would that have been? And what if I'd chosen to come out? Or, if I were outed? Would my parents have disowned me? My straight friends shunned me? Would I have found worthwhile work, been able to keep a job, enjoy the same partnership benefits as a straight spouse, the same legal rights?

+ + +

One thing was certain: If I were gay I wouldn't have been a cop. There *were* no gay cops then. You laugh? Hey, we were sure of it, the brotherhood and I.

During the screening process I'd been hooked up to a lie detector and asked if I'd ever been involved in an "unnatural sex act." I didn't know whether that included oral sex so I asked for clarification. The polygraph operator said, "You know. Do you have an unusual fondness for barnyard animals? Have you ever done it with a *man*?" If you copped to getting it on with a member of your own gender, or lied, you were automatically rejected. So, we *knew* there were no gays in the police ranks.*

---

* Federal law does not specifically prohibit interview or polygraph questions about sexual orientation, but more than a dozen states and many cities have banned the practice.

Not until Sgt. Larry Lamond, who'd recently left the department, went on national TV and told the world he was gay. (Some of my colleagues were sure he'd "turned homosexual" *after* he left the department). Much admired by his peers and superiors, his "confession" rocked our world— and caused a lot of cops to start looking funny at one another.

I don't remember when the word *homophobia* entered mainstream communication, but it was on the heels of Lamond's coming out that I added bigotry against gays to my public recitation of grievances against the profession. I decided to confront homophobia, like racism or sexism, wherever I found it. At my gym, a stockbroker/lawyer-type made some crack about "faggots." I said, "I find that offensive." He quickly wrapped a towel around his privates.

"Why? You gay or something?"

"What difference does it make?" He shook his head, slammed his locker door, and headed for the shower. I couldn't, I wouldn't remain silent anymore. As they say, if you don't stand for something you'll fall for anything. I stood for human rights, which now included gay rights.

+ + +

By the early nineties, SDPD had become, arguably, the most progressive police department in the country. We'd pioneered community policing, revolutionized our handling of domestic violence, opened the department to citizen participation in everything from policy making and program development to police shooting reviews. We'd conducted a whole-hog investigation into racism within the ranks, and moved aggressively to combat it. Thanks to affirmative action, relentless training, and the personal commitment of chiefs like Bill Kolender and his successor Bob Burgreen, we were one of the most diverse organizations anywhere. Burgreen and I (now the department's number-two guy, wearing my eighth badge) had marched several times in San Diego's annual gay pride parade.

Then came the toughest test of our progressive credentials. It was triggered by a mugging series in Hillcrest, home to the city's largest openly gay population. The crimes were vile. Elderly couples walking home from an evening meal, gay men headed for a movie or a drink, shoppers returning to their cars—all struck from behind with baseball bats and pipes. Money was taken in a few of the assaults, but amusement, not robbery, seemed to be the primary motive, and gay victims were clearly being singled out for the most vicious attacks. It was just a matter of time before someone got killed.

When it finally happened, two blocks from my home, the victim was a frail seventeen-year-old kid. He and a couple of pals had come to the big city from the burbs to sip espresso and soak up the atmosphere of a pre-Starbucks, independent coffeehouse on University Avenue.

Out of the grief and recriminations that followed the murder came a commitment to organize a citizens' patrol. Officer John Graham, the first openly gay cop within our ranks, stepped forward to offer the hundred or so citizen volunteers a class in personal protection. So did Chuck Merino, a friend of Graham's. Merino was an El Cajon cop and scoutmaster for his department's Explorer troop.

The citizens' patrol, sponsored by the PD, was a first for San Diego (and the country) so it got a lot of press. Which is how the Boy Scouts of America, which sponsors police Explorer posts, learned that one of their scoutmasters was gay. BSA wasted no time firing Merino. It didn't matter to them that he was an outstanding police officer in his hometown, a man of sterling character, a volunteer who had made an extraordinary contribution to our department, and to the people of Hillcrest.

To his credit, Jack Smith, Merino's chief, wasted no time telling Boy Scout leaders to pack up their tents and camp stoves and remove their bigoted butts from the premises. Smith formed his own, unaffiliated youth "scouting" program. And put Merino in charge.

To the credit of my own chief, Burgreen asked me to chair a special meeting of SDPD's senior staff. The agenda: Should we follow suit and file for divorce from the Boy Scouts of America?

Graham, who taught in our Explorer program, was not technically "at risk," since he wasn't a scoutmaster. But there was an important principle involved, namely discrimination and the will to stand up to it. There was also the matter of solidarity with another agency whose employee had been helpful to us, and whose chief had stuck his neck out for his guy.

There were an even dozen members of our senior staff—black, white, Latino, women, men, civilian, sworn. Several of the men, traditional police managers (some with grievances against the "liberal" chief of police and his even more "liberal" assistant chief), were ex-scouts themselves. I pictured them as kids: the straight-male bonding, the campfires, the knot-tying. This was not going to be a slam-dunk meeting.

I predicted at best a fifty-fifty outcome, with Burgreen having to make the call at the end of a rancorous meeting. By our rules everyone was required to speak his or her mind—no passing, no ass-kissing, no "group-think" allowed. We heard first from Chief Smith, then from the regional poobah of BSA. I thanked them, excused them, and started around the room. A deputy chief . . . a commander . . . our civilian personnel director . . . another a deputy chief . . . another commander . . .

Shaping up in the seventh-floor conference room that morning was one of the biggest shocks of my career. By the time I turned to the last member of the team, the "vote" was 11-0. The last person, our most senior member in age and tenure, one of our last "dinosaurs" and an ex-scout, made it unanimous: If the Boy Scouts of America would not stop discriminating against gays, and if Chief Justice Rehnquist's Supreme Court kept insisting they didn't have to, the San Diego Police Department would also send the scouts packing. I'd never felt more proud of my organization.

And the rank and file? They'd never felt more ashamed or embarrassed by their department. They went ballistic. So did three-quarters of the community and at least half the city council. So, too, did Bill Kolender, who'd moved on to become head of the California Youth Authority. "Jesus, Normy," he said, after our decision made headlines. "You and Bobby really fucked up on this one." I wanted a good comeback, but couldn't quite remember the quote. I went home that night, pulled out my journal, and found it:

> In Germany they first came for the communists and I didn't speak up because I wasn't a communist. Then they came for the Jews and I didn't speak up because I wasn't a Jew. Then they came for the trade unionists and I didn't speak up because I wasn't a trade unionist. Then they came for the Catholics and I didn't speak up because I was a protestant. Then they came for me—and by that time no one was left to speak.
>
> —Pastor Martin Niemöller

+ + +

Cut to Seattle, 1994, ninth and final badge. I'm the city's new police chief, having traveled a thousand miles up the Pacific coast. "You're not really going to be out there, are you?" said Norm Rice.

"Yeah, I was planning on it."

"You mean you're gonna *march?*"

"Sure."

"Well, I'll be damned." I think he was used to the chief before me, a man who'd rather have had his canines pulled than stroll along in the city's gay pride parade. For me, there was no way I *wouldn't* be there.

"Yeah, well, those are my people."

The morning rain had stopped and the sun was out in full force. A festive crowd of ten thousand lined Broadway from Pike to Prospect on Capitol Hill. Rice and I milled about with groups of city employees, including several gay and lesbian cops and firefighters. Local businesspeople, musicians, straight parents of gay children, politicians courting votes, six-foot-tall men in drag—all wandered over to say hi to the mayor and meet his new police chief. As we prepared to step out, a large, loud contingent of "Dykes on Bikes" roared past us to take their customary place at the front of the parade. Many were bare-breasted but for pasties; a few were bare-cheeked as well. They straddled "hogs" and Hondas and Kows, maybe even an Indian or two. The parade was under way.

As we turned onto Broadway we were met by half a dozen sign-toting Christian fundamentalists who, when they recognized me in uniform, shouted greetings like "You ought to be ashamed of yourself, Chief!" and "You're gonna burn in hell, Chief!" A few feet up the road the crowd turned friendlier. In fact for the rest of the parade spectators kept breaking from the sidelines to shake my hand, plant a kiss on my cheek, or press candy into my palm. Oh, yes, and to do the same with the hugely popular mayor.

Coming on the heels of a widely publicized incident in which a Seattle cop had (unlawfully) arrested two men for smooching in public, my appearance in the parade was "nothing short of astonishing," said a civil rights activist. People went out of their way to express appreciation, and none seemed more grateful than my own lesbian and gay police officers.

Others weren't so happy. On Monday morning the phone started ringing and wouldn't stop. Letters poured in for days (my favorite: a man informing me that I was a "dried up, useless scrap of scrotum"). Straight cops lit into me. Who did I think I was, disgracing the uniform like that? What message had I conveyed to upstanding, God-fearing, law-abiding citizens? Cal Thomas, the syndicated right-wing swill-pitcher, devoted an entire column to my reprehensible act. One of the local dailies ran a cartoon of the city's new chief dressed as a drum major*ette*—I've thrown my baton into the air and it's come down and landed in my eye.

There was more parade fallout: Two days before the event, one of my assistant chiefs, with my blessing, turned down a request for Christian police officers to participate, in uniform, in that Saturday's "March for Jesus." When word about that got out, hellfire rained down like a late-summer lightning storm.

I spent a good part of my first year as Seattle's chief fielding questions, asserting the principle of separation of church and state, and reassuring my cops that I was neither the Antichrist nor a sodomite—although I did let them know that my sexual orientation, like theirs, was nobody else's business.*

I also told my cops that as proud as I was to be their chief, I was also the *community's* chief of police. And, yes, as I clarified to a particularly testy lieutenant, "community" does include leather-clad, chain-dragging, bare-butted men and topless dykes on bikes.

+ + +

What did I mean when I said gays were "my people"? It wasn't meant condescendingly. I simply felt great warmth and affection for the gay community, a fondness derived, in part, from my own years of prejudice and bigotry. It was a reflection of my admiration for those who live courageously in the face of so much hostility in our society, and of gratitude for the way the gay community had embraced me in San Diego and in Seattle. Also because, yes . . . *some of my best friends are gay.*

* Nor is it the business of Supreme Court Justices Rehnquist, Thomas, and Scalia, who voted against the majority in the *Lawrence* case striking down Texas's sodomy law—a decision which, if there is a God, will pave the way for full gay rights, including legal marriage.

As I battled my homophobic demons I must have, along the way, replaced an old stereotype with a new one. Today, I believe that openly gay women and men are generally more "real" than straight folk, more honest with their emotions, easier to talk to, more likely to understand, care about, and confront the oppression of others. And, all in all, they're a hell of a lot more fun to be around.

+ + +

When I retired from SPD in 2000 a party was held in my honor at an upscale conference center on Seattle's waterfront. My whole senior staff was there, but only a smattering of rank and filers. In any event, the police presence was swamped by hundreds of community members, black, white, Latino, Asian, American Indian. And gay.

Judy Osborne walked up and gave me a hug just before the program began. "Happy?"

"Yeah, I am."

"Good," she said. "No sadness at all?" Tears had formed in her eyes.

"Oh, sure. A little. Mostly I feel . . . finished, complete." She knew what I meant. We'd come a long way together.

At the beginning of my last year as chief, Osborn, a member of my Sexual Minorities Advisory Council (we'd tried for a better name but "Chief Stamper's Lesbian, Gay, Bisexual, Transgendered, Polyamorous, Queer, and Questioning Advisory Council" wouldn't fit on the business card) asked to talk to me after one of our regular meetings. "You're not comfortable with me, are you? With *us*?"

I was taken aback. My lord, hadn't I reached out to her community? Aggressively confronted bigotry, discrimination, hate crimes? Made SPD a whole lot more hospitable for gays and lesbians? "What are you talking about, Judy?"

"The transgender community. Me, Suzanne, Barb . . ."

"Oh, come on. You know me better than that. You . . . you . . ." I didn't know what to say. I thought of Suzy. I looked into Judy's eyes—the first time I had allowed myself to really look at her. "Ah, shit. How did you know?"

"We know these things. We can tell."

"Yeah, but *I* didn't know."

"I know."

CHAPTER 27

THE FOURTH ESTATE:
A CHIEF'S LAMENT

HERMAN "HERM" WIGGINS WAS one of the least gifted cops in the San Diego Police Department. How do I know? I was his sergeant. Night after night I had to kick back his reports which contained ten or twelve spelling errors, and not just those tricky words like *surveillance* or *defendant* but *kidnap, car, knife*. His verbs waged war with his nouns. Not once did he write an acceptable report on the first try. A hulking man, the kind you love to see in the apex slot in a riot formation, Wiggins was friendly, outgoing, respectful. We were all rooting for him. But there was no way the guy was going to make it, not with his inability to write a report. (The real puzzler was how he'd ever graduated from the academy. Or junior high school.)

But Herm Wiggins was desperate to be a cop. He spent hours on his own, reading, studying the rules of grammar, applying himself to the task of writing an acceptable report. He schlepped around a log, which he labeled his "Dumb Book" and into which he dutifully recorded each word he'd misspelled.

His diligence paid off. A year later, working for a different sergeant, it still took him twice or thrice the time it took others, but he was finally able to turn in a satisfactory report. Wiggins made his probation. A few years later he won a Burglary assignment.

His superiors in Investigations were impressed with him from day one. He carried a huge caseload. He made more arrests than several of his peers combined. He won numerous convictions, and earned many commendations.

Then someone discovered a discrepancy. Then another, and another. An internal investigation was opened. Wiggins, it turned out, had been writing fiction. He invented and planted evidence (his specialty was phony fingerprints).

He perjured himself in arrest reports and on the stand. He sent innocent people to jail.

Herman Wiggins was a liar. Just like Pulitzer Prize–winner Janet Cooke of the *Washington Post*, Jayson Blair (felony-level liar) and Rick Bragg (misdemeanor-level liar) of the *New York Times*, Jack Kelley of *USA Today*, Stephen Glass of *The New Republic*, Daniel C. Hartman of the *Iowa State Daily*, Angele Yanor of the *Vancouver Sun*, Christopher Newton of the Associated Press . . .

How many reporters fudge facts, manufacture news, steal from their colleagues? Ten years ago I would have guessed, naïvely, a handful, a negligible number. Today? Today I ask, how many *don't* lie? In fact, I'm convinced that reporters are just as likely as police officers to fake or fudge the truth. Often with equal if not greater harm to the public.

I used to see the press as a pesky but honorable watchdog over my own institution: Were we behaving effectively, responsibly? Even after the *Los Angeles Times* muddied my image, deservedly, when I used a light-duty San Diego police officer as my personal valet, I retained positive feelings about the fourth estate. I was happily invested in Jefferson's belief that the purpose of the press was to comfort the afflicted and afflict the comfortable. Even if I happened to be the haplessly "comfortable" one being afflicted.

Then I moved to Seattle.

+ + +

For the first five years I could do little wrong in the eyes of *The Seattle Post-Intelligencer* (a certain political cartoon notwithstanding) and *Seattle Times*. Sixty months is a hell of a long honeymoon in my business, and I never took it for granted.

My predecessor, a former NYPD assistant chief, had maintained tight control over "media relations," dictating who could speak for the department—and what they could say. I turned that approach, common to most police agencies, on its head. My policy, imported from San Diego, was that any SPD employee could speak to any reporter at any time on any subject. The homicide detective, communications dispatcher, precinct captain, beat cop—each could speak for himself or herself.

I even went so far as to encourage my employees to tell the *truth* to reporters. If my cops were unhappy with something I'd done (like marching in the gay pride parade), they were free to say so. If they choked on my policies (such as affirmative action) they were free to say so. I believed that openness and honesty were good, in and of themselves, but also essential to my campaign to "demilitarize" and "democratize" the police department.

There were restrictions: My cops couldn't speak for the entire agency and they weren't permitted to release information barred by law. (Nor could they choose to ignore policies they didn't like.) But, repeatedly, I told them: *You're free to talk, just tell the truth as you see it.*

Every six months, my senior staff and I met with representatives of the local print and electronic media to field questions and complaints, of which there were many. Reporters griped about access to people and crime scenes and reports, the timeliness with which we furnished information, and police staffers who failed to return calls. Not once was I at odds with these concerns. (This was the meeting that had so incensed my chief of staff, who felt we were altogether too open to the press.) I instructed SPD's chiefs, directors, and media relations officers to be responsive, twenty-four hours a day, seven days a week to reporters in the field.

It was a policy borne, in part, of my empathy for working stiffs in *any* line of work.

Like us, reporters had a job to do. I've never understood the attitude, pervasive in police work, that it's okay to jerk reporters around—make ourselves scarce when they need a quote, refuse to return their calls, purposely withhold information, or delay answers until after the reporter's missed a deadline. That's just plain rude.

I think I can claim an "enlightened" approach to police-media relations in Seattle. But my views and values would be put to the test, big time, in my final year as police chief.

+ + +

1999 was the year I recalibrated my high opinion of the integrity and the motivations of the press and joined the rest of the world.

The year had begun propitiously for the department. Fueled by the region's smoking-hot, hi-tech, dot-com economy, SPD was no longer taking it in the shorts at budget time; in fact we'd just received additional funding for more cops and for crime prevention and victims' services. We'd made tremendous progress, developing one of the nation's best responses to domestic violence, working to institutionalize community policing, building positive relations with communities of color, with the gay and lesbian community, with (most of) our own cops. We'd recently adopted a new system of internal accountability that melded personal responsibility with a bracing software package that would soon improve the overall quality of just about everything we did. And the World Trade Organization had not yet seen fit to bless our city with its presence.

Yes, things were looking rosy that cold, wet winter. And compared to many of my colleagues across the country, I was still engaged in a veritable love-fest with the local media.

Then in the spring, Dan Bryant, one of my assistant chiefs, asked to see me privately following a staff meeting. "You're really going to love this," he said. It seems one of our senior homicide detectives, Sonny Davis, a thirty-year veteran, had lifted $10,000 from a homicide scene. His junior partner, Cloyd Steiger, who'd witnessed the theft, pointedly suggested that the evil-doer put the money back where he got it. Davis refused, though he did offer half the loot to his partner. Steiger snitched Davis off to their sergeant, Don Cameron. The next day Cameron took Davis back to the scene where he oversaw the replanting of the dough, the rediscovery of the dough, and the eventual impounding of the dough.

Oh my! Was that how the supervisor, a legendary thirty-eight-year veteran with more than a thousand homicide investigations to his credit, thought he should handle a *felony*? Would he have allowed a burglar or a stickup man or an embezzler to return the next day to the scene of the crime, put the loot back, and waltz away without penalty?

With the money safely, legally accounted for, Steiger began jawing about the incident to several cops, including "informally" and "confidentially" an Internal Investigations sergeant—who sat on the information for months.

I took stock: I had a slam-dunk felon working homicide; a sergeant who swept the crime under the rug; a right-minded detective who, once he'd properly blown the whistle, did everything wrong; an internal affairs investigator who'd imprudently promised confidentiality then inexcusably refused to breach it; and several employees plugged in to the whole thing, none of whom had come forward to report it.

I shouldn't have been surprised—the cop culture is notorious as a festering breeding ground of silence and complicity. It just is. But I *was* surprised; I thought we'd come a lot farther than that.

+ + +

Residents of big East Coast and Midwest cities laughed at our version of police corruption: *Let me get this straight. A cop takes something, gets caught, puts it back—and you label that "corruption"? What you got is a crooked and/or stupid cop. And a sergeant, though misguided, who tried to do the right thing. Corruption? I don't think so.*

Richard Pennington, now chief in Atlanta, told me that on his first day on the job as New Orleans's chief in the mid-nineties, he added yet one more dirty cop (who'd stolen a ten-thousand-dollar Rolex) to a long list of Big Easy officers who were under investigation, under indictment, or in jail or prison for crimes ranging from extortion to murder. Other major cities' chiefs chuckled over the contrast between our two departments. But, to me and to Seattle, a city that had battled back from decades of systemic police and political corruption, and which prided itself on its squeaky clean reputation, this was no laughing matter.

+ + +

But neither was it, as the Seattle *Times* suggested, the *Crime of the Century! Bigger than O. J.! Bigger than Rodney King! Bigger than Pee-wee Herman!* Not only that, to hear the *Times* tell it, the theft was just the tip of the iceberg. There had to be, lurking below the calm surface of our increasingly progressive, community-oriented PD, a churning ocean of venal and mortal sins. And, by God, their ace investigative reporters would fish until they reeled those sins to the surface.

Thus began a transparent, clumsy hatchet job—on me. I witnessed sole-source reporting, references to ancient history, the invention of non-existent "patterns" of police misconduct, and yes: a reliance on the proverbial "disgruntled employee"—including individuals I'd disciplined, refused to promote, or fired. A couple of ace investigative reporters from the *Times* gave voice to cops who were too lazy, too incompetent, too bigoted, or too dishonest to warrant promotion, or retention. Now, they were elevated to "informed sources." And, given my own press philosophy and policy, utterly free to talk to reporters. Maybe my chief of staff had been right?

For months, cops and ex-cops who were unhappy with my policies dished and dissed: I cared more about community policing than catching crooks; I delegated too much; I hired an "outsider"—a *female!* a *civilian!*—to run the Community Policing Bureau;* I made "affirmative action" appointments, passing over more deserving white male candidates; I was aloof; I spent too much time in the community; I didn't know what the hell was going on in the department; I, too, was an *outsider.*

This indictment, presumably *symptomatic* of why none of us at the top had learned about the Sonny Davis theft, was offered up, according to the *Times*, "by more than a dozen" sources, most of them tapped over and over. Yet, the steady drip-drip-drip, splash-splash-splash of "revelations" took its toll.

+ + +

The *Times* was in full feeding frenzy, and I couldn't figure it out. Why were they not even *trying* to be "fair and balanced"? Why did it feel so—so *personal?*

Because it *was* personal, according to an "informed source," a mole deep within the bowels of the newspaper. The *Times* had made a decision to target the police and was deliberately "beating up" SPD, me in particular.

The newspaper had just announced it was moving from an afternoon to

---

* Nancy McPherson, an internationally recognized expert on community policing and problem solving. I brought her in to build and run the new bureau. Her outsider/civilian status did not keep her from winning the hearts and minds of many cops, in Seattle and beyond. Detractors, however, chafed at her power and influence. They claimed that, together, we ran the department. The "Norm and Nancy Show," they called it.

a morning paper. That signified nothing less than mortal combat with the city's existing morning paper, the *Seattle Times*, also known as the *PI*. No informed observer believed the Puget Sound area could or would support two morning papers. (The two newspapers have been warring in the courts for several years now, the *Times* striking first but losing a recent case to the *PI*—which is hanging on by a thread.)

It's funny: in a more innocent day I would have pooh-poohed the mole's "scoop," chalked it up to a conspiracy-happy theorist . . . or one of the paper's own disgruntled employees. But I accepted its veracity the second I heard it. It made perfect sense: I'd been caught in the crosshairs of a newspaper shooting war.

But was it true? It didn't matter. Any casual misgivings I'd had about the basic truthfulness or fairness of reporters had ripened into a mordant distrust of "the media."

Within a couple of months, with some genuine as well as cosmetic PD reforms in place, the whole thing blew over. I regained my emotional resilience (it's hard not to buy in to the characterizations when you're constantly referred to in the press as "beleaguered" or "embattled") and reclaimed my sense of humor. But the experience left me deeply concerned about the effects of "campaign journalism." And not just on policing.

+ + +

The Pew Research Center for the People and the Press found that the "believability" of the daily newspaper has dropped from 80 percent in 1985 to 59 percent in 2002. The Project for Excellence in Journalism reported in 2004 that the press's "credibility crisis" is part of a "cultural divide." "Journalists think they are working in the public interest. The public thinks they sensationalize and report articles to make money . . . This sense of a lack of professionalism and sensationalizing to sell papers was clearly seen following the scandal in 2003 at the *New York Times*, particularly the news that the reporter Jayson Blair had engaged in extensive fabrication. But one of the saddest revelations to come from the scandal was that many people thought such unethical conduct was typical of newspapers."

The Pew survey in 2003 revealed that 22 percent of Americans believe that Blair-level dishonesty happens "frequently," while 36 percent believe it happens "occasionally." And 58 percent think journalists do not care about complaints of inaccurate reporting. I'm surprised the figure is that low.

+ + +

I see some obvious parallels between policing and reporting. Cops work under constant pressure to meet the traditional expectations of their bosses: investigate crimes, develop snitches, make arrests, write reports, stick around until the job's done. Reporters work under similar stress, ever on the lookout for newsworthy stories, being assigned stories, cultivating their own sources of information, writing their copy daily, getting it in on time—often under pressures that demand double (or, occasionally, triple) shifts. Most cops, like most reporters, want to get ahead. To do so they must please their bosses. In order to do that, some of them, like Herm Wiggins and Jayson Blair, resort to "shortcuts," a euphemism for cheating and lying.

The parallels at the executive and management levels of the two institutions are also striking. Whether you're a police chief or an executive editor of a newspaper, you want your people to "produce." You demand timeliness and top quality. Your push for results might be interpreted by the rank and file as authoritarian, top-down management. When you observe and reward the kind of work you want done you can be accused of "favoritism." If you believe in cultural diversity, in giving everyone an equal shot at plum assignments, you may be accused of failing to see the failings of women or people of color.

I liked Howell Raines's book on fly-fishing, but from what I've heard of his management style I suspect he would have been as large a failure as a police chief as he was an executive editor at the *New York Times*. According to his replacement, Bill Keller, the "Blair fiasco . . . was made possible in part by a climate of isolation, intimidation, favoritism, and unrelenting pressure." Publisher Arthur Sulzberger, Jr., claimed surprise at the "depth of anger and frustration" within the ranks of the *Times*.

The recent scandal involving the *Chicago Sun-Times*, *Newsday* of Long Island, and the Spanish-language *Hoy* points to top-level corruption. They've all admitted inflating their circulation numbers by the tens of thousands—for years. How does this qualify as corruption? *Ad rates.* They're based on circulation. According to the *New York Times,* fifty car dealers are suing *Newsday* for $125 million. As Lauren Rich Fine, a Merrill Lynch analyst who studies "profits and the press," wrote, "Newspapers are not supposed to be the subject of scandal, they are supposed to report on it."

+ + +

The Seattle Police Department had a thieving homicide detective, the *New York Times* a lying reporter. Outside experts in both instances, impaneled to investigate what went wrong, homed in on structural and cultural changes to prevent recurrences of such behavior. In police work it's always: Give your cops more training, create a civilian review board, fire the bad apples.

Well, the *New York Times* recently imposed a ban on "anonymous pejorative quotations" (*Seattle Times:* Make a note). That's terrific, it really is. But it speaks to *policy.* What about changes to the infamous *structure,* the *workplace culture* of the newspaper? How do you penetrate the deeply ingrained hubris of that venerable institution? How do you relieve untoward pressures on reporters to "produce"—to the point that production becomes "manufacturing"?

Most PDs have detailed standards of performance and conduct. They recruit and screen using these standards. They don't hire anyone they haven't vetted through a background investigation—which, in the best agencies, includes shoe-leather tracking of previous employment, academic records, family and other personal relationships, crime and traffic records, and financial responsibility. They subject prospective employees to rigorous psychological screening. Some departments polygraph their candidates. Once hired, every recruit undergoes an intensive training program. Periodic (usually annual) retraining is mandated by law. Officers are supervised, evaluated, and inspected on a regular, formal basis. At least that's the theory, the official policy.

Compare this to a typical news organization. Most newspapers "prefer" but don't require a bachelor's degree in journalism; many extend internships solely on the basis of success on a high school or college newspaper. Candidates for full-time jobs are hired on the basis of their resumes and portfolios, usually following a phone call or two to previous employers. To say that prospective reporters are "screened," beyond a reading of their work and on word-of-mouth assessments? That's a real stretch.

Yes, I know. Journalists are not responsible for protecting public safety. They don't have the power to detain and arrest people. With rare (and usually bizarre) exceptions they don't pack heat. But they affect the lives of many people, including the subjects of their reporting and their readers, who rely on them for accuracy and honesty. I'm not suggesting journalist candidates go through as exhaustive a process as most police officer candidates are exposed to. But shouldn't their bosses know who they're hiring? Shouldn't they know whether their prospective reporters are more at home with journalism than fiction?

Even the nation's best newspaper is vulnerable to the hiring of a Jayson Blair. I read Blair's book, *Burning Down My Masters' House.* His tortured account of his trials at the *Times* makes crystal clear that the man should never have been hired in the first place.

Every once in a while, randomly—or not randomly in a case of suspicion—a story should be reinvestigated, top to bottom and inside out. Why? Because despite the most rigorous screening, the closest supervision, and the sterling reputations of reporters, it's possible for an individual journalist to lie and get away with it—for years. We do this with cops. "Inspection," it's called. The news media ought to do the same.

Put every reporter on notice: We're going to check up on you from time to time. We understand how important it is that you enjoy flexibility and discretion in the reporting of newsworthy stories. But the truth is more important than your feelings. If you fabricate a story, purposely report unfairly, steal someone else's words, or violate other provisions of the Society of Professional Journalists' code of ethics* you're likely to get found out. Hopefully before you do too much damage to reputations: yours, the people you write about, and that of your news organization.

+ + +

---

* Contrary to the opinion of 99 percent of police officers, the press does have such a code.

Being singed by sensational reporting caused me to lose confidence in the fourth estate. I can no longer read an article, whether on a controversial police shooting or on Moby's New York tea shop, without wondering if the reporter told the truth.

In case you're wondering, I've taken a leap of faith every time I've quoted a reporter in this and all other chapters of this book. I've tried to support my observations and assertions with more than "sole-source" reporting. But you may want to do your own fact-checking.

It's a sorry thing to lose one's innocence at sixty. But I'm optimistic. If the fourth estate will clean up its act, as it's constantly urging the police to do, then people like me can take comfort in the realization that the Jayson Blairs of the world are, in fact, an anomaly. Like Herm Wiggins and Sonny Davis.

CHAPTER 28

SNOOKERED IN SEATTLE: THE WTO RIOTS

I WAS "OUT OF the loop" on the decision to invite the WTO Ministerial Conference to Seattle (November 29–December 4, 1999). I'm not sure how I would have voted anyway—for all I knew, "W-T-O" were the call letters of a Cleveland radio station. I will say this, though: Having your ass kicked so completely—by protestors, politicians, the media, your own cops, colleagues from other agencies, and even a (former) friend—does give cause for pause and reflection.

Local politicians were ecstatic that Seattle had beaten out San Diego, the only other U.S. finalist for the honor of hosting the WTO Conference. Our city of 530,000, with its police department of twelve hundred cops, was *delighted* to accommodate eight thousand delegates, the president of the United States, the secretary of state, dozens of assorted other dignitaries, hundreds of reporters from throughout the world, and tens of thousands of antiglobalization protesters.

No one was more tickled than Mayor Paul Schell. He wrote in an issue of his "Schell Mail"* (No. 39): "As the whole event comes to a peak during the days of the actual Ministerial our streets and restaurants will be filled with people from all over the world. Issues of global significance will be addressed in our conference halls and public spaces. School teachers will use local news to teach international civics lessons. (And our many visitors will be bringing something like $11 million of business to our town.)"

---

* A folksy missive from the mayor to thousands of Seattleites, inside and outside government, issued as events dictated or inspiration struck. His opponents accused the mayor of using "Schell Mail" to advance a political agenda—particularly with respect to mayoral dreams (including re-election), programs, and budget requests. As one of his cabinet members, I found the Schell Mail messages informative.

Schell had that very morning met with Michael Moore (no, not *the* Michael Moore, but the secretary general of the WTO). He wrote of the meeting, "Ex-Prime Minister of New Zealand, ex-construction worker, with a background in labor, and an author, he's got a good sense of humor and a great mind. We had fun giving him a big round of 'g-day, mate.'" Then he turned serious: "Though there's been a lot of talk about protests and demonstrations, without question these are overblown." Everyone (except us killjoys in law enforcement) seemed unable to curb their enthusiasm about the event. Especially the antiglobalization forces.

One city council member invited protesters from around the world to come to Seattle to join in the "dialogue." He issued urgent public appeals to Seattleites to find room in their homes to house the hordes.

+ + +

Early in '99, before pre-event speculation heated up, Ed Joiner, my Operations chief, and I walked the few blocks down to the local FBI office to learn what this WTO thing was all about from the "law enforcement perspective." Special agent in charge "Birdie" Passanelli and her fellow feds offered a primer. The World Trade Organization was established in 1995 to "oversee rules of international trade, help trade flow smoothly, settle trade disputes between governments, and organize trade negotiations." Simple enough, I thought. An innocuous mission with an emphasis on the bureaucratic and the diplomatic.

The WTO stood for the facilitation of *free* trade while its opponents favored *fair* trade. "Free," "fair"—what the hell was the difference?

I boned up on the controversy. "Free trade," I came to understand, means, essentially, the Clinton agenda—NAFTA, an opening of markets throughout North America and, beyond that, the reduction or elimination of trade barriers such as tariffs and quotas. Advocates claim that global free trade would reduce poverty, encourage greater economic and political freedom, increase corporate profits, and even enhance the environment. The most succinct free-trade argument I found, invoking Adam Smith, free enterprise, and the evils of socialism, came from Milton Friedman and Rose Friedman in "The Case for Free Trade" (*Hoover Digest*, 1997, No. 4).

In the view of its legions of disparate critics, however, free trade means devastation of rain forests and other irreplaceable ecosystems; loss of small American farms, businesses, and jobs to global conglomerates, agribusiness, and foreign sweatshops; world hunger; expansion of American imperialism; exploitation of laborers and the use of child workers in Third World countries; political imprisonment; a crushing subjugation of countries like Tibet; corrupt business practices by the multinational corporations; abridgment of intellectual properties; and denial of basic human and civil rights.

The last ministerial conference, in Geneva in May 1998, had attracted thousands of demonstrators, and it had turned violent. But President Clinton, a big supporter of the WTO, offered up the United States anyway. He was probably thinking, *No problem. I mean, how long has it been since the country has seen* violent *political protest? Twenty-five years? Thirty?*

+ + +

Seattle had handled, since the general strike of 1919 and through the antiwar and civil rights uprisings of the sixties and seventies, an unending stream of political demonstrations. Even in the mid-nineties it was like the city was frozen in time—or, depending on your politics, ahead of its time.

Seattle *is* a progressive town, one that can always muster several hundred, or several thousand, to protest social service budget cuts or police brutality or the conditions of migrant farm workers on the other side of the Cascades. I felt privileged to live and work in a town whose people still cared enough about social justice to get off their butts and help bring it about.

+ + +

We launched a regional planning effort on the heels of that FBI meeting. Joiner headed up a "Public Safety Executive Committee" consisting of ranking officials of SPD, King County Sheriffs, Seattle Fire Department, Washington State Patrol, the FBI, and the United States Secret Service. In all, twelve local, state, and federal agencies plus sixteen collateral agencies joined the planning effort.

Joiner and his group formed subcommittees to address every imaginable challenge: intelligence, venues protection, demonstration management, access accreditation, transportation and escort management, criminal investigations, communication, public information and media relations, hazardous materials (including weapons of mass destruction), fire and emergency medical services, tactics, logistics, personnel, finance, and training.

Their mission? Put together a plan to protect *people*—conferees, demonstrators, residents, business owners, shoppers, and dignitaries (the secretary of state, the secretary of labor, the president himself, maybe even Fidel Castro, who'd been rumored to be on the list of uninvited but expected guests). And *property*—the streets, the convention center, downtown hotels, Old Navy, Starbucks, Nordstrom, Nike, the Gap, independent news and espresso stands . . .

My purpose as a cop, as a chief was to make our streets safe—for everyone. When people asked me to describe the mission of SPD I gave them a stock answer: to stop people from hurting other people. It didn't matter to me whether the danger was in a couple's apartment in Greenlake or on downtown streets jammed with demonstrators.

The police would, in the mayor's words, "make sure that, for the citizens of this city, life can go on more or less as usual." The conference would be taking place at the peak of the holiday shopping season. "The carousel will be up at Westlake, shoppers will fill the stores, the holiday lights will be up, the PNB [Pacific Northwest Ballet] will be dancing The Nutcracker. This is still Seattle in December, after all," wrote the mayor.

+ + +

Joiner presided over the most exhaustive event planning SPD had ever done. Almost ten thousand hours of training was provided: over nine hundred SPD personnel, through the rank of captain, went through an initial nine-hour "crowd management" (riot control) class. Then weekly, then twice-weekly squad drills. There were three four-hour platoon-level exercises and a four-hour session with all platoons drilling together. There was extra training on the department's new chemical agent protective masks, and eight-, sixteen-, and twenty-four-hour classes on "crisis incident decision making" (a disciplined approach to analyzing and responding to crises of all kinds) for supervisors and commanders. Thirty SWAT officers traveled to Ft. McClellan, Alabama, for a four-day course on WMDs. Several SWAT supervisors and commanders attended an additional twenty-four hours of WMD and incident command system training. The Secret Service gave two days of dignitary protection and escort training to all motorcycle officers from the five agencies that would be contributing cops to the cause. The FBI and Secret Service ran two intensive tabletop exercises.

I monitored the training we provided to our officers. It started with classroom instruction on the short history of the WTO, the protest methods used in Geneva, and what they could expect, from best- to worst-case scenarios. Next, the student-officers were herded into an abandoned hangar at the old Sand Point military facility where they were subjected—against the audible background of an actual riot (a *loud* actual riot, recorded during recent political protests in Vancouver, B.C.)—to simulated protest strategies and tactics, including violent attacks. Back and forth the cops went, first as missile-chucking "demonstrators," then in their real role as frontline cops confronting those missiles. They rehearsed tactics, prepared mentally for things likely to come.

All along, I'm thinking, *We've got this sucker covered.*

But my cops? They weren't so confident. They appreciated the training, they loved the new equipment—all that all-black "hard gear," from catcher-like shin guards to ballistic helmets, making them look like Darth Vader. But they were convinced the city was in for a real shitstorm.

There *were* some ominous signs—Internet organizing and mobilizing, Ruckus Society training, anarchists threatening to descend on the city and muck things up not only for the conferees but also for the throngs of peaceful protesters.

I was familiar with such pre-event refrains from a segment of police officers who always sound like Chicken Little, as well as the shut-it-down braggadocio of the lunatic fringe of protesters. I'd heard the voices of "extremists" many times in my career. Back in the seventies in San Diego, a wild-eyed lieutenant warned of the day that fundamentalist religious sects in the Middle East would migrate to our shores and do bad things to innocent Americans. He prophesied acts of terrorism, like blowing up

airplanes and buildings . . . if you can imagine that. The brass labeled him
"Ol' Bombs and Rockets"—and kept him away from the armory.

Of course there would be demonstrations downtown. Of course there'd
be knuckleheads who'd try to bait the officers. But even though Seattle was
a small city in a small county in a small state, I was confident my PD was
ready. Joiner had asked for help from state and regional agencies, and
gotten it.* Washington State Patrol, King County Sheriffs, Port of Seattle,
Bellevue PD, Kent PD, and the combined forces of Auburn, Renton, and
Tukwila committed a total of fifty-three motorcycle cops, seventy-five
patrol officers, thirty-one SWAT officers, five bomb cops, two communica-
tions/media personnel, and three explosives-detection K-9 teams. Washington State Patrol and King Country Sheriffs also committed a total of 145
officers for "demonstration management" duty in the event they were
needed. All of this was to supplement the core forces of Seattle's police. On
a normal day SPD would field about one hundred cops at peak times. For
the WTO we would have more cops on the streets than at any time in PD
history. In all, nine hundred SPD officers would be suited up for WTO, all
of them working twelve-hour shifts. It sure *seemed* like a lot of cops.

+ + +

Things were moving apace when shortly before the conference, Schell
insisted on visiting roll calls. He wanted to offer words of encouragement,
let the officers know he was there for them—and to tell them to behave
themselves. Maybe he thought they wouldn't play nice with our global visitors, that they might not show proper restraint if provoked. I went with
him to the roll calls, stood by his side. The first few sessions were
uneventful, if not dull. The mayor was a bright, articulate politician but
when it came to rallying the cops he was no Knute Rockne.

---

* From everyone, that is, but Tacoma. Their chief sent a letter declining to ante up *any* officers. I
tracked him down at a DV conference. "We really could use your help, James." *James:* "We're short-
handed." *Me:* "Aren't we all, aren't we all. But this thing could really blow up on us." *James:* "I've got
my own city to police." *Me:* "But we're always there for *you,* James. Sure you won't change your
mind?" *James:* "No." *Me:* "Well, that really blows." *James:* "But if things get out of hand up there you
can count on us." Thanks, James. Thanks a bunch.

The last roll call was at the West Precinct, in a spanking-new facility, spacious, comfortable, and, unlike so many police facilities, designed and built with cops and police work in mind. It had that new-building smell, nice and fresh, and its opening had been a joyous occasion for the West Precinct cops, mostly because of the pit they were leaving. And because the plan called for free parking—just like PD employees at the other precincts enjoyed. But Schell had changed all that, and the cops were in a foul mood. In fact, they were lying in wait as we walked in.

There they sat. A roomful of disgruntled cops staring at a politician who had the nerve to ask them to make a good impression for the all the world to see, even as he stuck it to them on the parking. They glared, they griped, they grumbled. When one guy complained about WTO, hizzoner finally snapped. "Look, if you can't handle the job I'll find someone who can!"

Fighting the urge to throttle the guy, I stepped forward and reminded the cops of my confidence in them. But the damage had been done, and the mayor wasn't through yet. Right after roll call and within earshot of officers filing out of the room he turned to his police chief, shook his head and said, "I sure don't envy you *your* job."

The next day he said he was sorry. "Tell it to the cops," I said.

"I was *tired,*" he said. "And *hungry.* I hadn't eaten since lunch." Well, sir, neither had I. And the cops you were talking to? They're headed for long hours with no sleep, no food, not even a place to pee.

+ + +

As the conference approached, I began to have some of the same doubts my officers felt. I took my concerns to Joiner, who brought me back to reality. The first WTO ministerial conference had been held in Singapore, which meant, of course, there had been exactly *no* demonstrations. And the violence at that second one in Geneva? A "European phenomenon." Besides, Seattle PD had had a ton of experience and enjoyed a well-earned reputation for handling big political protests (while still in San Diego I'd heard positive things about SPD's approach to demonstration management). Moreover, Joiner planned to use only known and trusted SPD personnel at the most sensitive posts.

Ed Joiner had solid credentials as a strategist and tactician. His planning team included some of the best minds on the department. Plus every stakeholder, from the regional bus system to local hospitals, was involved in the planning. Also comforting was the FBI's threat assessment of "low to moderate." (I later learned they were talking about *terrorist* threats.)

And how's this for reassurance? The head of the local Secret Service office told the mayor and me at a meeting in Schell's office just moments before kickoff: "If things turn to shit it won't be for of a lack of planning." As a matter of fact, he had "never seen a better job of planning and preparation."

+ + +

Things started well. There were a couple of small-scale demonstrations downtown on the Friday before the Monday conference opening. On Saturday three daredevils rappelled themselves over a bridge and hung an anti-WTO banner over Interstate 5 (they went to jail). Sunday there were demonstrations on Capitol Hill, but what else was new? Later that night a collection of anarchists broke into and occupied an abandoned building near the West Precinct. Even that wasn't all that troubling—it allowed Joiner and his crews to keep an eye on the comings and goings of the "outside agitators." Further, it would have been problematic at that late moment to commit the dozens of personnel necessary to raid the place, scoop up the trespassers, sort out their undoubtedly counterfeit identities, and jail them—a decision that was a mistake, in hindsight.

But, it wasn't a bad weekend. All the more remarkable given that the conference was gearing up at the same time the city was playing host to the Seattle Marathon *and* a Seahawks game—both of which demanded much from our force.

Early the next morning officers discovered evidence of a possible break-in at the convention center. They'd been guarding the facility (a sprawling, multistory building, with a complicated layout, in the heart of downtown) throughout the night. But as Lt. Robin Clark, our SWAT commander, showed me, it looked like someone could have slipped through the outer perimeter, scaled a temporary wall at the back of the facility, busted open a padlock, and entered the place.

This was serious. Police commanders had not taken as idle the threat by militant protesters that they would, indeed, "shut down the WTO." It wasn't hard to imagine the mess they'd make if they'd breached security of the main WTO venue. They could set off the fire sprinklers and flood the interior, spraypaint choice antiglobalization slogans all over the walls, unleash stink bombs. Or real bombs. Officers *had* to search the whole convention center. So they did. Meticulously, with SWAT and police dogs. It took hours.

The opening ceremonies were delayed, and a few delegates got their noses bent out of shape—mostly because they got yelled at a good bit by throngs of raggedy demonstrators as they stood in line in their western business suits and native attire. One of them, a "minister," pulled a gun on some demonstrators.

A couple of hours later everyone was safe and snug inside the building. We breathed a collective sigh of satisfaction, and I returned to the streets to resume my "roving."

+ + +

In the Incident Command System, which we had adopted (and trained for) long before WTO entered the picture, the chief of police has, by design, no "operational" role. His or her name and title might appear at the top of official documents, but if you searched those documents for a job description you'd find none.

There are compelling reasons to keep police chiefs out of the operations arena. They are simply too busy, across a broad range of organizational and community duties, to master the kind of continuously updated specialized expertise needed to handle a SWAT incident, a crime scene, or a major demonstration.

The last thing you want is a police chief actually running the show. So, I "roved."

I walked the streets, encouraged my cops at their posts, stopped by the various hotels set aside for WTO delegates and dignitaries, and moved in and out of the convention center. I spent time with my commanders in the Multi-Agency Command Center (MACC), the Seattle Police Operations

Center (SPOC) next door, and the Emergency Operations Center (EOC) at the fire station at Fifth and Battery. (My four assistant chiefs, with Joiner taking the point, were split between the MACC and the EOC, each pulling twelve-hour shifts, for around-the-clock coverage.) I received regular updates and teamed up with the mayor and the fire chief to make frequent announcements to, and to field questions from, the huge international press corps.*

The first press briefing on Monday was upbeat. I had just come from an intersection clogged with demonstrators. David Horsey, two-time Pulitzer Prize–winning political cartoonist with *The Seattle Post-Intelligencer*, had been standing next to me as a local protester approached. She told us she'd traveled downtown for two reasons: to protest globalization, and to keep people from hurling insults and/or bottles at her cops. She wanted me to know how much she respected and admired the job our officers were doing. It was one of those lovely peace-love-harmony moments. I envisioned the next morning's political cartoon, and felt all warm and fuzzy.

+ + +

Veteran cops told me they'd never seen so many people on the streets. There was sea of sea turtles and anti-WTO signs, choruses of chanting, and street theater performances, replete with colorfully costumed actors on stilts playing out the various points of opposition to globalization. That night, thousands of protesters filed into Key Arena where the Sonics and the Storm play their basketball. They heard speeches from local politicians, including the mayor (who at one point bleated, "Have fun but *please* don't hurt my city") and various protest leaders and organizers. There were songs by Laura Love and other politically active musicians. Day One ended peacefully.

Which was in stark contrast to the way Day Two began. Starting at two in the morning (those protesters needed a union!), demonstrators began assembling, quietly, but not unobserved (cops do work 24/7). Throughout

---

* One of my answers at one of the press conferences would infuriate my cops, but that wouldn't come until later.

the night the MACC and the EOC fielded reports from officers monitoring the increasing size of the crowds. By five-thirty a large group had formed at Victor Steinbrueck Park just north of Pike Place Market. Sprinkled within the crowd were gas masks and chemical munitions. At seven-thirty large groups began marching to the convention center from five different locations. Between seven-thirty and eight o'clock, seven distinct, large-scale disturbances erupted within a two-block radius. At nine minutes after nine the incident commander authorized the use of chemical irritants. One minute later he put out the call for mutual aid.

I stood in the rain at the intersection of Sixth and Union and witnessed a single line of ten King County Sheriff's deputies holding off more than a hundred raucous demonstrators who were trying to penetrate the underground parking at the Sheraton. The militants taunted the deputies, pushed up against them. I worried for the thin tan line, the tiny handful of county cops who rarely saw this kind of "big-city" action. And realized, for the first time, that we didn't have *nearly* enough cops to get the job done.

Moments later hundreds of demonstrators surged into the middle of the intersection and took a seat. They completely choked off Sixth Avenue up to University, a block east. If a police car, a fire truck, or an aid car had to get to an emergency in or around any of the high-rise buildings it would have been impossible. Police commanders had spent months negotiating with protest leaders, but this wasn't in the plan. There was no choice but to declare an unlawful assembly and clear them out. Which wouldn't be pretty, given what the sitters did next.

In response to the command to leave the intersection, protesters locked arms, making themselves one massive knot of humanity. Only force would unlock them from one another. A field commander told them they were in violation of the law, and that they would be arrested if they didn't leave the intersection. He did it by the numbers: He used the proper language, stationed cops around the perimeter to verify that the bullhorned warning could be heard, and warned them and warned them and warned them. Then he warned them again. Then he gassed them.

Why didn't he and his squads just wade in, pull the protesters apart, and haul them off to a prisoner transportation unit? This particular demonstration wasn't violent, after all, but a classic civil disobedience tactic. But there simply weren't enough cops to pluck them off one at a time. And violence had broken out at several other locations around the convention center.

At noon, a scheduled AFL-CIO march left Seattle Center in the shadow of the Space Needle and headed downtown. It grew from twenty thousand to forty thousand on the way, and soon converged with another ten thousand demonstrators already on the streets of downtown. Suddenly, my minuscule police force seemed microscopic.

Even the reinforcements from other agencies, streaming in and en route, struck little confidence into the hearts of police staffers. Our cops were clearly in trouble. The department had co-planned with organizers from the AFL-CIO and other groups, and had gotten assurances that they would largely police themselves. These were honorable people who'd kept their word in the past. One could only hope they'd be able to hold their own against interlopers.

Those hopes were dashed when even before the tail end of the march reached downtown, self-described anarchists and Beavis-and-Butthead recreational rioters unleashed a round of criminal acts.

Thugs in uniform—black with black bandannas—popped out of the throngs of peaceful protesters and chucked bricks and bottles at cops, and newspaper racks through shop windows. They even smashed a Starbucks window and ripped off bags of Arabica, Colombian, and French roast (a hanging offense in Seattle). Then they scurried back into the crowd where they cowered behind senior citizens, moms with jogging strollers, and kids dressed up in those cute little sea turtle costumes.

I walked into a hastily called meeting at the MACC, Joiner's windowless headquarters. The mayor was there, so was Washington governor Gary Locke, Chief Annette Sandberg of the Washington State Patrol, King County Sheriff Dave Reichert, and a couple of feds who were in town to do advance work for the president's visit. Clinton was due in late that night. The meeting had one item on its agenda: whether to declare a state of emergency and call in National Guard troops. Tension in the room was palpable, as you might expect with a city under siege. But there was also an undercurrent of something else.

+ + +

The place reeked of fear. It couldn't have been a fear for our own safety—
we were, for the moment, safely hunkered in and bunkered down, far
away from the din of battle. So what were we afraid of? I can't speak for
the others, but here's what I was afraid of: (1) My cops were out there on
the streets, taking a licking; (2) nonviolent protesters, store owners, office
workers, and shoppers faced a clear and present danger; (3) the president of
the United States, leader of the free world, wouldn't be able to address the
ministers—if he could get in to the city at all; (4) my beloved city looked
more like Beirut, or Baghdad; and (5) I didn't know what the hell to do,
other than close down the city and call in the National Guard.

Mostly, I was afraid I'd failed. I had let down a lot of people I cared
about. Sitting next to me in the MACC was Sheriff Reichert who wanted
nothing more than to get back out on the streets to kick some ass and take
some names. Reichert, angry at our insufficiently "aggressive" plan for
dealing with the demonstrators and disgusted by the dithering in the room,
leaned over and whispered, "Let's just throw the damn politicians out of
the room." I liked the sound of that, but we needed them: the mayor to put
the official request for a declaration of a "state of emergency" to the governor, the governor to act on it.

+ + +

Joiner, still in charge in the MACC, remained calm and cool. He held out
for accurate updates from the field. Through his own "shock and awe" at
what had unfolded that day, he was still very much the kind of operations
commander you want calling the shots.

Now, however, *everybody* wanted to run the show—or at least judge it.

Sandberg sighed audibly, rolled her eyes, and murmured under her
breath when the conversation took a turn she didn't like. The feds
migrated to a corner of the room, mumbled, crossed their arms, put their
heads together and shook them vigorously. (Paraphrasing, their position
was: *Just clear the fucking streets, for God's sake! We don't care what it takes.
We got the Big Guy touching down in a matter of hours. POTUS* [the Secret

Service abbreviation for "President of the United States"] *shouldn't be exposed to this . . . this riffraff.*) And Reichert? The poor guy was apoplectic, his blood boiling over every time Schell opened his mouth.

Those individuals most capable of bringing reason to the table and advice to the decision makers, like West Precinct captain Jim Pugel, weren't in the room. They were, by popular demand, out there on the streets. Pugel was doing a hell of a job under hellish conditions. He and other field commanders reported in regularly, but the situation kept changing, of course, from one minute to the next.

So there we were, a roomful of leaders, accustomed to running things, taking risks, making decisions, getting things done. As individuals we made things happen. Now we were suddenly thrust together as a body, as a *team* of leaders—though hardly a cohesive one. It occurred to me that planning and preparation for WTO should have included at least one tabletop exercise for the "rovers"—the very people in that room.

At 3:52 the mayor declared a civil emergency. The governor called out the National Guard.* A curfew, which covered most of the downtown area, was imposed for that evening and the next.

I left the MACC and headed back out on the streets. If anything, the situation was worse. Police officers were being pelted with an amazing array of missiles: traffic cones, rocks, jars, bottles, ball bearings, sticks, golf balls, teargas canisters, chunks of concrete, human urine shot from high-powered squirt guns. Gas-masked militants fired their own teargas at the cops, hurled ours back at us, and flung barricades through plate glass windows. Some moron(s) flattened all four tires on a herd of parked police cars. By nightfall it was no better. Most of the action simply moved to Capitol Hill where innocent café diners got gassed along with rioters.

But at least POTUS made it in to town safely. At about one-thirty in the morning he was put to bed at his favorite Seattle hotel, the Westin.

---

* In a script that could have been written by Joseph Heller, Joiner had asked in advance that the National Guard be placed on alert. *We can't do that unless a state of emergency exists.* But we're trying to *prevent* a "state of emergency." *Well, we can't mobilize unless a state of emergency exists.* Can't you just have your people standing by, say, in Kent or SeaTac? *Nope. Have your emergency first, then give us a call.*

At five o'clock Wednesday morning, having established a "police perimeter" to keep demonstrators from getting too close to the WTO venues, officers observed people carrying crowbars, rocks, masonry hammers, and bipods and tripods (from which to suspend intrepid activists high in the air, in the middle of intersections). The cops confiscated what they could and began arresting the first bunch of the hundreds who would be jailed that day. Against a backdrop of full-scale urban rioting, police officers and Secret Service agents escorted our national leader and his entourage from one venue to another—from the Westin to the Bell Harbor Conference Center on Elliott Bay to the Four Seasons Hotel. Officers continued to take a pelting but POTUS was never touched.

By mid-morning the ACLU filed for a temporary restraining order in U.S. District Court seeking to overturn the "police perimeter." A police commander had to break away from his duties to summarize the department's defense of the tactic, but it paid off. The court denied the request. (As if the demonstrators were paying any attention at all to the so-called "no protest zone.")

All that day and into the night, with action shifting once again to Capitol Hill, cops fought the fight, ducking often as protesters chucked unopened cans of soup and other objects. A platoon commander's car was surrounded by a fun-loving crowd that jumped up and down on the vehicle, then attempted to flip it over. (The lieutenant, who had himself been an antiwar demonstrator at the University of Washington back in the days, told me later, "I've been on every kind of call there is, Chief. But I've never been more scared than I was that night. I thought sure they were going to pull me out of the car, grab my gun, and . . . and who knows what.") Officers dispersed that group with gas and rescued their boss.

Moments later an employee at a gas station on Broadway called 911 to report that the station had been taken over by rioters who were filling small bottles with gasoline. One officer witnessed an individual dressed in black carrying a Molotov cocktail. A crowd of three hundred to four hundred broke off from the Broadway festivities and moved to the 1100 block of East Pine where they threatened to take over SPD's East Precinct.

At two-fifty Thursday morning the precinct was still under siege, the crowd having grown to somewhere between a thousand and fifteen hundred.

The officers protecting it were no longer surprised by the pelting they took, or by the infinite variety of projectiles.

A combination of chemical agents and rubber pellets finally secured the peace. The building, which contained weapons, injured police officers, and prisoners, was never breached.

Downtown at dawn was much quieter than it had been the past two days, a portent of positive things to come. Clinton flew out of town at ten, and the "no protest" perimeter was shrunk. A crowd circled King County Jail at about one in the afternoon (triggering a lockdown), but other than that it was peaceful. Most of the violent demonstrators were either in jail, lying low, or scurrying out of town. As day turned to night the crowd continued to hang around the jail, listening to speeches from protest leaders, criminal defense attorneys, and other activists. At seven-thirty they split up, half of them sticking around, the other half, under police escort, heading up to Capitol Hill where they continued their mostly peaceful ways.

On Friday, the final day of the now-truncated WTO conference, the drama ended. (If the demonstrators had been shouting "Truncate it! Truncate it!" instead of "Shut it down!" they would have achieved their goal.) All that remained of the protests was a hastily negotiated, legally sanctioned march by organized labor. It drew a decent crowd, maybe eight hundred to a thousand, but by then the focus had shifted from the WTO to claims of police brutality and to condemnation of the curfew and the perimeter. At its conclusion the marchers headed back to the Labor Temple.

A hundred or so of them broke from the group, marched over to Fifth Avenue, and swarmed the main entrance to the Westin—did they think POTUS was still inside? (Protesters earlier in the week had effectively made hostages of a furious Secretary of State Madeline Albright and U.S. Trade Representative Charlene Barshefsky—both of whom were unable to leave their hotel rooms for the better part of a day.) Several of the demonstrators chained themselves to the front door of the hotel. It was a lame tactic—the Westin had other obvious entrances but there were too few protesters left to cover those doors. I walked into one of those other entrances and took the elevator to the twenty-first floor where a suite had been set up for officers assigned to dignitary protection at the hotel. I helped myself to a bottled water and walked over to the window. It was dark outside. A good-size crowd had gathered to cheer on this last hurrah. We could hear the muffled chants from behind the thick glass. A couple of hours later, the chains came off and what was left of the crowd either went home or over to the jail to shout words of encouragement to their imprisoned brothers and sisters. The riot was over.

+ + +

Saturday, December 4. I made one last round of the still-operating venues, stopping finally at the MACC where I informed the deputy mayor I that I was turning in my badge.

My decision made headlines. And a Horsey cartoon which had the chief of police falling on his sword. Its caption: "I figured I'd do it myself before someone did it for me."

+ + +

It took great self-discipline for me not to blurt out publicly what I thought of the mayor. But had I done it, it would not have been for the things the mayor was being accused of (hubris, naïveté, lack of foresight—all of which, if it fit him, also applied to me). In fact, I strongly believe that Schell got a raw deal for his role in the battle. It just wasn't his fault, any of it. The guy wasn't a cop, or a tactician, or a "demonstration management" expert. Hell, he'd only been a politician for two years. But the mayor had acted the fool on other fronts, and it was those occasions that had riled me. First and foremost were his reckless remarks to and about Sheriff Reichert.

Riding around at the height of the rioting with King County Executive Ron Sims, Reichert had observed an act of vandalism. Telling Sims he'd seen enough, he bailed out of the car and gave chase. He didn't catch the suspects, but his actions produced a satisfying sound bite on the evening news—and endeared him to my cops, who had plenty of other reasons to favor the county lawman over their own chief.

As the mayor and the sheriff walked out of a hall following one of Clinton's speeches, Schell cornered Reichert. He told him he didn't appreciate the sheriff "acting like a fucking hero out there," or words to that effect. He blocked Reichert's path, and continued to berate him. The sheriff ignored the mayor, and pushed past him. Schell, always the gentleman, shouted after him, "I'll personally destroy you!" The many witnesses to the mayor's actions were not impressed.

After the dust had settled, Schell presided over a special cabinet meeting. He praised all the city departments who'd played any kind of a role during the week (especially the crews who'd cleaned up around Westlake Park over the weekend and made downtown sparkle once again). He thanked us for our personal sacrifices, and so on. It was a gracious statement. Then he said, "You know, *everyone* did a terrific job under incredible stress. Everyone except our lunatic sheriff."*

I cornered the deputy mayor after the meeting, Schell having scooted off. "I'm sick and tired of your boss's character assassinations." I told her he was acting like a "narcissistic sociopath," and urged her to put a muzzle on him.

"I know, I know," she said. "He's been under such pressure . . ."

It wasn't that I didn't understand. The week had taken a personal toll on everyone. I, myself, had gone home to my condo in the middle of the night, four nights in a row with only enough time to shower, air out my gas-saturated uniform, and try to squeeze in a couple of hours' sleep. Bone tired, I found it next to impossible to get to sleep. Some nights I could still hear the *whoop-whoop-whoop* of Guardian One, the sheriff's helicopter I'd ridden in with the governor in order to get an eagle's-eye view of the proceedings. As with a song you can't get out of your head, I'd be wracked by a rerun of the day's other noises: drums, police whistles, chants, screams, rocks landing on police helmets and on the face shields of our horses, dueling bullhorns, glass shattering. I replayed over and over in my mind the frantic radio call of one of my mounted officers as the cop reported

---

* Running a Bush "Mini-Me" campaign—support for the war in Iraq, opposition to reproductive rights, support for a constitutional amendment banning gay marriage, opposition to federally funded sex education, support for oil drilling in the Arctic National Wildlife Refuge, opposition to stem-cell research—the "lunatic" won election in November 2004 to the eighth Congressional District from Washington.

being pulled from his horse. I'd responded to that one, Code 2, turning onto Pine Street just in time to catch a faceful of CS gas.

With eyes shut I saw Technicolor images of bipods and tripods, looters, Dumpster fires, intersection bonfires. I saw cops being baited and assaulted. And I saw a cop kicking a retreating demonstrator in the groin before shooting him in the chest with a rubber pellet. That particular scene, caught by a television camera, was flashed around the globe, over and over, Rodney King–style.

Then there was the cop who, spotting two women in a car videotaping the action, ordered one of them to roll down her window. When she complied, he shouted, "Film *this!*" and filled their car with mace.

+ + +

If Paul Schell wasn't responsible for this mess, who was? I was. The chief of police. I thought we were ready. We weren't. I thought protest leaders would play by the rules. They didn't. I thought we were smarter than the anarchists. We weren't. I thought I'd paid enough attention to my cops' concerns. I hadn't. All in all, I got snookered. Big time.

To this day I feel the pangs of regret: that my officers had to spend long hours on the streets with inadequate rest, sleep, pee breaks, and meals, absorbing every form of threat and abuse imaginable (including, for a number of officers, a dose of food poisoning, from eating vittles that had been sitting out all day); that Seattle's businesses were hurt during the rampaging; that the city and the police department I loved lost a big chunk of collective pride and self-confidence; that peaceful protestors failed to win an adequate hearing of their important antiglobalization message; and, yes, that Paul Schell's dream of a citywide "dialogue" had been crushed.

+ + +

When I think back to that week in 1999, which I do probably too often, one event stands out. It's three in the morning. I've just walked into my darkened condo on Lower Queen Anne.

I check for phone messages. There's only one. I'm sure it's from one of my cops. Friendly and jovial on Day One, the officers had joked with me, shown off their new equipment, passed along compliments they'd heard from protesters. But this was Day Three, and now they were shooting me nasty looks. Why?

Word had spread through the ranks that I'd answered "yes" to a reporter who wanted to know if I'd seen any police conduct that disturbed me. Well, I sure as hell had, and I wasn't about to lie about it. That I'd lavishly praised the sterling performance of my officers at a string of press conferences made no difference to many of my cops. I'd broken an important provision of "the Code." Like the Republicans' "Eleventh Amendment," police officers are not to speak ill of one another—even if one of them has assaulted an unarmed, retreating demonstrator. Or maced innocent women.*

I punch in the code and retrieve the message. It's not from a cop, after all. It's from a friend. A doctor friend I have dinner with several times a year. I sigh. *Thank God, I can use a little support right about now.*

"I can't believe what I'm seeing on TV," says the friend's voice, dripping with venom. "Your cops are worse than the fucking Gestapo. I'm totally repulsed that you're allowing this. You're a sorry, miserable excuse of a human being and I'm appalled that you're our chief."

But at the end of the week there was this: My cops hadn't killed anyone. Given fatigue, provocation, and ample legal justification to employ lethal force on numerous occasions, they'd held their fire. The Battle produced not a single death (and fewer than a hundred injuries, the most serious of which was a broken arm).

+ + +

The Battle of Seattle was an important event in the history of American social and political protest. Whereas ten years ago a thousand people might have shown up to protest the WTO, there were fifty times that number on

---

* In neither of these incidents was a Seattle police officer involved. The "kicker-shooter" belonged to Tukwila PD, the "macer" was Reichert's. Both agencies responded immediately, taking their cops off the streets—and later imposing stiff penalties.

the streets of Seattle in the fall of '99. I believe that's a testament not only to the power of the Internet (which has all but replaced posters on fences, campus leafleting, and telephone trees as the primary means of organizing and mobilizing protest) but also to broad, intense antiglobalization sentiment and to a deep mistrust of our government's policies. Witness the awesome numbers of protesters who took to the streets locally (as well as globally) to protest America's invasion and occupation of Iraq.*

+ + +

Seattle was, in the end, just too damned small to pull it off. If you're thinking about hosting such an event you need to be able to count your cops in the thousands or tens of thousands, not hundreds. Hell, the city wouldn't have had enough cops had we called in every officer in the state.

We learned many lessons from the Battle, foremost of which are: (1) line up as much help in advance as you possibly can, then find more; (2) plan for "force multipliers" (i.e., volunteers), but don't become overreliant on them; and (3) keep demonstrators at a much greater distance from official venues. No matter how much they bitch about it.

And finally, my gift to every police executive and mayor in cities the size of Seattle's: Think twice before saying yes to an organization whose title contains any of the following words: *world, worldwide, global, international, multinational, bilateral, trilateral, multilateral, economic, monetary, fiscal, finance, financial, fund, bank, banking,* or *trade.*

---

* Prediction: With the reelection of George W. Bush and the continuation of his foreign policies, America's cities will experience wave after wave of street protests, with demonstrations that could rival or exceed the scope and intensity of the antiwar movement of the sixties and seventies.

CHAPTER 29

COMMUNITY POLICING:
A RADICAL VIEW

"WE'RE REALLY INTO COMMUNITY policing," said an East Coast police chief at a conference in the late 1990s. "We've got cops on bicycles, on foot, on horseback, even ATVs." *What, no skateboards?*

Although two thirds of all police departments claim they are engaged in "community policing," most of them practice nothing more than an arid, cynical form of public relations. Real community policing is predicated on the potentially frightening notion that people in a democracy have the right and the authority to act on their own to make their communities safe. And to hold their police accountable for *helping* them do so. Community policing is the community policing itself.

In chapter 26, I mention a community meeting I attended when I was San Diego's assistant chief. Called on a day's notice and held at Rick's, a gay bar on University Avenue, the place was packed. The agenda? Public safety—and anger and fear following the slaying of a seventeen-year-old kid as part of a vicious gay-bashing spree by skinheads. Introduced first, I outlined the mugging series and provided details on the murder. I thought I was doing a terrific job—sensitive to cultural issues, forthcoming on the facts of the homicide, encouraging people to work with us to help solve the crimes. But, from the back of the room came the loud, grating voice of a man who had a less high opinion of my talk. "Look, Chief. Here's how it is . . ." The room went silent as heads turned toward the speaker—a short, muscular, middle-aged man in a red tank top. "If you don't catch these assholes, we will."

I opened my mouth to give the speech I'd given hundreds of times: *Whoa, now, mister. You don't want to resort to* vigilantism. *Don't put yourself in harm's way—or violate the civil liberties of your fellow citizens. No, this is the one part of community policing you want to leave to the pros. Now, if you'll just work with us* . . . But my jaw snapped shut as my brain registered the hypocrisy of what I was about to say.

I'd been professing since the early seventies that we were the "people's police," that the police in America (unlike so many other places around the globe) *belong to the people*—not the other way around. Yet, here I was about to inform "the people" that they must let us, the police, take care of everything—or at least take the lead. The people had no *right* to take to the streets, to reclaim their own neighborhood.

An epiphany, sprung on you in public like that, can produce kind of a meltdown, especially when you've been wedded all your career to a truth that no longer rings true. But I kept it together, thanked Tank-top, seconded his "motion," and asked him what his police department could do to help. Thus was born America's first PD-sponsored citizen's patrol.

The following day I received a call from John Witt, San Diego's city attorney. "Tell me it's not true," he said. "Tell me you didn't authorize a 'citizens' patrol' last night."

"Well, I'm not sure what you mean by 'authorize.' A group of citizens told me that if the PD couldn't catch the bastards who killed that kid, they would. I just figured they had that right. It's their community."

"Did you tell the group you'd provide training?"

"Yes."

"Did you allow them to schedule their 'patrols' out of that big police van?"

"Yes."

"Did you promise to broker the donation of cell phones for them to use?"

"Yes."

"And have you found those phones?"

"Well, I called PacBell who referred me to PacTel who sent me to Pac-Cell, and, yes, I found them six phones."

"Do you realize you've just made these, these . . . *lay* people, these *citizens* our agents?" That meant the City would be liable for anything that might go wrong.

"Hmm. I thought *we* were *their* agents."

"What?"

"Don't we belong to them? Aren't we the *people's* police?"

"Ah, cut the political craptrap, will ya? Do you have any idea what our exposure is on this?"

"Yeah, I think so." The city was self-insured, meaning if we screwed up and it cost us in civil damages the money would come out of the city budget, most likely the PD's. The *people's* budget.

"Well, I'm putting you on notice. I can't order you to cease and desist; I don't have that authority. But," he paused. "I plan to take this up with the city manager and the city council. In the meantime, consider yourself *officially advised*."

"Thanks, John. I hereby consider myself officially advised."

+ + +

Today, many San Diegans patrol their own streets, some of them using SDPD vehicles, many of them carrying SDPD radios. Citizens with disabilities write parking citations to selfish, arrogant citizens who park illegally in "handicapped" zones. Seniors patrol retirement communities, doing security checks, writing parking tickets, checking on shut-ins. Up to a thousand others are scurrying about the city or working in the department's various divisions, engaged in all kinds of "self-policing." (For an exquisite example of community policing in unexpected places, see sidebar.)

COMMUNITY POLICING AT 36,000 FEET

Three days after 9/11, with commercial flights resuming and passengers and crews understandably skittish, if not terrified, a remarkable thing happened on United Flight #564 from Denver International to Washington Dulles. Widely reported at the time (and replicated, in essence, on other flights), I've drawn this account from David Remnick's "Talk of the Town" column in *The New Yorker* posted on October 8, 2001. He cites the pilot's speech, as transcribed by passenger Kathy Rockel of Virginia:

"First, I want to thank you for being brave enough to fly today. The doors are now closed and we have no help from outside for any problems that might occur inside this plane. [The pilot was quoted by other passengers as saying,

---

> "If you have a bomb no need to tell me or anyone else; you are already in control."] As you could tell when you checked in, the government has made some changes to increase security in the airports. They have not, however, made any rules about what happens after those doors close. Until they do that, we have made our own rules and I want to share them with you. . . .
>
> "Here is our plan and our rules. If someone or several people stand up and say they are hijacking this plane, I want you all to stand up together. Then take whatever you have available to you and throw it at them. Throw it at their faces and heads so they will have to raise their hands to protect themselves. The very best protection you have against knives are the pillows and blankets. Whoever is close to these people should then try to get a blanket over their heads. Then they won't be able to see. Once that is done, get them down and keep them there. Do not let them up. I will then land the plane at the closest place and we *will* take care of them. After all, there are usually only a few of them and we are two-hundred-plus strong. We will not allow them to take over this plane. I find it interesting that the U.S. Constitution begins with the words 'We, the people.' That's who we are, the people, and we will not be defeated."
>
> A flight attendant "then asked the passengers . . . to turn to their neighbors on either side and introduce themselves, and to tell one another something about themselves and their families. For today, we consider you family. . . . We will treat you as such and ask that you do the same with us."
>
> Community policing at 36,000 feet? Why not?

In the early 1970s, Police Chief Ray Hoobler was under intense attack from many San Diegans—especially people of color, whom he'd offended repeatedly with his less than sensitive public remarks about "stoop laborers" and "wetbacks" (along with more discreet references to "niggers"). His popularity had plummeted within City Hall in direct proportion to the antagonisms he fostered between the PD and the politicians' constituencies. His job at risk, Hoobler was desperate to be seen as more community "orientated."

As luck would have it, I'd just finished writing a proposal that would at least in theory bring about a shift in Hoobler's image: a kinder, gentler, more "community-orientated" chief. I was a lieutenant at the time, heading up Planning, Research & Systems Analysis.

Hoobler and I flew to Washington, D.C.—he sat in first class while I was wedged into a center seat in coach—to ask for money from the Police Foundation. The Foundation is a private organization established in the early seventies by the Ford Foundation to stimulate, sponsor, and evaluate reforms in American policing. "Remember," said Hoobler as we walked into a hotel suite of academic heavies the next morning. "No running off at the mouth with your liberal bullshit. Just stick to the plan."

The "plan" was to randomly select twenty-four patrol cops from our Northern Division, put them through an intensive (and ongoing) training program in methods of community analysis, community organizing, interpersonal communication, and problem-solving skills, then have them "profile"* their beats. The officers would then apply their ongoing learning over a one-year period, exercising far greater decision-making authority and coming up with innovative approaches to fighting crime and solving problems. Their accomplishments would be judged against a control group of twenty-four other patrol cops. Hoobler had warned me against "team policing," against "letting the community dictate police actions," against anything "smacking of communism" (he actually said it) or, his pet bugbear, "rule by committee."

Hoobler was a traditional cop, brought up under a system that, while nominally valuing "teamwork," was invested in a highly centralized system of authority. It was a system that defined good cops as those who kept their noses clean, shoes shined, hair trimmed, and their police cars free of Jack-in-the Box trash, sunflower seeds, and cigar butts; wrote legible reports; generated lots of "activity" (principally traffic tickets, field interrogations, and arrests); and met an assortment of other bureaucratic requirements. It

---

* A term with unfortunate implications today. To the project, it meant police officers becoming increasingly, *systematically* more well educated about demographic, socioeconomic, crime, traffic, and other community issues, particularly the *trends* and *patterns* in their assigned communities. To guard against understandable fears that our "profile cops" would build dossiers or otherwise pry into the private lives of individual citizens, we formed a citizens' advisory group of university professors, a student activist, a business representative, and an ACLU attorney—and gave them complete access to *everything*. They read profile reports, had unfettered access to the officers' daily journals, rode along with the cops, and without supervision questioned individual project officers. Their report at the end of the project was glowing: not a single abuse of police authority did they find.

was a rigidly traditional, "Lone Ranger" system, a mentality that placed no value—in fact it placed a *minus* value—on beat cops' involvement in the *prevention* of crime, or in teaming up with other officers or, heaven forbid, the community itself to solve problems. The rule: Chase calls, harvest numbers, please your sergeant (and, by implication, the rest of the chain of command), and to hell with *results*. Hoobler's administration saw to it that those who exceeded these internal, bureaucratic standards went to dicks or got promoted, thus perpetuating the system.

I, on the other hand, was passionately committed to opening up the PD to the community, engaging department personnel and citizens in joint crime fighting and problem solving, encouraging collaboration, experimentation, and innovation within the ranks, and ending the PD's "quota system"—which I saw as an instrument for perpetuating "attitude" arrests and other oppressive police tactics. I'd read George E. Berkley's *The Democratic Policeman* (1969), and had written a senior thesis at SDSU on the need to replace the police paramilitary bureaucracy. My motive in proposing the profile project was to launch a campaign, subversive by necessity, that would fundamentally reorient policing and the community-police relationship. I envisioned San Diego cops working in authentic partnership with the community—with the latter as senior partner. I believed that police performance and conduct should be evaluated not solely by department supervisors but by the community, and that the community should be involved in helping to set policies and priorities and in helping to design programs and procedures.

The chief and I were on a collision course.

Hoobler went first during our presentation in D.C. He told the research experts that unlike other cities experimenting with such concepts as preventive patrol (Kansas City) or "team policing" (Cincinnati), which brought detectives, traffic officers, and beat cops together as a team to police specific geographical areas, San Diego would offer a "back-to-basics" approach to police work.

"Our officers will continue to do the all the same things cops have done for years," he said. "We'll just do it much more efficiently." The remark sent shivers down my spine. We would become more efficient in our unilateral approach to police work, more efficient at oppressing people of color, youth, our critics. "The project I'm asking you to fund," he continued, "is an 'old-fashioned, cop-on-the-beat' approach to police work. It will emphasize *individual* beat accountability. There will be no venturing off into nontraditional, *non-cop* activities . . ."

If he only knew.

When it came time for me to speak, I echoed Hoobler's "back to basics" theme, but offered as diplomatically as I could a fundamentally different, ideologically freighted definition of the term: police work with a more open, democratic, *publicly accountable* flavor.

+ + +

In the early 1830s, official contingents of New Yorkers, Philadelphians, and Bostonians crossed the Atlantic to examine Great Britain's "Metropolitan Police Act." At that moment in history, U.S. cities were suffering the same social problems that led the English to form the first organized, nonmilitary police force in a democratic society.

The brainchild of Home Secretary Sir Robert Peel, such a force was urgently needed to contend with an explosion of lawlessness in and around London—highway robbery, burglary, theft, rape, arson, stranger-on-stranger killings. Spawned by the Industrial Revolution (and the vast migration that accompanied the transition from rural to urban, farming to manufacturing), it was starting to look like the country's crime "spree" would become a permanent condition in Great Britain.

Yet even in the face of unprecedented crime and the elevated fears of its people, Parliament balked at Peel's proposal. They feared that an organized police force would bring about its own onerous social problems. That it would spawn police nepotism and corruption, heavy-handedness, intrusions into the private lives of individual citizens, and other violations of British civil liberties. Peel, who entertained these same reservations, worked hard to engineer critical safeguards into the act. Even so, it took the home secretary seven years of intense political maneuvering to convince British lawmakers to enact the legislation.

The new law stipulated that police officers had to be "morally fit," with no hint of past wrongdoings. Explicit policies and procedures would be formulated to *control* the police, to make them responsive, accountable, courteous and nonthreatening to the people they would serve. British police would carry no firearms. And all one thousand of the first "Peelers," later to become Sir Robert's "Bobbies," had to be at least six feet in height. Their tall hats, still worn today, were designed to make Bobbies literally "stand tall" in the eyes of the citizenry so that they might patrol their beats with psychological versus physical force. Britain's cops were intended from the beginning to serve as role models, exemplars of good government and civility. Not mercenaries, or thugs in uniform.

Cut to the Yanks who traveled to Great Britain. These city officials and civic leaders fell in love with this new approach to social control. They returned to their respective cities with tremendous enthusiasm for it—but with little or no regard for the precautions Peel and Parliament had so painstakingly built into the British model.

Predictably, from their birth as full-time police forces in the mid-1880s the New York, Boston, and Philadelphia police departments were instant havens for corrupt beat cops—and for the fathers, uncles, in-laws, cousins, and ethnic ward lackeys who "supervised" them. The process of becoming a nineteenth-century police officer in New York was straightforward: You simply went to the local ward leader or alderman with the requisite sum of money. The same was generally true for every other city police force of the nineteenth and early twentieth centuries, including the Seattle Police Department (established 1869) and the San Diego Police Department (1889).

+ + +

Having endured police abuses into the 1890s, "progressive elites" began what Robert M. Fogelson called the first of two "waves" of police reform.*
The first, culminating in the Wickersham Commission report (1931), was aimed at wresting control of the police from local political machines.

---

* Fogelson, Robert M. *Big-City Police.* Harvard University Press, 1977.

Appointed by President Herbert Hoover in 1929 (pursuant to an act of Congress), and headed by former U.S. Attorney General George Wickersham, the blue-ribbon panel was charged with "studying exhaustively the entire problem of the enforcement of our laws and the improvement of our judicial system, including the special problems and abuses growing out of the prohibition laws." The commission's principal finding, which led to widespread adoption of civil service merit systems, was that incompetent agency leadership was responsible for "police lawlessness."

Fogelson's second wave of police reform, begun in the 1930s, was generated within the law enforcement community itself—and was largely a response to initiatives pushed for years by August Vollmer (who wrote most of the Wickersham Commission's final report).

A former letter-carrier with a sixth-grade education, Vollmer became police chief (originally city marshal) of Berkeley, California, in 1905. The uncontested "father of modern policing," he pioneered automobile, bicycle, and motorcycle patrols, the police radio, record-keeping, polygraph exams, crime and fingerprint analysis. His was the first department to employ a scientist to help the police prevent and solve crimes. And he developed a program of police-community relations. But it was his attitude about police education, and police behavior toward citizens, including criminals and ethnic minorities (he was said to hate prejudice) that won him the support of progressives of the era. (These included his pal, Alameda County district attorney Earl Warren, who would go on to become the state's attorney general, three-term governor, and, finally, chief justice of the Supreme Court.) Vollmer wrote, "The policeman's job is the highest calling in the world. The men who do that job should be the finest men. They should be the best educated. They should be college graduates . . . And what are they? Dumbbells."

One of Vollmer's cops in Berkeley (and one of his students when Vollmer became a professor at U.C. Berkeley) was Orlando Winfield Wilson, who went on to become superintendent of police of the Chicago Police Department from 1960 to 1971. "O.W." Wilson is probably the better known of the two men within police circles because he essentially wrote the book on how PDs should be organized—bureaucratically, with an emphasis on centralization, specialized units, and a steep hierarchy of "command and control."*

Wilson's reforms, focused as they were on efficiency and anticorruption, had the effect of helping to clean up a lot of dirty police departments. But they also functioned to distance police officers from the communities they served—the inevitable effect of a civil service mentality, the paramilitary-bureaucratic structure, and the "professional" model. Call it the law of *intended* consequences: Reformers at least through the mid-1960s did not *want* police officers getting close to the community. They correctly saw that coziness with business interests and with ward politicians would be a slippery slope to corruption.

+ + +

Clean or dirty, cops in America have always served the elites: white, moneyed, propertied, the politically entrenched. It's not hard to understand why people of color, the poor, and younger Americans did not, and do not, look upon the police as "theirs."

Policing, *in theory*, is a neutral, nonaligned institution, existing, *in theory*, to serve the legitimate interests of public safety and criminal justice. But even today it serves the interests of politicians over "the people," landlords over tenants, merchants over consumers, whites over blacks, husbands over wives, management over labor—except when "labor" is the police union. Never, as an institution, has policing lived up to the lofty language of its Code of Ethics:

> As a law enforcement officer, my fundamental duty is to serve mankind, to safeguard lives and property, to protect the innocent against deception, the weak against oppression or intimidation,

---

* I was fortunate to inherit O. W. Wilson's personal library, and kept it in my office in San Diego for years. It was full of his and others' writings on these cutting-edge management theories. (It also contained a first edition of LeMoyne Snyder's classic *Homicide Investigation* [1945], replete with page after page of the most gruesome murder scenes you'd ever want to see.)

and the peaceful against violence or disorder . . . and to respect
the Constitutional rights of all men to liberty, equality, and
justice. . . .*

Compare and contrast: Are the police, *as an institution*, known for their protection of "the innocent against deception" or do they deceive the innocent? Do the police protect "the weak against oppression or intimidation" or do they oppress and intimidate the very people they're sworn to protect?

+ + +

The Police Foundation gave us our money, and with it an opportunity to usher in a "third wave" of police reform. Hoobler was ebullient. He slapped me on the back and upgraded my ticket for a boozy, shoulder-to-shoulder, first-class return trip to San Diego.

A few months later we kicked off the "community policing" training program for twenty-four randomly selected cops—whose view of and approach to police work would never again be the same again. They worked beats north of Interstate 8, from upscale La Jolla on the west to the Wild Animal Park in the northeast corner of the city. They patrolled Mission Valley, with its long strip of hotels, golf courses, car dealerships, and sprawling shopping malls; Linda Vista, an economically depressed, densely populated community and home to the division's only significant black population; the wall-to-wall industrial parks of Sorrento Valley; a part of Clairemont known for its intractable landlord-tenant problems at huge low-income apartment complexes; Rancho Bernardo, a sprawling suburban retirement community; and Mission Beach, where hordes of "Zonies" descend each summer from Phoenix and Tucson to escape the heat, guzzle beer by the keg, fight with the locals, and throw rocks and bottles at the police. The vast, diverse area gave us a superb lab within which to test the theory of community policing.

---

* Embraced by most states and cities, and many other countries, the code was written in the late 1950s by a former San Diego police captain, Gene Muehleisen, who later became the first executive director of the California state commission on Peace Officer Standards and Training.

The officers discovered on the first day of training that they were in for something quite different from their academy days. I'd hired research associates who, while amiable and sociable and able to get along marvelously with cops, were unyielding political progressives. They were wary of the authority of the police and critical of many department practices. (It was from one of them, Rubén Rumbaut, a brilliant sociologist, that I picked up the term "people's police.") Together, we'd spent months designing an exceptional educational experience that we believed would capture the imaginations of our officers and challenge them to rethink some of the most basic preconceptions of their work.

It was critical that our cops question the assumption that policing was something you do *to* the community, rather than *with* it. We wanted them to challenge the notion that their superiors knew better than they what to do about problems on their beats, that they had to raise their hands for permission to try something different in order to fight crime or solve a problem.

If we were to attack these assumptions in a training setting, we knew we'd have to make that setting comfortable and nonthreatening, and populate it with extraordinary instructors armed with persuasive ideas—and an ability to relate to cops.

We brought in some of the finest minds, and most approachable teachers, in the country. Among them were Professor Egon Bittner of Brandeis University (who spent a day talking with our cops about the unsustainable role of police officers as "soldier bureaucrats") and Professor Nicos Mouratides of San Diego State (who talked about the "sociology of work," helping our officers see that theirs was a truly noble calling, and not "shit work," as many of them had come to view their craft). We did the initial training in a weeklong session—morning, afternoon, and evening blocks each day—in a "residential retreat" format at a resort (directly across the street from the Del Mar racetrack).

Our cops appreciated being treated with respect, living like the "big boys" in the corner pocket, and being given an opportunity to reexamine their daily work, and to make it more productive, more satisfying. It was one of those transformative, "mountaintop" experiences. The kind that leaves you praying that reentry into the *real* world won't be *too* jarring for the cops.

At the end of the week Gene Chouinard, our most senior police officer with more than thirty years on the job, shared with me privately what the experience had meant to him. We'd just finished the last evening session and were sitting in the bar. "Unbelievable!" he said, shaking his head. "Unbelievable."

"What's that?"

"*This* is what I hired on to do, over thirty years ago."

"Yeah?"

"Yeah. But I've spent my whole career chasing calls and collecting numbers. And thinking all that time I was doing police work. But *this* is police work—what we've been talking about all week. It's almost like a dream come true. The chance before I retire to actually make a difference in people's lives. And to think for myself."

"I'm glad you feel that way, Geno. But everyone knows you're a hell of a cop."

"Yeah? Well. Thanks. But I've always done police work in *spite* of the system, not *because* of it. What this project is telling me is that I can get out of my car, work with people, solve problems—and not have to worry about my five-two-and-one." (The five shakedowns, two traffic citations, and one criminal arrest beat cops were expected to produce during an eight-hour shift.)

"That's right," I said. "And, if there's a God we'll put a permanent end to the numbers game. You'll never have to worry about your sergeant hounding you for 'activity,' so long as you're out there fighting crime and solving problems—with the community."

"Amen," said Gene Chouinard.

Fueled by a couple of drinks, we took our conversation outside. It was raining hard but that didn't stop us. We walked the grounds for an hour or so, talking shop, jawing about what was in store for him and the other project officers.

+ + +

For the next year our project cops did things they'd never done before. They *studied* their beats, systematically. (At least two of the officers had been unable to tell us their beat boundaries at the beginning of the training. Their attitude was, what difference did it make, so long as they continued to shag their numbers and stuff them into the PD's centralized "productivity" machine?) They analyzed demographic and socioeconomic and crime and traffic and called-for-services data. They researched "institutional patterns of life" on their beats, examining the various services of community-based organizations and introducing themselves to agency employees. They devoted hours to "mapping" their beats, identifying key geographical and topographical features, and where the neighborhoods' biggest problems were.

They didn't just study their beats, of course. They worked them according to a new set of values, strategies, and tactics (which included traditional approaches well worth preserving). While they didn't encourage direct citizen patrols (I wouldn't have allowed it in those days), they did work intimately with the community to develop joint approaches to solving problems and fighting crime. And because they were allowed to use their own discretion in coming up with innovative strategies, they *invented* several new approaches to police work. And not once were they pestered for numbers.

It's old hat today, but in the early seventies patrol officers didn't carry walkie-talkies (ours did); they didn't put citizens in the passenger seat to let them ride along and see police work up close and personal (ours did), and to strategize together how best to solve problems (ours did); they didn't attend, much less host, community meetings (ours did); they didn't take up advocacy of safety around schools or speak at school board sessions (ours did).

We had one officer who, at the beginning of summer, took paint to paper and created a colorful poster which he then plastered all over Mission Beach. "So, You Want to Have a Party?" it read. Below that: a cartoonish picture of a young hippie grasping a beer can in one hand and flashing the peace sign in the other. The poster acknowledged the fun that beach parties promise, as well as the downside for residents (and for the cops), and it extended an invitation to meet with the self-same officer/artist to do a little "pre-party planning." It turned out to be a wildly successful intervention. Meetings were held all over the neighborhood, and not a single bash got out of hand that summer. That had to be some kind of a record.

We had another cop who worked with tenants and landlords in a neighborhood notorious for conflict. He spent hours researching the law and relevant policies and programs. Then he held joint meetings with all parties at which he provided training—and during which he mediated conflicts. Result? Dramatic reduction in calls, dramatic improvement in landlord-tenant relations.

Most of our project officers worked with groups, numbers of people. One, however, a rookie, singled out an individual as his beat's biggest problem.

+ + +

Officer Ray Pulsipher made a project of "Robbie Hawkins." Pulsipher, a cherubic, soft-spoken man who looked even younger than his twenty-two years, had struggled during the training. Not only was he one of the cops who didn't know his beat boundaries, he'd guessed wrong on just about every demographic or socioeconomic characteristic of his beat, including this: Beat 122, the Linda Vista area of San Diego, was not, as he believed, "ninety percent black." It was eight percent black. Nor did Beat 122 generate the "highest crime rate in the city"; it had the second *lowest* crime rate of the twenty-eight Northern Division beats.

What these misconceptions revealed was that in his short time on Beat 122 Pulsipher had spent most of his nights patrolling a tight circle within the Linda Vista community. A circle of black faces. Sure, there was crime in that neighborhood, too much of it. But Pulsipher had made the same mistake most rookie white cops make while patrolling black communities. He equated "black" with "crime" and he ignored those parts of his beat that he assumed were "safe," or at least relatively so: the vast white residential areas of Linda Vista.

Pulsipher confessed to his ignorance. He also copped to "having trouble speaking to 'the blacks.' " He told a story during a training session of taking a teenage shoplifter home to her mother. Pulsipher couldn't understand it when mom lit into him; he thought he'd done her a favor by bringing the kid to her and not to Juvie (Juvenile Detention). We pressed him. What had he said to the woman? *How* had he said it? He told her he'd arrested *lots* of teenagers and that "not all of them are black." "I swear I'm not prejudiced," he told the class. Then he paused. "At least I don't think I am. And if I am, I need to know it. I just can't seem to stop putting my foot in my mouth."

Back on the streets after the training, Pulsipher radically changed his approach to patrolling Beat 122. He studied the numbers, the census and crime data. He discovered his biggest (i.e., the *community's* biggest) crime problem: daytime residential burglaries committed by truant white kids in white neighborhoods. Pulsipher teamed up with the cop working days, went out in plainclothes, on a bicycle, with a walkie-talkie in his backpack, and solved that problem in two days.

And he acted on his vow to learn to talk with people in the black community. Every night, after taking a quick survey of his beat by car, he'd park the vehicle, get out and start walking. And talking—and *listening*—to people, white and black. Some of these conversations were field interrogations, but most were merely friendly chats. He attended numerous community meetings in black neighborhoods, honing his listening skills, sensitizing himself to "hot button" words, searching for ways to make a human connection with African-Americans, people he was beginning to see as no different from himself—except in "positive ways."

It was early in this real-world tutorial that he came across the black youth, Hawkins. Sullen and snarly, Robbie Hawkins was a member of one of the most notorious families of offenders and ex-offenders in the city. Every one of them, Robbie especially, had a rap sheet that went to multiple pages and included burglaries, robberies, thefts—and assaults on police officers. I hadn't even graduated from the academy when I first heard the family name. San Diego cops from the Tijuana border to Del Mar knew of the rabidly "anti-police" family in Linda Vista.

Having left a party one night, Hawkins was walking up Linda Vista Road. Pulsipher spotted him and pulled over. "Hey, Robbie. How you doing?"

"None of your fucking business."

"Okay."

"Why you always jacking me?"

"I thought I'd offer you a ride. If you want one, I mean."

"Why, man?"

"No reason, I guess. Just seemed a little chilly tonight. Looks like you got a long walk ahead of you."

"Yeah, it is a ways."

"Well, hop in if you want to."

"I guess." Hawkins reached for the back door of the cage car.

"No, no," said Pulsipher. "Up here." He reached over and opened the front seat passenger door. Hawkins slid in. Our police officer had just violated every officer-safety rule in the book. But he was willing to take the risk.

"Never rode up here before," said Hawkins.

"How come you're walking?"

"No reason."

"Where's your car?"

"Home." Pulsipher knew Hawkins had lost his license, but he didn't want to rub it in. At least the kid was obeying the law tonight.

"Well, I'm glad I came along. Happy to give you a lift."

"They took my motherfucking license," said Hawkins. Pulsipher saw his opportunity and took it.

"Well . . . maybe I can help you get it back."

Which he did. He got Robbie Hawkins his license back. Why? Because he had concluded that Hawkins was redeemable, and that he might be able to make a difference in the young man's life. If nothing else, maybe this gesture would neutralize *some* of the ill will Hawkins felt toward the PD. Pulsipher understood that people, even neighborhood hoodlums, are less likely to attack the few cops, or the one, they know and trust.

Hawkins never thanked Pulsipher for going out on a limb for him. But he never forgot it. How do I know?

Because of an armed 211 (robbery) call at L.V. Liquor in the 7100 block of Linda Vista Road. The clerk had been shot through the shoulder. Pulsipher was one of the first officers to arrive at the scene. The suspect was long gone, but as he drove onto the lot Pulsipher spotted Hawkins standing by a car. Another unit was across the parking lot, broadcasting suspect information. Hawkins gestured to Pulsipher, a motion so slight that no one else would have picked up on it. Then he walked behind the liquor store. Pulsipher waited a moment then followed, into a pitch-dark recess.

Hawkins was standing on the other side of a Dumpster. Had the kid set him up? Pulsipher wouldn't let himself believe it but the thought crossed his mind. He walked up to Hawkins.

"What's up, Robbie?"

"I saw it, man."

"The stickup?"

"Yeah."

"Who was it?" said Pulsipher. Hawkins told him. Then he told him where the robber would likely be found.

Pulsipher still had a nagging feeling that the whole thing might be a setup—cops in black communities were taking a fair amount of rocks, bottles, and, on occasion, sniper fire in those days—but he called for backup and drove to the location Hawkins had given him. Four units were in place, sitting on the house when the suspect pulled up moments later. Pulsipher and another cop took him down. Within forty minutes of the robbery, they'd impounded the gun, the money, the getaway car, and the stickup man. Score one for the value of community policing, and of building positive relationships on the beat.

This incident, though, paled by comparison to what would happen a couple of months later, a deadly incident involving Pulsipher and his new pal.

Pulsipher got a call to an apartment complex, a loud stereo complaint. He pulled up to the curb, having asked radio for a "call back" to the complainant, sometimes an effective anti-ambush tactic. The din of the stereo suggested it wasn't a trap. He walked up a flight of outdoor stairs and down a walkway to the offending apartment where he knocked on the door and announced himself to a collection of young black men. Without warning, a man bolted through the screen door, grabbed Pulsipher, and pushed him across the landing to the wrought-iron railing. Taken by surprise and teetering over the railing, Pulsipher was sure he was a goner. He pictured himself falling, his head splitting open on the concrete below. Then, as quickly as it had happened, he felt the man being jerked off him. "Nah, man," said the familiar voice. "*This* dude's okay." Hawkins may not have thanked Pulsipher in a conventional way, for the officer's positive intervention in his life, but his gratitude was conveyed unambiguously that night.

+ + +

By the end of our "demonstration project," we'd proved that cops, freed of the numbers game (both psychologically and operationally) and other bureaucratic nonsense, *can* make a difference. Our project cops arrested more felons and answered as many radio calls, but wrote fewer traffic citations, as their control-group counterparts. Our analysis, and that of an independent on-site evaluator, found that the increase in arrests was the result of greater citizen confidence in the police, a willingness to come forward with suspect tips and other important information.

Those fewer traffic tickets? Chalk it up to a refusal on the part of our project cops to write "wobblers," or chickenshit citations. Our officers worked to *build* relations with the community, not tear them down.

At project's end, we brought three of the cops into Hoobler's office to talk about what the experience had meant to them. Over lunch a couple of days earlier, I'd cautioned them to avoid certain trigger words with Hoobler, but they used them anyway: *partnership* with the community, *collaboration* with social workers and others, *sharing* information, and credit for successes. The chief sneered a couple of times, but took it all in. On the strength of the statistical results and some splendid anecdotal accounts of the success of the project, he accepted our recommendation to implement community policing citywide.

Hoobler's stock had been dropping steadily during the yearlong project, confidence in his leadership plummeting by the day. The man *had* to be seen as far more sensitive to the community and quick. It was Hoobler who coined the now-common phrase *community-oriented policing*, although he continued to stick with "orientated."

I'd like to say that citywide, departmentwide implementation of community policing was a smashing success. But it wasn't. Far from it.

+ + +

Within two years the thing was dead—or as I preferred to put it, *dormant.* We'd tried hard, our small band of advocates and True Believers, putting on some of the best departmentwide training the agency had ever seen, devising systems to help ensure accountability in the absence of the numbers game, and so on. But we just couldn't keep it together, even when Hoobler got the sack (for lying to his boss) and Bill Kolender, his young assistant chief with impeccable community credentials, took over.

Community policing was an idea whose time had not come.

It had worked wonderfully in a hothouse environment, with a mere twenty-four cops and a sizable, dedicated staff to teach, encourage, challenge, and support the officers around the clock. But in the hostile, often toxic, culture of the department at large, community policing—San Diego–style—rolled up into a little ball and went to sleep.

We continued for years to assert that we were a community-oriented police agency, and for years visitors from around the country and around the globe streamed into the city for canned pitches on the marvels of "community policing." But it wasn't until 1988 when a woman named Nancy McPherson showed up on our doorstep that community policing was roused from its slumber.

+ + +

Hired by the Police Executive Research Forum (Washington, D.C.) to help us implement a pilot program in "problem oriented policing," McPherson came from a background in political science and public administration. Smart, skillful, and respectful, she'd had no experience working with the police. But she worked tirelessly, first to educate herself about the history and culture of our institution, then to help individual police officers learn how to become better problem solvers.

In 1989, Bob Burgreen was named SDPD's top cop. A more enlightened, risk-taking chief you'd not find anywhere. McPherson, Burgreen, Captain Jerry Sanders, and City Manager Jack McGrory led the process of institutionalizing community, or "neighborhood," policing in San Diego. As Burgreen's new assistant chief, in charge of all day-to-day operations, I was generally confined to the role of cheerleader.

The city manager, in particular, was critical to the success of neighborhood policing. McGrory understood that only through the purposeful, collaborative, and *sustained involvement of all city departments* could true community-based policing become a reality. From cleaning up graffiti to shutting down crack houses, from providing recreational facilities and programs for the city's youth to filling potholes in the street (another metaphor for "broken windows"), *every* city employee needed to understand his or her role in helping the community police itself.

It was never radical enough for my blood, those late eighties initiatives. It never really achieved the promise of legitimate, grassroots community direction and oversight of police practices. But it sure beat the hell out of everything else out there. And it reestablished San Diego as the preeminent community-policing city in the country.* This time, when visitors showed up to be educated SDPD actually had something to teach them.

As did Seattle in the late 1990s.

+ + +

On a cold, wet day in 1996 I walked a beat in Seattle's International District with Tommy Doran and his partner. I was there to observe "improvements" over what I'd seen just months before. I did see progress, mostly in the form of modest cosmetic changes to storefronts. But I also saw conditions that made me wonder whether Chinatown, in the heart of the ID, would ever become a model of "community policing" success.

Chinatown had had a recent history of drive-by shootings and other youth gang violence, street muggings, and car prowls. Aggressive panhandlers and passed-out drunks ruled Hing Hay Park on South King Street. The police and the community, historically, had been unable or unwilling to break through cultural stereotypes to build a durable peacekeeping partnership. Further, the "Wah Mee Massacre" was still on the minds of many cops and residents—and in the thoughts of would-be tourists and investors.

---

* A dear friend, Joe Brann, insists that Santa Ana beat San Diego to the punch in institutionalizing community policing (he's been wrong before). I'd met Brann when he was a lieutenant in Santa Ana. We've maintained our friendship through his work as Hayward (Calif.) chief of police and in his role, during the Clinton years, as director of the Justice Department's Community Oriented Policing Services (the "COPS Office") in Washington, D.C. A consultant these days, Brann is much in demand not only because he knows community policing inside and out but because he backs the theory with dozens of real-world success stories culled from hundreds of on-site visits.

On February 18, 1983, three young Chinese-American men had stormed the Wah Mee, a Chinatown nightclub that hosted big-stakes illegal gambling. Armed to the teeth, the suspects hogtied the fourteen people present, shot them all (only one survived), and fled with tens of thousands of dollars. (Two were captured immediately, and the third was extradited from Canada two years later. All three were convicted and received life sentences.)

Our hope was that a 1995 "Community Safety Initiative" grant from the Local Initiatives Support Corporation (LISC) would help us turn things around in Chinatown–International District. Headquartered in New York and chaired by former Treasury Secretary Robert Rubin, LISC "helps resident-led, community-based development organizations transform distressed communities and neighborhoods into healthy ones—good places to live, do business, work and raise families."* It sounded perfect, just what Chinatown needed. But months into the project I was beginning to despair that Seattle's "CSI" could do much more than put a better face on the ID. I saw little evidence that Doran's work with the community, to that point, would ever *transform* it into a permanently safe, "good place to live, do business, work and raise families."

Under and adjacent to Interstate 5, and close to the center of Chinatown, was the "Jungle." Home to a small army of the homeless, the Jungle spawned continuing waves of crime and other conduct that terrorized and demoralized the community: belligerent begging, public urinating and defecating, robberies, assaults, rapes, murders. I'd been pestering Doran to take me there. With an hour left in the shift, he said, "You ready?"

We walked east up Jackson Street, a broad four-lane that if taken west would put you in Pioneer Square, a block from the King Dome. Follow it a few blocks more to Elliott Bay and you can board a ferry for Bainbridge or other lovely wooded islands in the Puget Sound. It was daylight as we started under the massive freeway overpass, but it seemed more like midnight—dark, dismal, foreboding. The dozens of parked cars jammed into a makeshift lot on the south side of Jackson seemed to be shivering, as if

---

* It has invested over $3 billion in 1,700 local "community development corporations" in forty-one cities. It's helped build or rehabilitate 100,000 affordable homes, and created over eleven million square feet of commercial and community space.

they were cold, or afraid. Doran had asked the Department of Transportation to light the place up, but they had other priorities.

We walked across the street and started up the steep bank to the heart of the Jungle. "Careful," said Doran. "That's not mud." We slipped and slid our way to the top of the bank where a homestead had been established in the crease between turf and concrete bridge abutment. The camp was deserted, its inhabitants scurrying off in response to an early-warning system activated when we'd been observed crossing the street below. Strewn everywhere were used syringes and condoms, mud-encrusted blankets, cardboard boxes, some used for storage, others flattened out and used for beds, filthy articles of clothing, and a treasure trove of crime evidence, most of it the empty cases of cameras and binoculars and other personal belongings lifted from the cars—and the persons—of Chinatown tourists.

Over the next three years I heard clashing accounts of what was happening in the district. Lisa Belsky, New York director of LISC's CSI projects, and her colleague Bill Geller of Chicago were optimistic, but they saw problems. Mostly with us, the police. Doran's captain, Tag Gleason, and his sergeant, Mike Mehan, were extremely supportive of their cop. But some of Doran's fellow officers were resentful of the time he spent in "non-cop" activities—when he was out there organizing and mobilizing and attending meetings, when he was off forging partnerships with nontraditional partners, when he was *walking* his beat, his fellow patrol officers had to pick up the slack on 911 calls. Certain others in the chain of command were no happier. I asked Belsky and Geller, "Do you want me to intervene?" No, they suggested. "Just keep supporting the project but let Tommy and Tag and Mike work it out." They'd let me know if it got bad enough for the chief of police to start dictating. Our goal was to *institutionalize* community policing, not order it.

During those three years I made numerous visits to the ID, taking lunch or dinner in one of the many tasty Chinese, Japanese, Thai, and Vietnamese restaurants, walking long stretches of the district, attending and/or speaking at community meetings. The "cosmetic" changes I'd noted on my first tour with Doran? I watched them become irreversible and, in the process, inspire other improvements. Storefront by storefront, block by block. But the biggest change of all was to the Jungle.

Tommy Doran and his CSI allies (Belsky, Geller, and from the community Michael Yi and Aileen Balahadia, and from the local Community Development Corporation, Tom Lattimore, et al) spearheaded a movement to put a permanent end to the dangerous, unhygienic jungle. They started by enlisting as partners homeless agencies, other city departments, private enterprise, and, yes, the Washington State Department of Transportation.

Phuong Le, a reporter for *The Seattle Post-Intelligencer*, joined several of us on a tour in November 1999. Harvard's John F. Kennedy School of Government had just published a case study on our project. Here is part of what Le wrote:

> To see how a partnership between police and community can change a neighborhood, hit the streets of the International District. ... Start at Hing Hay Park, where the aromas of roasted duck and steamed dumplings have replaced the pungent odors of urine and booze that once dominated. ... Seattle police and community members got merchants to voluntarily stop selling high alcohol wine and fortified beer. They put in tree lights, a restroom and game tables in the park and reduced public boozing, brawls and urination. These days, the park is a place where children come to skate, where the elderly play Chinese chess and residents practice tai chi. ... The tour ... started at Hing Hay Park and moved to the Phnom Penh restaurant where [the project] helped owner Kim Ung negotiate to buy the property about three years ago. Under previous owners the restaurant had been a trouble spot where drive-by shootings and gang activities were so common that gang unit officers were there on most weekends.

Doran then led the tour up to where the Jungle used to be. The concrete columns under the freeway had been clad in bright red with yellow Chinese characters. The parking lot was lit up to make the darkest days and nights bright and cheery (was that a smile on that Nissan?). Across the street and up the bank? The Jungle had been graded, making the bank even steeper. And it was paved over, in a not unattractive sandstone color. Its former occupants had been linked up to homeless agencies (where some of them would actually take advantage of the proffered assistance). And immediately to the east, where the Jungle had begun to encroach, construction was under way on the Pacific Rim Center, a multistory combination of affordable housing and small commercial businesses.

As Le wrote, "In the International District, community policing isn't a buzzword. It's a creative way of doing business." To end the article, she quoted Doran: "I love the energy, this is a great community. So many things have happened so gradually that all of a sudden you see [the neighborhood] has changed."

+ + +

Like each of the eleven agencies that made up Seattle's CSI project, Nancy McPherson grasped the true meaning of community policing. Along with her mentors, John Eck at the University of Cincinnati and University of Wisconsin professor Herman Goldstein (the "Father of Problem Oriented Policing" and the author of the 1977 classic, *Policing a Free Society*), McPherson recognized that three conditions must be present in order for an agency to proclaim itself a genuinely community-oriented PD: (1) a *problem solving* orientation (Eck's "SARA" model—*s*canning, *a*nalysis, *r*esponse, *a*ssessment—provided the most widely accepted approach to the discipline of problem solving); (2) an authentic *partnership* with the community; and (3) a demonstrable commitment to *organizational transformation*.

That last one is crucial because without such a commitment it's simply not possible to conceive of community policing taking root in any city. The structure and culture of policing must change, fundamentally, for that to happen. All bureaus, divisions, sections, units—all *members* of the department must be on board. A handful of specialized patrol officers, a pontificating police chief, an idealistic lieutenant running some demonstration project—that's not community policing, no matter what the propaganda claims.

+ + +

In San Diego and Tallahassee, in Milwaukee and Brooklyn, in Seattle and Santa Monica, neighborhood "justice centers" have opened in recent years.

Created, among other reasons, to help disputants resolve differences not with fists or guns out in the street but in a safe environment, these geographically dispersed centers are involved in conflict resolution, mediation, and sometimes arbitration. Some of the centers embrace a "restorative justice" concept, which means that the suspect in a crime is often brought face-to-face with his or her victims. Stolen articles are returned or replaced. The feeling of having been "violated" is addressed, apologies rendered, restitution ordered. Sometimes the wrongdoers are forgiven, sometimes they're not. But the driving force behind restorative justice is just that: the restoration of fairness, of safety, and of that which has been lost to crime—tangibly or psychologically.

Staffed variously by attorneys, trained mediators, magistrates, and volunteers, justice centers operate *in the community*. The centers don't replace the centralized courthouse or jails or prisons—those components of the criminal justice system must remain available for cases that can't or ought not to be handled within the community. Major crimes, including sex offenses, domestic violence, and other violent and/or repeat offenses are best handled by the more formal system.

San Diego has pioneered a remarkable "one-stop shop" for dealing with the entire range of family issues, from DV safety planning to nutrition to pregnancy services to counseling.

Often community-driven, these initiatives, along with their public-private partnerships, are extremely promising. But there's a big problem looming—and too many jurisdictions are ignoring it.

+ + +

Just about everyone convicted of a crime and serving time in prison today (short of a capital or aggravated murder case or a "third strike" offense) will be "de-incarcerated" soon enough. Six hundred thousand of the two million people in jail or prison at this moment will be returning to the streets over the next year.

According to an October 2004 study by the Bureau of Justice Statistics (citing reports of the National Recidivism Reporting Program and the Survey of Inmates in State Correctional Facilities), the average number of ex-offenders who will be rearrested within three years of their release is

69.1 percent. On this basis alone, not to mention the moral duty, our police and other social institutions have a major stake in helping ex-offenders successfully reenter the community. If over two thirds of all ex-offenders return to the habits that put them in jail in the first place they will do serious damage to the best-laid plans of community policing.

Jeremy Travis, formerly of the Urban Institute, the Department of Justice, and now president of John Jay College of Criminal Justice, offers a novel proposal: require that the sentencing judge preside over the community reentry process, convening all stakeholders—community and family members, police, parole officers, et al. The judge, familiar with the case, would lay down the law to the ex-offender and at the same time see to it that all appropriate resources are marshaled to help the ex-offender's reentry.

Dennis Maloney, president of Community Justice Associates, and former director of Deschutes County (Oregon) Community Justice (note that it's "community" not *criminal* justice), writes and speaks compellingly on the need for "earned redemption." In his capacity as director of both adult and juvenile correctional facilities, Maloney developed some of the most innovative programs in "balanced and restorative" justice. Graduates of his program, who are required to *work* their way back to freedom—and responsibility—recidivate at dramatically reduced levels.* Maloney's graduation ceremonies, in which a key, symbolizing the community reconstruction work of his ex-offenders, is passed from one graduate to the next. The moment is dramatic, the audience often reduced to tears. Among those in attendance at most graduations? The cops who'd busted the offenders, and many of the victims of those offenders.

+ + +

Community policing is not for everyone. Just ask Daryl Gates. As the two of us debated the concept in Seattle, the ex-LAPD chief stunned the audience

---

* The work can be privately financed but usually involves mandated community service. Street and graffiti cleanups, restoration of watersheds, filing and other clerical work for social service agencies, building homes for Habitat for Humanity are but a few examples of the kind of work performed by ex-offenders.

with one of his frequent outrageous remarks. "Community policing, my friends," he said to the roomful of wealthy businessmen and business-women of the Young Presidents Organization, "is a sham, a hoax. You have absolutely no obligation to your neighbors. Your duty is to yourself, and no one else." His rationale? You pay taxes for police service, so let the cops do it all. "Your responsibility for public safety ends at the sidewalk in front of your house. Take care of yourself, your family, and your home, and leave the rest of it to us—the police."

I don't know, maybe Gates was playing to the audience, those wealthy, youthful presidents of corporations, CEOs, chairs of corporate boards, managing partners, publishers. Gates may have *thought* he was preaching to the choir, but he couldn't have gotten it more wrong—and the audience let him know.

But Gates is far from alone in the belief that policing should be left to the police.

+ + +

In 1993 I spoke to a business group in Orange County, California. I'd given what I thought was an inspired, rousing talk on community policing, denouncing particularly the mentality behind guarded and gated communities.

I'd told a hypothetical story of a "wealthy male head of household" (whom we'll call WMHH) who every morning slides behind the wheel of his silver Mercedes S-Class, pulls out of his four-car garage, waves good-bye to Sammy the Guard as Sammy the Guard salutes him and raises the gate. WMHH then motors toward his manufacturing business in the inner city.

The streets he travels undergo a striking transformation: from broad, winding, and shaded to clogged, treeless, smog-filled. Now, they're bordered by apartment buildings and small stores, some shuttered, most sporting bars over the windows, all awash in graffiti. WMHH passes youngsters on the way to school, drunks passed out in doorways, homeless people with their shopping carts, their cardboard pleas for spare change. Crack houses abound. Bangers and drug dealers control the streets.

Hookers cover all three shifts, syringes and used condoms at their feet. Knots of seniors sit outside mom-and-pop grocery stores in plastic and aluminum lawn chairs, shaking their heads, clucking their teeth, telling each other how it didn't use to be like this.

WMHH pulls up to his place of business. An employee jumps up, rushes over to push open the ten-foot cyclone gate. WMHH pulls in, parks in his designated space. Another safe trip into the heart of the jungle. In the evening, before dark if he can manage it, he reverses the journey. And sighs deeply, relieved, as Sammy the Guard opens then shuts the gate behind the S-Class. WMHH clicks open the garage door to his palace, drives in, punches the security code to the house, strides into the kitchen, shakes and pours himself a martini, walks out to the deep aqua pool in the backyard, and decompresses.

"Wouldn't it be swell," I concluded, "if each of us took responsibility for improving conditions in the communities where we *work* as well as where we live? Questions?"

The first came from a tan, balding, decidedly rich-looking man who'd been giving me the stinkeye from the moment I started my talk. He didn't have a question but he wanted me to know that he pays taxes, a lot of taxes, for police protection, and that it is the job of the police to protect him and his family. The Gates offense. He was afire with anger (and only in part because I'd unknowingly described the man to a T, all the way down to the make and model of his automobile).

We made zero progress, WMHH and I. I just wanted to eat my free lunch and get back on I-5 as soon as possible.

What would I have *liked* WMHH to do in his community? Simple. Turn over the deed of his faux-Tudor mansion to a battered women's shelter and grant them his fleet of luxury vehicles—or sell them and donate the proceeds to charity or give one each to his gardener, housekeeper, nanny, and personal trainer. I'd have him, his spouse, and their 2.5 children move into the inner city, to within a few blocks of his business. Think of the convenience! They wouldn't need a car; they could take the bus, like so many of their neighbors—sometimes transferring as many as three or four times to get to work in the morning then home again at night. They could rent an apartment or a house, perhaps one formerly used as a meth lab (they could get it for a song). They could send their kids to the neighborhood school where the average eighth grader reads at third-grade level, and the whole family could take advantage of the community health clinic for all their medical needs. Oh, and I'd have him sell his boat and his vacation home in Palm Springs, cash in his stocks, bonds, annuities, and other paper assets, then transfer the money directly into the accounts of organizations like the Boys and Girls Club and Big Brothers, Big Sisters.

Okay, that's fantasy. But what if Mr. WMHH—motivated by guilt or genuine concern for his community decided he *wanted* to get involved? He'd be limited only by his imagination.

He could introduce himself to the neighbors around his business, get to know them. Let them get to know him. He could slip into his grubbies on a Saturday and pick up litter, paint over graffiti. He might even organize a work party to paint that decrepit old house on the corner—the one occupied by the elderly woman whose arthritis is so advanced she can hardly pour herself a cup of tea, much less wield a paintbrush. Maybe the plumbing or the wiring or the heating or the yard needs work. WMHH could create a neighborhood/business watch program, invite neighbors into his conference room, serve refreshments, launch a citizens patrol. He could donate time to the school's or the library's reading program (few things brought me greater joy as a chief in Seattle than reading stories to schoolkids in poor neighborhoods). He could become a Big Brother. Or a mentor, teaching some lucky kid how to become a thriving capitalist. He could walk a couple of blocks over to the Boys and Girls Club, volunteer his services, write them a shockingly big check. He could do the same for the battered women's shelter and/or the little league and/or the neighborhood health clinic and/or the center for services to immigrants and/or the ex-offender reentry program and/or the city's rec center and/or . . .

The point is that community police is really *community building*. And community building is character building.

+ + +

There are understandable reasons why some people don't want to get involved in policing their own communities. Families are busy. They spend their days and nights juggling multiple and colliding priorities—Sarah's soccer, Mark's orthodontia, Lucy's clarinet lessons, choir practice, PTA meetings. Both parents, or the solo parent, work long hours, often at more than one job. The last thing they have time for is patrolling the streets or volunteering at an after-school program for teens or hosting a neighborhood watch program.

Or, like me—they simply don't *want* to get involved with neighborhood watch or citizen patrols. Personally, I've had enough of it. I guess I've over-dosed on crime. The less I have to think about it, the less often I see a police car (as a reminder of crime—or, depending on my mood, of government oppression), the happier I am. I live in a cabin on a mountain on an island. I neither see nor hear my neighbors. My "community" is the woods, its diverse wildlife, and Gunther, my long-haired miniature dachshund. This is a painful confession, coming from a lifelong advocate of community organizing, and a man who still loves big-city diversity and amenities. But it is what it is.

Yet, if someone steals my street sign down by the main road *one more time* . . .

Most of us have, I suspect, an "involvement threshold" which, if crossed, would motivate us to get involved. A series of home-invasion robberies the next block over. Your car stolen out of your driveway. The rape or murder of a neighbor's child. The theft of a sign. Whether we stick it out for months, years, a lifetime, or merely until the immediate threat has ended, we'll come together as community. Organizing, mobilizing, and working with one another and with the police to make our homes, schools, work-places, and streets safe.

No matter how much money we make, how steep our police-supporting taxes, how busy our lives, or how "alone" we prefer to be there are times when we just must act—together.

+ + +

That citizens patrol we formed to help catch the murdering skinheads? Well, they did it! Trained by some outstanding police officers (and having been vetted by voluntary criminal records checks), they reported for duty at our command van. They received their assignments, donned orange vests, and patrolled Hillcrest and North Park in VWs, Camrys, and Ford Fiestas. Armed with cell phones, suspect information, and instructions on how to avoid recklessly endangering themselves or violating the rights of their fellow citizens, they worked night after night, observing and collecting information. They prevented (simply by their highly publicized, conspicuous presence) untold crimes. And they caught, in the act, several muggers—which is to say they got on those cell phones immediately, followed the suspects, and called us to swoop in and make the arrests.

And it was information provided by the citizens patrol that led to the arrests and convictions of the suspects who killed that kid.

CHAPTER 30

CULTIVATING FEARLESS
LEADERSHIP

YOU'RE A POLICE CHIEF. You want to move your department from where it is today to a better place. What do you do? You surround yourself with good people, set the agency on the right course, and establish and enforce tough standards of performance and conduct. Then you do everything in your power to make sure that, when your time comes, you are replaced by someone who'll do the job better than you.

This means promoting the *personal growth* and *professional development* of each and every employee. (That's why you delegate responsibility and authority, not because it's the fashionable thing to do.) You want your cops, and all your employees, to make the right decision, for the right reasons—when you're not around.

In one of the all-time best books on the subject, *Leadership* (1978), James MacGregor Burns draws a distinction between *transactional* and *transformational* leadership.* The transactional form, common in political and corporate leadership—and pervasive in policing—is all about "brokering" deals, e.g., vote for me, I'll rezone your property; do a good job for me, I'll recommend you for dicks; lie for me, I'll lie for you . . . . Transactional leadership is efficient, and it's often enough to get the job done—if you're satisfied with barely adequate (or barely ethical) performance, and the preservation of the status quo.

Transformational leadership, on the other hand, promises profound change ". . . so comprehensive and pervasive . . . that *new cultures and value*

---

* He has updated the work in *Transforming Leadership: The Pursuit of Happiness.* Atlantic Monthly Press, 2003.

systems take the place of old" (emphasis added). It sets out, consciously and deliberately, to transform followers into leaders and leaders into moral agents.

"Moral agents"? Individuals who are deeply, demonstrably committed to liberty, justice, and equality. A police department that embraces these values would, by definition, reject racism, sexism, homophobia, and every other brand of bigotry. It would work *with* the community to achieve safe streets and social justice. It would nurture a workplace in which diversity of opinion is appreciated, and whose employees treat one another with dignity and respect, regardless of rank or status.

It should be apparent why this kind of leadership is so arresting to me, given my conviction that American policing—its culture, value system, and structure—is in need of "comprehensive and pervasive" change.

In Seattle, I taught these and other leadership principles in classes open to all employees, as well as members of the community. The theory of transformational leadership was embraced enthusiastically. In fact, my cops hungered for such a workplace—even as they acknowledged the gaping chasm between classroom theory and the real world. What then, stood in our way? In a word, *fear.*

+ + +

Fear (or at least the expression of it) is a socially unacceptable emotion in the police culture, something you learn the first day on the job. It's okay to tell your buddies in the cop bar how you almost peed your pants when you came face-to-face with the gunman. But that's just a figure of speech. Your peers must experience you as the ass-kicking, fearless hombre you've worked so hard to personify. It's the same persona that many cops bring along with them as they ascend the promotional ladder, thereby creating a police leadership culture of fake fearlessness.

Looking back, I wouldn't trade my own fears for anything. I hurt people because of them, and I feel shame for many of my actions. But the struggle to understand my behavior taught me, as it continues to teach me, that most abuses of power flow from fear.

+ + +

I've talked about the need for police officers to be tough and gentle at the same time. They can't do that if they're living and working in a state of perpetual fear. In my leadership class I diagrammed how fear works in the body.* To develop fearlessness you have to *lean into your fears.* You have to become a *warrior.*

When I picture warriors I don't see the "jarheads" described in Anthony Swofford's 2003 chronicle of the Gulf War. I see: Nelson Mandela, Joan of Arc, Martin Luther King, Jr., Mahatma Gandhi, Harriet Tubman, Vaclav Havel, Eleanor Roosevelt, Viktor Frankl, Sojourner Truth, Branch Rickey, Rosa Parks, Franklin Delano Roosevelt, Mother Teresa, Anne Frank. Men and women who who went into battle armed only with a moral compass and a passion for justice. They changed the world, these warriors.

As have warriors armed with more conventional weapons of war—and the requisite skills, tactical wisdom, and capacity for physical violence: the samurai of Japan who fought valiantly, without regard for personal glory. Sitting Bull, the Hunkpapa Lakota chief who, with the Oglala Sioux chief Crazy Horse, prevailed at the Battle of Little Bighorn. ("*Hoka Hey,*" said Chief Sitting Bull, appropriating the Sioux war cry—"It is a good day to die." Which I take to mean: *I've lived honorably, told the truth, taken a stand against evil and injustice. I am at peace.*) I think of E Company, 506th Regiment, 101st Airborne: the "band of brothers" who in darkness parachuted into Normandy and fought their way through France, including an implausible stand at frigid Bastogne (where, according to Stephen Ambrose, the rallying cry was, "They got us surrounded, the poor bastards"), all the way to Hitler's Eagle's Nest atop Obersalzberg.

---

* In *Arianna Online* ("Appealing to Our Lizard Brains: Why Bush is Still Standing," October 13, 2004), Arianna Huffington cites the work of Dr. Daniel Siegel who describes the physiological origins of fear. Whether we're conscious of it or not, when a fear-inducing stimulus presents itself to the amygdala (an almond-shaped structure deep in the brain) the most primordial of all questions is raised: *Is it safe?* If the answer is "no"—and we have not learned to be fully conscious of, or *in touch with* our fears—the less fully evolved part of our brain, the reptilian "old brain," will simply take over, and rule our reactions. The essential strategy of the Bush-Cheney presidential campaign, says Huffington, was to create a relentlessly reinforced image of the terrible things that would happen to us if we didn't vote for them. As she wrote, "Fear paralyzes our reasoning and literally makes it impossible to think straight." Sure worked for Bush-Cheney in 2004.

Common to these armed warriors is uncommon grace. Gentle of spirit, but capable of astonishing ferocity. Peace-lovers, but not pacifists. Some warriors fight out of love of humanity, for social justice, for human rights. But many fight and die not for their "homeland" (and certainly not for pusillanimous politicians who, over the centuries, have sent them to fight unwise or immoral wars), but for the love of their fellow warriors.

Police officers in Japan are modern-day samurai. Carefully selected for their interpersonal competence as well as their physical prowess, Japanese cops receive instruction in Confucianism, Bushido (the way of the samurai), and psychology to promote their "social skills and moral judgment."* It is the tradition of the samurai to learn flower arranging before swordsmanship.

+ + +

How do we get American cops, and police chiefs, to abandon *fake* fearlessness —bravado and/or cruelty—in order to achieve genuine warriorlike courage? It begins, I believe, with a decision to think about and to experience fear in a fundamentally different way, a conscious choice not to dread fear, but to embrace it. An illustration from "Meeting the Demons," from *No Enemies Within* by Dawna Markove:

> Once upon a time, a long time ago, and very far from here, a great Tibetan poet named Milarepa studied and meditated for decades. He traveled the countryside, teaching the practice of compassion and mercy to the villagers he met. He faced many hardships, difficulties, and sorrows, and transformed them into the path of his awakening.
>
> Finally, it was time to return to the small hut he called home. He had carried its memory in his heart through all the years of

---

* Alas, the Japanese seem to have little regard for female warriors in blue; women make up less than 2 percent of the force, carry no firearms, handle a tiny range of low-prestige duties such as traffic direction and parking enforcement, and serving tea to station visitors—and to their male colleagues. I appreciate cultural differences as much as the next guy, but this strikes me as a bit of a blind spot in Japanese "moral judgment."

his journey. Much to his surprise, upon entering, he found it filled with enemies of every kind. Terrifying, horrifying, monstrous demons that would make most people run. But Milarepa was not most people.

Inhaling and exhaling slowly three times, he turned towards the demons, fully present and aware. He looked deeply into the eyes of each, bowing in respect, and said, "You are here in my home now. I honor you, and open myself to what you have to teach me."

As soon as he uttered these words, all the enemies save five disappeared. The ones that remained were grisly, raw, huge monsters. Milarepa bowed once more and began to sing a song to them, a sweet melody resonant with caring for the ways these beasts had suffered, and curiosity about what they needed and how he could help them. As the last notes left his lips, four of the demons disappeared into thin air.

Now only the one nasty creature was left, fangs dripping evil, nostrils flaming, opened jaws revealing a dark, foul, black throat. Milarepa stepped closer to this huge demon, breathed deeply into his own belly, and said with quiet compassion, "I must understand your pain and what it is you need in order to be healed." Then he put his head in the mouth of the enemy.

In that instant, the demon disappeared and Milarepa was home at last.

+ + +

To my comrades in blue: Whether facing peril on the streets, untoward peer pressure in the squad room, a bully of a boss, or tough political choices at headquarters, lean into your fears. Strengthen your skills, build emotional resilience, keep your sense of humor, strive for balance in life. As Anne O'Dell, of domestic violence prevention fame, appends to her e-mails, *Work like you don't need the money. Love like you've never been hurt. Dance like you do when nobody's watching.*

When a fear-inducing situation presents itself, embrace it. Reject the methods I employed in the past: burrowing under your fear, vaulting over it, weaseling around it. Open your body and soul to the fear. Keep your eyes open, your mind alert, the goal always in sight. Soon, you'll reach the "half-life" of that fear. As you step into the daylight on the other side, you will have been rendered *fearless*. You are a warrior.

America's cities need warrior mothers and fathers, warrior teachers, warrior role models of all types to help make our streets, our schools, our homes safe. We need warrior cops and warrior police chiefs who fight as hard to uphold civil liberties as they do to fight crime, who treasure human decency and social justice as much as they love catching crooks.

CONCLUSION

I WAS TWENTY-FOUR, a new sergeant with my own squad of patrol officers. A white officer from another squad went off on one of my cops, an African-American, calling him "boy." When I found out about it, I drove Code 2 from East San Diego to headquarters and, in a rage, hammered out a memo. It was "one thing for a black officer to be subjected to community abuse, quite another to be exposed to the blatantly racist attitude of a fellow officer," I wrote. A department commander responded by labeling me a "social crusader." He spat out the term as if it had fouled his tongue. But his accusation was accurate, and I would wear the mantle for the rest of my career.

Today, at sixty, both public safety and social justice continue to motivate me. How do we make life safer for that kid in National City who grew up scared of his own shadow? How do we create a safe, sane world for people of all ages? A heartbreaking number of Americans live with emotional and physical violence in their own homes. Many Americans, reacting to predatory street crime, are forced to change the way they live. Many suffer the effects of open-air drug markets, street prostitution, gang violence. Many are mistreated by their own police, some for no other reason than the color of their skin. And many do not receive the full protection and services of law enforcement they pay for.

It's distressing to think about the numbers of beat cops, police chiefs, lawmakers, attorneys general, and presidents who lack passion about safe streets *and* civil liberties. In a democracy, it's these officials' *job* to care about, and to aggressively pursue these complementary goals. Many, of course, do take the responsibility seriously, and they deserve to be recognized for it. But far too many of our officials take home a check for doing the job ineffectively, or improperly.

As suggested throughout *Breaking Rank*, inept crime fighting and police misconduct are largely the product of (1) defective lawmaking, (2) weak or haughty politicians, (3) the police paramilitary structure, and (4) the workplace culture of police agencies. It's the *institution* of policing, not rank-and-file cops, that is in need of an "extreme makeover."

391

+ + +

As a reformist cop, I generated and absorbed a good deal of heat during my career. I've been called a "pinko" for agitating for social justice and civil liberties, and for criticizing police practices publicly. My vision has been labeled "naïve," the ideas I promote "impractical." But critics of reform are often, to put it kindly, cynics. And, as Oscar Wilde wrote, "A cynic is one who knows the price of everything, and the value of nothing." Cynics can tell us what a transformative change in public safety will *cost*—in dollars, in organizational instability, in political risks—but they're obstinately blind to the benefits of reform. And to the costs of doing nothing.

Firsthand experience causes me to conclude that most station-house critics of police reform are *bystanders*—the kind of cops who watch passively as fellow officers club and kick a passive traffic violator, or shove a broom handle up a man's rectum. Bystanders don't take risks. They're obsessed with preserving the status quo, covering their tails, hiding behind the blue wall of silence, or the union label. Cynical chiefs and cynical political leaders cannot seem to get beyond the bureaucratic mindset. Change threatens "disruption" of their lives. Or their re-election.

How do reformers confront this resistance? First and foremost, by *listening* to and *respecting* one's opponents. Whether right or wrong, everyone deserves to be heard.

+ + +

Early on as a police reformer I was a terrible listener. I couldn't understand how my peers could be so stubbornly resistant to my desire for them to change. (Didn't they realize their willingness to change themselves would make me a happier person?)

Tom Murton, who pushed fundamental reforms as the warden of the Arkansas prison farm system, was an early inspiration.* I remember a dinner, held in the early 1970s in Murton's honor at the home of Tom Gitchoff, SDSU

---

* Murton's book, coauthored with Joe Hyams, *Accomplices to the Crime* (1969), became the basis for the 1980 film *Brubaker*, starring Robert Redford.

professor and longtime friend. A novice reformer at the time, I cornered Murton and asked him how he kept his sanity working in a field with so many "ideological opponents" (I think I used the word *assholes*). He told me he worked hard to practice a philosophy of collaboration and compromise with his enemies—however repulsed he might be by their conduct.

Sometimes it was easy: If Governor Winthrop Rockefeller wanted the prison's barns painted green, Murton would "paint the damn barns green"—even though he was partial to traditional red. On matters of principle, however, he refused to make concessions.

Murton exposed legislators and other state officials who for years had driven their Cadillacs and Lincolns up to the back gate of the Tucker and Cummins prison farms, where they'd toss sides of taxpayer-funded beef into their trunks. He fired guards, and "demoted" trustees who couldn't be trusted to perform competently, or to behave responsibly. He disconnected the "Tucker telephone"—a sinister device (literally a modified telephone) wired to the testicles of uncooperative prisoners, who were then made to endure excruciating "long-distance" calls. And he unearthed the bodies of murdered prisoners whose deaths had previously been attributed to "natural causes."

Murton understood that when it comes to incompetence, corruption, or brutality you simply don't "collaborate."

+ + +

Resistance to even modest changes in law and in the structure and policies of policing is as natural as sun in San Diego or rain in Seattle. But we need to get on with it. How, then, apart from becoming a good listener, do we proceed?

I think where you start depends on where you are. Are you a student of political science, public administration, sociology, criminal justice? An analyst of government's failed approaches to "social control"? A survivor of domestic violence or other crimes? A victim of official abuses, and official excuses? A black mother, frightened that your young boys won't be coming home after a run-in with the local police? A beat cop, bothered by what you've seen, or done, and willing to "break rank" to atone, and to help improve your police department?

Whatever your motives (and it's important to understand them), here are some basic "dos and don'ts" I've learned during my many years in police work, and in community-police politics.

DO:

Become a student of that which you seek to change. Learn everything you can about policing. Are the laws your police officers are called upon to enforce sensible? Do they add to, or subtract from, community safety? Are they humane?

What is the stated mission of your police department? Its goals, objectives, and core values? Is the agency organized efficiently, and appropriately, to get the job done? Does it recognize that domestic violence is a precursor to all other forms of violence, and does it place its highest priority on DV prevention and DV law enforcement?

Does your department take advantage of the latest developments in management, technology, and forensic sciences? Is it adequately funded to carry out its mission? Does your community have enough cops? Enough civilian personnel? Who gets chosen to be a police officer? How are candidates selected? How are new cops welcomed into the department—trained, educated, *acculturated*? Who gets promoted? How and why?

What are your local agency's enforcement priorities? How is individual police performance appraised? How is organizational effectiveness evaluated?

How are allegations of poor service or misconduct, including racism, sexism, and homophobia, investigated? Are such investigations timely, and of high quality? Are citizens meaningfully involved in complaint investigation and adjudication? If not, why not?

How are officers disciplined? Are police officers, civilian employees, supervisors, and managers expected to treat one another, and the community, with respect? Does accountability for performance and conduct operate at *all* levels of the organization, from the cop on the beat to the chief in the corner pocket?

Your police department belongs to you and your fellow citizens. You have a right to ask these questions, and your department has a duty to answer them. (If they won't, try the Freedom of Information Act. It'll frustrate police administrators and records personnel, but it works wonders.)

Strengthen your own capabilities. You are the most critical agent of your vision. Are you *effective?* Do you demonstrate the knowledge, technical and political skills, and interpersonal competence necessary to persuade others? Are you trustworthy? Do you refuse to take yourself too seriously, even as you demonstrate the seriousness of your purpose?

Organize and mobilize. "Those who profess to favor freedom and yet deprecate agitation, are men who want crops without plowing the ground," wrote Frederick Douglass. *Change is never unopposed.* It rarely happens because it should, even less often because you want it to. Protectors of the status quo outnumber and usually "outrank" you and your fellow agents of change. Further, they are at least as deeply wedded to stasis as you are to transformation.

It's true that an *individual* can make a difference, and I would never denigrate the efforts of courageous, single-minded, "Lone Ranger" reformers. But it's easier, faster, usually much more effective, and frankly a lot more fun when people band together and agitate for positive change.

Show a little respect. The "rule of reciprocity" says if you treat people with respect, they'll treat you with respect: Give them information, they'll give you information; trust them, they'll trust you. Of course "reciprocity" is rarely a fifty-fifty proposition in the real world, each party exhibiting equal courtesy, openness, generosity. But a diligent, persistent, collective, and *respectful* campaign for change *will* bring about transformation—or at least visible progress.

DO NOT:

Make an ass of yourself. One of the reasons cops don't listen to their detractors is that detractors often shout so loud they can't be heard. Or they resort to obscenities, name-calling, and/or threats. I recently saw a photo of a demonstrator at an International Monetary Fund conference in Washington, D.C. She was holding aloft a large sign that read, "Ramsey [chief of police]: Clean Up Your Pigpen." Such rhetoric may satisfy on a visceral level, but it's stupid, and self-defeating.

Be docile. There's no immediate danger of the meek inheriting the earth—quite to the contrary. Passive or *overly polite* people get steamrolled every time they attempt to effect changes in policy. You don't have to be obnoxious about it, but be assertive, stand your ground. Do not relinquish your rights as an American.

Give up. Journalist I. F. "Izzy" Stone, that marvelous warrior for social justice, wrote:

> The only kinds of fights worth fighting are those you are going to lose, because somebody has to fight them and lose and lose and lose until someday, somebody who believes as you do wins. In order for somebody to win an important major fight 100 years hence, a lot of other people have got to be willing—for the sheer fun and joy of it—to go right ahead and fight, knowing you're going to lose. You mustn't feel like a martyr. You've got to enjoy it.

+ + +

However much one enjoys being a cop or a police chief—and I loved my three and a half decades in police work—there are moments of unspeakable horror. And sadness. I've seen raped and murdered children, bloodied spouses, the maggot-infested bodies of society's "throwaways." I've participated in, witnessed, and later punished brutal, racist, or corrupt police behavior. I've attended far too many cops' funerals, choking on the lump in my throat as the "last call" for a fallen officer is broadcast live over the police radio. Labor of love or not, there are times when being a cop just leaves you sick at heart.

But through it all, there is this: There's no other job with greater potential for making a difference in the lives of one's fellow citizens. Police officers stop people from hurting other people. They render assistance when individuals and communities are most in need of it. They save lives.

As I used to tell my officers, misery is optional. If you're able to keep a sense of humor, to rejoice in the humanity of policing and even police politics, you can have a ball being a cop. I know I did.

ACKNOWLEDGMENTS

With endless gratitude to my exceptional Nation Books editor, Ruth Baldwin who, with Carl Bromley, Jerry Gross, Meg Lemke, Sherri Schultz, and my agent, Elizabeth Wales, offered up sound advice, a keen eye, and uncommon patience at every step.

And to Sarah Buel, Adrienne Casey, Steve Casey, Anita Castle, Dr. David Corey, Don Drozd, Jack Mullen, Anne O'Dell, Ann Rule, and Paula Russell whose wisdom and insights added so much to my understanding of their specialties.

And to esteemed SDPD and SPD colleagues who taught me, and often fought me. In *San Diego*: Rulette Armstead, A.D. Brown, Bob Burgreen, Don Davis, Bill Kolender, Ken O'Brien, and Mike Rice. In *Seattle*: Harry Bailey, Janice Corbin, Robin Clark, Jim Deschane, Harv Ferguson, Ed Joiner, Clark Kimerer, Nick Metz, Debbie Nelson, and Lisa Ross.

And to civic, academic, and community leaders who've inspired me and held my feet to the fire for years. In *San Diego*: Rev. Robert Ard, Irma Castro, Dr. Dennis Doyle, Bonnie Dumanis, Jon Dunchack, Scott Fulkerson, Murray Galinson, Maria Garcia, Dr. Stu Gilbreath, Dr. Tom Gitchoff, Dr. Kenji Ima, Ernie McCray, Jack McGrory, Helen McKenna, Sherry Silver, George Mitrovich, Dr. Joyce Ross, Dr. Rick Ross, Dr. Janet Sherman, Andrea Skorepa and Rev. George Walker Smith. In *Seattle*: Aileen Balahadia, Debbie Barnes, Guadalupe Barnes, Robin Boehler, Connie Bown, David Bown, Bert Caoili, Terrence Carroll, Rev. Ellis Casson, Dr. Robin DiAngelo, Dr. Roy Farrell, Dr. Camilo de Guzman, Rebecca Hale, Sheila Hargesheimer, Alma Kern, Anne Levinson, Jan Levy, Dr. Hubert Locke, Lonnie Lusardo, Dr. Sandra Madrid, Roberto Maestes, Dorothy Mann, John Morefield, Mark Murray, Todd Nelson, Vanna Novak, Judy Osborne, Margaret Pageler, Kate Pflaumer, Norm Rice, Deborah Terry-Hays, Richard Wildermuth, Mark Sidran, Harriett Walden, and Jo Ellen Warner.

And to cherished pals who've stuck by me through good times and bad, whose professional expertise, personal mastery, and dedication to social justice is evident in all they do: Lisa Belsky, Joe Brann, Bill Geller, and Nancy McPherson.

INDEX

CPSIA information can be obtained at www.ICGtesting.com
Printed in the USA
LVOW08s2059190116

471140LV00001B/1/P